THE LABOR MOVEMENT
IN THE UNITED STATES
1860-1895

THE LABOR MOVEMENT
IN THE UNITED STATES
1860-1895

A Study in Democracy

BY

NORMAN J. WARE, Ph.D

ASSOCIATE PROFESSOR OF ECONOMICS IN WESLEYAN UNIVERSITY
AUTHOR OF "THE INDUSTRIAL WORKER, 1840 TO 1860"

GLOUCESTER, MASS.
PETER SMITH
1959

TO

LEO WOLMAN

*Toutes choses sont à leur place dans ce
monde misérable, même le pathétique désir
d'un monde meilleur.*

—GEORGES DUHAMEL

PREFACE

ACKNOWLEDGMENT is made of assistance in this study to John W. Hayes, the last leader of the Knights of Labor, who placed at the disposal of the author all his material on the Order, including letters of great value from Mr. Powderly; to David J. Saposs for the loan of much material, including the original manuscript copy of the "treaty" offered the Knights of Labor by the committee of trade unionists who shortly after formed the American Federation of Labor; and to Miss Eunice Miller, late of the New York Public Library, whose untimely death has robbed research students in economics of the most efficient aid rendered graciously under all circumstances.

N. J. W.

CONTENTS

x CONTENTS

APPENDICES

INTRODUCTION

"THE Noble and Holy Order of the Knights of Labor"
began in 1869 in Philadelphia, the cradle alike of America's
political and industrial life; became in 1886 the most imposing
labor organization this country has ever known; and closed
the doors upon its long-departed glory in 1917, when John W.
Hayes, its last master workman, stored the remains of its records and furnishings in a leaky shed behind an insurance office
in Washington, D. C. But the Order was dead long before
Hayes buried it, and this history will take it down only to 1894,
when its importance as an industrial society ceased.

The subtitle, "A Study in Democracy," indicates a primary
interest of the writer. Democracy, once worshiped as the hope
of mankind, is now abused unconditionally by intellectual
aristocrats like H. L. Mencken and Dean Inge, by the eugenists
who offer a new panacea, and by the self-appointed spokesmen
of the proletariat. Mencken perhaps is not to be taken seriously because he addresses the democracy with the same pro-
fane gusto one keeps for one's friends, but no one will question
the seriousness of Dean Inge, the eugenists, and the communists.

Yet few of them have taken the trouble to study any specific
democratic movement, a process less interesting perhaps than
invective, but necessary, it would seem, to a just estimate. The
Knights of Labor are commonly supposed to have had a highly
centralized government, and it may be objected that they cannot be regarded as truly democratic. But the highly centralized nature of the Order's government was more formal than
real, and anyway it is best not to define "democracy" before
examining it. Unquestionably the Knights of Labor was a

popular movement, and this is all that is meant in this place by "democratic." If this popular movement became highly "undemocratic," that is perhaps what democracy does.

A large part of this study will be taken up with the emergence of the trade unions and the American Federation of Labor, and comparisons are likely to creep in. Professor Ely wrote when the Knights were at the height of their power and prestige, and he looked kindly upon them. Professor Commons wrote when the Federation was in the saddle, and he was not enthusiastic about the Knights—which proves only that even economists are human. The bitterness that grew out of the old conflict between the two organizations has evaporated. Even Samuel Gompers let sleeping dogs lie. There was nothing inevitable about the failure of the Knights and the success of the Federation. Explanations of both can be found in the circumstances and the men. The economic interpretation of history, even or especially for labor organizations, has been overdone. Individual ambitions, hatreds, strengths, and weaknesses played their part. The Knights were outmoded in many ways, but there were anachronisms in the Federation too. Generalizations are interesting but lack proper modesty, and meanings can be found in details.

One may say on the whole that the Knights tried to do a much bigger thing than the Federation—bigger and vaguer. For a few months in 1885-86 it looked almost as if they might succeed. Then they crashed, and the American Federation of Labor emerged from the wreck under the banner of an older and perhaps greater *débâcle:* "Sauve qui peut!" In a sense the American Federation of Labor was not an advance of the American labor movement, but a strategic retreat of a few craft unions disturbed for their own safety by the remarkable but "unhealthy" growth of the One Big Union. The Locomotive Engineers had done the same thing earlier when they refused further aid to the shopmen and through Chief Arthur declared that they were not a labor union. That this withdrawal meant immediate security for some is not questioned, but later developments have not proved that this security was well founded.

Three main strands can be discovered in the labor movement of the United States: pure and simple trade unionism, reformism, and politics. But no single organization or group or organizations has confined itself to any one of these. All that can be said is that a certain union or group is or was predominantly one thing or another. Pure and simple trade unionism accepts the wage system as a *fait accompli* and makes the best of it, but it may branch out into large schemes of reform and political action. Reformism, perhaps the oldest tradition in the American labor movement, involves various methods of escape from, or adaptation to, the economic *milieu*. And politics is ordinarily the outgrowth of reform or engrafted upon the movement by the farmers or the radical fringe of socialists and communists of one stripe or another.

Each interpreter of the Knights of Labor has found it to be that sort of organization which the interpreter through sympathy or antipathy requires. For one it was political; for another coöperation was its major interest; for another, the boycott; and for others, strikes, arbitration, education, insurance, or what not. This is natural enough because the Order tried them all. But what the Order stood for was not a function but an idea. It grew out of disillusionment with politics on the one hand and pure and simple trade unionism on the other. Its most marked characteristic was reformism which the Knights themselves called "education" and which one is privileged further to translate into "propaganda." Stephens and Powderly were both agitators rather than executives, as were most of the other leaders of prominence.

Thus one may not speak too glibly about the failure of the Knights in this or that. As propagandists, organizers, and experimenters they had remarkable if ephemeral success. They put the labor movement on the map. They reached groups that had never been reached before. They taught many things about land, money, immigration, government ownership—many things perhaps that were not so, or if so, not important. But these were side issues. They had one major idea or sentiment —the idea of solidarity. There was no expression that so caught the popular imagination of the time as the motto of the Order, "An injury to one is the concern of all." It was not a new idea but one that is never old. It was a shibboleth, a catchword, but it is in such terms that men think, and if men must think in such terms, this one was better than most. The idea of course was not enough. Some way had to be found to work it out. The Knights tried one way and failed, but it is pertinent to ask, who has found another way and succeeded?

It must be admitted too that the Knights did not always live up to their motto. They deserted Albert Parsons and allowed him to be hanged for a crime he did not commit. But they welcomed the negro, and at Richmond had a colored delegate introduce Powderly when the latter responded to Fitzhugh Lee, then Governor of Virginia. After some hesitation they accepted women and treated them with due if not excessive consideration. They capitulated for a time to the anti-Chinese mania but not overmuch. Though Powderly was disgusted with the "new immigrant" in the steel and coal regions, the Knights organized among all nationalities, races, creeds, and grades of skill. They went to England, Ireland, France, Belgium, Italy, Australasia, and set up assemblies.

It is a mistake to think that the American labor movement has outgrown the Knights of Labor. In functions, organization, and ideas, perhaps, but not in sentiment. With the Knights solidarity ended in chaos. With the American Federation of Labor exclusiveness has reached something like sterility. The great mechanized industries which the Knights once held have since been lost. They cannot be regained by the point of view that once saved the cigar makers, carpenters, and printers. When Gompers and McGuire conducted their successful retreat and saved the remnants of the labor forces out of the confusion of 1886, they did a neat and perhaps necessary job. But they never forgot, and it is more important, the psychologists say, to forget than to remember. For some time the exclusiveness of the American Federation of Labor was diluted by the presence of two remnants of the Knights of Labor—the miners and the brewers. But the brewers are now as innocuous as their products, and the miners are making a losing fight for existence.

The Knights started on their national career in 1878 with a brave platform, but for a long time it was impossible to discover what they were doing. They were in sympathy with everything and involved in nothing. An assembly would organize, go through the founding ritual, elect officers, initiate new members with due solemnity, pay the tax, do a little charity work and employment-finding for the brothers, and pass out. In 1879 each local was required to give some time to the discussion of certain labor problems, including the following: "How can the toiler receive a just share of the wealth he creates?" According to Powderly, the Order was engaged on a Crusade, but he had trouble in pointing to any Holy Sepulcher worth the winning. The rank and file grew impatient at the leisureliness with which the officers awaited the millennium. There was a popular demand for "something immediate." "They say," complained Litchman, "and with much truth, that while our Order deals with measures for the future emancipation of labor, the present necessities should also be considered. . . . The number of men seems very few who can plan and then patiently wait until time brings the fulfillment of their hopes." Litchman had, of course, no plan other than to hold his job, but Powderly was cogitating, and in 1884 the result was revealed.

"We are," he said, "the willing victims of an outrageous system. . . . We should not war with men for being what we make them, but strike a powerful, telling blow at the base of the system which makes the laborer the slave of his master. . . . So long as a pernicious system leaves one man at the mercy of another, so long will labor and capital be at war. . . . In what direction shall we turn? . . . Far be it from me to say that I can point out the way. . . . I can only offer a suggestion that comes to me as a result of experience. . . ." And while the General Assembly hung breathless on his words, words that would lead them out of the wilderness of "wage slavery," he suggested, "to abolish the wage system!"

This was Powderly's contribution, the sum and substance of it. He was a windbag whose place was on the street corner rousing the rabble to concert pitch and providing emotional compensation for dull lives. They should have thrown him out, but they did not. Instead, with the stupid loyalty of a dog for an abusive master they clung to him as to a savior. He offered, even pleaded, to resign over and over, but they refused to listen. For fourteen years they kept him at the head of their organization in spite of obvious disqualifications for the job. That was loyalty, a virtue much praised by the philosophers.

And the reason—one hesitates to suggest for fear of derision in these sophisticated days—the reason was that the labor movement of the 'eighties was not a business but a religion, not a doctrinal religion like socialism, but a vague, primitive, embryonic sentiment, a religion in the making. The local assembly was something like a congregation living in times of persecution. The early Christians had their catacombs, and it is not irreverence that suggests that the Knights had their secret "sanctuaries."

There were no movies, Fords, radios. The workingmen's homes were unattractive, and the saloon was in official disfavor. Meeting places were built coöperatively with a store on the ground floor and an assembly hall above. This sanctuary became the center of the members' lives, their club, union headquarters, school, church, in one. Out of it came most, if not all, of the labor leaders of the future. They came out with some enthusiasm for ideas, a vague humanitarianism, and the conviction that the Knights were "noble and holy." It wore off. A hard-boiled generation now knows better. The wage-earner of today may get his inspiration from Gloria Swanson or Tom Mix. But the Knights had no such opportunities. They were serious-minded, highfalutin, sentimental, a little ridiculous, but engaged on a crusade of some sort which in some way seemed to them important. They talked of "honorable toil," of the "sufferings of the masses," of "emancipation from wage slavery," of "justice," and of "rights and wrongs," with never a suspicion that their children would be talking of silk stockings, carburetors, wave lengths, and liquor, so-called. But the Knights may not be blamed or praised for this. These things are beyond praise or blame.

The rapid advance of the Industrial Revolution in the middle of the last century convinced the more intelligent workers that their special skills would not long serve to protect their standards. Machinery, the factory, and industrial combinations, so-called monopolies, reached during and after the Civil War unheard of proportions and, by discounting craftsmanship, broke down special living standards in every direction. This bore most heavily upon the shoemakers, iron and steel workers, machinists, molders, coopers, and cigar makers, and it was from these that most of the labor leaders of the mid-century came. Miners and railroad workers were less affected by mechanical changes than by industrial and financial conditions peculiar to their trades or times, but the shopmen suffered as machinists as well as railroad workers. The special conditions of the coal-mining industry were like those of the present day, while the railroads were overexpanded, undernourished, and the prey of the speculator. Jay Gould and the Knights of Labor were contemporary luminaries in the American scene. The latter were forming their first local when the former was preparing Black Friday. Gould broke the Telegraphers in 1883, but was beaten by the Wabash men two years later. In 1886 he dealt the Knights the severest blow of their career when Powderly capitulated in the Southwest strike.

The lesson of the time was obvious, and the Knights were not slow to point it out. The Industrial Revolution as it progressed was bound to do two things, to create on the one hand a dead level of labor in which craft distinctions would be practically wiped out, and, on the other, huge consolidations of capital with economic and political authority unchallengeable by any but a consolidated labor movement. It was to fight consolidated capital that the Order tried to create an integrated labor society to replace the isolated craft alliances and conventions of reformers that had preceded. When the Knights began, the trade unions were almost destroyed. They seemed incapable of organizing or of getting anywhere when they did. The solidarity of labor was fast becoming an economic reality if not a psychological fact, and it was the business of the Order to make the organization of labor fit the conditions of work. Emphasis on the principle of solidarity is the beginning of understanding of the Knights of Labor. Strange and grandiose names and titles, rituals, secrecy, forms of organization, even activities, were secondary. The Order tried to teach the American wage-earner that he was a wage-earner first and a bricklayer, carpenter, miner, shoemaker, after; that he was a wage-earner first and a Catholic, Protestant, Jew, white, black, Democrat, Republican, after. This meant that the Order was teaching something that was not so in the hope that sometime it would be. It failed, and its failure was perhaps a part of of the general failure of democracy—or is it humanity?

N. J. W.

THE LABOR MOVEMENT
IN THE UNITED STATES
1860-1895

THE LABOR MOVEMENT
IN THE UNITED STATES

CHAPTER I

FROM THE CIVIL WAR TO THE PANIC OF '73

NOTHING was left after the panic of 1857 of the labor agitations of the forties and fifties but three small "national unions" so-called: the Printers, Stone Cutters, and Hat Finishers. In 1859 the molders and the machinists were organized nationally, but their unions declined in the first years of the Civil War. Their leaders, William H. Sylvis and Jonathan Fincher, were active in the reform and political movement of the sixties in part because of this decline of the unions they represented.

The early war depression lasted until the summer of 1862, when currency inflation and military needs began to stimulate industry to feverish activity which culminated in the boom year of 1865. Labor activity followed rising prices and full-time employment, first in the formation of local trade unions and city trades' assemblies, and later of national trade unions. The dominant factor in the labor movement of the sixties is found in the mixed trades' assemblies. The national unions were weak and ineffective and national in name only. Unlike England the national unions in America did not take the leadership of the labor movement until very late, after the formation of the American Federation of Labor in 1886. The reason is obvious. The concept "nation" in America has been a constantly expanding one, economically even more than politically, and a "national" union of one decade has seldom survived into the next. When the officers of national unions were active in the general labor movement, it was frequently because their organizations had died on their hands.

The first general labor activity in the United States was in the mixed trades' assemblies of Philadelphia and New York in the twenties and thirties. The same thing is found in the New England Workingmen's Associations, and, tempered by reformers, in the Industrial Congresses of the forties and fifties. Again, during the Civil War the first sign of a general labor activity was the formation of a trades' assembly in Rochester, N. Y., March 13, 1863. By the end of the year these trades' assemblies had been set up in every important industrial center in the East. One of the strongest was in Philadelphia, the home of the first, and in it were James L. Wright and John Samuel who later went into the Knights of Labor.

The trades' assembly or city central was a mixed body covering a city or town and its vicinity and composed of delegates from local trade unions, workingmen's clubs, and reform societies. Its chief function was propaganda or agitation leading readily into local politics, but it occasionally engaged in collective bargaining, supporting boycotts and labels, aiding strikes, organizing demonstrations, and giving advice. Its jurisdiction was territorial and with the rise of the national union and a changed industrial order its importance has declined.

Inevitably the trades' assemblies reached out toward national organization, and in April, 1864, the Louisville body sent a letter to the trades' assemblies of the United States and Canada suggesting that a convention be held in July. The president of the Louisville assembly was Robert Gilchrist, the antiwar labor leader of 1860 He tried a second time in August to interest the assemblies in a national convention with better success. On Sept. 21, 1864, a convention met with twelve delegates from eight city assemblies. Among them was Richard Trevellick, ship carpenter, veteran labor agitator, and later, organizer at large for the Knights of Labor. This convention formed the International Industrial Assembly of North America and its constitution made provision for a strike fund to be raised by a per capita assessment and held by the constituent bodies on order from the international society. This was on paper only, but it is significant because it was very like the Resistance Fund later established by the Knights of Labor, and the more effective "equalization of funds" still later set up by the Cigar Makers and the basis of the claim made for the latter to the title, "The New Unionism."

The International Industrial Assembly did not meet again. A new national movement displaced it, but its structure and aims later found expression in the district assemblies of the Knights of Labor and their relation to the national body.

THE NATIONAL TRADE UNIONS

At the outbreak of the Civil War and for four years thereafter the few national unions were in a sad way. They were national in name only, without funds, and lacking control over their constituent locals. The Typographical had survived from 1850 largely because of its benefit features. The Stone Cutters had maintained some sort of organization from 1853 and the Hat Finishers from 1854. The Molders and the Machinists, both organized in 1859, hardly maintained themselves through the Civil War. The president of the Machinists did not bother to attend the 1861 convention because he did not expect any delegates ppear. The Molders' national organization seems to disappeared in 1862 and its leader, Sylvis, lost faith in trade unionism and turned to coöperation and politics.[1]

The revival of the national unions came in 1864, was halted by the depression of 1867, and reached its height in 1873, the year of the panic.[2]

THE EIGHT-HOUR MOVEMENT, 1864-65

The premature death of the International Industrial Assembly of 1864 left the labor movement without a head for two years of great industrial activity and reform agitation. The intellectual leader of the period was Ira Steward, the eight-hour fanatic, who succeeded to the rôle of George Henry Evans, the land reformer of the forties and fifties. Evans had added the ten-hour plank to his land-reform program to gain the support of the New England Workingmen's Associations, but the Homestead Law of 1862 took the sting out of land reform and left the way open for the eight-hour movement that Steward was ready to lead.[3]

---

[1] For this survey the facts, where not otherwise stated, are derived from Commons and Associates, *History of Labour in the United States*, Vol. II. The section on Nationalization, 1860-77, was done by John B. Andrews.

[2] The national unions were organized in this period as follows: 1861, The American Miners' Association; 1862, The Sons of Vulcan (boilers and puddlers); 1863, The Locomotive Engineers; 1864, Cigar Makers, Ship Carpenters, Curriers, Plasterers; 1865, Carpenters, Bricklayers, Painters, Heaters, Tailors, Coach Makers; 1866, Silk and Fur Hat Finishers; 1867, Spinners; 1868, Knights of St. Crispin (shoemakers), Railroad Conductors; 1869, Wool Hat Finishers, Daughters of St. Crispin, Morocco Dressers; 1870, Coopers, Telegraphers; 1871, Painters (reorganized); 1872, Wood Workers, Iron and Steel Heaters, Rollers and Roughers; 1873, Roll Hands, Furniture Workers, Miners, Railroad Firemen, German Typographia.

[3] Professor Commons' effort to find in Steward's eight-hour philosophy —"a reduction of hours, an increase in wages"—a revolutionary wage theory does not alter the fact that the eight-hour movement of the sixties was a continuation of the ten-hour movement of the forties and fifties. In both cases the change was to be gained by legislation and

Steward began his eight-hour agitation in 1864 by break-ing away from the Workingmen's Assembly of Boston and creating *ex nihilo* the Labor Reform Association, the name itself harking back to the ten-hour movement of the forties and fifties. In 1865 he formed the Grand Eight-Hour League of Massachusetts and the Republican state con-vention in September put an eight-hour plank in its plat-form, while the Republican candidate for governor signed on the dotted line. Steward's practice was exactly that of Evans and the ten-hour reformers to secure pledges from regular party candidates to their measures. It was as en-tirely political and reformist as anything in the labor move-ment. But the state elections were disappointing. In 1865, only twenty-three members of the new legislature were pledged and the alternative of a new political party gained followers.

In February, 1865, the New York State Workingmen's Assembly had called a national convention to meet in New York in July to "devise the most eligible means to secure to the workingmen, eight hours' labor as a legal day's wcrk." In November, the Grand Eight-Hour League of

---

was promoted in the sixties and fifties but not in the forties by "labor reformers."

There were three short-hour theories: the "make work" doctrine of the trade unions founded upon an economic fallacy but very real, immediate facts; the argument for leisure and opportunities for culture; and Steward's standard-of-living theory, that shorter hours would mean increased wants which would in turn increase production and thus work and wages. Steward's theory was thus a combination of the other two, an interesting combination with as much truth in it as in most economic theory. It required the notorious "in the long run" assump-tion so common in classical economics but this assumption has never appealed to wage-earners who have to live from day to day. The wage-earner could understand more leisure or more work but it was too much to ask that he appreciate the "in the long run" economics of Steward or any one else. The wage-earners sometimes put Steward's phrase in preambles but they clung to leisure and "make work" ideas. Steward was just another economist.

Indiana was formed and immediately suggested the holding of state conventions to elect delegates to a national convention of "workingmen." On March 26, 1866, representatives of all but two of the national unions met in New York and called a convention to be held in Baltimore on August 20. Each local was to have one delegate, each trades' assembly two, and the eight-hour law was to be the principal business of the meeting.[4] The Workingmen's Union of New York City protested against this action of the officers of the national unions as "an assumption by a few individuals," and in May the Buffalo Trades' Assembly called for a trades' congress for legislative action. A compromise was arranged and the call for a national congress was issued jointly by the trade union officers and the Baltimore Trades' Assembly. All labor organizations were invited, including the eight-hour leagues.

THE NATIONAL LABOR UNION, 1866-72

The result of these involved birth pangs was the first convention of the National Labor Union or Congress at Baltimore, Aug. 20, 1866. It was of mixed origin as can be seen from the above, the result of spontaneous agitation from many sources: trades' assemblies (city and state), eight-hour leagues, and officers of the national unions. But its main strength came from the trades' assemblies and in this respect it was a renewal of the International Industrial Assembly of 1864. Once more the American labor movement had a national head.

At the first convention of the National Labor Union there were 77 delegates: 50 from 50 local trade unions; 17 from 13 trades' assemblies; 7 from 5 eight-hour leagues, and

---

[4] Although the officers of the national unions called this convention it is worth noting that they did not bother to give representation to the national unions as such.

3 from 2 national trade unions. The two national u
represented were insignificant ones: the Coach Ma
organized the previous year, and the Curriers, organized in
1864.[5]

The National Labor Union was a politico-reform body
from the start. It appointed committees on all the ancient
subjects that had agitated American reformers and labor
leaders from the beginning: hours; public lands and the
national debt (the national debt issue was a new one because the debt was new); coöperation and prison labor; an
address to workingmen and a conference with the President. Its committee on strikes reported against strikes and
in favor of arbitration through committees of the trades'
assemblies. There was nothing to differentiate this new
society from the industrial congresses of the forties and fifties and the politico-reform agitations that had marked
the course of the American labor movement from the start,
nothing but the change from a ten-hour to an eight-hour
demand and the addition of the national debt to the reformers' worries. The committee on the eight-hour plan,
instead of adopting Steward's economics or the "make
work" doctrine of the trade unions, reverted to the old
reformist grounds for short hours, "more time for moral,
intellectual, and social culture." It refused to recommend
political action by the convention and left each locality to
be governed by its own predilections, "whether to run an
independent ticket of workingmen, or to use political parties

[5] Mr. Andrews (Commons *et al.*, *op. cit.*, Vol. II, p. 97) attempts to
show that the representation from the national unions was really 10
because their presidents and secretaries were allowed to sit and speak
but not to vote, and because 4 delegates from other organizations were
at the same time officers of national trade unions. This, however, shows
only that the national unions were uninterested as compared with their
officers. In spite of the fact that 1866 marked the peak of postwar
industrial activity, the national unions were insignificant factors in the
general labor movement.

already existing." But the report was not "political" enough and opposition developed, an opposition which came in part from the trade unions, from Alexander Troup, representing the Boston Workingmen's Assembly but treasurer of the Typographical Union, from William Harding, president of the Coach Makers' International, from A. C. Cameron who best represented himself, and from a Lassallean socialist, E. Schlagel.[6]

The nonpolitical report was defeated and A. C. Cameron, editor of the Chicago *Workingmen's Advocate,* another name reminiscent of Evans, was appointed to redraft it. The new draft proposed, in no uncertain terms, the formation of an independent labor party to enact an eight-hour law. Like the report of the committee, this was passed and later opposed, this time by Roberts from the Philadelphia Trades' Assembly and delegates from Virginia and Maryland who were afraid this action would hurt their chance of regaining the vote. The political action report was then recommitted and came out with the same recommendation for a labor party, but qualified by the comforting addition "as soon as possible." In this form it was adopted with only one dissenting vote.[7]

The land question took second place and Evans' old slogan, "the public lands for actual settlers only," was reiterated. Coöperation and convict labor received some consideration along with "sewing women, factory operatives and daughters of toil."

[The American labor movement was in full swing under the wing of the reformers, among whom must be numbered some of the outstanding leaders of the national trade unions.] Had Evans been there, or Brisbane, or even Robert Owen, they would have felt completely at home. They had heard

---

[6] Commons *et al., op. cit.,* Vol. II, p. 99.

[7] *Ibid.,* pp. 96-100.

it all before. "Pure and simple" trade unionism was still a long way off.

The convention announced the formation of a National Labor Union to meet in annual congress. [Representation was to be from "every trades' union, workingmen's association and eight-hour league"] one delegate for the first 500 members or fewer, and one more for each additional 500 or fraction thereof. The unimportance of the national unions is again seen in the fact that they were not specially mentioned.

After adjournment a committee of the convention met President Andrew Johnson and presented a speech on the hours of labor, public lands, pauper immigration, and convict labor. The President pointed with pride to his record, but remained reticent as to his intentions.

Postwar prosperity came to a stop in 1867 and the effects of deflation were seen in a more varied representation at the second convention of the National Labor Union at Chicago, Aug. 19, 1867. Representation was as follows:

Farmers' societies, 6; national unions, 6; trades' assemblies, 9; local unions, 33; eight-hour leagues, 9; state convention, 1.

This shows the new farmer representation, the increase in the numbers of national unions and eight-hour leagues, and the falling off of local trade unions and trades' assemblies. The new constitution gave greater recognition to the national unions, allowing them each three representatives and a vice president at large, but it deplored their tendency to act independently. "Heretofore," read the preamble, "the highest form labor associations have taken is the national union of some of the trades. Between these organizations, however, there was no sympathy or systematic connection, no coöperative effort, no working for the attainment of a common end, the want of which has been experienced for years by every craft and calling." [8] State organizations were given two representatives and all other trade and labor societies one each. The time of the convention was taken up with Greenbackism and political action.

Prosperity returned in 1868 and continued with a slight recession in 1870 to 1873. The National Labor Union flourished, and though the farmers dropped out, their loss was more than made up by the addition of political unions, offshoots of the National Labor Union itself, and woman suffrage societies. Greenbackism remained the major issue. A new demand for a Department of Labor was added. A permanent lobby was to be established in Washington and A. C. Cameron was sent to the International Workingmen's Association at Basle.

The first negro delegates were present at the 1869 convention but the "negro question" was avoided. In 1870, it was decided to call a separate political convention to form the long-delayed labor party and with the Burlingame Treaty of 1869 giving China most-favored-nation treatment, the ugly Chinese labor question raised its head.

From 1870 the National Labor Union rapidly declined. The political convention met Feb. 21, 1872, and nominated Judge David Davis of Illinois for president, with the platform of the National Labor Union adopted as that of the National Labor and Reform Party. Davis declined the nomination after a qualified acceptance and the political movement died. What remained of the industrial organization met at Cleveland, Sept. 16, 1872, with only seven persons present: Trevellick, Campbell, Foran, J. C. Sylvis, Sheldon, Fay, and Manly.

The National Labor Union at no time in its career had

---

[8] George E. McNeill, *The Labor Movement: The Problem of To-day*, p. 136.

the slightest resemblance to the American Federation of Labor which followed it fourteen years later. It was a typical American politico-reform organization, led by labor leaders without organizations, politicians without parties, women without husbands, and cranks, visionaries, and agitators without jobs.

THE INDUSTRIAL CONGRESSES, 1873-75

The Industrial Congress of 1873-75 was an attempt to revive the National Labor Union without its posthumous child, the Labor Party. Not that any one who was prominent in either organization was opposed to politics but that politics seemed opposed to them. Powderly has expressed it quite clearly. "There were a number of men," he said, "in the convention [of 1868] wise, cautious and farseeing who saw that to take action either way [immediate political action or none at all] would not result in harmony, and they advocated the adoption of a platform containing such measures as were political in their nature without suggestion as to how they were to be enacted into law." This was perhaps a trifle too subtle for the ordinary intelligence, but "it was the belief of these men who took the conservative middle ground that education would in time bring these measures prominently to the front and make friends for them with men of all parties." [9]

Independent political action having broken down, the idea was to shelve it for the nonce in favor of organization and consolidation of the forces of labor and reform. The chief weakness of the old National Labor Union was that it was simply a congeries of societies brought together annually at the call of a few enthusiasts and having no integral structure or body of its own. Any one could get up a convention in those days for almost any purpose, but un-

---

[9] T. V. Powderly, *Thirty Years of Labor*, p. 45.

less it had at least a nucleus of permanent and reasonably like-minded groups behind it, it soon broke up into sects centrifugally inclined. To meet this difficulty the National Labor Union had attempted to organize locals and attach them directly to itself. They were, however, political clubs rather than labor unions, with little unity and permanence. The Industrial Congress proposed to do the same thing and create state and subordinate locals of its own. In each case organization came from the top and worked down. Neither the National Labor Union nor the Industrial Congress was a bona fide movement from the bottom up, and in this respect, as in others, they differed from the Knights of Labor, the first truly national labor organization in the United States.

The initiative of the new movement for an Industrial Congress came from a few leaders of the national trade unions, but this does not imply that the new congress was to be like the future American Federation, as Mr. Andrews suggests. It is always a mistake to write history as it were *post facto*, to look at the American labor movement through the eyes of the American Federation of Labor instead of looking at the American Federation of Labor through the eyes of the American labor movement. The point of view and experience of the trade union leaders of the sixties was reformist and political. They were not delegates but free lances. "Pure and simple" trade unionism resided only in the locals and they paid little attention to the antics of their national officers. It is true, as Mr. Andrews points out, that a new trade union leadership was growing up, best represented by Siney of the miners. But Siney left the Industrial Congress in disgust and the national unions had to wait for McGuire, Strasser, and Gompers in the eighties.

The first call for the Industrial Congress was addressed

to the presidents of the national trade unions by Foran (Coopers), Fehrenbatch (Machinists), and Saffin (Molders), all three the legitimate heirs of the labor tradition of Fincher and Sylvis. The national presidents ignored the call and the meeting at Cleveland, Nov. 19, 1872, was attended only by Foran and Fehrenbatch. Another call was issued May 3, 1873, signed by Saffin, Fehrenbatch, Foran, and Collins (Printers), to form a national organization "such as was contemplated at Baltimore in 1866." This was addressed not to trade unions alone but to "every trade organization in the United States, be it local, state or (inter)national, and every anti-monopoly, coöperative or other association organized on purely protective principles." This was certainly wide enough and proves that so far as representation was concerned the new congress was to differ not at all from the old. It was promised, however, that the new organization would not, if the sponsors could help it, "deteriorate into a political party . . . but shall to all intents and purposes remain a purely industrial association, securing to the producer his full share of all he produces."[10] An address to the organized workingmen of the United States, prompted in part by the Paris Commune of 1871, protested that the originators of the movement had no Agrarian ideas—Agrarianism being the contemporary equivalent of Bolshevism—and no connection with the Commune. It mentioned, too, the conspiracy laws, Chinese labor, unemployment, monopolies, the rising cost of living, bureaus of labor statistics, coöperation, the apprentice system, and arbitration.

The first of the new Industrial Congresses met at Cleveland on July 15, 1873, with 70 delegates. Of these, 44 came from 5 national unions (Coopers, Machinists, Molders, Sons of Vulcan, and Knights of St. Crispin). There

---

[10] Commons et al., op. cit., Vol. II, pp. 157-58.

were 5 miners' delegates led by John Siney, 2 from Typographical locals and one each from Cigar Makers' and Tobacco Workers' locals. Five trades' assemblies sent delegates and 5 labor unions, the offshoots of the old National Labor Union. The Pittsburgh National Protective League was admitted and two old reformers, Cameron and Trevellick, were given seats without votes.

The first Industrial Congress steered clear of politics and, while passing the usual resolutions, proposed as its immediate task the organization and consolidation of the forces of the producing masses "as a stepping-stone to that education that will in the future lead to more advanced action through which the necessary reforms can be obtained." This cryptic declaration is quoted, not for what it elucidates, but for what it tries to conceal. And what it tried to conceal was the fact that no sort of unanimity could be secured as to what a national labor organization had best do. It was agreed that independent political action was out of the question for the moment. It was agreed, too, that a national labor organization should be built up. But the trade unionists and the reformers were at outs as to how this should be done. There were already trade unions in the field but they were useless "for more advanced action." The congress fully recognized "the power and efficiency of trade and labor unions, local and international, as now organized in regulating purely trade matters." But for the congress, that was not enough. "On all questions appertaining to their welfare as a whole the influence of these organizations without closer union must prove futile."

The result was a compromise. Education was to be substituted for the time being for politics and the labor movement, in some way as yet undetermined, was to be consolidated. This consolidation was attempted along the lines laid down by the National Labor Union, by organizing, after the first congress, thirteen industrial unions (mixed locals) and two industrial councils (city assemblies), chartered directly by the national congress. At the same time two new national unions were granted charters. This marks the second beginning of a unified, national labor organization, but the panic of 1873 stopped it. It is to be doubted, however, if it would have gone much further had there been no panic, for it involved the old weakness of Evans' Industrial Congress and the National Labor Union. It was organized from the top down.

The compromise of 1873 settled neither the problem of politics nor of organization. At the second congress at Rochester, N. Y., April, 1874, the position on politics, whatever it was, remained intact; but the organization question became further complicated by the appearance of delegates from two new, secret societies, the Industrial Brotherhood and the Sovereigns of Industry.

Little is known of the Industrial Brotherhood. It had only one representative at Rochester, A. Warner St. John of Missouri. Powderly said that it had at that time forty branches throughout the country [11] and it is evident from its methods—it initiated members regardless of their affiliation with other organizations—that it was intended to supersede existing trade unions. The name may have come from the subordinate units of the Industrial Congresses of the forties and fifties and may indicate the persistence of reformist tendencies. It maintained the principle of solidarity in terms not unlike those later adopted by the Knights of Labor. "The condition of one part of our class," it affirmed, "cannot be improved permanently unless all are improved together." [12]

---

[11] Powderly, *op. cit.*, p. 66.
[12] *Ibid.*, p. 67.

The Sovereigns of Industry was a coöperative society confined practically to New England, a revival of the tradition of the Associationists and Coöperators of the forties and fifties. It was organized as a national body in 1874 by William H. Earle and grew so rapidly that at Rochester it threatened to absorb the Industrial Congress. It reached its height in 1875 with nearly 28,000 members, but declined rapidly and disappeared in 1880. From 1874-76 John Orvis, formerly of Brook Farm, editor of the *New Era,* and an enthusiastic Coöperator, was one of its organizers. It had a personal connection with the Patrons of Husbandry (the Grangers), a farmers' society founded in 1868 by O. H. Kelly, a government clerk, for education and mutual aid. Earle was a friend of Dudley Adams, and when the latter was made head of the National Grange, he delegated the former to organize the farmers in Massachusetts. But Earle found the soil of Massachusetts unreceptive to farmers' organizations and followed the line of least resistance which, in New England, was always either coöperation or short hours.

The 1874 congress spent most of its time listening to arguments on the respective merits of these two societies as constitutional models. President Robert Schilling (Coopers) wanted an organization like the Patrons of Husbandry and "intimate coöperation with the Farmers' movement," but he had no intention of fusing the congress with any other society. Earle wanted fusion with his own organization and St. John put forward the claims of his.

The result was another compromise. The old constitution was retained with the omission of its reference to politics and trade unionism and a committee was appointed to "prepare a definite plan of organization with constitution and by-laws for National and State Congresses and subordinate industrial unions." This meant that the original plan of creating a complete, new labor organization from the top down and on national, state, and local (mixed) lines was to be continued. Earle refused to accept this, but St. John agreed, so that when the new constitution was finally printed it bore the name and character of the "Industrial Brotherhood."

Schilling immediately sent out a circular to all labor organizations, informing them that an organization among workingmen somewhat similar to the Grangers had been provided for, and appointed organizers for each state to establish local and state unions. John Siney, president of the Miners' National Association, who had left the congress because it promised no help for the miners,[13] was made organizer for Pennsylvania. He refused the job and Terence V. Powderly, a machinist, recommended by Fehrenbatch, was appointed in his place. Powderly found the trade unions jealous of the proposed mixed locals of the Industrial Brotherhood, careful of their trade autonomy, and exclusive in their attitude toward unskilled labor.[14]

The 1875 and last Industrial Congress represented only the new mixed unions, the industrial councils.[15] The committee on the constitution found that "a unification of the existing labor organizations was an impossibility" and proposed a new constitution with state, city, and county industrial councils as a framework. This was simply putting on paper what had already been attempted, the creation of an entirely new national organization from the top down, largely because there was nothing with which to build from the bottom up.

By a strange coincidence the Industrial Congress, in its last gasp, resolved that on July 4, 1876, the eight-hour

---

[13] Rochester, N. Y., *Democrat and Chronicle*, Apr. 18, 1874.
[14] Powderly, *op. cit.*, p. 69.
[15] One printer was present.

system would go into effect "by a united movement on the part of the working masses of the United States"; just as the dying Federation of Trades and Labor Unions in 1884 was to do for May 1, 1886, but with very different results.

It was easier for the reformers of that day to draw up imposing lists of demands than to create an organization to carry them out. The preamble and in part the platform of the Industrial Brotherhood, written by Schilling in 1874, hung around for four years until it was tacked on to the Knights of Labor when they formed their national organization in 1878. Preambles and platforms do not mean much, and in the case of the Knights they meant less than usual because they were borrowed from a defunct society. This one was complete and high sounding as will be seen.

THE KNIGHTS OF ST. CRISPIN

Another important source of the Knights of Labor's ideas and personnel is found in the remarkable shoemakers' society, the Knights of St. Crispin, organized secretly May 7, 1867, in Milwaukee, Wis., by Newell Daniels.[16] The career of this society overlaps the local and district development of the Knights from 1869 to 1878, but in origin they were quite unrelated. The decline of the Crispins left a large body of shoemakers without any sort of organization, and first their leaders, and later the rank and file, drifted into the Order and became the largest single trade element within its fold.

Shoemaking, one of the oldest crafts, was affected by the factory system in the forties, before the introduction of machinery. In the fifties the sewing machine was introduced for stitching, but it was not until 1862, with the invention of the McKay pegging machine, that the male shoemakers began to feel the full effect of the Industrial

---

[16] Daniels had migrated from Milford, Mass.

Revolution. Numerous minor inventions followed, specialization and the factory system developed, "green hands" or
semiskilled workers replaced the older craftsmen, and the
Knights of St. Crispin grew up in protest. Like the Cigar
Makers later, they opposed the machines and refused to let
their members teach their craft. They tried coöperation
and strikes but they were fighting a losing battle and their
decline was as spectacular as their growth.

The first meeting of the International Grand Lodge,
Knights of St. Crispin, was held in Rochester, N. Y., July,
1868. In 1870 its membership was perhaps 50,000, by far
the largest trade union in the country. Its numerous strikes
in 1869-70 were generally successful, and in the latter year
the manufacturers of Lynn, Mass., were forced to sign a
trade agreement. But they, too, combined and in 1872
were able to break the union. From 1872 to 1874 the
Crispins were consistently beaten and the Order disappeared
in the latter year. In 1875 an attempt was made to revive
it, with the intention of substituting arbitration for strikes.
This too failed, and the Crispins had entirely disappeared
by 1878.

The experience of the Crispins with strikes was common
to the trade unions of the sixties and especially of the
depressed seventies, and the idea that arbitration should
replace strikes was general. The National Labor Union
and the Industrial Congress took the same position. It
was, in fact, almost a truism of the period that strikes were
dangerous and ineffective, did more harm than good, and
should be supplanted by peaceful and intelligent methods
for the settlement of industrial disputes.

The term "arbitration" as used in the sixties and seventies
did not mean what it means to-day—the settlement of
disputes by an outsider under voluntary agreement or legislative act. It meant simply any peaceful settlement as

opposed to strikes, what would now be called collective bargaining or negotiation. This might, of course, result in arbitration, but the real meaning of the term is found in its repeated juxtaposition to strikes.

The Crispins were Coöperators—old style. They could hardly be otherwise with their strength in New England and in a craft that was being engulfed by the Industrial Revolution. They held fast to the ideal of self-employment (producers' coöperation) in place of the wage system and when they entered the Knights of Labor, they carried something of this tradition with them. As the Industrial Revolution advanced the self-employment ideal became more and more fantastic, but each new industry as it became involved in large-scale production had to learn this lesson for itself. The Crispins were interested in consumers' coöperation too, but that was revolutionary only when used to promote self-employment.

The last convention of the Knights of St. Crispin was held in Boston in 1876. Joseph N. Glenn, a delegate from Cincinnati, was initiated into the Knights of Labor in New York on his way to this convention. On his return to Cincinnati he organized in April, 1877, Local Assembly No. 280 of the Knights of Labor with Hugh Cavanaugh one of the charter members. Charles Litchman, grand scribe of the Crispins, was made grand secretary of the Knights of Labor at its first convention in 1878. Litchman was a typical labor leader of the old school—trade unionist, reformer, politician, and publicist in one. He was born in Marblehead, Mass., April 8, 1849. His father was a shoe "manufacturer" and he went on the road as a salesman for the concern. He studied law and went into business but evidently failed, for in 1874 he was employed in a shoe factory. As a Republican he was twice defeated for the general court of Massachusetts. In 1878 he ran as an independent and supported Ben Butler for governor. He was elected by the Greenback-Labor Party and served one year in the lower house. In 1880 he went to Washington as a delegate to the conference which called the national convention of the Greenback-Labor Party, and he attended the Chicago convention as a delegate from Massachusetts. After holding office in the Knights of Labor off and on for fourteen years, he resigned in 1892 to return to his first love, the Republican Party.

Litchman was a Mason; past grand and past chief patriarch, etc., of the Grand Encampment of Massachusetts I.O.O.F.; grand senior sagamore of the Great Council of the United States Improved Order of Red Men; past regent of the Royal Arcanum; member of the American Legion of Honor and of the Order of the Golden Cross. After this, one wonders not at the highfalutin terminology of the Knights of Labor but that they were so modest for their time.[17]

---

[17] *The Journal of United Labor,* June 15, 1880, p. 1880. Hereafter referred to as the *Journal.*

Another Crispin who was equally prominent in the Knights was Richard Griffiths. He was initiated by Litchman in 1877 in Chicago and organized the first local, No. 400, in that city. He became master workman of District Assembly No. 24 in 1878, worthy foreman of the General Assembly in 1879, and grand treasurer in 1882.

CHAPTER II

TOWARD NATIONAL ORGANIZATION

WHILE the National Labor Union and the Industrial Congresses were trying vainly to establish a national labor organization from the top downwards; while the national trade unions were weak, isolated, and uninterested in or incapable of unification; nine unknown garment cutters in Philadelphia reorganized a dying local from which grew naturally and slowly a bona fide, national trade and labor society, the first in the history of the American labor movement.

Every previous attempt at a general national organization had been more or less artificial, the result of a "call" by some individuals, who, while they held official positions, rarely represented anything but themselves. These calls had been answered by other individuals often holding quite different views and equally unrepresentative. Attempts to unite these individuals and the groups to which they belonged had gone little further than platform making, at which they were all adepts. The platform makers had learned that they could hope for no sort of permanence until they could find, or create, a real organization behind the bold front of their convention demands. The trade unions were not strong enough or interested enough to supply the need. The reform societies were ephemeral and doctrinaire. The attempts of the National Labor Union and the Industrial Congresses to create an entirely new structure from the top down failed. Something new had to happen, and that something was the first local assembly of the Knights of Labor.

Stimulated by war-time conditions in the clothing industry, a benefit society, the Garment Cutters' Association of Philadelphia, was organized in 1862 and managed to keep together until December 9, 1869, when they met for the last time, divided their funds, and dissolved. A few of the members were reluctant to see the thing die, and after much discussion during the previous summer they had decided to reorganize the elect in a secret society. This they did in the hall of the American Hose Company on Jayne Street after the dissolution of the old society. Only nine members of the old went into the new, and the first local assembly of the Knights of Labor was formed,[1] though the name was not adopted until the third meeting on December 28. In the meantime, the "secret work," the chief concern of the new society, was elaborated and the obligation taken at the third meeting by Stephens, Wright, Hilsea, Keen, Kennedy, Cook, and McCauley. This was the first permanent organization and two days later five new members were taken in.[2]

On Jan. 6, 1870, the first regular officers were elected. The retiring presiding officer, James L. Wright, was made venerable sage and Uriah Stephens was made master workman. The initiation fee was set at $1.00, refreshments were served to keep the members away from the saloons, and on May 10 the following advertisement was placed in the Philadelphia *Ledger*:

---

[1] The nine men were: James L. Wright, Uriah S. Stephens, William H. Phillips, Robert McCauley, William Cook, James M. Hilsea (or Hilsee), Joseph S. Kennedy, Robert W. Keen, David Westcott.

[2] G. W. Cook, H. L. Sinexon, W. C. Yost, Samuel Wright, G. W. Hornberger, and James Barron. Although not among the original members, Sinexon, according to Powderly, was, with Stephens, the real originator of the new society.

This record follows Powderly, *Thirty Years of Labor*, 1890 edition.

Fountain of Power—K. of L. officers and representatives—
a special meeting will be held on Thursday the 12th instant
to act on the first report from the State Labor Union giving
aid to the Garment Cutters' branch, to resist the attempt of
certain oppressive houses in the trade to reduce the wages of
skilled workmen; secondly shall the patronage of the industrials
be given to establishments that refuse just remuneration?

By Order

L. A. SMITH, M. E. W.

At the meeting on May 12 which followed this cryptic
announcement, Stephens explained that he had signed the
call "Smith" to avoid detection, that L.A. meant "Labor
Advocate" and that "M.E.W." was suggested by Sinexon
and meant "Most Excellent Workman." Powderly explained
that the reference to the State Labor Union was "to have it
appear that there was a strange new organization in existence
in the city, one which had connection with a national association."

It is evident that the new society differed little from any
local trade union except in its extreme secrecy and its
ritual. The announcement in the *Ledger* suggests the possibility of a strike against·a reduction of wages and the use
of the boycott. Secrecy in fact was the major concern of
the Order in its early years and the cause of most of its
troubles. A prospective member was told nothing. He
was questioned as to his opinions on "the elevation of labor"
and, if his answers were satisfactory, his name was brought
before the assembly and a committee was appointed to
investigate his qualifications. If the committee were satisfied the candidate was voted on, and if rejected, he remained
in ignorance of the existence of the society. If elected, his
proposer would get him to the meeting place on some pretext
and he was given to understand that his proposer was there
for initiation too. Thus if he refused to join he would not
know that his friend was a member of the society. Secret

societies were of course not uncommon and no special explanation is needed for this one. There was some danger from employers no doubt, but more important perhaps was the general human desire for self-aggrandizement by means of secrecy, signs, and mysteries.

But the new society soon discovered that it could have too much secrecy, so much as to interfere with its growth and influence. On Aug. 11, 1870, it was agreed to allow a member to reveal to prospects his own membership in the organization, provided he did not reveal the name of any other member.

On Oct. 20, 1870, the first "sojourner" was proposed in the assembly. The idea of the sojourner, like the ritual, was probably derived from the Masonic Order. The sojourner was a worker of some other craft than garment cutting, who was initiated into the cutters' local until such time as enough members of his craft could be secured to "swarm" and form an assembly of their own craft. The sojourner was not a full member of the local. He was there temporarily, had no voice in trade matters, and was not required to pay dues. "The sojourner," says Powderly, "was admitted that he might become a missionary among his fellow tradesmen."[3]

This subject is treated in some detail because it touches on a problem that later became important. There is a rather general impression that the Knights of Labor assemblies were predominately "mixed," i.e., composed of members of different trades, and thereby unlike trade unions whose locals admitted only members of one trade. The general question will be taken up later, but here it should be noted that the original assembly was composed entirely of cutters, and that the entry of the sojourner did not involve any breakdown of this principle. It was simply a means of

[3] Powderly, op. cit., p. 77.

extending the organization and for some time only Local Assembly No. 1 admitted sojourners. Local Assembly No. 1 was a strictly craft society, more strictly craft than the ordinary trade union of the time, and though the practice of admitting sojourners later made possible the development of the mixed assembly, it was more by accident than intention.

Only two of the original members of the Garment Cutters' assembly had any labor "past," and it is in them that there will be found any ideas beyond the pure and simple trade unionism of the first assembly.

Uriah S. Stephens was the founder of the Order of the Knights of Labor. He was master workman of the first local, the first district, and the first national assemblies. He resigned the second year of the national organization (1879), after being defeated on the Greenback ticket for Congress in 1878. He recommended Terence V. Powderly or Richard Griffiths as his successor and the former was chosen. In 1881, when the ritual was changed by the elimination of Scriptural passages and the oath of secrecy— a pledge being substituted to meet the objections of the Roman Catholic Church—Stephens quarreled with Powderly and threatened to withdraw himself and Local Assembly No. 1 from the Order.

Stephens was born Aug. 3, 1821, at Cape May, N. J. His maternal ancestry was Quaker and he was educated for the Baptist ministry. He must have carried over from his early training some Greek as he undoubtedly did strong religious sentiments and a familiarity with the Bible. After the panic of 1837 he was indentured to a tailor and later taught school. In 1845, he moved to Philadelphia where he worked at his trade, and in 1853 he made a tour of the West Indies, Central America, Mexico, and the Pacific Coast. He stayed in California five years and returned in

1858 to Philadelphia. He supported the antislavery cause and worked for Frémont in 1856 and for Lincoln in 1860. In 1861, he attended the national convention of workingmen in opposition to the war. Perlman, in Commons' *History of Labour*,[4] says that Stephens visited Europe in the sixties and there "doubtless came in touch with the Marxian Internationalists." But there is no evidence that Stephens ever visited Europe, and no support for the legend among American Socialists that Eccarius gave him a copy of Marx's writings including the Communist Manifesto.[5] Mr. Perlman rightly points out that Stephens did not adopt the essential ideas of Marx but that is putting it mildly. There is no hint of Marxianism in anything Stephens said or did that is recorded.

In 1878, Stephens was nominated for Congress from the 5th District of Pennsylvania. He made a vigorous campaign resigning as grand master workman of the Knights of Labor to give all his time to it, but was defeated. He was elected grand master workman a second time in his absence and attended the second General Assembly in January, 1879. He resigned by letter at the third General Assembly, September, 1879 (a change of date had brought two meetings of the General Assembly in one year), and though he retained office in his local he lost touch with the Order as a whole.

Stephens was a Mason, an Odd Fellow, and a member of the Knights of Pythias. He died in 1882, estranged from his successor, Terence V. Powderly, over changes in the ritual and modifications of the policy of secrecy. These were his peculiar contributions to the Knights, and are explained by his religious background and his connection

---

[4] Commons and Associates, *History of Labor in the United States*, Vol. II, p. 197.
[5] *Der Sozialist*, March 3, 1888.

with secret fraternal societies. His philosophy of the labor
movement is best summed up by the term "solidarity."
The trade unions of the sixties and seventies were isolated
and therefore weak, and he preached the "benefits of amalgamation and affiliation with our great brotherhood." [6] His
political interests were common to all the labor leaders of
the period.[7]

James L. Wright, the second founder of the Knights of
Labor with a past, was born Apr. 6, 1816, in County
Tyrone, Ireland. His family moved to St. John, N. B.,
and later to Philadelphia. He was educated at Mt. Vernon
Grammar School and the private academy of one Charles
Mead. He served a six years' apprenticeship as tailor to
George W. Farr and, in 1836, became a member of the
Tailors' Benevolent Society. He went into business for
himself at Frankfort near Philadelphia in 1847, and in 1854
he became manager of a large clothing house. The depression of 1857 threw him back into the ranks of the wage-
earners. He helped organize the Garment Cutters' Association of 1862, and was its president when it dissolved in
1869.

The Philadelphia Trades' Assembly was formed in
October, 1863, and Wright was made treasurer. He was
temporary chairman of the first local assembly of the
Knights of Labor and later venerable sage and master workman. In 1878, he received 54,000 votes as Greenback-Labor
candidate for state treasurer and 82,000 votes for Secretary
of Internal Affairs of Pennsylvania.[8]

The significance of Stephens' and Wright's careers is

---

[6] *Proceedings,* January, 1879 General Assembly of the Knights of
Labor, p. 55.

[7] Powderly, *op. cit.,* McNeill, *The Labor Movement: The Problem of
To-day,* and *Journal,* pp. 137-38.

[8] McNeill, *op. cit.,* and Commons *et al., op. cit.,* Vol. II, p. 25 and
n. 20.

found in the light they throw upon the way in which the labor leaders of the mid-century moved in and out of the wage-earning class. The opportunities which America offered for economic betterment have often been elaborated, but the industrial instability which wrecked careers as fast as it made them was equally important. Both Stephens and Wright had seen "better days" and their experience was not uncommon. They were not class conscious in the European sense—could not be, in a country and time when classes were fluid.

The Knights of Labor grew very slowly and it was not until July 18, 1872, that the second assembly was organized by ship carpenters and caulkers of Philadelphia who had sojourned in Local Assembly No. 1. All the early assemblies were trade bodies. The mixed assembly did not appear until comparatively late. The founders of the Order undoubtedly expected to organize all trades, but there is no proof that they wanted to mix all trades in the same local assemblies. They deplored the exclusiveness and narrowness of the trade unions, but they proposed to remedy this by gathering the trade locals into one big union. The idea of the mixed local probably came from the National Labor Union and the Industrial Congress and in that case it entered the Order when the General Assembly was formed in 1878. But there were some local mixed assemblies before that, due in all probability to the fact that they were organized in neighborhoods where there were not enough men of one craft to form a trade assembly.[9]

---

[9] No. 1 garment cutters December, 1869; No. 2 ship carpenters and caulkers July 18, 1872; No. 3 shawl weavers December 21, 1872; No. 4 carpet weavers; No. 5 ship riggers March 27, 1873; No. 6 carpet weavers; No. 7 stone masons May 8, 1873; No. 8 bag makers May 8, 1873; No. 9 machinists and blacksmiths; No. 10 stone cutters; No. 11 wool sorters; No. 12 machinists and blacksmiths and boiler makers; No. 13 tin plate and sheet iron workers; No. 14 steel workers; No. 15

By the end of 1873 more than eighty locals had been organized, all of them in Philadelphia or its vicinity. Expansion beyond Philadelphia began with the organization of a gold beaters' assembly, No. 28, in New York City, January, 1874, and the stone cutters of Trenton, N. J., December, 1873, or January, 1874, probably the latter. The ship carpenters and caulkers of Camden, N. J., and Wilmington, Del., were organized as locals, Nos. 31 and 30, about the same time, and in March, the first local in Massachusetts was formed at Boston of gold beaters (No. 55) by Frederick Turner who later became secretary of the General Assembly and was throughout an important cog in the "machine." [10]

In the fall of 1873, before the effect of the panic was felt, Local Assembly No. 1 appointed a five-member committee on progress and invited other assemblies to do the same. The result was a joint meeting of the representatives of the locals and the formation of the first district assembly, Philadelphia, Dec. 25, 1873. Each local sent three delegates. The district assembly was the first delegate, mixed body in the Order. In many respects it was like the

---

pattern makers and molders; No. 16 shop smiths; No. 17 machinists, blacksmiths, and boilermakers; No. 18 house carpenters; No. 19 bricklayers; No. 20 gold beaters (Powderly, *op. cit.*, p. 98). All these were in Philadelphia.

Numbers 20 to 27 inclusive are simply mentioned by Powderly as having been organized at one time but they too were probably trade assemblies, for two lists, one dated Jan. 1, 1882, and the other not dated, give No. 23—the only one of these numbers represented in either list—as composed of carpet weavers.

There were two mixed assemblies represented at the convention, July 3, 1873.

[10] It is impossible to locate all the early assemblies and their numbers do not always indicate the order in which they were formed. Organizers were given groups of numbers to avoid repetition and this practice destroyed historical continuity. Many of the early assemblies had disappeared before the first complete list was issued in the *Journal* in 1882 and many of the numbers may never have been used.

city centrals or trades' assemblies but more homogeneous in that it represented only the Knights of Labor. Throughout the history of the Order, Philadelphia remained the center of trade as New York became the center of "mixed" senti- ment. Thus the Knights in their early locals carried on the tradition of the local trade unions, and in their dis- tricts, the tradition of the trades' assemblies, the two most important units in the early history of trade unionism. The peculiar contribution of the Order lay in combining the exclusiveness of the one with the larger purposes of the other.

Nearly a year passed before the formation of the second district assembly at Camden, N. J., Oct. 14, 1874,[11] but this was simply an extension of the Philadelphia growth, leaving the Order still confined as to district organization to its original home. The first important expansion was westward through Reading[12] to Pittsburgh and into the coal and iron districts, where the more rigid craft ideas of Philadelphia began to break down. On Jan. 9, 1873, John M. Davis began the publication of the *National Labor Tribune* at Pittsburgh. Davis went to Philadelphia and was initiated into Local Assembly No. 53 (cigar makers) in October, 1874, and on his return to Pittsburgh organized Local Assembly No. 81 (iron workers). He pushed the organization of the Knights in the west and on Aug. 8, 1875, formed District Assembly No. 3 of Pittsburgh.[13] But while organization was rapid and 100 locals were formed in the Pittsburgh district by January, 1876, internal differences

---

[11] Composed of locals Nos. 22, 31, 52, 54, 60, and, shortly after, 66 and 69.

[12] Local Assembly No. 86, May 19, 1875, Reading, Pa.

[13] Composed of No. 96 (miners), Coal Valley; No. 98 (cabinet makers), Pittsburgh, which died a few months later; Nos. 100-106, the last at Gallatzin; and No. 88 (stationary engineers), Scranton, May 15, 1875.

forced District Assembly No. 3 into what Powderly called a reorganization in June, 1876.[14]

The first local at Scranton, Pa., No. 88, was organized May 15, 1875, by Frederick Turner and James L. Wright and transferred from District Assembly No. 1 to District Assembly No. 4, Reading, on the formation of the latter district, Jan. 23, 1876. It followed closely the Philadelphia tradition of secrecy and craft exclusiveness and for some time did not accept sojourners. A second visit of Turner and Wright was necessary when, with great reluctance, the local admitted some miners to its ranks. These swarmed July 3, 1876, and formed a local, No. 216, in Providence, the upper end of the city. In the same way the carpenters left No. 88 and formed No. 217 and, on Oct. 14, employees of the Dickson Manufacturing Company (locomotives) organized Local Assembly No. 222. Terence V. Powderly was initiated into the Order in Philadelphia in 1874, but "could learn nothing of its whereabouts" until he was admitted to No. 88 at Scranton, Sept. 6, 1876. He was elected master workman of Local Assembly No. 222 when it was organized. District Assembly No. 5 (Scranton) was formed Feb. 24, 1877, and by July 1 it had 107 locals within its jurisdiction.

The expansion of the Order through the western coal regions is explained by the condition of the miners' organizations. The bituminous miners had district, but no

---

[14] Powderly, *op. cit.*, p. 101. In 1876 district assemblies were formed at Reading, No. 4 (January 23), Connellsville, Pa., Akron, O., and in West Virginia. The locals going into District Assembly No. 4 were: Nos. 86, 99, 125, 126, 127, 128, 130, 165, 172, 173, of Reading; 91, 92 of Allentown; 118, Pottstown; 129, Royersford; 90, 133, Bethlehem; 88, Scranton. Other locals were organized at: Scranton, 216 (miners) July 3, 1876, 217 (carpenters) Aug. 29, 222 (locomotive shopmen) Oct. 14, and 227; Carbondale, No. 223; Wilkes-Barre, 224; Danville, 225 (machinists and blacksmiths); Dunmore, 226, 228, 229; Mill Hollow (miners) 230, 231.

national organization until October, 1873, when John Siney resigned as head of the anthracite national union, and at Youngstown, Ohio, combined the existing state organizations among the soft coal miners into a National Miners' Association.   Siney was aided by John James, president of the Illinois Miners' Union, and by Alexander McDonald, a Scotch labor leader.   The policy of the new national was that of the British union of the same name, a policy of opposition to strikes and preference for negotiation and arbitration.   In December, 1874, the employers of the Tuscarawas Valley, led by Mark Hanna, decided to reduce the scale from 90 to 70 cents, and offered to confer with the union.   Three representatives were chosen from each side and Judge S. J. Andrews was made chairman of the scale committee.   The decision went against the miners, the base rate being set at 71 cents.   One company, annoyed at a previous refusal of the operators' association to support it against the union's demand for a check-weighman, offered the men 80 cents.   This was accepted and the employees of other operators appealed to the union to be freed of the arbitration award.   The union officers agreed and the operators were forced to pay 80 cents, but the practice of joint conference and arbitration was destroyed for a decade.   At the end of 1875, the National Miners' Association had 35,000 members, but incessant striking and the arrest of Siney and Parks in Clearfield County, Pa., June, 1875, for "conspiracy and inciting to riot," destroyed the association.   By 1876 the soft coal miners were without a national union.

In the anthracite field a similar condition was found. From 1868 to 1871 there existed trade agreements between the Anthracite Board of Trade and the Miners' and Mine Laborers' Benevolent Association.   But the "long strike," December, 1874, to June, 1875, completely destroyed the union and put the disorganized miners in the power of the Molly Maguires.

The Molly Maguires was a secret, inside ring which controlled the lodges of the Ancient Order of Hibernians. They appeared in the United States as early as 1852. They opposed the draft in the Civil War; were important factors in local politics, interested chiefly in those offices which controlled the expenditure of funds; and murdered and maltreated mine owners and bosses throughout Pennsylvania, more for personal and political than for industrial reasons. In 1869, Franklin B. Gowen became president of the Philadelphia & Reading Railroad which, like most of the Pennsylvania railroads, was also owner of a large number of mines. He employed the Pinkerton Detective Agency, then just entering labor disputes, to stop the Maguires. In October, 1873, they sent James McParlan, Irish and Catholic, into the mining region and he, claiming to be a fugitive from justice, worked himself into the Mollys under the name of McKenna. The Mollys had controlled the strike of 1874-75 and forced the union to hold out against reductions longer than it would otherwise have done. There was great suffering among the men but they were afraid to return to work, with the Mollys, who were not particular about whom they killed, in command. When, on June 1, 1875, the union ordered the men back as individuals to make what terms they could, the Maguires remained intransigent and by intimidation were able to prevent resumption for some time. A riot resulted from the attempt of the Philadelphia & Reading to open its mines and the Maguires seemed to have won at the expense of the union. But McParlan had his evidence, arrests were made in the fall of 1875, and late in 1876, 24 Mollys were convicted, 10 were hanged, and 14 sent to jail for terms of 2 to 7 years. This finished the power of the

Molly Maguires, but it also left the anthracite miners without a union.

The "long strike" left the way open for organization by the Knights of Labor, but the murderous activities of the Mollys and their bloody end tended to discredit secrecy. This innocent practice, borrowed by Stephens from the fraternal orders, had taken on a dangerous complexion. Secrecy in the coal districts meant murder and theft, the fear and antagonism of the public and especially of the Church, and the first major problem of the Knights began to emerge.

The Order was spreading rapidly from two centers, Philadelphia and Pittsburgh, and there was no adequate understanding between the two. Conflict arose because, though Philadelphia was the parent center, Pittsburgh was the more active. There was, too, a conflict of ideas. Philadelphia was the oldest trade union center in the country. It had the longest tradition of "pure and simple" unionism and had seldom followed the strange gods of reform. It was conservative, law-abiding, and dominated by middle-class ideals. Pittsburgh, on the contrary, was western, aggressive, rough, politically minded, and influenced somewhat by socialist thought. The Pittsburgh cabinet makers were socialists and Davis was involved in the Pittsburgh convention of April 17, 1876, called by a Greenback society, the Junior Sons of '76, and invaded by the New York socialists under P. J. McGuire.[15] Greenbackism was in the air and the eastern socialists were beginning their long

---

[15] This Pittsburgh convention though controlled by Knights of Labor had nothing to do with the Order. It was called by a political society and adopted a Greenback platform. Its only significance is that it permitted the New York socialists for the first time to cross the Alleghenies in force and practice their best trick of withdrawing from any meeting they could not dominate. But compare Commons *et al., op. cit.*, Vol. II, p. 235 for a very different account of this convention.

series of forays into the labor movement with the intent to capture it for the revolution. What they could not capture they were frequently able to destroy and District Assembly No. 3 of the Knights of Labor was one of their earliest victims.

To secrecy, socialism, and the antagonism of east and west was added the natural need of a central authority for the growing Order. Two district assemblies with the same number—5—were organized, one from Philadelphia at Scranton in June, 1877, and another by Pittsburgh at Raymond City, W. Va. This was not corrected until the first meeting of the General Assembly when the number of the Scranton district was changed to 16. It is in this West Virginia district, No. 5, that the first mixed assemblies can be definitely located. This district was composed of locals Nos. 158 Raymond City; 392 Coalburg; 393 and 395 Cannelton; and 394 Lewiston. In a record of Jan. 1, 1882, purporting to contain a full list of existing locals, Number 158 is described as "mixed," "mining, farming, etc."; Numbers 392 and 393 as "miners and laborers," though this probably means miners and mine laborers; Number 394 as "mixed" and Number 395 as "miners and laborers." [16] But this record of 1882 is not a reliable guide as to the nature of the local when first organized. It gives for instance Local Assembly No. 31, Camden, N. J., as "mixed," whereas Powderly states definitely that it was organized by ship carpenters and caulkers. Nevertheless, a semirural district like West Virginia was likely to be the original home of the mixed local.

In 1877, the year of the great upheaval among miners and railroad workers in Pennsylvania, the Order expanded rapidly in the West, in Pennsylvania, West Virginia, Ohio, Indiana, and Illinois. In all, 11 new district assemblies

---

[16] *Journal*, p. 189.

were organized, bringing the total up to 14 before the fall
of 1878 and the first General Assembly.[17]

---

[17] This total includes the two District Assemblies numbered 5.   The
district assemblies formed in 1877 were:
District Assembly No. 5 Scranton, Pa., February 24.
District Assembly No. 5 West Virginia, May 5.
District Assembly No. 7 Akron, O., May 8.   The first local of this
district was No. 120, organized by Christopher Evans at New Straitsville Sept. 23, 1875.   Evans was, with John McBride, one of the outstanding leaders of the Ohio miners.   Local Assembly No. 169 organized
at Shawnee Feb. 5, 1876, was another important miners' local in District
Assembly No. 7 and between them they supplied many of the leaders
of the Miners' National Trade Assembly No. 135, organized in 1886,
and the open unions which finally merged to form the United Mine
Workers of America.
District Assembly No. 13 Springfield, Ill., August 1, composed of
Local Assembly Nos. 271 Springfield, 346 Hollis, 360 Kingston Mines,
415 Limestone, and an assembly at Peoria.
District Assembly No. 11 Connellsville, Pa., September 11, composed
of Local Assembly Nos. 234 Frost Station, 239 Dunbar, 245 Scottsdale,
279 Connellsville, 290 Fairchance, and 297 Mount Pleasant.
District Assembly No. 12 Youngstown, O., organized about the same
time; no record.
District Assembly No. 14 Knightsville, Ind., September 13, composed
of Local Assembly Nos. 299 Cardonia, 303 Brazil, 318 Knightsville,
455 Harmony, 456 Carbon.
District Assembly No. 8 Pittsburgh glass blowers September 23, composed of locals Nos. 281, 300, 305, 319, 322, 484.   This district collapsed
in 1880 but was immediately reorganized (May 8, 1880) by the merging
of locals Nos. 300, 305, 322 as Window Glass Workers Assembly No.
300, the first and most successful national trade assembly in the Order.
District Assembly No. 6 New Haven, W. Va., October 20, composed
of Local Assembly Nos. 338 New Haven, 339 Clifton, and three others
whose numbers were changed because they had been duplicated to 1432
Minersville, 1501 Syracuse, O., 1502 Pomeroy, O.   The *Journal*, Jan. 1,
1882, gives the Clifton number as 329 and does not mention 338.   It
calls 329 (339) and 1502 mixed assemblies.
District Assembly No. 9 West Elizabeth, Pa., October 23, composed
of Local Assembly Nos. 96 Coal Valley, 109 West Elizabeth, 124
Noblestown, 140 Walkers Mills, 147 Fayette City, 151 Coal Bluff, 157
Elizabeth, 162 Monongahela City, 168 Greenfield, 178 Hope Church, and
198 McKeesport.
There is no record of District Assembly No. 10.
District Assembly No. 15 Elmira and Canisteo, N. Y., must have
been organized sometime in 1877 because it sent delegates to the first
General Assembly in January, 1878, but Powderly, from whom these

THE PHILADELPHIA CONVENTION, JULY 3, 1876

Once the Knights had grown beyond Philadelphia the demand for some central body to coördinate the locals and districts was certain to arise. New points of view and interests at variance with those of the founders emerged and among them was the attitude to be taken toward the original policy of secrecy. In the fall of 1875, a New York local, No. 82 (flint glass workers, Brooklyn), asked District Assembly No. 1 as "head of the Order" to take steps to make the name of the Order public, in place of the five stars which were then used. It was the profound conviction of the founders that complete secrecy was an important factor in the success of the movement, and they were reluctant even to consider so minor a change as the publication of the Order's name involved. In a way they were right. Secrecy was an important factor in their success; but, as the Order grew and spread, some modification in this policy was necessary, especially under the conditions created by the Molly Maguires and the opposition of the Church. Stephens was probably influenced in his attitude by the success of the fraternal organizations whose longevity was in striking contrast to the ups and downs of the trade unions. If so, he misunderstood the cause of the fraternal societies' success. They lasted longer not because they were secret, but because they were fraternal. Then, too, Stephens was a Baptist, and therefore not disturbed by the attitude of the Roman Catholic Church, while many of the newer members were Irish and Catholic.

The pressure of growth and the problems arising from it forced District Assembly No. 1 to act and a call was sent to the assemblies that were known to a convention

---

particulars are compiled, does not include it in the list of districts in existence at the time of the first General Assembly.

in Philadelphia, July 3, 1876. Thirty-five delegates attended, representing 28 trade locals, 3 district assemblies, 2 mixed locals, and 2 localities which may or may not have had assemblies. The convention unfortunately represented practically only Philadelphia and Reading. Twenty-two of the delegates came from these two cities, only one from Pittsburgh, 3 from Brooklyn and New York, 2 from Allentown, and one each from Chester, Pottstown, Camden, Pottsville, Greenland. The trades represented were: iron workers (5), iron molders (4), machinists (3), boiler makers (2), painters (2), house carpenters (2), stove molders, heaters and stove cutters, garment cutters, shoemakers, carpet weavers, flint glass blowers, railroad workers, safe makers, stocking weavers, and cigar makers (one each). James L. Wright was made president and all the officers but one were from Pennsylvania and all but two from Philadelphia and Reading.[18]

The need for some central authority was evident from the confusion over the delegates. J. Fortner was not on the list of representatives but he appeared for Local Assembly No. 28 (gold beaters) of Brooklyn, the first local to be organized outside Philadelphia and its environs. He explained that his assembly was defunct, owing to the negligence of its founder and that its number had been given to a Reading local of boiler makers. A similar confusion arose over Local Assembly No. 82. Powderly states that this convention was called because of a protest of Local Assembly No. 82, flint glass workers of Brooklyn.

---

[18] The officers were: president, James L. Wright, Philadelphia; vice presidents, George E. Rieff, Reading, Samuel Lamond, Philadelphia, and George (or Charles) Stroud, Chester; secretary, William Farrell, Philadelphia; assistant secretaries, Millard F. Smith, Philadelphia, Joseph Auchenbach, Reading; treasurer, James McCambridge, Philadelphia; doorkeepers, J. Fortner, Brooklyn, and Samuel Burkhart, Reading. There were no highfalutin titles in this organization and only one of the officers, the president, was known to the labor movement.

But the convention seated a delegate, Jacob Umstead, for Local Assembly No. 82, cigar makers, Philadelphia, while the Brooklyn flint glass workers were organized as Local Assembly No. 84. Powderly may simply have made a mistake, but there were two delegates from Local Assembly No. 82 in the convention, and one of them spoke in favor of greater publicity. It would seem that this speaker was from Brooklyn and with Fortner constituted the opposition to the Philadelphia policy. It is true, at any rate, that the convention was dominated by the Philadelphia delegates, and while the question of secrecy was supposed to be the point at issue, it was completely ignored.

This convention is of great significance for an understanding of the Knights of Labor, because it represented them in their virginal simplicity as yet unspoiled by itinerant reformers and politicians with delusions of grandeur. A resolution to make the Order a benefit one was defeated, as was another to take political action; and a resolution was adopted to admit to membership none but "men of good moral character, sober and industrious and thoroughly understanding the trade which he follows." In other words these men were pure and simple craftsmen and made no provision as was afterwards done for the entry of non-wage-earners.

The main work of the convention was the adoption of a constitution, a simple matter in marked contrast to the difficulty experienced by the heterogeneous Industrial Congress. No platform or preamble seems to have been thought of and no grandiose terminology rooted in an inferiority complex. The name of the national body was to be, to members, simply the National League and "to the public should it be considered expedient" to reveal any of the proceedings, the National Labor League of North America. It was to be made up of two delegates from each district and one from each local assembly, thus giving both direct and indirect representation with the local influence predominating. Had this basis of representation been followed when the General Assembly was finally formed, many of the characteristics of clique government might have been avoided and the mixed influence in the Order weakened. The *Adelphon Kruptos,* or secret work, was retained with some amendments.

The object of the proposed league was simply to bring the local assemblies "into closer fraternal union," "to share each other's burdens," and "to enable them to agree upon such modes of procedure as will make the members of the Order a band of true pioneers of labor reform." An executive committee of five was to be appointed before the adjournment of each convention to carry on the work of the Order during the year. This committee was given "sole power to decide by majority vote all disputed points as to exact meaning of the A.K.,"[19] or the constitution, the decisions to be final unless set aside by the following convention. All legislative powers not specifically vested in the League (residual powers) were to be exercised by the districts, and those not vested in the districts, by the locals, *i.e.,* federalism. Any five or more locals were to be allowed to form a district provided that they were not in arrears to the district to which they had belonged and that no two districts should be created in any one congressional district, town, or city without the consent of all the assemblies therein. This provision had nothing to do with politics but was meant only to prevent overcrowding. An assessment of 5 cents per member per annum was to be paid to support the executive committee and it was agreed that no one should go to work before the regular hours. The convention adjourned to meet in Pittsburgh—

---

[19] *Adelphon Kruptos*—secret work.

probably to placate the sulking District Assembly No. 3 —in July, 1877.

This then was the beginning of a bona fide general labor movement, the first in the history of American labor. It had no philosophy, no reforms, no political ambitions, no strange and ambitious titles. It was as pure and simple as the national trade unions, and differed from them only in its ambition to include all trades and in its secrecy which was not unknown among them. Fortunately or unfortunately the Knights were not to continue in the strait and narrow path. When they created their permanent national organization in 1878, they accepted the tradition of the older national bodies, dressed themselves in preambles, platforms, and titles, and launched upon the country, in theory if not in fact, another reform society. But much water flowed under the bridge before they reached this stage.

THE PITTSBURGH CONVENTION, MAY 14, 1877

Pittsburgh had almost, if not quite, ignored the Philadelphia convention, and the Pittsburghers were not placated by the decision to hold the second meeting in their home town. The question of secrecy had been avoided at Philadelphia, there had been no politics and no proper recognition of the fact that the Order was growing from Pittsburgh in a way to leave Philadelphia, the place of its birth, very much behind.

In 1874, a semisecret political society, the Junior Sons of '76, was organized in the Pittsburgh region after the Patrons of Husbandry with a Greenback platform. This society called a national convention at Tyrone, Pa., Dec. 28, 1875, which was attended by Greenbackers and socialists, among them P. J. McGuire who was then in his socialist stage, but later became a Knight and still later a trade unionist; George Blair of New York, a member of the Order; and John M. Davis, master workman of District Assembly No. 3. Davis was made president of the convention and Blair secretary. A second meeting was held in Pittsburgh, April 17, 1876, at which James L. Wright was made temporary, and John M. Davis permanent chairman. Politics was in the air and some of the leaders of the Order were deeply involved.

At the Pittsburgh convention of the Junior Sons, the socialists and Greenbackers split, the former withdrew and nothing more was heard of this movement. Wright and Davis were further involved in politics in August, 1877, when an attempt was made to organize a Greenback-Labor Party, and in Pennsylvania when they both ran for office on the Greenback ticket.

This constitutes one of the early ventures of the leaders of the Knights into politics and it was no exception to the rule. Stephens, Wright, Davis, Blair, Powderly, Litchman, Bailey, Beaumont—practically all of the leaders went political as individuals at one time or another in their careers. Not only that, but, as was repeatedly pointed out, most of the demands of the platform of 1878 could be secured only by political action of one sort or another, and the Order after its decline as an industrial body went into politics. But from its beginning throughout its active career the Order as such kept out of politics and can in no sense be considered a political organization. It lobbied a little and some locals and some districts were on occasion politically active. It had a politically minded group within it just as it had groups representing almost every sort of idea. But as an Order it kept remarkably clear of politics in the hope, however fatuous, that its membership would one day be educated to act intelligently at the ballot box. It was realistic in this sense, that only as a gesture of despair did it ever pretend that such a condition of intelligence had been reached.

On May 14, 1877, the Pittsburgh Knights proceeded to create a national organization in opposition to the National League, and Wright, though president of the Philadelphia convention, was made national past master workman, and George Blair, on the executive committee of the League, was made worthy foreman of the new national. John Davis was elected master workman.

This would suggest that the difference between the west and the east hinged upon politics, but there is nothing in the meager proceedings of the Pittsburgh convention to bear this out. Neither could the difference have been a conflict of east and west because Wright was from Philadelphia and Blair from New York. Only one thing then remains—secrecy—which Philadelphia ignored and Pittsburgh dealt with. To-day one might think this a small matter, but it was not in the seventies, and the Molly Maguires had given it a new significance. At the same time there remains the very strong suspicion that the political inclinations of Wright, Davis, and Blair had much to do with the split in the ranks of the Order.

The Pittsburgh convention decided to make the name of the Order public, and although this did not involve discarding secrecy, it was as far in that direction as any one at that time proposed to go. Wright, as past master workman, was delegated to instruct the new members of the Roman Catholic faith that there was nothing in the rules of the Order to prevent them from receiving the sacraments or attending confession. The Philadelphia constitution was adopted with some amendments and the next convention was set for Washington, D.C., on the first Monday in January, 1878.

Neither the Philadelphia nor the Pittsburgh convention

was representative of the Order and a new attempt had to be made at national organization. The proposed second convention of the League at Pittsburgh, July, 1877, did not take place. The Great Upheaval intervened.

THE GREAT UPHEAVAL OF 1877

The story of the railroad strikes of 1877 amounting almost to a revolution without revolutionary intent is well known. Only the outline need be recorded here as a background for the further expansion of the Knights of Labor and the formation of the General Assembly in 1878.

In 1877, the United States was coming to the end, without knowing it, of the longest depression in her history. From the fall of 1873, when a panic was precipitated by the Cooke failure and the collapse of railroad speculation, to the latter half of 1878, industrial stagnation had held the country in its grip.[20] Unemployment demonstrations like the Tompkins Square incident in New York in the winter of 1873-74 had been ruthlessly suppressed by the police. Wages had been reduced all along the line and a new tyranny had been created in Pennsylvania by the Pinkertons and the coal and iron police. On top of previous wage reductions, the Pennsylvania, the Baltimore & Ohio, and the New York Central proposed to make further 10 per cent cuts in June and July of 1877.

In the "long strike" of 1874-75, President Gowen of the Philadelphia & Reading got rid of the anthracite miners' organization and, shortly after, of the Molly Maguires. There was little organization among the railroad men. The Locomotive Engineers had lost two strikes in April, 1877, one on the Boston and Albany and the other on the Penn-

---

[20] Information as to business conditions used here and elsewhere in this volume is taken from Willard L. Thorp, *Business Annals*, National Bureau of Economic Research publications, 1926, pp. 127-38.

sylvania. Gowen evidently decided that the time was ripe to make a clean sweep of unionism and ordered the engineers to withdraw from the Brotherhood under penalty of discharge. They staged a surprise strike on April 14, but the Pinkertons had tasted the blood of the Molly Maguires, and Gowen with their tactful aid was ready. The surprise strike was no surprise, the strikers' places were filled, and the Brotherhood practically ceased to exist on this road. Many of them along with other railroad workers went into the Knights of Labor.

When the Pennsylvania proposed a reduction of wages to take effect in June, a committee, composed mostly of engineers, visited President Scott and agreed to a reduction with the understanding that the old scale would be restored when conditions improved. Other trainmen charged that the engineers had sold out, and a secret Trainmen's Union of employees of railroads with termini at Pittsburgh was organized to resist the reduction. The first local lodge of this new organization was formed by Robert H. Ammon June 2, 1877, in Allegheny City. He was later called Boss Ammon because he controlled Allegheny City throughout the strike and prevented rioting and bloodshed that occurred elsewhere. The new union expanded rapidly on the Pennsylvania and leased lines out of Pittsburgh, on the Baltimore & Ohio, the Erie, and the Atlantic & Great Western. The intention was to organize all trainmen including the engineers on the three trunk lines "into one solid body" and strike simultaneously. Forty men were sent from Pittsburgh to call the strike for June 27, but dissension arose and some of the leaders went west saying the strike was off. The whole movement collapsed.

Spontaneous outbreaks followed, first at Martinsburg, W. Va., on the Baltimore & Ohio, July 17, where the engineers participated only half-heartedly. Local militia failed to control the situation and the strikers held sway until 200 Federal troops arrived. At Baltimore, the management stopped running freight trains to avoid trouble, and Governor Carroll ordered the 5th Baltimore regiment and two companies of the 6th to Cumberland on July 20. The two companies of the 6th were trapped in the armory by a mob before they could leave the city. They marched out under a hail of missiles freely using their rifles and reached the depot. At night the mob tried to fire the depot and attacked the firemen, but fortunately for the firemen and militia the police arrived and rescued the "soldiers." The next day Federal troops went in and as usual the strike ended.

The real war was in Pittsburgh against the Pennsylvania Railroad, always a union breaker, and at that time very unpopular with the citizenry. Nothing much happened when the reduction was enforced on June 1, but on July 19 insult was added to injury by the introduction of "doubleheaders"—freight trains of 34 in place of 17 cars drawn by two engines. This was too much and a strike followed. Trains were held up. Mobs gathered. The company called on the mayor for protection but the mayor failed to respond. Local regiments of the National Guard were ordered out and because they were expected to fraternize with the strikers, six hundred troops were sent from Philadelphia. The Pittsburgh militia did what was expected of them but the Philadelphians on Saturday, July 21, reached the city and dispersed one crowd by killing twenty-six people. No attempt was made to run trains, and the Philadelphia militia, finding the job too big for them, took refuge in the lower roundhouse and machine shops. There they were disbanded by their commanding officer on the advice of citizens and left to their own devices. The mob laid siege to the roundhouse and set fire to the shops and cars. The unfortunate Philadelphians fought until morning when they retreated out of the city leaving the mob in undisputed possession. Looting and rioting followed for a full day, and at night every one went home tired and satisfied. Five million dollars' worth of railroad property had been destroyed.[21]

The Pittsburgh affair was not properly a strike but a revolt of the community against the Pennsylvania Railroad. Other disturbances occurred at Harrisburg, Philadelphia, Reading, Altoona, Scranton, Buffalo, Toledo, Louisville, Chicago, St. Louis, and San Francisco. At Reading, Federal troops had to be sent in to restore order. At Scranton, the miners were more active than the trainmen.

The effect of the riots of 1877 was enormous. For the first time in America the head of labor revolution was raised. Until then, the labor movement had been ignored except by those in immediate contact with it. A few intellectuals had talked about it in sentimental terms. Its hopeless struggle against forces it could not understand, its unhappy experiments with self-employment, its pathetic ventures into politics, its petty bargaining had gained the sympathy of preachers and editors like Channing and Greeley, but a hardened community could well afford to treat it with contempt. The Great Upheaval revealed a great discontent, and what was more significant, a great, if unwieldy power. Civil authority had been brushed aside. The militia were toy soldiers at the mercy of destructive mobs. Only the regulars could deal with them, and the United States was coming to a pretty pass when Federal troops had to rush into every village to maintain law and order.

So the lid was clamped down. The courts began to see

---

[21] In Allegheny City, Boss Ammon managed the division for four days without trouble.

a riot in every strike, and a Molly Maguire in every trade unionist. The doctrine of conspiracy was revived and in Pennsylvania and elsewhere strengthened by statute law. Labor became an outlaw, the wage-earner a member of a subcommunity or class, separate and distinct from the general community to which he had, at least in theory, always belonged. Credence was given in fact to the "un-American" theory of class war.

And labor learned, too, the danger of strikes that develop into riots, and of breaks in their ranks like that between the engineers and other trainmen. If it did not become class conscious over night it did become suspicious and secretive, fertile soil for doctrines of class war. Labor's answer to the rioting of desperate men and the reprisals of the community was, first, an orgy of politics, and then the Knights of Labor grown to national proportions. By some freak of fortune Stephens' idea of 1869 of labor unity and solidarity became, in 1877, the obvious need of the American wage-earner. Trade unionism was down if not out. A labor consciousness was in process of formation and it was obvious too that this had to be expressed in other ways than by strikes and rioting.

But there were dangers in any national organization, the chief of them that the older leaders brought up in the middle-class, politico-reform tradition would devitalize by over-ornamentation the clear lines of labor solidarity upon which the Order had been founded. Superficially, and perhaps a little more, this is what happened. The national organization formed in 1878 was not the simple and straightforward National League of 1876. It got itself a gorgeous preamble and platform from the Industrial Congress, representing not present and future needs, but past hopes and disappointments. But the new idea was there too, uncertain and confused, but becoming more clear in the light of the burning roundhouse at Pittsburgh. The old, master-journeyman relationship was gone forever. Great corporations owning mines and railroads, employing private police and semiprivate "detectives," calling vainly for state but more successfully for Federal protection, influencing if not controlling courts and legislatures, were set over against labor masses, ignorant and unorganized, daily losing their one possession, their craft skill, as suspicious of one another as of their common enemy, and aroused to futile action only as a result of long depression.

A monopoly against monopolies, said the Knights. After that they did not know, but time would tell. So they advanced toward solidarity, followed every trail that promised to lead them out of the morass of the wage system or make it conformable to them, threw the nation into hysteria, and departed, making the way clear for business unionism and the bankruptcy of ideals.

A POLITICAL INTERLUDE, 1877-78

The long depression had aroused political dissatisfaction among the farmers. The Greenback movement of 1876 was purely agricultural. The depression behavior of the wage-earners is found in the riots of 1877 but its inadequacy contributed to a renewal of political agitation. In most states workingmen's parties appeared in 1877, and the leaders of the Knights of Labor plunged into the political arena: Schilling in Ohio, Blair and Ralph Beaumont in New York, Davis and Wright in Pennsylvania, were all nominated on Greenback-Labor tickets. In February, 1878, at Toledo, a national Greenback-Labor Party was formed. Trevellick was temporary chairman of the convention and Schilling, Beaumont, and Stephens were delegates. In the spring Powderly was elected mayor of Scranton.

The peak of the Greenback-Labor campaign was reached

in the congressional elections of 1878. The Greenback vote was over one million, and fourteen representatives were sent to Congress. At the Pennsylvania state convention of the Greenback-Labor Party in 1878, Thomas Armstrong, associated with John Davis on the *National Labor Tribune,* just missed the nomination for governor. Wright was nominated for Secretary of Internal Affairs, and Stephens for Congress from the 5th District (Philadelphia).

On Jan. 1, 1879, the Resumption Act went into effect and the *raison d'être* of Greenbackism disappeared. The volume of currency increased and prosperity returned. Another national convention, held in Washington, Jan. 8, 1880, was attended by Albert Parsons and Litchman. Weaver was nominated for president. Powderly and Wright attended the Pennsylvania convention of that year but the movement had lost its labor support.

THE STATE OF THE TRADE UNIONS, 1877-78

The development of national trade unions during and after the Civil War had come to an end with the panic of 1873, with perhaps a total of thirty-three or thirty-four national unions. From 1874 to 1878 most of these disappeared altogether, and the formation of only five new nationals is recorded: the Horseshoers, 1874, probably a revival of a part of the Machinists and Blacksmiths; the Amalgamated Association of Iron and Steel Workers, 1876, not a new union but an amalgamation of three organizations formed before 1873; the Granite Cutters, 1877; and the Lake Seamen and Cotton Mill Spinners, 1878.

The oldest and steadiest trade union in the country, the Typographical, had 9,819 members and 106 locals in 1874, but declined to 4,260 members and 69 locals in 1878.[22]

---

[22] George E. Barnett, *The Printers,* Pubs. Am. Econ. Assoc., 3d series, Vol. X, no. 3, October, 1909; app. VII, p. 375.

In 1877, the *Labor Standard* listed only nine national unions in existence: the Molders, Locomotive Firemen, Miners, Coopers, Iron and Steel Workers, Granite Cutters, Machinists and Blacksmiths, Cigar Makers, Carpenters and Joiners. Even this list is not correct, though it may offend in omissions as well as additions. The miners for instance, as has been shown, lost their national organization in both the anthracite and bituminous fields in 1875 and 1876. It was not until 1879 that the miners revived, and then it was in the Pittsburgh district among local assemblies of the Knights of Labor.[23]

The cigar makers formed their national union in 1864 with 21 locals, 12 of them in New York state. In 1869, they had 5,800 members, but the fight against the mold and the inability of the national officers to control local strikes weakened them until their membership had fallen to 3,771 in 1873. In 1874, they had only 54 locals and 2,167 members, and when they decided in 1875 to take in bunch breakers and rollers many of the old locals either broke up or seceded. From 1875 to 1877 the Cigar Makers' Union can hardly be said to have existed at all. It was a rarity to see a traveling card. The New York tenement-house strike of 1877 further weakened the organization, and it reached its lowest point at the Rochester convention in September of that year, with 21 locals and 1,016 members. Revival did not come until 1880, when the membership rose to 3,159. In 1881 the Cigar Makers had 8,300 members but the secession of the Progressives nearly destroyed the International.[24]

The *Labor Standard* list includes the Locomotive Firemen and not the Engineers, but there was practically no organi-

---

[23] Andrew Roy, *A History of the Coal Miners of the United States*, 3d edition, Columbia, O., 1907.

[24] McNeill, *op. cit.*, app., pp. 585-95.

zation among either. The Firemen seem to have passed out of existence and though the Engineers had 3,500 members in 1877, most of them were lost in the spring strikes and the uprising of the summer.

The Iron Molders and the Coopers had practically given up trade unionism for coöperation in the sixties, and if they had organizations in the late seventies they were paper ones. The Coopers had declined from 7,000 members in 1872 to 1,500 in 1878.

The Bricklayers, not mentioned in the *Labor Standard* list, had 43 locals and 5,332 members in 1873, but only three unions were able to send delegates to the convention of 1879.

From 1873 to 1876 all the unions in the cotton and woolen mills of New England were dissolved.

The German Furniture Workers, organized in 1873, had only 9 locals in 1876 and held no national convention from that year until 1880 when 8 locals were represented.

The Associated Brotherhood of Iron and Steel Heaters, organized in 1872, held its last meeting in 1876 with only 412 members. The Iron and Steel Roll Hands Union (1873) held no convention in 1875. These two—largely because of their weakness—amalgamated with the Sons of Vulcan in 1876 with a total membership of 3,000 as the Amalgamated Association of Iron and Steel Workers.

The Machinists lost two-thirds of their members in 1877.

After the disappearance of the Knights of St. Crispin the shoemakers had no organization outside the Knights of Labor.[25]

It was in this condition of trade union desuetude that the Knights of Labor formed their national organization. The unions began to revive shortly after, but the Knights were not unwarranted in their conclusion, from their own

---

[25] Compiled from McNeill and Commons.

growth in the seventies and the complete disruption of the trade unions, that the day of the isolated open trade union had passed, and that of one big union, combining all trades under the veil of secrecy, had arrived. All through the eighties the trade unions were placed on the defensive and it was not until the unhappy seventies were forgotten that they were able to reach back and pick up the scattered threads of their tradition. That tradition itself was weak enough and had to be buttressed by the allegedly pure and simple tradition of the British trade unions which, as a matter of fact, was more benefit than bargaining, and more political than was thought.

CHAPTER III

THE FIRST GENERAL ASSEMBLY

THE Philadelphia convention of 1876 had decided to hold its second meeting in Pittsburgh in July, 1877. The recalcitrant Pittsburgh convention of May, 1877, had agreed to meet in January, 1878, at Washington. The Great Upheaval of the summer of 1877 prevented the July meeting and helped somewhat to wipe out the antagonism between east and west. Neither the Philadelphia nor the Pittsburgh convention had been representative of the Order. Powderly, who was secretary of District Assembly No. 5, Scranton, Pa., received no notice of the Philadelphia convention and only learned of the Pittsburgh affair when it was over. He was a good fixer and opened up a correspondence with Singer of St. Louis, Griffiths of Chicago, Blair of New York, Litchman of Marblehead, Mass., and Turner of Philadelphia, to get a full record of all the locals. District Assembly No. 1 agreed to postpone the July meeting until September, but by that time the political orgy was in full swing and the date was set over to Jan. 1, 1878. To avoid further jealousies, a compromise location was agreed upon and Reading, Pa., was chosen as the place of meeting of the first General Assembly of the Knights of Labor.

On Aug. 2, 1877, a notice was sent from District Assembly No. 1 signed by Frederick Turner, secretary of the district, calling a convention at Reading, Jan. 1, 1878, "for the purpose of forming a central assembly . . . and also for the purpose of creating a central resistance fund, bureau of statistics, providing revenue for the work of organization, establishment of an official register giving the number, place of meeting of each assembly, etc. Also the subject of making the name public together with all business appertaining to the perfection of a National body."[1]

Each district assembly was allowed three delegates and states having no district assembly were allowed the same. No direct representation was given to locals in contrast to the procedure of the earlier Philadelphia convention. Assemblies were instructed to vote on the proposal to make the name of the Order public and report the results through the delegates to the convention. A two-thirds vote was declared necessary to make public the name of the Order.

The three major purposes of the first General Assembly were: to form a national organization; to create a strike fund;[2] and to decide on a modification of the policy of secrecy.[3]

Though delegates were not invited from local assemblies some of the most influential came in in that way, Charles Litchman of Marblehead, Thomas Gallagher of St. Louis, Jacob Christ of Waverly, N. Y., Thomas Crowne, New York City, and after much argument John Langdon of Youngstown, Ohio.

The trades represented were: miners 9; machinists 4; shoemakers 4; glass workers 3; locomotive engineers 2; and engineers, molders, printers, boiler makers, nail packers, carpenters, coopers, blacksmiths, garment cutters and teachers one each. These designations must be taken with reservations as "politician" or "labor reformer" would have

---

[1] T. V. Powderly, *Thirty Years of Labor*, p. 126.

[2] There can be little question but that the original purpose of the Resistance Fund was to support strikes. It was later misappropriated and diverted to other uses.

[3] The Knights never gave up secrecy though there is an impression to the contrary. The only proposal involved here was that of making the name of the Order public. Changes were later made in the ritual, and the oath was made a pledge of honor.

more realistically characterized men like Litchman and
Beaumont and even Powderly and Stephens.

There were 33 delegates distributed as follows: [4]

District Assembly
No. 1 Philadelphia 3
     4 Reading 3
     5 Scranton 3
     5 St. Albans, W. Va. 1
     6 West Clifton 1
     7 Akron, Ohio 2
     8 Pittsburgh 3
     9 Pittsburgh 2
    11 Connellsville 2
    12 Leetonia, Ohio 1
    14 Knightsville, Ind. 1
    15 Elmira, N. Y. 3
     Unnumbered
       (Hazelton, Pa.) 3
                                  ——
                                  28
From locals 5
                                  ——
Total 33

The absence of District Assembly No. 3 of Pittsburgh
is noticeable. Either it had not recovered from its early
pique or had broken up. The presence of delegates from
two other Pittsburgh districts suggests the latter explanation as does the fact that the General Assembly decided
to give District Assembly No. 3 locals new charters without
additional cost if they could prove that they had paid
charter fees to L. J. Booker (District Assembly No. 3) or
to others claiming authority.[5] District Assembly No. 2,
Camden, N. J., had probably died and District Assembly
No. 10 never existed. District Assembly No. 13 of Springfield was not represented.

---

[4] The *Proceedings,* First General Assembly, Knights of Labor, 1878,
p. 26, give only thirty-two delegates, but this was due to the omission
of Langdon of Youngstown who was thrown out.

[5] *Proceedings,* 1878 General Assembly, p. 23 footnote.

The delegates were with few exceptions men unknown in the labor and political movements of the time. The exceptions were Charles Litchman, Ralph Beaumont, Robert Schilling, and Uriah Stephens. Committees were appointed on the constitution and ritual, and on the national resistance fund. The latter committee recommended that all local assemblies collect 5 cents per member per month to be held by the treasurer of the local "for such cases of emergency as may from time to time arise." The fund was not to be used at once but allowed to accumulate for two years from Jan. 1, 1878. That this was intended as a strike fund is evident from the following stipulation in the committee's report: "When the Board of Arbitration fails to adjust a grievance it shall notify the national Master Workman . . ." who "shall direct the District assemblies . . . to forward not more than ten per cent of the Resistance Fund then in the treasuries of the subordinate assemblies."

This was a very awkward and indefinite arrangement. The locals were to collect the fund and hold it for two years. After that, when the district board of arbitration failed to settle a dispute, it was to inform the national master workman and he was empowered to order all districts to "forward" 10 per cent of the fund in the hands of the locals. It does not say how the districts were to get the money, if any, away from the locals nor where to send it, though the presumption is that they were to send it, on instructions from the master workman, to any district or local in trouble. The report caused a great deal of discussion. It was resubmitted and the second report was attacked. It was then sent to the constitutional committee and finally appeared as Article VII of the constitution. In its final form it provided for a 5-cent levy per month per member to be set aside for two years to be used at the expiration of that time as the General Assembly might provide. This left the matter entirely in the air.

The question of secrecy came up on the second day when G. Gallagher (Missouri) moved that the name of the Order should be kept secret. This was ruled out of order but the matter came up again in connection with a rather curious incident that throws some light on the seriousness with which the Knights took themselves and their practices.

On January 3, John Langdon of Youngstown, Ohio, over whose credentials there had been much dispute, was reported to the convention as having been seen "in suspicious intimacy" with a reporter of the Reading *Daily Eagle,* "and it was feared that the objects of the convention as well as the name of the Order had been divulged and made public." A committee was appointed to deal with the matter and the *Eagle* reporter told them that while he had seen Langdon and had talked with him, the latter was too drunk to give any information "fit to publish." The committee was unable to find the offender though they had "reliable information" that he had called at three houses of ill fame in the city and was expected to return to one of them. The reporter evidently exaggerated Langdon's condition, for a long article on the convention appeared in the *Eagle* exposing some of the secrets of the Order. At this point Uriah Stephens left the assembly, in part no doubt in disgust with the roving Langdon, but also because of "business engagements," possibly a euphemism for politics in which he was at that time deeply engaged. He resigned as master workman but was reëlected in his absence. With Stephens gone the question of secrecy again came up. A vote was taken on making public the name of the Order and was defeated by twenty-two to five. The constitution was adopted, St. Louis was chosen for the next meeting, and the following officers elected for the year:

Uriah S. Stephens .... Grand master workman,
Ralph Beaumont .... Grand worthy foreman
Charles H. Litchman ...... Grand secretary
John G. Laning .... Grand assistant secretary

and an executive board of five. The officers were drawn from Pennsylvania, West Virginia, Ohio, New York, and Massachusetts.[6]

The constitution adopted at the first General Assembly was borrowed with modifications from the Industrial Brotherhood of 1873-75. Both Schilling and Powderly had been in the Industrial Brotherhood, the former as president and the latter as delegate and organizer. Both of them brought copies of the constitution of the Industrial Brotherhood to the first General Assembly of the Knights of Labor and had no difficulty in foisting the preamble and platform upon the new organization. But the Knights had grown up so far as local and district units were concerned with a constitution of its own. Though it lacked a preamble and platform it had what was, perhaps, more important, an organized body of wage-earners. Thus the new constitution had to be modified to avoid disturbing the existing district and local machinery, and in fact it left them pretty much as they were. It was then chiefly the preamble and platform that came from the old congress and even this was changed in many important respects.[7]

The history of labor is cluttered up with a too rigid insistence upon forms of organization and Professor Hoxie was right in stressing function in place of form. But the Knights of Labor cannot be fitted into any conceivable classification of form, function, or theory. There was no form of organization they did not possess at one time or

---

[6] *Ibid.*

[7] See Appendix I for the preamble and platform of the Industrial Brotherhood with changes made by the Knights of Labor.

another, no function they did not perform or attempt, and almost no theory they did not hold either officially or unofficially. They differed, it is true, from their successor, the American Federation of Labor, but less in form, function, and theory than in sentiment, and in locus of authority. Mr. Gompers always insisted that the federalism of the American Federation of Labor was in keeping with that of the United States and therefore better adapted to this country than the centralization of the Knights of Labor, which presumably corresponded more closely to the political government of England.

But Mr. Gompers' constitutional history was a little weak. The American Federation of Labor resembles much more the Confederation of 1777 than the Federal Union of 1787; and Gompers failed to note that the whole trend of American political life has been to strengthen the position of the Union at the expense of the powers of the states. The American Federation of Labor is a very loose confederation, too loose effectively to represent the American labor movement. Admitting the value of federalism for this country it should be remembered that a desperate Civil War was fought to put down the doctrine upon which the American Federation of Labor was founded and to which it still holds.

Superficially, that is, constitutionally, the Knights of Labor was a highly centralized form of government. The General Assembly was the supreme authority and made laws governing the locals and districts. But many of the locals and fifteen of the districts preceded the General Assembly in point of time, and most of them were more homogenous, more active, and did much as they pleased. In almost every case the action of the general officers was forced upon them by previous action of locals or districts. There was little of discipline. Expulsions seldom stuck.

The window glass workers formed a national trade assembly within the Order when the laws were all against it, and they were able to get the general executive board to plead their case before the General Assembly. District Assembly No. 49 of New York was expelled for insubordination, but it not only forced itself back into the Order but gained control of the national officers. An insignificant district in Iowa wrote a very rude letter to the general secretary daring the Order to expel it for refusing to pay an assessment, and received no censure. Only when Powderly's personal feelings were hurt was authority exercised, and then it was upon individuals and not upon locals or districts. Looking at the constitution of the Order one is warranted in the belief that it was a highly centralized government and it did come under the control of cliques. But watching the general officers running hither and yon at the beck and call of every local and district it becomes evident that centralization was a myth. When the Order wanted to take in the national trade unions it offered them all the autonomy that even the most extreme of them could wish.

The Glass Workers dragged the Order into lobbying at Washington. The executive board initiated only one boycott out of thousands, and that because of personal pique at treatment not becoming to its dignity. It engaged in only one coöperative venture into which it was drawn by the previous action of a local. It regarded itself in bargaining as an arbitrator and in general as the servant of the locals and districts. When aggressive or arbitrary action was found it was almost without exception taken by a district. The Cigar Makers' fight was not with the Order, but first with a left wing movement in its own ranks, then with District Assembly No. 49, New York, and with the general executive board only when District Assembly No. 49 had gained control of that body. The Order never called a strike and seldom supported one.

Thus the only basis for the assertion that the Knights were highly centralized in fact rather than in law was the development of a clique rule through the Home Club of District Assembly No. 49, and later the creation by Powderly of a personal machine. This is proper ground for criticism of the Order, but it is not especially rare in labor unions or elsewhere. It happens in most societies whatever form of government they have. The American Federation of Labor is certainly in no position to object to the Knights on this account.

Therefore while it is necessary to describe the formal constitution of the Order it is well to remember that the real condition was found in practice and not in law. Surely the Eighteenth Amendment has proved that.

The Knights of Labor never clearly distinguished between fundamental and other law, and the constitution underwent continual change by the simple process of legislation. The business of the General Assembly was to make laws and this it did with an enthusiasm common perhaps to the American people. Many of these laws were contradictory, many were ignored, and it would take a regiment of Philadelphia lawyers to untangle the mess. Most, if not all, of the important changes are considered under the special heads and it is necessary here only to outline the broad character of the organization. On the whole it can be said that the Order moved from local to centralized control in theory, and after the first General Assembly from central to local control in fact. As the Order grew it got out of hand. It was only after decline set in that Powderly became supreme, and even then he had no interest in exercising his authority except to get rid of his enemies.

The Knights of Labor differed from the national bodies

representing all trades that preceded it, in that it began from the ground and worked up. It was a natural growth and not artificially created by reformers. The older bodies were simply conventions which sometimes tried to reënforce themselves by organizing labor unions from the national convention down. The Knights of Labor was the first national trades and labor society in the United States.[8]

---

[8] See Appendix II for a detailed description and discussion of the constitution.

CHAPTER IV

GROWTH AND EXPANSION

THE early spread of the Order from Philadelphia, before the formation of the General Assembly in 1878, is covered in other chapters. Here it is only necessary to give a general picture of the rise and decline in members as a national organization, and an estimate of the character of the personnel, especially in the years of greatest growth.

Statistics of trade and labor union membership in the eighties and nineties are very unsatisfactory. There are few contemporary records and in many cases it has been necessary to fall back upon the memories of trade union leaders, years later. The membership figures of the Knights of Labor are, however, an exception to this rule. While they may not be entirely accurate, they are, for the eighties at least, sufficient to give a correct impression of the strength of the Order. Unlike the old Federation of 1881-86, and unlike the American Federation of Labor, the Knights of Labor was an integrated body and every member was directly a member of the Order and not indirectly through an affiliated organization. The old Federation was little more than a congeries of trade unions, trades' assemblies, and reform societies, holding an annual convention with a few officers and a legislative committee. There is no way of knowing what its membership was. It was supposed to have a per capita tax of 3 cents, but when the American Federation of Labor was formed in 1886, the Typographical Union, which had been in the old Federation, refused to pay a per capita tax. It wanted to do what it had done in the old Federation and pay simply its pro rata of the expenses of the annual convention.[1]

As the largest annual income of the old Federation was $700, its membership on the basis of a per capita tax of 3 cents could not have been more than 24,000 at any time.[2]

The figures for the membership of the Knights of Labor are based upon the per capita tax and compiled from the *Proceedings* of the General Assemblies. It is possible that the district assemblies in some cases paid the tax out of their funds to maintain their representation, and Powderly said that the membership of the Order never exceeded 600,000.[3] But Powderly said this after the Knights had lost half its membership under his personal administration and it is well to discount his statement. The following table gives the official membership of the Order for all the years in which it was published:

Year	Membership	Members in Good Standing
1879 (Oct. 1)	9,287	.....
1880 (Oct. 1)	28,136	.....
1881 (Oct. 1)	19,422	.....
1882 (July 1)	42,517	.....
1883 (July 1)	51,914	49,458
1884 (July 1)	71,326	60,811
1885 (July 1)	111,395	104,066
1886 (July 1)	729,677	702,924
1887 (July 1)	548,239	511,351
1888 (July 1)	259,518	221,618
1889	220,607	.....
1890	100,000	.....
1891	.....	.....
1892	.....	.....
1893	74,635	.....

[1] See Chap. IX on Trade Unions, *The Printers*.

[2] There is, however, no meaning in membership figures for the old Federation.

[3] T. V. Powderly, *Thirty Years of Labor*, p. 336.

This table shows a large and continuous growth to 1886 with the exception of the year 1881. It is likely that the drop in 1881 should be spread over the two previous years as a reading of the *Proceedings* of the General Assembly gives the impression of decline. The remarkable jump in membership from about 100,000 to about 700,000 in 1886 is the most significant feature of the Order's history, and the decline after 1886, though less rapid than the rise, was about as fast as an organization could dissolve under the most favorable—for dissolution—purposes. The publication of official membership was given up in 1891 for obvious reasons, and the stray figure for 1893 is not very reliable.

The membership of the Order was very unstable; for though in theory it was very strict about initiation, the practice that grew up of paying organizers' commissions out of charter fees made for "unhealthy" expansion. The initiation fees and dues were low and there were no compulsory benefits. This explains in part the remarkable jump in 1886. Thousands who had once belonged to the Knights and had dropped out because nothing much was happening, flocked back after the strike, boycott, and other successes of 1885. Old locals were brought to life again and new ones created as fast as the organizers could run through the ceremonial. One organizer formed three new assemblies in one night, though the rule was that an organizer must attend at least five weekly meetings of the new assembly before a charter could be issued.

From July 1, 1885, to June 30, 1886, there were more locals formed than in the previous sixteen years of the Knights' existence. The Order became in fact more observed than Congress, and the Washington *Gazette* prophesied that it would name the next President.[4] But

---

[4] *John Swinton's Paper,* March 14, 1886, quote.

while the real growth was phenomenal enough it was nothing to the rumors that circulated about it. Estimates of membership ran as high as 2,500,000. The treasury was reported to contain $12,000,000, and of the 1,412 strikes of the year, more than twice the usual number, three-quarters were attributed to the Knights.[5] "Never in all history," Swinton orated, "has there been such a spectacle as the march of the Order of the Knights of Labor at the present time."[6] And the Knights themselves claimed to have 10,000 assemblies and a membership of over a million.[7]

The peak of the growth came in February, 1886, when 515 assemblies were organized in one month. The general executive board was alarmed and ordered the suspension of organizing for forty days to permit the gains to be consolidated.[8] But, according to Powderly, organizing went on, the organizers simply holding back the charter fees until the forty days had expired.[9] In May, Powderly had 300 applications for organizers' commissions but refused to approve them until the fall meeting of the General Assembly.[10] At the special session at Cleveland in May and June, all organizers' commissions were withdrawn,[11] but new commissions were issued from July to November and 800 new assemblies were formed in that time.[12]

By 1884, the Knights were established in England and Belgium and in the southern states. Richmond, Va., had two district assemblies, one composed entirely of negroes. Attempts to organize in North Carolina and Georgia were not very successful except among the Atlanta mill workers.

---

5 Villard, *Les Chevaleurs du Travail*, pp. 285-86.

6 Swinton, *op. cit.*, March 14, 1886.

7 *Journal*, December, 1886, p. 2233.

8 *Ibid.*, March, 1886, p. 2019.

9 Powderly, *op. cit.*, pp. 80-81.

10 *Journal*, May, 1886, p. 2066.

11 *Proceedings*, special session of the 1886 General Assembly, p. 20.

12 *Journal*, January, 1887, p. 2244.

In 1885, Powderly started on a southern tour but fell ill and had to return. Among the railroad workers of the west the Order spread rapidly from 1884 to 1886. In 1885 A. G. Denny was sent to Europe as organizer for the glass workers and formed locals at Sunderland, England; Charleroi, Jumet, and Brussels.[13] Assemblies were formed in Australia and New Zealand and at least one in Ireland.

The decline of the Knights was less spectacular than their rise, but sufficiently impressive. It began, not after the Richmond assembly of October, 1886, and the expulsion of the Cigar Makers, but in May, with the loss of the Southwest strike, the failure of the eight-hour movement, the Haymarket bomb, and the growing dissatisfaction of the trade unions. "It seemed last March and April," said Swinton in July, "as though the Golden Age were at hand, and it now seems as though they had been deceived by a will-o'-the-wisp." [14]

Success had gone to men's heads. They had rushed into innumerable strikes and agitations: curriers in Massachusetts, collar and cuff makers at Troy, knitters at Amsterdam and Cohoes, mill operatives at Augusta, stove molders at Troy, horse-car men in New York, packers in Chicago, glass blowers in New Jersey, textile workers in Philadelphia, and so on. And to top it all were Powderly's vacillations, internal intrigues, the "rule or ruin" faction, and the unpreparedness of any group of men to ride a hurricane.

Professor Commons has suggested that the extraordinary growth of 1886 was due to the "rush of the unskilled into the Order," and has explained the opposition of the trade unions to the Knights as based largely upon this fact. It is true that the "unskilled," *i.e.*, the new class of semi-

---

[13] *Proceedings*, 1885 General Assembly, p. 55.
[14] Swinton, *op. cit.*, July 25, 1886.

skilled workers who were replacing the old craftsmen, did rush into the Order, but that does not explain the opposition of the trade unions. The complaint of the trade unions was that the unions were rushing into the Order, as they undoubtedly were. Swinton, an impartial observer, is quoted in another place to the effect that local trade unions were daily changing into local assemblies, and Joseph Buchanan, who was no friend of the administration, said that the growth of the Knights in 1886 "was in large measure due to the affiliation of trained, able and active trade unionists" which began in 1882.[15] The complaints that the trade union committee took to the Order at Cleveland were not that the Knights were organizing the unskilled, but that they were taking in "unfair craftsmen." This, one is privileged to assume, was a euphemism. The unions could hardly complain that the Knights were getting their members. The mere fact that a craftsman or a local left the national union made it "unfair." But the term did not alter the fact that the unions were being invaded by the Order and raped of their strength. In a few cases it was intentional upon the part of the district officers, but in most it was simply the result of abnormal growth.

The complaints of the unions that the Knights accepted expelled members of the trade organizations were disingenuous. If the unions suffered, the Knights suffered much more. The Knights expelled by the hundreds and never suggested that any other organization should pay attention to an applicant's past in relation to the Order. But even so, the number of expelled trade unionists was insignificant enough to throw grave doubts upon the sincerity of the complaint. The real trouble was simpler. The Knights were stepping perforce upon the toes of the unionists, good, bad, and indifferent.

---

[15] Joseph R. Buchanan, *The Story of a Labor Agitator*, p. 48.

If the Order had expanded only or chiefly among the unskilled there would have been no complaint. The trade unions had no interest in these. No realist can imagine Strasser, McGuire, Weihe, and other signers of the "treaty" which the unions presented to the Knights at Cleveland, being interested in the "unskilled."

The fact is that the accessions to the Order in 1886 were from every class, but especially from the specialized workers created by the Industrial Revolution of whom the strict craft unions were afraid. But the policy of the Knights in this, though it was less a policy than a spontaneous development, was in line with industrial change. If the hand cigar makers chose to ignore the bunch breakers, rollers, and packers, these naturally looked to the Progressives and the Knights for aid. If the iron and steel unions thought only of the disappearing distinctions between boilers, puddlers, heaters, rollers, and the new labor in and about the mills, they might keep the Knights out but were soon themselves to go under. The only case in which the Order caused trouble by organizing really unskilled workers was that of the coal handlers of New York, and there the difficulty was not the organization of the coal handlers but the demand by District Assembly No. 49 that the skilled brewers, stationary engineers, and railroad trainmen support them. Among the packing-house workers in Chicago who won the eight-hour day in May, 1886, and lost it in the winter, were the skilled butchers as well as the semiskilled operatives and unskilled labor. The major strikes of the Knights in 1885-86 were among the railroad workers, including in two instances the trainmen and in all the shopmen. The shopmen had been machinists but were then specialized workers of the modern sort.

Industrial development had passed beyond the craftsman stage upon which the trade unions were founded, and though the Knights of Labor were unable for many reasons to adapt the labor movement to the changed industrial situation, they at least made the attempt.

The unskilled were taken in too, and the new immigrant. Requests were constantly made to the General Assembly to translate the *Adelphon Kruptos* into German, Italian, Polish, French, Bohemian. The Polish membership in Chicago was between eight and ten thousand and in Milwaukee nearly three thousand.[16]   In 1885, the *Adelphon Kruptos* had been translated into French, the German translation was in the press, and the Scandinavian was daily expected.[17]

---

[16] *Proceedings*, 1886 General Assembly, p. 195.
[17] *Journal*, January, 1885, p. 883.

CHAPTER V

THE ORDER AND THE CHURCH

The secrecy of the Knights of Labor had, in part, an economic justification common to all labor organizations in their infancy. It was protective coloring desirable if not necessary until the society grew strong enough to "declare itself to the world." It had, too, a psychological significance in that, combined with impressive rituals and names, it gave a fictitious importance to those whose standing in the world in which they worked and lived was not high. One hesitates to use the term inferiority complex, but undoubtedly the labor leaders, if not the rank and file of the period, suffered from that distressing malady. But the secrecy of the Knights was further complicated by the thing they tried to conceal. There was in Stephens, and in the ritual that he and Sinexon created, a strong religious sentiment which the founder regarded as the most important element in the new society.

The Industrial Revolution had cut across old lines of demarcation, had broken old ties of neighborhood, creed, sex, color, nationality, making wage labor the new common denominator of them all. But while it had forced all sorts of diversities into one common status it had not destroyed their differences. Though they became wage-earners they did not cease to be white and black, male and female, American, Asiatic, European, Democrat and Republican, Catholic, Protestant, Jew. It was the stupendous job of the labor movement to create from this diversity a psychological unity on economic lines.

Nothing, in Stephens' opinion, could do this but a religious sentiment, a sort of Comtean humanitarianism, "Universal Brotherhood"; and the veil of the sanctuary was to the early Knights what the gloom of the catacombs was to the early Christians. "Creed, party and nationality," said Stephens, "are but outward garments and present no obstacle to the fusion of the hearts of the worshippers of God, the Universal Father, and the workers for man, the universal brother."

It must not be inferred from this however that the early Knights were ready to acquiesce in the wage system and the status to which it had reduced the free citizens of America. The wage system was still comparatively new, and the success with which it had been crowned was due largely in Stephens' opinion to the old antagonisms and diversities which he proposed to break down. Behind the veil and unified by humanitarian sentiment the Knights were preparing—how they did not know—"the complete emancipation of the wealth producers from the thraldom and loss of wage slavery." In Christian and republican America had grown up "the great Anti-Christ of civilization manifest in the idolatry of wealth and consequent degradation and social ostracism of all else not possessing it, and its baneful effects upon heaven-ordained labor."

The Bible occupied the most prominent place in the sanctuary and the whole original ritual was couched in religious language. The vow of the new candidate for membership read:

I . . . do truly and solemnly swear [or affirm] that I will never reveal by word, act, art or implication, positive or negative, to any person or persons whatsoever, the name or object of this Order, the name or person of any one a member thereof, its signs, mysteries, arts, privileges or benefits, now or hereafter given to or conferred on me, any words spoken, acts done or objects intended; except in a legal and authorized manner or by special permission of the Order granted to me.

I do truly and solemnly promise strictly to obey all laws, regulations, solemn injunctions and legal summons that may be sent, said or handed to me.

I do truly and solemnly promise that I will to the best of my ability defend the life, interest, reputation and family of all true members of this Order, help and assist all employed and unemployed unfortunate or distressed Brothers to procure employment, secure just remuneration, relieve their distress and counsel others to aid them, so that they and theirs may receive and enjoy the just fruits of their labor and exercise of their art.

All this I swear [or affirm] without reservation or evasion to do and perform until death or honorable discharge [an accepted resignation] and bind myself under the penalty of the scorn and neglect due to perjury and violated honor as one unworthy of trust or assistance. So help me God and keep me steadfast unto the end. Amen.

While Stephens and most of the founders of the Order were Protestants, it had spread most rapidly from Pittsburgh among Irish Catholics and the Roman Catholic Church was historically opposed to secret societies in general, and in especial to secret religious bodies with rituals and vows that might interfere with the confessional. The priests in the mining districts were doubtful of the new Order and at least one of them openly attacked it in sermon and writing. This was responsible for the decision to publish the name of the Order and the statement of the Pittsburgh convention of 1877, that prospective members of the Roman Catholic faith might be told that there was nothing in the Order to prevent them from receiving the sacraments or keep them from confession. At Philadelphia, in 1876, the Protestant element had kept the name of the Order secret.

Another danger came from the tradition of the Molly Maguires. This organization had been destroyed in 1876, but its reign of terror in the mining districts was not easily forgotten. Any secret society of wage-earners was bound to be confused with it. Allan Pinkerton, in 1878, although in possession of the innocuous ritual of the Industrial Brotherhood, was convinced that the Knights of Labor was "an amalgamation of the Molly Maguires and the Commune." "In the vicinity of Scranton and Wilkes-Barre," he wrote, "two-thirds of the workers belong to it," and it promised "the destruction of all government by the ballot (sic) and if that shall fail, by force when the proper opportunity arrives." [1] Pinkerton's alarm must be accepted with some skepticism—his business depended upon alarm—but there is no doubt that the Knights and the Maguires were confused in the public mind.

Although Archbishop Wood of Philadelphia seems to have given his sanction to the Order,[2] a priest in Schuylkill County, shortly after the first General Assembly, launched a furious attack upon the Knights. This caused a loss of members and brought the growth of the Order to a halt in that region. Stephens' hand was forced, probably by Powderly who was a Catholic, and on May 16, 1878, he issued a call for a special session of the General Assembly at Philadelphia, June 6. The call cited an "emergency of vast and vital importance," and stated that the business of the special session was "to consider the expediency of making the name of the Order public for the purpose of defending it from the fierce assaults and defamation made upon it by the press, clergy and corporate capital. . . ." [3]

Fifteen delegates attended the special session and the majority of them were in favor of making public the name of the Order. A resolution was introduced to give the

---

[1] Allan Pinkerton, *Strikers, Communists, Tramps and Detectives,* pp. 88-89.

[2] *National Labor Tribune,* March 13, 1875.

[3] T. V. Powderly, *Thirty Years of Labor,* p. 134.

grand master workman and the grand secretary the power to permit districts and locals under the General Assembly to publish the name upon request made by a two-thirds vote. This very mild letting down of the veil of secrecy would have passed but for a ruling of Stephens that it was a constitutional amendment and therefore required a two-thirds vote. The vote was: yeas, 9; nays, 6; lacking one vote of the necessary two-thirds. If the meeting had not been held in Philadelphia, or if notice had been given sooner and more delegates had attended, there is little doubt but that the resolution would have passed.

It was agreed however that the following propositions should be put to a vote of the districts and of locals under the General Assembly:

1. To make the name of the Order public
2. To expunge from the A. K. all scriptural passages and quotations
3. To make such changes in the initiation ceremony as would tend to remove church opposition
4. To dispense with the founding ceremony for districts and locals

This compromise came from Powderly, and even the suggestion must have been a severe blow to Stephens who regarded the rituals as essential because the expression of the religious character of the movement.

At the next General Assembly in St. Louis the delegates were to vote on instructions from the districts and from locals attached to the General Assembly, and a two-thirds vote of the entire membership was to be necessary to make the change. An informal vote was asked from each local to be recorded with the grand secretary not later than Dec. 1, 1878. [4]

---

[4] *Proceedings,* special session of the 1878 General Assembly, pp. 44-45.

At St. Louis, January, 1879, Secretary Litchman reported that the returns from the locals were so meager that he was unable to tabulate them—whatever that may have meant. He found however that the majority of the locals were against making public the name of the Order while a majority of the votes were in favor of it. The majority of both locals and votes were against the other three proposals. Litchman concluded that the movement to make public the name of the Order came from special localities, and recommended local option.[5]

District Assembly No. 3 of Pittsburgh was not actually represented but three of its locals sent C. C. Burnett to St. Louis with a request that they be allowed to form a new district assembly as District Assembly No. 3 was in the hands of officers whose locals had lapsed but would not give up their charters. This was agreed to and the three locals (771, 791, 862) were recognized as constituting District Assembly No. 3.

There were twenty-five delegates at St. Louis, a decline of eight since the first General Assembly. District Assembly Nos. 4 Reading: 6, West Clifton; 11 Uniontown, Pa.; 12 Leetonia, Ohio; 15 Elmira, N. Y. were not represented but six new districts appeared in their places: District Assembly Nos. 17 St. Louis; 18 Upper Lehigh, Pa.; 20 Mahanoy Place, Pa.; 22 Streator, Ill.; 24 Chicago; 26 Moberly, Mo.

Schilling, Blair, Beaumont, Trevellick, Wright, Armstrong, in fact, the whole political crew were absent except Stephens, Powderly, and Litchman. The Greenback successes of 1878 had drawn them away. An attempt was made to prevent officers of the General Assembly from running for public office but it failed.

A resolution to make the name of the Order public was reported out of committee with the following recommendation: "The committee recommend that the G. A. be governed in its decision by the number of votes cast in favor of the 'first proposition' submitted to the Order at the special session of June 1878."

The secretary had said that the majority of locals were against the first proposition—making public the name of the Order—while the majority of the votes were for it.

[5] *Ibid.*, 1879 General Assembly, pp. 62-65.

The adoption of the committee's recommendation therefore should have involved the publication of the name of the Order. But it did not, and one may suspect from the wording that a loophole was intended to be created to placate the grand master workman.

Powderly again came to the rescue with one of his compromises, which was accepted: that a district assembly, or a local assembly under the General Assembly, might make the name public by a two-thirds vote of delegates or members present at a regular meeting. Such publication, however, was to be restricted to the locality of the district or local assembly taking such action, and in no case might a member disclose the name of another member or the place of meeting of any branch. It was further agreed that no member might make known any secret of the Order before April 1, 1879, "except such members as hold private consultations with the clergy for the good of the Order."

Powderly was undoubtedly winning, and this last provision was evidently intended to allow him or some one else to see members of the Roman Catholic clergy to discuss changes in the ritual which would make it acceptable to the Church.

The third regular General Assembly was held in Chicago, Sept. 2, 1879, making two regular assemblies in one year, the date of meeting having been changed from January to September with the expectation of influencing legislation. Stephens was absent and Powderly, who had been elected grand worthy foreman at St. Louis, acted in his place. A letter of resignation was received from Stephens suggesting either Powderly or Griffiths as his successor. Stephens' withdrawal was due in part to his interest in politics and the financial losses his campaign involved, but also to the movement of the Order away from "first principles" of which secrecy and religion were the chief. Powderly was his natural successor as the outstanding man in the Order to cope with the conflict with the Church. [6]

The Order was not growing. Something—many began to suspect that it was secrecy—was holding it back. Locals were impermanent and easily gave up. But nothing was done to change the Powderly compromise on secrecy adopted at St. Louis, possibly because its author was not ready. Terence V. Powderly succeeded Stephens as grand master workman.

TERENCE V. POWDERLY

In the history of labor too much attention has been paid to structure and programs and too little to personalities. In old institutions, where forms are set and traditions established, leadership may mean little. "The King is dead! Long live the King!" The so-called leader is simply the head and must conform to a pattern of long standing and stability of which he himself is a part. But the labor movement in America is comparatively young and amorphous. Certainly in the last century it was in the experimental stage in a milieu that was rapidly changing. There were no established institutions of any strength or permanence, a condition in which the personality of the leader became of first importance.

Terence V. Powderly was the head if not the leader of the Knights of Labor from 1879 to 1893, that is, over its

---

[6] There were only twenty delegates at the third General Assembly representing thirteen District Assemblies: Nos. 1, 2 (Vineland, N. J., replaced Camden), 3, 7, 13, 14, 16, 17, 24, 25, 27, 30. The secretary's report showed twenty-three district assemblies paying dues to the General Assembly of $956.05 as against twenty-two the previous year paying $1,223.26. The number of local assemblies paying dues had fallen from 174 to 156 and the amount of their payments from $1,197.13 to $921.33. Although the secretary had over 700 locals on his list only 142 had reported to him during the year.

whole active career. This fact in itself is of importance. There should perhaps have been a change, for the Order changed from weakness to strength, from an insignificant handful to a prominent mass, from defense to aggression, and from ideas of brotherliness and mutual aid to revolutionary ardor. Labor societies seem not to have learned what political societies have long known. There is no anti-third-term sentiment among them, and they often retain their leaders long beyond their effectiveness. This is due to the same conditions that operate in all human societies, an instinctive conservatism of the rank and file, a fondness for office in the leaders themselves, and the discomfort attendant upon doffing the official regalia, with its perquisites, for mufti. But in labor societies these conditions were peculiarly strong. There was no future for the union official outside of politics and no retreat outside the shop. After a few years in office it was difficult if not impossible to go back to the shop, and there was nowhere else to go. The remuneration of the union official was not sufficient to lay up a competence and he would have been eyed with grave suspicion had he done so. He was almost forced then to spend most of his time repairing his fences, building up a machine within the organization to keep him in his job. Only the Bureau of Labor at Washington, bureaus of the various states, and a few other political shelves were available as retreats for men who had given their best years to building up and leading the trade and labor unions. Powderly through most of his career as head of the Knights of Labor had other jobs. In 1886 he received a good salary for that time, but all that was left for him when he was discarded by the Knights was a minor position in Washington.

Powderly was born at Carbondale, Pa., Jan. 24, 1849, of Irish parents. He became a switch tender at sixteen years of age and at seventeen went into a machine shop. In 1869 he moved to Scranton and joined the local of the Machinists and Blacksmiths. He was initiated into the Knights in Philadelphia in 1874 and entered Local Assembly No. 88, Scranton, Sept. 6, 1876. He organized Local Assembly No. 222 (machinists) on October 14 and became corresponding secretary of District Assembly No. 5 (later No. 16) when it was organized Feb. 24, 1877. In 1876 he entered the Greenback-Labor campaign and he was elected mayor of Scranton in 1878, a position he retained until 1884. [7]

In 1878 Powderly passed the preliminary examination in the courts of Luzerne County and began the study of law. He expected to be admitted to the bar in 1880.[8] But in September, 1879, he was made grand master workman of the Knights of Labor and gave up his legal career. He seems to have been health officer of Luzerne county for many years. He was prominent in the Irish Land League and was its second vice president in 1883. In 1880, he attended the Greenback-Labor convention which nominated General Weaver for President of the United States. He accepted a membership card in the Socialist party from Van Patten, its secretary, but seems never to have been a "practicing" socialist. [9]

In 1882 Powderly invested $1,000 in a tea and coffee business started by his brother-in-law in Scranton. The brother-in-law died the same year and Powderly carried on the business with his sister-in-law until it failed in July, 1883. Through the early eighties he had too many irons in the fire. He was at one time mayor of Scranton, health

---

[7] George E. McNeill, *The Labor Movement: The Problem of To-day*, p. 613, and Powderly, *op. cit.*, pp. 103-4.

[8] *Journal*, p. 409.

[9] *Proceedings*, 1887 General Assembly, pp. 1536-37.

officer of the county, part owner and manager of a grocery store, and head of the Knights of Labor. His frequent refusal of a larger salary as head of the Order is explained by his unwillingness to give his full time to the job and his even more frequent threats to resign, which usually got him what he wanted, grew out of the same condition. Even after he was given a salary of $5,000 a year in 1886, he spent most of the next three years writing *Thirty Years of Labor*.

In 1884, when the Federal Bureau of Labor Statistics was first organized, Powderly applied for the position of chief. He advertised in the *Journal* for the support of the Knights and went to Washington with 1,000 recommendations. President Arthur chose Jarrett of the Amalgamated Iron and Steel Workers, but discovered later that he was a political enemy, and Carroll D. Wright of the Massachusetts Bureau of Labor Statistics landed the plum. Powderly was very poor at the time, after the failure of his grocery business, and if his job-hunting efforts seem less than dignified, his methods were the only ones open to one who was not a Republican.

Powderly was a slender man, under average height with mild blue eyes behind glasses. Blond mustache hides his mouth and bends down to below his chin. Light brown hair in curves that are neither waves nor curls rests on his coat collar, heavy behind but almost burned away at the top. Wears at convention double-breasted, black, broadcloth coat, stand-up collar, plain tie, dark trousers and narrow small shoes. He looks and behaves like a man of good breeding, accustomed to the usages of society, but is unlike the average labor reformer in appearance. All around him are strapping big fellows with hands and shoulders formidable to the eye, unpolished gems in the main. English novelists take men of Powderly's look for their poets, gondola scullers, philosophers and heroes crossed in love but no one ever drew such a looking man as the leader of a million of the horny-fisted sons of toil.[10]

---

[10] John Swinton, *John Swinton's Paper*, Oct. 17, 1886.

Powderly was not physically strong. He was very susceptible to colds and hated to travel. Letter writing was his chief and favorite occupation, and though he constantly complained of the burden of his correspondence, there was method in his complaint. He wanted to be relieved of other duties. In 1883 he refused a salary of $1,000 and tendered his resignation because he was unable "to devote his entire time to the Order." [11] It was agreed that he was not required to travel "or visit any portion of the Order" [12] and his salary was set at $800 a year. In 1884 his salary was raised to $1,500 and he was required to devote "his time to attending to the duties of the office and 16 weeks in the year to visit assemblies. . . ." [13] He made an attempt to fulfill these conditions but after a short trip to the South he was "overtaken by quinsy," had an operation on his throat in Cincinnati, rushed back home and published an hysterical screed in the *Journal* against letter writers who wanted him to visit their assemblies, against picnics and picnickers and all other annoyers of his peace. "I will talk at no picnics," he screamed. "When I speak on the labor question I want the individual attention of my hearers and I want that attention for at least two hours and in that two hours I can only epitomize." No truer word was ever spoken in anger. "At a picnic where . . . the girls as well as the boys swill beer I cannot talk at all. . . . If it comes to my ears that I am advertised to speak at picnics . . . I will prefer charges against the offenders for holding the executive head of the Order up to ridicule. . . ." [14]

As Swinton said, Powderly did not look like a labor

---

[11] *Proceedings*, 1883 General Assembly, pp. 514-15.
[12] *Journal*, p. 475.
[13] *Proceedings*, 1884 General Assembly, p. 735.
[14] *Journal*, March, 1885, p. 931.

leader but he might have said further that he did not act like one. He acted more like Queen Victoria at a national Democratic convention.

Never was the adulation of the masses—and he had that adulation—received with less amenity. And he did not change. Just after the Richmond assembly of 1886, which had raised his salary to $5,000 and might have expected a kind word in return, he issued a secret circular full of the old complaints, "I am literally deluged with letters. . . . I am pestered with invitations to attend banquets, entertainments, etc. I am besieged from every quarter to lecture. . . . I will not go. My throat is not strong enough to speak in public . . . the Order has grown and is growing stronger every day, but I am not growing stronger and must have relief from unnecessary labor. . . ."[15] He was then only thirty-eight years old. "The position I hold," he again complained in 1887, "is too big for any ten men. It is certainly too big for me and I am only too willing to hand it over at once to whoever may be selected." But at this time he was the last man in the world to give up his job, and when he was finally ousted he did everything in his power to destroy his opponents and the Order with them.

The position was undoubtedly too big for him—too big for any one perhaps—but he made only desultory attempts to fill it. In 1892, when the Order was but a shadow of its former self, he received a wire from Wisconsin asking him to go there to prevent a strike of 1,500 men. "We never had a meeting yet," he wrote Hayes, "that some such thing did not turn up to hamper and embarrass us."[16] And this was, throughout, his point of view. Something was always turning up to spoil his meetings.

Powderly was very sensitive and vain and had something

---

[15] *Ibid.*, Jan. 29, 1887, p. 2265.
[16] Letter from Powderly to Hayes, May 1, 1892.

of an inferiority complex, as it seems most of us have. His full signature "Terence V. Powderly" ran across half a page of ordinary business letter paper. He always talked big, but his actions, unless some personal slight were involved, never matched his words. He had a rather dangerous habit of disingenuous rabble rousing, as when he spoke of rifles and machine guns with his tongue in his cheek, and as at Richmond, when he used a passing regiment to point a moral.

Light is thrown on his vanity and humor in a letter he wrote to the editor of a paper called *The Watchman*.

Your issue of March 7 contained a villainous-looking wood-cut of some person, and underneath I find my name. . . . That picture is not mine. I am a temperance man and the man who sat for the first copy must have been as drunk as an orator on the 4th of July or he never would have left the bridge of his nose at home when posing for his picture. Then again the cheek extends away around to the back of his neck. . . . Some one has imposed on you . . . the intention is to press that picture into duty on the front of a patent medicine bottle. If the medicine don't kill the victim then one steady look at that portrait will do the work. Whoever saw a man with a pair of wings flapping out from the bridge of his eyeglasses? Besides, that picture looks as though the man who sat for it was bald or nearly so. I intend visiting Michigan soon and if you don't take it back before I get there you had better move your establishment into the next state. I was never an advocate of dynamite until I saw that picture together with the announcement that I was the alleged original. Now I am an advocate of anything that will annihilate the wretch who, with malice aforethought, sprung that mixture of wings, mustache and eyeglasses upon an unsuspecting public and named it after me.

I do not object to the cut so much as to the sketch of my life which accompanies it. Seriously speaking it is not true. It says that I am of "humble origin" [Ah! there's the rub.]. . . . I can say of my blood what the so-called noblemen of Europe cannot say of theirs—I know where it came from. [Can erudition go further?] You will pardon me then if I say in correction of your sketch that instead of being of humble I am of noble origin. I am a free-born American citizen and nobler birth than that the son of mortal cannot have.[17]

If this letter were only a joke it might be passed by. But it was serious too. In 1888, when the Order was on the down grade Powderly asked Hayes not to send newspaper clippings concerning his own "general depravity" but to "fish out a line or two of a complimentary nature." "When I hear any bad news," he said, "it sickens me . . . and for hours I am unfit for duty." [18] "Bad news" for the grand master workman was personal criticism.

But Powderly was not so careful of the feelings of others. He had, in fact, a very sharp tongue. He was intelligent and found a great many fools in the world, and he did not suffer them gladly. Some "fool," for instance, sent him a letter asking if "God" in the ritual did not mean "good." "The being whom God created," he softly replied, "with as little sense as to deny His existence is a fool. He may if he chooses have a spite against God for not furnishing him with a full stock of wit; but he should not ask others —who have—to take sides with him against their Maker." [19] There was a great deal of intellectual arrogance in the man, and for his personal enemies he had no mercy. Gompers was one of those "Christ sluggers," Barry either "bovine or canine," [20] Crandall was for free silver—"anyway he is for silver for Crandall." [21]

As a manager of popular assemblies and of political intrigues he had few equals. "My machinery is working nicely," he wrote in 1888, " . . . some one will have to get off the Board pretty soon or be expelled. I have written

---

[17] *Journal*, March, 1885, p. 940.
[18] Letter from Powderly to Hayes, September, 1888.
[19] *Journal*, p. 10.
[20] Letter from Powderly to Hayes, July 10, 1888.
[21] *Ibid.*, May 23, 1892.

Charlie [Litchman] a seven page letter to-night which will make him as cross as hell for I speak plainly in it. . . . He may get mad enough to resign. If he hands you the document freeze to it at once." [22] He got rid of his enemies with astonishing rapidity after 1886, but the smoother ran his machine, the faster ran the Order down into oblivion. "It will go out to the Order in a stiff circular," he wrote to Hayes, "that all provisionals and secret cliques are enemies of the Order . . . that their names must be dropped from the rolls at once.[23] But his own secret clique of "Governors" was excepted.

Powderly's strength—and the above is not intended to suggest that he was a weak man—lay in his oratory, and his close touch through correspondence with the rank and file. He was a rabble rouser and dealt with those glamorous generalities so loved of the people. He had a few strong convictions, the strongest perhaps on the "temperance question," but aside from these he was easily influenced by the last man who got hold of him. Personally he had little faith in coöperation but when coöperation swept the Order he was for it. The same was true of insurance, eight hours, trade assemblies, or anything that came up. On the liquor question he was obdurate and throughout his career he was a land reformer and opposed to strikes and politics for the Order.

Land reform was his major ideal. "In my opinion," he said, "the main, all-absorbing question of the hour is the land question. . . . Give me the land and you may frame as many eight-hour laws as you please yet I can baffle them all and render them null and void. . . ." [24] "Miners," he said, "instead of asking for more pay should agitate the question, 'Who owns the coal lands?'" A wage program

---

[22] *Ibid.*, Feb. 22, 1888.
[23] *Ibid.*, Feb. 24, 1888.
[24] *Proceedings*, 1882 General Assembly, pp. 282-83; *Journal*, p. 477.

he considered "shortsighted work." [25]   He was interested
in the Irish Land League and represented the Agrarianism
of G. H. Evans combined with Irish anti-landlordism. He
believed not only that no more public lands should be given
to corporations and speculators, but that those already distributed should be restored to the people. He spoke for
Henry George in 1886 in the New York mayoralty campaign, but he was not a single-taxer and the Order paid
little attention to his land reform ideas.[26]

After land came temperance. "The temperance question," he said, "is most important and sometimes I think
it is the main issue." He was constantly denouncing the
"rum seller" and the "rum drinker." But he was not a
prohibitionist. He had too much respect for personal lib-
erties to demand that others drink only water because
it suited him. The Women's Christian Temperance Union
was his firm friend but his temperance ideas helped to
alienate the coopers and brewers.

Powderly was altogether opposed to strikes, and though
he talked arbitration he was a poor and reluctant negotiator. In connection with the Southwestern strike he said,
"I was forced to interfere after it had started without any
advice from me," and he could have said the same thing of
all the strikes of the Order with which he had anything to
do. He called off the Chicago stockyards strike when it
was perhaps nearly won, and kept out of the Reading strike
entirely, for fear of the criticism that his action had in-
jured the prospects of the men. He did everything he could
to prevent the strike on the New York Central but failed.
Public opinion was his great bogey. His idea was always
to settle a strike and have it over with on almost any
terms. His complete failure as a negotiator was due largely

---

[25] Letter from Powderly to Hayes, Apr. 29, 1887.
[26] *Proceedings*, 1888 General Assembly, p. 9.

to the fact that his heart was not in it. He believed in the peaceful settlement of disputes but he believed even more strongly in not having disputes to settle.

And finally, Powderly had great faith in what he called "education" or "agitation." He was a born agitator himself and continually insisted that something be agitated. In 1884 he said:

Our work heretofore has been but preliminary, educational. Up to the present day we have been sowing the seed; from this time forward we must bend our energies to gathering in the harvest. Men have grown eager and anxious. Longing for results they have overlooked the fact that full and complete preparations have not yet been made [for what, he was never quite sure]. To attempt to carry out the idea of the founders of this organization in a week or a year or a decade would be folly. . . . No hasty or ill-advised action . . . must be taken. . . .

He blew hot and cold. In one sentence it was time to do something. In the next nothing could yet be done. In the last analysis the "something," when the time came, would be politics, but the time did not come until after the Order had ceased to be of importance. Powderly was politically minded, but he kept the Order out of politics until very late. He thought first to create a labor public opinion which sometime, somehow, would affect legislation. The Knights before the American Federation of Labor had a nonpartisan policy of rewarding friends and punishing enemies. They had a lobby and in later years tried to unite with the farmers politically. Powderly rejected a nomination for office in Pennsylvania and after he became grand master workman refused to run for any political post. He remained mayor of Scranton until 1884, but always insisted that he was a labor mayor and not the representative of any party. He belonged to no political party but took an active interest in legislation, especially in Pennsylvania.

This then was the man who led the Knights of Labor or was led by them from 1879 to 1893. He was a talker, writer, agitator, but lacked executive ability and inclination. He was an introvert where an extravert was needed. His successor as head of the American labor movement, Samuel Gompers, was almost the exact opposite. They could never understand each other and there was distrust on both sides. This explains as much as anything the split which brought into being the American Federation of Labor.

By 1880 the long depression had passed and the Knights of Labor picked up. The Resumption Act had killed the Greenback movement and the politicians returned. The new grand master was a Catholic and unembarrassed by strong religious feeling as compared with Stephens. The General Assembly of that year was held in Pittsburgh, the center of the Order's strength among the Catholic miners. But nothing was done to change the status of secrecy.[27]

The Order declined in 1881,[28] due in part to its secrecy.

---

[27] At the fourth regular General Assembly at Pittsburgh, September, 1880, there were 40 delegates representing 24 district assemblies and 10 locals. In May, 1880, the Order had 31 district assemblies working and 868 local assemblies (*Journal,* p. 15, May, 1888). At least 8 new district assemblies had been added during the year while 173 new locals were formed and 70 or 80 reorganized (*Journal,* May 15, 1880). Quarterly reports were received in September from 32 districts. Thirty-four districts had made payments to the General Assembly of $4,431.48 and 138 locals had paid $1,566.23. The membership of the Order had increased from 9,287 on Oct. 1, 1879 to 28,136 on Oct. 1, 1880.

[28] At the fifth regular session at Detroit, September, 1881, the membership had fallen from 28,136 in 1880 to 19,422 in October, 1882. There were 33 delegates at the General Assembly, representing 15 districts and 18 locals. Only one new district assembly had been added and District Assembly No. 2 of Camden, N. J. seems to have revived. Powderly complained that the Order had made little progress in the year and blamed it on prosperity and secrecy. He wanted to resign. Litchman was in trouble over the Defense Fund and was replaced by Robert D. Layton of Pittsburgh.

In January some of the members had been arrested in Somerset County, Pa., for conspiracy and for membership in an organization "which encouraged crime, arson and theft." This was a revival of the feeling against the Maguires. In June, the *Journal of United Labor* [29] carried a warning, that after giving up secrecy locally, in 1879, "where the name of the Order has been made public the leaders have been singled out, black-listed and victimized." Much of Powderly's time in 1881 had been spent in writing to the clergy in various parts of the country to explain that the Order was not dangerous nor subversive of religion and law. But this had little effect. He found that many members were faced with the alternative of leaving the Order or the Church. He even went to the clergy personally in eight places, carrying with him no doubt the rituals and secret work, but while he was well received, the oath of secrecy and the religious character of the initiation ceremony were insuperable obstacles to peace. Many if not most of the districts had made the name of the Order public though the General Assembly had not.

Secrecy and prosperity did not in fact go well together. In the bad seventies, when employers had the whip hand and advantageous collective bargaining was impossible, the open unions were at a disadvantage while a secret body was able to grow. But with the return of prosperity and bargaining, the Knights of Labor was handicapped rather than helped by secrecy. The 1881 General Assembly met in gloom and despondency. Many went away feeling that another session would never be held, and it was for this reason that the Knights were so strongly represented at the Pittsburgh Federation convention in November. It is doubtful if secrecy was the only reason for the condition of the Order but it was the chief. The publication of the name

---

[29] Powderly, *op. cit.*, p. 23.

was, however, not enough. The real difficulty was in the vow and ritual.

The 1881 General Assembly decided that the name of the Order should be made public generally by proclamation by the grand master workman, Jan. 1, 1882. The five stars were to be discontinued, and the adjectives "Noble and Holy" before the name, discarded. But more important than this was the fact that the oath was deleted from the initiation pledge and a simple promise substituted for it. It read from then on, "I . . . do truly promise on my honor." And finally the *Adelphon Kruptos* was rid of all Scriptural passages and language. Powderly did not issue the proclamation making public the name of the Order [30] because it would be "silly." The name was practically public before. But he got what he wanted, and what the Church required, by the change in the secret work and the removal of the vow. This does not mean that the Order gave up secrecy in 1881. What it gave up was the coating of religion. In many places the utmost secrecy was maintained throughout, and in all, the doings of the assemblies remained behind the veil.

Opposition to the change appeared immediately from two centers, Philadelphia and New York. The Detroit General Assembly (1881) had put Uriah Stephens on a committee to compile a history of the Order, but on Oct. 22, 1881, he wrote to Powderly refusing to act and asking that some one else be at once appointed in his place, so that his name would not appear in the proceedings.

He wrote:

The Order has drifted so far away from the primary landmarks, has so completely changed from the original, that a strong feeling begins to manifest itself in my local assembly to sever its connection with the organization. In this feeling I also

[30] *Journal,* p. 247.

coincide. Neither the assembly nor myself intend to act hastily or unadvisedly but the subject is up for consideration and action will ultimately be taken as mature deliberation may seem to dictate.

If the assembly decides to surrender its charter I shall go with it regretting to sever affiliation with yourself and many others whose friendship I highly prize. . . .[31]

Powderly answered October 25, making light of the changes made at Detroit, and followed his letter by a visit to Philadelphia. There he discovered that Stephens had a personal reason for his dissatisfaction. The New York crowd had tried to get Stephens to lead a secession and had told him that Powderly had bitterly attacked him at Detroit. According to his own story, Powderly was able to placate Stephens who promised to oppose the withdrawal of Local Assembly No. 1 from the Order. Perhaps Stephens was not completely convinced, but he died Feb. 13, 1882, and the schism could go no further. The Masons and other fraternal orders were invited through the press to his funeral, but the Knights of Labor was not.

District Assembly No. 49 of New York was not at that time in existence, but the New York and Brooklyn locals were represented at Detroit by Theodore Cuno, James Connolly, and Henry Taylor. They opposed the publication of the name of the Order and the changes in the ritual. New York never gave up secrecy. It remained fundamentalist, and constituted the opposition to Powderly which, in 1886, won him over and precipitated the war on the unions.

Theodore Cuno, a fanatical socialist, was made general statistician at Detroit, and on Oct. 24, 1881, he wrote Powderly that there was a good deal of grumbling in the New York and Brooklyn locals because of the changes in the ritual. He reported that William Horan, master workman of Local Assembly No. 1562, "the principal kicker,"

---

[31] *Proceedings*, 1887 General Assembly, p. 1515.

was "of Stephens' old school and says that no man in the world has a right to change the fundamental work of the Order." Powderly replied with a characteristically emphatic declaration "that if the object of the Order was to waste the time of each meeting in a long rigamarole of senseless phrases . . . then the old A.K. by all means. But if bare, stern realities, without any glossing, frighten any members then let them go. I will have no insubordination. As soon as the new work goes into effect it must and will be obeyed."

Further light is thrown on Powderly's attitude toward the early ritual in a letter to George K. Lloyd, New York, November 24.

> For years I have been opposed to the old style of initiation—it took too long. I did not favor an oath for I considered a man's word to be sufficient. During all these years the best part of each meeting in the local assembly was taken up in initiating new members, in instructing them in the use of symbols, in hymns and formula that could not be put in practice in the interest of labor outside the meeting room. During a part of these years I tramped up and down the land looking for work and all the ceremonies of the A. K. did not throw a single ray of light on my pathway to show me how to get a situation or to better my condition. . . .[32]

District Assembly No. 49 of New York was organized in the early part of 1882 and maintained secrecy to the end. "The Knights of Labor in this city," wrote Swinton in 1884, "maintain a degree of secrecy unknown to the Order in any other part of the country. Outsiders are kept in the dark as to their place of meeting, their active questions and other things which in other cities are fully published through the press."[33]

The year 1882 was one of great growth, in part due no

---

[32] *Ibid.*, p. 1516.
[33] Swinton, *op. cit.*, Jan. 27, 1884, and Aug. 2, 1885.

doubt to the changes in the ritual and the elimination of the oath.[34] The only fly in the ointment was a lack of interest among the members after organization. They hardly knew what to do with themselves. "To dress up after a day's toil and go to an assembly room to hear the same old program," complained one, who had no idea how soon his needs would be met by a change of reel at least once a week, " . . . becomes monotonous even to the most energetic and enthusiastic of our membership. The lack of interest is due to the fact that there is nothing growing and forming into a permanent reality." [35]

This was indeed the basic weakness of the Knights. The trade locals did not need weekly meetings to manage their affairs while most of the mixed locals had few affairs to manage. The weekly meeting had little to do but ceremonialize, play politics, or study. The leaders harped upon education, the writing and reading of essays, the study of "political economy," coöperation, insurance, public questions. For a time at least some locals did go in for study. Perhaps the Knights made the first bona fide experiment in adult education in America. But it was—and still is—a heartbreaking business. It was only the general drabness of the time and the scarcity of respectable alternatives that kept them at it at all.

---

[34] Seventy-six delegates attended the New York General Assembly of 1882, representing 26 districts and a membership of 42,517. Nine new districts had been organized in the year while two had lapsed. There were 513 new locals organized in the year and 86 old ones reorganized. Thirty had lapsed. The total number of locals in September, 1881 was 349 and in September, 1882, 918. From July, 1881, to July, 1882, the membership had risen from about 20,000 to 42,517.

The New York *Herald,* Apr. 23, 1882, published an article, the information for which was given by Cuno, giving the membership as 140,000 showing the exaggeration of the strength of the Knights that became common at this time and of course influenced public opinion more than did the actual figures.

[35] *Proceedings,* 1882 General Assembly, p. 295.

At the New York General Assembly, Powderly referred briefly to the dissatisfaction in some quarters with the new ritual but argument was unnecessary in view of the great growth of the Order. From then on it represented in the eyes of the public the American labor movement. It had ceased to be a hole-in-the-corner affair. At the same time, if there were danger of members being victimized, "there was no good reason why the names or identity of members in any locality need be made more public than in the day when we practiced the utmost secrecy." [36]

Thus the secrecy-religion problem was solved until, in 1885-86, when, with the tremendous growth of the Order, it was raised again by American priests and especially by a Canadian Archbishop, and only the energy, intelligence, and influence of Cardinal Gibbons prevented the Pope from denouncing the Knights of Labor. Cardinal Gibbons' statesmanlike brief for the Order not only saved it from condemnation but, following Cardinal Manning in England, put the Roman Catholic Church, unwillingly perhaps, on the side of organized labor.

In September, 1884, the Holy See, after consultation with Cardinal Taschereau, Archbishop of Quebec, condemned the Knights of Labor and charged the bishops "to deter their diocesans therefrom." This the Canadian Cardinal did in a circular letter (No. 131) of Feb. 2, 1885.[37] In February, 1886, Powderly apologized for the Church by somewhat naïve reflections upon the French. "There are," he said, "so many anarchists in Canada they have reason to be suspicious. . . . [The] French are much harder to manage than our people. We have some anarchists in the United States but not of the dangerous class. The French are of a very different temperament. We can take our

---

[36] *Ibid.*, p. 276.
[37] Swinton, *op. cit.*, Apr. 17, 1887.

people and pack them in a solid mass from one end of Market Street to the other and there will be no harm. But take an equal number of Frenchmen and the result will be serious." [38] Powderly may have heard rumors of Paris but he did not know his Quebec habitant. Cardinal Gibbons, too, came to the rescue. "Archbishop Taschereau's condemnation should not be taken as the sentiment of the Church in regard to the Knights of Labor as an organization. I am not familiar with the labor troubles of Quebec but it is certain that the archbishop's hostility grew out of some local laws of the Knights which are contrary to the doctrines of the Church." [39] Cardinal Gibbons explained that the whole question of the attitude of the Church hung upon the nature of the oath taken by the Knights. If the initiate's oath of secrecy provided that nothing in the Order "shall be contrary to the laws of the land, to his conscience and religious tenets" no objection would be made. But about the same time Father McElrone, editor of the *Catholic Mirror,* declared that

some decidedly socialistic doctrines contained in the constitution of 1883 were submitted to it [the Roman Curia] with the usual interrogation. "Were they in accord with the doctrines of the Church? No. Was the body a fit one for a Catholic to belong to? No. Was a society of that kind condemned by the Church as unlawful? Yes." Armed with this, Cardinal Taschereau forbade Catholics to join the condemned society under pain of excommunication. Mr. Powderly and the conservative element at least admit the gravamen of the charges but declare that the condemned doctrines of the constitution of 1883 have been eliminated and in fact a new and unobjectionable constitution framed. . . . Far be it from me to condemn Mr. Powderly. He and others are struggling now to keep down this very inner cabal which has obtained only too strong a hold upon the Order in the United States. If it becomes mani-

---

[38] *Ibid.*, Feb. 28, 1886.
[39] *Journal*, May, 1886, p. 2070.

fest that the powers of darkness are at the helm of the Knights of Labor ship then all true Catholics will be called upon to come out of the doomed vessel just as it has happened in Canada.[40]

The Church was, in fact, under Pope Leo XIII, interested as much in socialism as in secrecy. But Father McElrone was misinformed. The so-called old constitution of 1883 was less "socialistic" than that of 1884. Nevertheless, the Canadian Catholics were forced out of the Order and the Catholics of the United States were none too comfortable. "If you do not listen to the words of our bishops," said the Superior of the Oblate Fathers at St. Peter's at Montreal in 1886, "and the teachings of the Holy Catholic Church you will commit a mortal sin and incur eternal damnation. . . . No Knight of Labor will be allowed to participate in the sacraments." [41]

In October, 1886, Cardinal Gibbons called the bishops of America together in Baltimore and Powderly was invited to meet them. The latter gave Cardinal Gibbons copies of the constitution and other documents relating to the Order, and explained that it was nothing more than a workingman's society with peaceful intent which hoped to get rid of the "violent element, the element of radical men who want to found a society of atheistic anarchy." [42]

After the meeting at Cardinal Gibbons' home, Bishop Spalding of Peoria is reported to have said that nearly all the bishops were unfriendly to the Knights and convinced that the objects of the Order were opposed to the views of the Catholic Church. "They could not condemn however without the Pope's approval of their course." [43]

---

[40] Swinton, *op. cit.*, Sept. 26, 1886, quoted.
[41] *Ibid.*, Dec. 5, 1886.
[42] *Proceedings*, 1887 General Assembly, p. 1644.
[43] Swinton, *op. cit.*, Nov. 7, 1886.

Whatever the bishops may have thought, Cardinal Gibbons was completely convinced, not only of the propriety of the Knights, but of the propriety of the Church supporting labor. He went to Rome and presented, along with the evidence supplied by Powderly, a statesmanlike document protesting against the condemnation of the Order. Cardinal Manning supported him, and on April 5, 1887, Cardinal Taschereau proclaimed that the Holy See had suspended until further orders the effect of his sentence against the Knights. He authorized the confessors to absolve the Knights of Labor under certain somewhat severe conditions. In March, 1887, Cardinal Gibbons gave the Order a clean bill of health.[44] But in 1888 Powderly insisted privately that the Vatican had not favored the Knights. "I would just as lief," he wrote to Hayes, "have the Vatican denounce the Order so that we could stand on our dignity and say we don't care a damn." [45]

For Powderly's troubles were not over. When the Catholic Church let up, some of the Protestant clergy began an attack. A Rev. S. M. Adsit of California and a J. G. White of Stanford, Ill., circulated reports that the Order was under the domination of the Catholic Church. Adsit quoted a letter from the Cardinal Prefect of the Sacred Congregation to Cardinal Gibbons dated Aug. 29, 1888, which said that the Knights might be "tolerated for the present," but that changes would have to be made in the preamble and that any words that "savor of socialism or communism" would have to be corrected. Mr. Adsit stated further that the Catholic Church had condemned the teachings of Henry George and forced the Knights of Labor to remove expressions of agreement with George from their constitution. He quoted a letter from Cardinal Gibbons

---

[44] *Journal*, p. 2316.
[45] Letter from Powderly to Hayes, July 8, 1888.

dated September 25 (no year) to Archbishop Elder of Cincinnati as follows:

"On the receipt of the letter of which the enclosed is a copy I wrote to Mr. Powderly requesting him to come and see me. He came on the 25th inst. . . . and cheerfully promised to make the emendations required by the holy office, and expressed himself in readiness to comply at all times with the wishes of ecclesiastical authority."

Powderly replied to Adsit pointing out that he himself was a single-taxer, that Henry George was a member of the Order, and that Father McGlynn, who was suspended by Archbishop Corrigan for adherence to George in the New York mayoralty campaign of 1886, was reinstated in 1893 without retractions. Powderly showed, too, that the land plank of 1886 and later was more "Georgian" than that of 1885. But he did not deny that he had promised Cardinal Gibbons to make the changes required, as the Cardinal's letter claimed.

The Rev. J. G. White, who seems to have been put upon, was reported as saying in Milwaukee: "I have convincing proofs that Pope Leo, Cardinal Gibbons, sixty clergy and bishops and ten archbishops are backing a man who is endeavoring to raise a revolution in this country. That man is T. V. Powderly who under the pretense of aiding and assisting the laboring man is plotting, with the aid of the Roman Catholic Church, to overthrow this country."

This, and numerous expressions like it, hurt Powderly deeply. His patriotism was perhaps a much profounder sentiment than his religion. He wrote a dignified and pathetic letter to Mrs. Stevens, editor of the Chicago *Vanguard*, who had defended him.

But the attacks of ignorant and ridiculous Protestant preachers, like those of a suspicious hierarchy, helped to destroy the Order as they wounded its leader. In no other relationship did Powderly show so great dignity and ability as in his handling of the problem of the Order and the Church.[46]

---

[46] *Proceedings*, 1893 General Assembly, pp. 6-20.

CHAPTER VI

RINGS AND REVOLTS

THE HOME CLUB

ALMOST any society will be subject to internal disaffection and schism. The Knights suffered from this disease or sign of growth, whichever it may be, throughout their whole career. They managed, however, either to ignore or suppress all malcontents with one exception. The Home Club, an inner ring of District Assembly No. 49 of New York, fought Powderly for years and, in 1886, got complete control of the organization.

Powderly's hold on the Knights was very strong. He had a great popular following which could not be ignored. He was a good constitutionalist and in the General Assembly was always able to find some technicality to disarm his enemies. He appointed most of the committees of the assembly, the committee on credentials in especial, and in the later years he had a machine of his own. It was only when his closest friend and associate, John W. Hayes, turned against him in 1893 that the combined socialist and farmer factions got him out.

The Home Club, a secret, oath-bound ring in New York, originated in what may be called the "Cuno affair" which, though not of importance in itself, was the beginning of the conflict between New York and the administration of the Knights which finally led to the fight with the Cigar Makers, the rise of Gompers and Strasser, and the break with the unions.

Theodore F. Cuno, a reporter on a German newspaper in New York, was one of the first of the "new men" to gain office in the Order. He was made grand statistician at Detroit in 1881. Cuno was aggressive, socialistic, somewhat scatter brained, and perhaps unscrupulous. He did not fit well into the respectable company of the general officers. His first report as statistician had to be censored by the general executive board before it was printed and then it read more like the Communist Manifesto than a statistical work. He wrote six hundred letters the first year, "explaining how to agitate the Labor Question and how to spread knowledge of the miserable conditions of laborers in all countries among those who are not aware of being slaves to capitalistic oppressors." [1]

On Oct. 24, 1881, Cuno wrote Powderly that Local Assembly No. 1562 of Brooklyn, and especially its master workman, William A. Horan, were opposed to the changes in ritual made at Detroit. Horan may have been, as Cuno said, "of Stephens' old school" but Cuno, Caville, and others in the local were not. They were socialists as can be readily seen from the long resolution against coöperation presented by Horan to the 1882 General Assembly and signed by Michael J. Heaphy, then master workman of Local Assembly No. 1562, and John G. Caville. The report advised the Order to concentrate its forces "upon the one great object: to create and enforce laws by which the present capitalistic, competitive system may be abolished and universal coöperation established." [2] This was an attempt at "boring from within" the Knights of Labor in the interest of the socialist ideal. At the same time a pious lamentation was uttered over the death of Stephens.

The New York socialists had adopted Stephens though

---

[1] *Proceedings*, 1882 General Assembly, p. 287.
[2] *Ibid.*, pp. 320-22.

there was little in common between them. They adopted Stephens simply to fight Powderly, who was if anything more of a socialist than his predecessor. New York socialism at that time was a European product, and the chief work of the New York socialists was to find some connection with the American labor movement, which itself had a socialist tradition of what the Marxians called the Utopian stripe. P. J. McGuire, Samuel Gompers, Adolph Strasser ran the whole gamut of socialist thought before they settled down to pure and simple trade unionism in 1886. They became in fact more royalist than the king. Having, as Marxians, repudiated Utopian socialism, they in turn repudiated Marx for benefit-bargaining trade unionism of the so-called English type just at the time that the English unions were going over to socialism and politics.

Cuno and Caville were not the first socialists in the Order but they were probably the first Marxians. Powderly himself had accepted the red card of the Socialist Labor Party in 1880 [3] and Philip Van Patten, national secretary of the Socialist Labor Party, had been a prominent representative in the General Assembly for some years. Van Patten however was a socialist of the old Utopian stripe and was accepted by the Marxians more for his Americanism than for his socialism. He opposed Cuno and McGuire in the Duryea matter.[4]

Early in 1882, on a complaint from Local Assembly No. 1562, Cuno had Secretary Layton issue a boycott on the Duryea Starch Company of Glen Cove, L. I., promising later to supply the evidence on which it was based. Layton issued the order and a member of the firm complained to Powderly. Cuno claimed that he had ample evidence to warrant the boycott and offered to produce it if the Duryea

---

[3] *Ibid.,* 1887 General Assembly, p. 1536.
[4] *Journal,* pp. 379-80.

company would pay for the investigation. Layton published this offer along with a sympathetic statement that Cuno had been discharged by his paper. The company seems to have paid for an investigation and Layton reported that Cuno's charges, the evidence for which no one had yet seen, were without foundation. In place of evidence Local Assembly No. 1562 issued a lament over the decadence of the Order and an appeal for return to secrecy.[5] This was rather interesting in view of the fact that Cuno was the first prominent member of the Order to publish its secrets.[6] Powderly charged Cuno with exceeding his authority as grand statistician and Cuno replied "that all capital is robbery and it is our duty to throttle it and stamp it out of existence; that the Duryea company was boycotted and attacked merely to show that we could do it and that even though the charges made against them were false we should still go on and punish them. . . ."

These sentiments naturally shocked Powderly who repudiated the boycott and asked for Cuno's resignation on the spot. This was refused.

On April 23, 1882, Cuno published an article on the Order in the New York *Herald,* revealing some of the secret work, the proceedings of the General Assembly and something of the history of the Order. It was probably intended to be a boost and perhaps to force the leaders into more aggressive ways. But it contained a very misleading and dangerous calumny.

The Knights of Labor was just coming into the public view. There was much curiosity about it and some fear. It had not quite lived down the memory of the Molly Maguires. Powderly, though the least aggressive of labor leaders in action, had a dangerous pen and was very fond

---

[5] *Ibid.,* pp. 358-59.
[6] *Herald* article, Apr. 23, 1882.

of using it to shock his followers into attention. There was in him something of the evangelist and his spectacular utterances occasionally got him into trouble. In the August, 1882, number of the *Journal of United Labor*—the official organ of the Knights—Powderly published one of his characteristic utterances. He vigorously attacked strikes as he always did, and advised temperance, coöperation, and education in their place. But in trying to be impressive he said that the next General Assembly ought to put a stop to strikes or prepare for bigger and better ones. This was one of his little jokes, carried a trifle too far when he suggested the following amendments to the constitution if a strike policy were to be accepted:

1. Each local shall levy a sum upon each member sufficient in the aggregate to purchase a rifle and bayonet; also one hundred and fifty rounds of ammunition for each member.
2. A like assessment shall be levied for the purpose of purchasing the latest improved style of Gatling gun for the use of this assembly.

Realizing perhaps that this might be misinterpreted he said further on "as a representative to the G. A., I for one shall vote against the rifle and Gatling gun."

Cuno, from malice, fanaticism, or ordinary dumbness, published this in the *Herald* article as a serious threat from the grand master workman and substituted "for" in place of "against" in the reference to the use of guns. Peter Cooper brought the matter to the attention of Congress, informing that body that the leaders of the Knights of Labor advised their members to save money "and buy for each organized company a gatling gun with 150 rounds of ammunition and three months' provisions for their families." The business community was disturbed. Powderly was furious, and the general executive board suspended Cuno until the next General Assembly should meet. On August 13 and 22, Local Assembly No. 1562 issued two circulars abusing the general officers, maintaining the Duryea boycott and charging that Cuno had been suspended without proper trial. Much of the time of the 1882 General Assembly was taken up with the Cuno affair and a committee was appointed to investigate and act on the Duryea boycott, the *Herald* article, and the circulars attacking the general officers. The committee found all the charges against Cuno and Local Assembly No. 1562 to be true, and on Nov. 27, 1882, the charter of the local was revoked and Theodore Cuno, Michael Heaphy, John Caville, William Horan, William Cowen, and P. J. McGuire were "expelled and forever debarred" from membership in the Knights of Labor. Heaphy and Caville were expelled for the circulars, and Horan, Cowen, and McGuire because, acting as counsel for the defendants, "they hindered the work of the committee and treated its members with contempt."

The Cuno affair solidified the socialist and fundamentalist sentiment in New York against the general officers and the long series of intrigues began which finally did much to disrupt the Order and create the American Federation of Labor. P. J. McGuire, who with Gompers later built up the American Federation of Labor, had thrown himself into the Cuno fight, and it was suggested that Cuno would have backed down if McGuire had not been behind him.[7] McGuire was about at the end of his radicalisms and was settling down as secretary of the new-formed Brotherhood of Carpenters and Joiners. Gompers in his autobiography speaks somewhat patronizingly of this young man, but the latter undoubtedly supplied what ideas the American Federation of Labor had for its foundation. McGuire had been expelled some time before this from a St. Louis assembly of the Knights of Labor but he was able—fraudulently it

---

[7] *Journal,* p. 379.

was charged—to join Local Assemly No. 1562.[8] After the Cuno affair he kept up a running fight within and without the Order. In spite of his expulsion he was on the rolls of the Brooklyn local as late as 1889.[9]

But, as has been suggested, there was another faction in New York opposed to Powderly—the fundamentalists, the strict constructionists of Stephens' gospel of secrecy and ritual. They and the socialists seemed to have had much in common, probably based on a misunderstanding of each other's position, and a common flair for intrigue. The fundamentalists were politically minded and opposed to trade unionism as were the socialists in spite of their protestations.[10] They were led by T. B. McGuire, John Morrison, George K. Lloyd, and James E. Quinn.

In October and November, 1881, Powderly received two letters from New York complaining of the changes in the secret work made at Detroit. One was from Cuno representing the attitude of Horan, and the other from Lloyd asking a dispensation to continue in the old way. District Assembly No. 49, New York, was organized July 1, 1882, and took in most of the locals of New York and Brooklyn but not Local Assembly No. 1562. The report of the investigating committee which revoked the charter of this local, 1562, and expelled its defenders was supposed to be final. The general executive board, however, afraid of such

---

[8] *Ibid.*, p. 380.

[9] Letter from Powderly to Hayes, Sept. 25, 1889.

[10] The Marxian socialists were trade unionists only as compared with the Lassalleans. The latter could wait for the Revolution to create trade unions: the former saw the chance of the revolution in their capture of the unions. To socialists there was a world of difference in these points of view but socialists are notorious and subtle dialecticians. No ordinary trade unionist could see the difference and when Gompers, Strasser, and McGuire dropped socialism they dropped all the 57 varieties. But compare Perlman in Commons and Associates, *History of Labour in the United States* for a very different interpretation.

drastic action, asked for the evidence upon which the report was based. This was not produced but the verdict was promulgated by the grand secretary in the *Journal* for December, 1882.

By September, 1882, District Assembly No. 49 had taken Local Assembly No. 1562 under its wing, admitting its delegates while the local was under suspension, and making common cause against the administration. The district appealed from the decision of the committee and ignored its discipline. Powderly protested but got no satisfaction, and in February, 1883, District Assembly No. 49 itself was suspended by Powderly's order, and District Master Workman Cook—an administration man—returned the charter to the general officers.[11] Members of District Assembly No. 49 continued to meet, led by James E. Quinn, "chairman of the committee of appeal." Powderly was forced to yield. The general executive board declared the suspension of District Assembly No. 49 illegal, returned the charter to Cook, and carefully notified Quinn. New York had won the first round in the battle for control. It was to win more.

On May 1, 1883, Cook, charter in hand, was refused admission to the district meeting and the general executive board was forced to renew the suspension but agreed to consider the appeal from the verdict of the special committee *in re* Local Assembly No. 1562 and investigate further as soon as the district was reorganized. The board went to New York in July, and on August 8 instructed the grand secretary that the special committee had conducted its inquiry "in an irregular manner" and had failed to produce evidence which warranted its decision. The committee report was therefore declared null and void. Local 1562 was reinstated and Cuno, Heaphy, Caville, McGuire, Cowen,

---

[11] *Proceedings,* 1883 General Assembly, pp. 447-48.

and Horan were taken back into the Order. Quinn succeeded Cook as master workman of District Assembly
No. 49.[12]

Thus began, under the leadership of Quinn, an inner ring
of District Assembly No. 49, later known as the Home
Club, in control of the second largest district in the Order,
of the Central Labor Union of New York, and finally, in
1886, of the Knights of Labor.[13]

The Home Club then had a dual origin, fundamentalist
and socialist. In January, 1881, a "Spread the Light" club
was organized in Brooklyn to carry on a night school to
instruct the master workmen of New York in their duties.
In May, 1884, T. B. McGuire, then district master workman of District Assembly No. 49, reported that a committee
had been established on the work of the Order which met
at least once a month for the instruction of officers.[14] And
finally the "Class" was organized by Victor Drury based
on the methods of the International. There were nine
members of the Class and each one went out to form another circle of nine, thus permeating the Order. The members were: Victor Drury, T. B. McGuire, James E. Quinn,
T. P. Quinn, Edward Kunze, secretary of District Assembly
No. 49, Harry E. Taylor said to be the right-hand man of
Frederick Turner, Hugh Carey, Paul Meyer, and George
Dunne.[15] They were said to control all the general officers
except Powderly and at the special session at Cleveland in
1886 they succeeded in electing four of their candidates to
the auxiliary executive board. John Morrison produced a
paper at Cleveland charging the Home Club with trying to
murder Powderly and numerous other offenses and a com-

---

[12] *Ibid.*, pp. 450-52.
[13] During the controversy Powderly threatened to resign for the
second time but didn't—a characteristic gesture.
[14] *Journal*, p. 705.
[15] John Swinton, *John Swinton's Paper*, July 3, 1887.

mittee was appointed to investigate the organization. Powderly opposed the washing of the Order's dirty linen in public and was accused of selling out to the Home Club. At Richmond his salary was raised to $5,000 and his term of office extended to two years. The committee exonerated or "whitewashed" the Home Club. Powderly was chairman of the credentials committee at Richmond which reported unfavorably on the credentials of John Morrison and others opposed by the clique.

In June, 1887, the Home Club was reorganized. Quinn was deprived of some of his powers and the committee on arbitration and strikes was abolished.[16] Gompers believed that the "better element" in the Order was trying to oust the antiunion officials.[17]

In 1893 the New York socialists under De Leon combined with the farmer element under Sovereign, and, with the aid of John W. Hayes, who was originally made a member of the general executive board by the Home Club, ousted Powderly. De Leon and Sovereign fell out in 1895, when the New York socialists were finally expelled from the Order. They retained the charter and seal of District Assembly No. 49 but Sovereign reorganized the District and "placed it in the hands of loyal members." [18]

In 1886, District Assembly No. 49 under the control of the Home Club took up the cause of the Progressive Cigar Makers and made the Progressives' fight with the International their own. The attack of the trade unions on the Order, which came to a head in this struggle and created the American Federation of Labor, will be dealt with in another chapter.

---

[16] *Ibid.*, July 3, 1887.
[17] *Union Advocate*, July, 1887.
[18] *Proceedings*, 1896 General Assembly, p. 43.

The first revolt from the Order was that which called the Terre Haute convention of 1881, and was later organized as the Federation of Organized Trades and Labor Unions. The Knights dropped out the next year and were later invited back, but this will be treated in another chapter. The second revolt originated in Baltimore in 1883 under the name "The Improved Order of the Knights of Labor." It was a political movement led by Washington and Baltimore Knights, some of them trade unionists. It protested against autocracy in the Order, heavy taxation for the support of strikes, and looked to "labor emancipation peaceably by means of the workingman's ballot."[19] There is some indication that it was a trade union movement but its political intentions were unmistakable.[20] Whatever it was, it did not last long. Its members were expelled from the Order in 1883 and nothing more was heard of it.[21]

A third attempt to form a separate organization was made after the 1883 convention at Cincinnati. An assembly was organized at Binghamton, New York, in opposition to another local. The organizer was expelled from his local and the general executive board supported the protestants. The organizer and some others then started a new society called the Independent Order with Excelsior Assembly No. 1 as a benefit society. They, like many other locals, objected to supporting the glass workers in their strike. The Independent Order died in the spring of 1884.[22]

At the special session of the General Assembly at Cleveland in May-June, 1886, the Home Club gained control of the Order. The trade unionists within and without were

---

[19] T. V. Powderly, *Thirty Years of Labor*, p. 294.
[20] *Proceedings*, 1883 General Assembly, p. 408.
[21] *Ibid.*, p. 495.
[22] Powderly, *op. cit.*, pp. 295-96.

ignored, and four out of the six men put on the auxiliary general executive board were Home Club nominees. Joseph Buchanan, the stormy petrel of the Knights, was one of the two non-Home-Club men put on the auxiliary board. At the regular General Assembly at Richmond in September, the Home Club ran wild and the cigar makers were expelled from the Order. In January, 1887, Buchanan left Denver, where for five years he had published the *Labor Enquirer,* and shortly after, Burnette G. Haskell, who with Buchanan was then a member of the International, published a long list of ridiculous charges against Powderly, and asked him to reply. Powderly went to Denver in May and answered Haskell's nonsense, but the *Enquirer* was not satisfied and continued to malign him.

Immediately after the Richmond assembly Buchanan issued a circular instructing the locals of his district to pay no attention to the order expelling the cigar makers. This of course did not add to his popularity with the Home Club, though in other places the order was discreetly ignored. It is doubtful if there were enough cigar makers in Denver to require a circular and the action of Buchanan was nothing more than a characteristic gesture. Though Buchanan had sold the Denver *Labor Enquirer* and had left the city for good, Powderly recalled his organizer's commission and when Buchanan's old district, No. 89 of Denver, sent him as its delegate to the Minneapolis assembly of 1887 he was rejected with the connivance of the grand master workman.

Two days after the Minneapolis assembly closed, about twenty-five of the delegates, dissatisfied with the direction in and under which the Order was moving, met at Chicago and organized a "Provisional Committee." It issued a manifesto asking the locals to refuse to pay dues to the General Assembly and gained the sympathy of some districts and of two members of the general executive board,

Thomas Barry and William Bailey. Barry was expelled and formed a new society, the Brotherhood of United Labor. The provisional committee broke up after a few weeks but it was responsible, at least the dissension it represented was responsible, for the withdrawal of many members from the Order. Even as far south as Charleston, S. C., there was a secession under the name of the Improved Order.[23]

In 1889, Powderly proposed to drop Turner by combining the offices of secretary and treasurer under Hayes. By this time the Home Club itself was in decline and Powderly had built up a machine of his own. Turner, Victor Drury, Henry Taylor, all connected with the Home Club, and R. N. Keen, R. C. McCauley, J. N. Kennedy, and James L. Wright, all charter members of the first local assembly, started a fundamentalist or founders' movement within the Order. They proposed to return to the early oath-bound secrecy and anti-Catholic sentiment. The ritual of the fundamentalists contained the question, "Are you prepared to bind yourself to use your own judgment . . . uncontrolled by any outside power and absolutely independent of the dictation of any church, prince, potentate, or authority whatsoever?"[24] Turner was an Englishman and a member of the St. George's society.

In 1887, the largest district in the Order, No. 30 of Massachusetts, split on the trade union question. Litchman led the administration forces against McNeill, Foster, Carlton, and Skeffington. The district lost 40,000 members in one year.[25]

Two more independent orders appeared, a political one at Washington in 1888 and a "trade union" one at New

---

[23] *Proceedings*, 1887 General Assembly, p. 1375.
[24] Powderly, *op. cit.*, p. 299.
[25] Swinton, *op. cit.*, July 17, 1887.

Orleans in 1894. The General Assembly of 1894 at New Orleans refused admission to fourteen delegates, six of whom were from national trade assemblies. These included the glass workers in Local Assembly No. 300 and the miners' National Trade Assembly No. 135. They met at Columbus, Feb. 14, 1895, and established a new Order.

In 1895, De Leon led a split in District Assembly No. 49 of New York. By that time there was not enough left of the Knights of Labor to be worth quarreling over, though this did not prevent much further quarreling.

CHAPTER VII

STRIKES AND THE ORDER

WITH the return of prosperity in 1880, the Knights became involved in a large number of local and district strikes, and, as there was supposed to be a Resistance Fund accumulating, the general officers were continually pestered for financial help. There were two good reasons why this was not forthcoming, one that it was not called in until after the 1880 General Assembly, and the other, that most of it had been spent by the secretary for printing.

The attitude of the Order toward strikes was determined largely by the experience of all the unions of the seventies. It was not peculiar to the Knights, but common to the trade union leaders who had gone through the disastrous depression of 1873 to 1879. Strikes in that period were failures, and the conclusion was unwarrantably drawn that the strike per se was a hopeless anachronism and should be discouraged. So far there was agreement. A difference of opinion grew up only as to the best method of discouragement. On the whole the trade unions, led by the Molders and Cigar Makers, decided to discourage local strikes by bringing them under national control and building up a financial system that would give support to official strikes with some chance of success. The Knights started out in the same way but were deflected from strike support to pure and simple discouragement with "arbitration" as a substitute. Thus the real difference between the Knights and the trade unions on strikes was not so much a difference of policy as a difference in execution. But it is also true that the weakness of the Order's execution was due in part to lack of unanimity as to policy. And the most decisive factor in deflecting the Order from its original idea was the accidental one that the first grand secretary had once smelt printer's ink.

While the Knights of Labor was opposed to strikes one of the first things it did was to create a strike fund. In the call for the convention issued by District Assembly No. 1, in 1877, which resulted in the formation of the first General Assembly, the second matter mentioned after national organization as the reason for the call, was the creation of a National Resistance Fund. The idea was like that of the trade unions, to create a strike fund under national control so that spontaneous local strikes would be discouraged, and, should the Order enter upon a strike, it could be prosecuted successfully, or the mere threat of the fund would enforce arbitration.

At the first General Assembly, January, 1878, a committee was appointed which recommended that 5 cents per member per month should be collected and held by the treasurers of the local assemblies for "such cases of emergency as may from time to time arise after the expiration of two years dating from January 1, 1878." That this was intended as a strike fund is evident from the further recommendation of the committee that "when the Board of Arbitration fails to adjust a grievance, it shall notify the National Master Workman . . ." who shall ". . . direct the district assemblies to forward not more than 10 per cent of the Resistance Fund then in the treasuries of the subordinate locals." This was an awkward arrangement but no more so than a similar one in the constitution of the Cigar Makers. It did tend to create a fund held locally under central control for the enforcement of arbitration and the support of strikes. The General Assembly was, however, not unanimous and the recommendation of the committee was amended so as to leave the use to which the Resistance Fund should be put, undetermined, "to be held for use and distribution under such laws and regulations as the General Assembly may then (1880) adopt." [1]

Had the General Assembly been intent upon creating trouble for itself, it could hardly have done better. The Order was poor. It had no headquarters nor equipment. Its secretary lived in Massachusetts and its head in Philadelphia. The *Proceedings* had to be printed, salaries paid, and the expenses of the general executive board defrayed. In 1880, the *Journal* was started. Naturally, with an undetermined windfall in the offing, there was much speculation as to how it might be spent. Stephens, still under the impression in 1879 that it was to be a strike fund to enforce arbitration, called it the "wisest measure ever inaugurated for the elevation of labor," sufficient "to enforce arbitration in any ordinary case." And he went into an elaborate statistical prognostication as to its size when the second year had expired, and concluded that it would be large enough to assure "that strikes . . . will be of rare occurrence and irresistible and effectual when they must be resorted to." They would be "least likely to be called upon to resist who are prepared." [2]

But while Stephens' reckoning may have been statistically correct it was humanly inaccurate. The fund did not accumulate according to schedule. The locals were re-

---

[1] Constitution, Art. VIII. Powderly became grand master workman in September, 1879, and in 1880 issued a decision that "neither the A. K. nor the constitution has anything to say with reference to strikes, and the grand officers cannot make a demand upon the Order to support a strike." All they could do was appeal for voluntary aid. *Proceedings*, 1880 General Assembly, p. 262. Decision 119, *Journal*, July 13, 1881, p. 35.

[2] *Ibid.*, 1879 Chicago General Assembly, p. 108.

luctant to collect money they were not allowed to disburse for a purpose at which they could only guess. And as it turned out, their parsimony was in the nature of wisdom. Then, too, the Order was growing beyond its original industrial boundaries. So long as it remained in Pennsylvania and the mining districts of Ohio and Indiana it retained its trade character and its interest in strikes and strike funds. But it had moved out into the Middle West among the small towns, where its locals represented not wage-earners solely but the last frontier of semi-itinerant craftsmen and small shopkeepers, who had no interests in the mass movements of the newly mobilized regiments of the wage-earning East. From an enthusiast in Onekama, Mich., two years later, a letter was received by the *Journal* [3] which throws an interesting light on the new personnel of the Order in the West. He reported that the assembly was new and small but that "quite a number of our best citizens . . . are coming to the front," endorse the Knights, and take a great interest in the assembly. East and West are one in this, that it is the habit of the "best citizens" everywhere to come to the front. But the "best citizens" of Philadelphia failed to follow the example of their peers in Onekama in entering the Order, and a cleavage appeared between West and East, most marked in relation to strikes and the strike fund.

In 1879, the general executive board was instructed to draw up regulations for the Resistance Fund and report to the 1880 General Assembly. The needs of the Order and purposes other than strikes and arbitration were given consideration. The name was changed from Resistance to Defense Fund and it was called in to be distributed as follows: 10 per cent for traveling organizers; not more than 30 per cent for strikes; 30 per cent to be held for coöperation; and 10 per cent for education. The remaining

---

[3] September, 1884, p. 801.

20 per cent was to be unappropriated until 1881. In 1880, coöperative sentiment was strong and the general executive board was reluctant to recommend strike help. It suggested that "brothers on approved strikes" should be "assisted into self-help by coöperative enterprises if possible." If relief was to be paid from the Defense Fund, the request had to be approved by local and district executive boards to be created for the purpose, before going to the general executive board.

But the Order's enthusiasm for coöperation did not go to the extreme of spending money on it. While 30 per cent of the fund was set aside for this purpose it was to be held intact for a year. "Coöperation," said the board, "is the order of human progress but as such imperfect ideas prevail in reference to its vital principle, it is deemed wise that this portion of the fund shall remain intact until the next session of the General Assembly." The 10 per cent for education was to be used "to stimulate and encourage the writing, printing and circulating among the members of the Order of tracts, pamphlets and other literature conducive to their education in organization, coöperation, political economy. . . . "

The suggestions of the general executive board were adopted with the modification that the local treasurers were required to pay to the trustees (the grand master workman, general worthy foreman, and chairman and secretary of the general executive board) the amount then in the fund and 15 cents per member per quarter in the future. Of this, 30 per cent was to be used for strikes and 10 per cent for education, the remaining 60 per cent to be held for productive and distributive coöperation after 1881. Strikes were said to cause as a rule more injury than benefit, and all attempts to "foment" them were to be discouraged. If a strike were contemplated the local was required to elect an arbitration committee to settle the dispute. If this failed a district arbitration committee was to take it up, and when that failed it was to be transferred to a third committee composed of one representative of each of the two nearest district assemblies and a third from the district assembly involved If this failed the matter was to be referred to the general executive board which, with the grand master workman and the grand secretary, were to take it under "advisement," and, if warranted, to order a strike. No strike unless thus sanctioned could be supported from the Defense Fund, and when money was taken from the fund for this purpose an assessment was to be levied at once to replace it. [4]

This was the second attempt at strike legislation by the Order, and shows a very definite trend against strikes and strike sentiment. It is obvious now, whether it was at the time or not, that strict adherence to the procedure laid down in 1880 would mean that practically no strike would ever receive help from the Defense Fund. The four separate series of "arbitrations" were carried through on only one occasion, and no ordinary body of potential strikers could have been held in leash for the length of time necessary to complete the negotiations required. But it made little difference. The Resistance-Defense Fund was to serve another purpose and the General Assembly had its fondness for legislation satisfied by one of its many elaborate schemes.

Charles H. Litchman was grand secretary of the Order. He was a reformer of the old style, a joiner, and for one year a member of the general court of Massachusetts. The Knights were short of funds and, according to his statement, which there is no reason to doubt, he carried the Order on his own credit. He was also a passionate publicist

[4] *Proceedings,* 1880 General Assembly, pp. 247-48.

and in 1880 had been made editor of the *Journal* in addition to his duties as secretary. Litchman quite naturally felt that publicity was the big job of the Order and he the big publicity man. He was always able to convince himself that the way to save a little money was to spend a lot. The 1880 General Assembly had set aside 10 per cent of the Defense Fund for "education" and Litchman needed a printing press to get out his circulars, the *Journal,* the *Proceedings,* and any other educational matter he might think of. So, like Stephens before him, he began to figure. Carefully multiplying the number of members per month from 1878 to 1880 by a nickel, he arrived at the interesting conclusion that the Defense Fund should amount to $25,000. Of this, "education" was to get 10 per cent, or $2,500, so Litchman proceeded to buy his printing press and pay the debts of the General Assembly to the amount of $4,691.64. This would have left a considerable deficit even if the Defense Fund had lived up to expectations. But it decidedly did not. Instead of $25,000 it amounted to $7,876.65 up to September, 1881, so that there was little left after the grand secretary had paid his bills. The board found that Litchman had used the Defense Fund illegally, removed him from office and ordered him to reimburse the fund. What remained was put in the bank to apply to the per capita tax of the locals who had paid in. [5] Thus the Resistance-Defense Fund, after much legislation as to its distribution, disappeared, and nothing was done about strikes.

When the Knights made it practically impossible to give financial aid to strikes, the general officers were probably pleased with their work because they believed that more could be secured by "arbitration," no matter how long drawn out, than in any other way. But they forgot the most

---

[5] *Ibid.,* 1881 General Assembly, pp. 312, 318, 331.

important sort of strike—for union recognition. If the union and its representatives were refused recognition, "arbitration" was an empty word. There could be no substitute other than the boycott for the strike for recognition, and in 1882 the Order was everywhere forced to face the problem of the iron-clad contract. Arbitration, or what the Knights called arbitration, might be the newer and better way to conduct industrial relations, but the employers as well as the employees had to be convinced of this before the strike could be forever junked as a "relic of barbarism." Employers in the eighties were unaccustomed to dealing with unions. They had had their own way in most industries for at least ten years and in many for much longer. Industries were rapidly expanding and could not be bothered with the incubus of union recognition and the slow process of debate, often atrociously annoying debate with stupid and willful people. A man's business was still regarded as his own, even when the man was that fiction the corporation, with all the rights of an individual. What use could Jay Gould make of trade unions? He could wreck half a dozen railroads quicker than he could negotiate a wage scale with his shopmen. And what, anyway, did he care about wage scales or about railroads for that matter, when there were so many things to wreck at a decent profit? And if it were a builder instead of a wrecker the situation was the same. Industrial America had got her second wind since the Civil War, and just as the wheels began to whir again, came a giant of labor saying "Halt, we want to talk this thing over." Little and big, the employers replied "Talk? talk? We're not in business to talk. Here, sign this." And out came the "iron-clad," usually in the mining districts accompanied by a house lease whereby the miners were required "to waive their right under the law to require notice to terminate the tenancy." [6] The "iron-clad" read in part " . . . And the party of the second part (the employee) agrees and binds himself to withdraw from and renounce his allegiance to the Order of the Knights of Labor, and not become a member of any secret labor organization while in the employ of the party of the first part. . . . " [7]

Of course there were then, as to-day, employers and employers, but the history of the labor movement pretty well establishes the principle that "good" employers are the product of "bad" labor unions. Recognition has seldom been handed out on a silver platter and when it seems to be, it is usually found that some other sort of recognition is knocking at the door with an ax. The following letter from a nonunion mine owner is not typical because very few employers, even in 1883, were as aggressive as this in print, but it represents an attitude that was more common then than now. It was written by William Wyant who signed himself "Operator Non-Union Mines" and was addressed to Robert Layton, secretary of the Knights of Labor, dated Feb. 8, 1883, from Fayette County, W. Va., where the tradition possibly still holds good. It is quoted in full for its flavor:

DEAR SIR,

I have noticed time and again of your sending papers and communications in the interest of the society called the Knights of Labor to Mr. Langdon Carter an employe of mine. Mr. Carter has signed a written agreement that as long as he is employed by me he is to have nothing to do with any labor organization, and especially the one known as the Knights of Labor. I employ some two hundred and fifty men and will employ no one that belongs to any labor organization, and will at once discharge from my employment any man who has anything to do with any labor organization.

Mr. Carter requests me to say to you that he wishes nothing

---

[6] *Journal*, p. 503.
[7] *Ibid.*

to do with you or any other agitator of labor troubles, as his past experience is that just such sharks as you who are too lazy and shiftless to earn their own living cause all the trouble among the poor but honest laboring men.

Now my advice to you is to mind your own business, and let other people's affairs alone, and if you still persist in your foolishness perhaps come in person and attempt to interfere in my business and I assure you that after one personal interview you will learn sense enough to attend to your own business hereafter. Hoping you will go to work and earn an honest living I remain

Very respectfully yours. . . .[8]

Powderly replied with a silly letter of abuse suggesting as "the oldest health officer in the state of Pennsylvania" that the gentleman was rotten, but he missed the point of the letter when he failed to see that his enthusiasm for negotiation and arbitration would not get him far with a man like Wyant. But if Powderly could not see it others could, and in 1882 the general executive board was flooded with appeals for help against union-breaking employers.

The strike law of 1881 involved too slow and complicated a process to do any good, but there seems to have been one attempt to make it work. Local Assembly No. 1709, carriage workers of Rochester, N. Y., had some trouble with Cunningham and Company which they tried to settle. It was passed on to District Assembly No. 44, and later to representatives of District Assemblies Nos. 9, 3, and 44, and finally to the general executive board. On Jan. 26, 1882, the general executive board sanctioned a strike and ordered an assessment of 15 cents per member.

In December, 1881, the general executive board issued an appeal for ax makers of Cleveland, Ohio, and Lock Haven, Pa., on strike for higher wages, and $2,113.94 was collected. [9] Another assessment of 10 cents per member

---

[8] *Ibid.*, p. 425.
[9] *Proceedings,* 1882 General Assembly, p. 332.

was levied in 1882 for District Assembly No. 25, miners of Maryland, who lost a strike of six months' duration against a reduction and the iron-clad. [10] And two more assessments were levied for locked-out pottery workers of East Liverpool, Ohio, and New Castle, Pa., one of 5 cents which netted only $1,500 and another of 10 cents. District Assembly No. 3, to which they belonged, could not help them because its resources had been depleted in maintaining 2,000 Knights of Labor steel workers called out by the Amalgamated.

In 1882 it became evident that there were strikes and strikes, and that while the Order might neglect an ordinary stoppage for wages, hours, or conditions, it could not afford to ignore a lockout, or a strike for recognition of the union, which often amounted to the same thing. Thus while the general executive board was emphatic in its opposition to strikes, and recommended that they be prohibited by law, it made an exception for "cases where the right to belong to the organization is denied by an employer or where brothers are victimized because of any action taken in carrying into effect the aims and purposes of our Order." [11] This paved the way for legislation covering lockouts and strikes for union recognition. It went in fact beyond that as almost any sort of strike could be interpreted as an attempt to carry out the purposes of the Order. An elaborate plan of conciliation and arbitration was offered by the general executive board, but nothing was done with it. [12] Instead, it was decided that no local should strike until the proposal was endorsed by a two-thirds vote of the local and approved by the district master workman. If the district master workman should refuse to sanction the

---

[10] *Journal,* pp. 364-65.
[11] *Proceedings,* 1882 General Assembly, p. 305, and *Journal,* pp. 364-65.
[12] *Proceedings,* 1882 General Assembly, p. 333.

strike the local could appeal to the district assembly which by a two-thirds vote could overrule the district master workman. Locals attached to the General Assembly were required to submit the matter to the general executive board. This resolution was passed over the adverse recommendation of the Committee on Laws by a vote of 26 to 17. [13] In addition to this, a special committee was appointed on lockouts and strikes for recognition, and a new strike law was adopted that where twenty-five or more members of the Order in any one district assembly or local assembly were locked out and refused employment because they belonged to the organization, "and not because they have made themselves obnoxious to employers as individuals," the general executive board should make an investigation, and if satisfied might assess the entire membership of the Order sufficient to sustain the locked-out members, but not more than 10 cents a week was to be levied at any one time. Any local failing to pay the assessments within thirty days was to be suspended unless exonerated by the general executive board for sufficient reasons. [14]

In 1870 a national union of telegraphers had been organized but was broken up by a strike in 1871. No further organization among the telegraphers appeared until 1882, when the Pittsburgh operators formed an assembly of the Knights of Labor and sent organizers into the eastern cities. At about the same time the Brotherhood of Telegraphers, an open union, was organized in the West and the two groups came together to form the Telegraphers National District Assembly No. 45. On July 19, 1883, John Campbell, district master workman of District Assembly No. 45, called a strike of all the commercial

13 *Ibid.*, pp. 324, 352.
14 *Ibid.*, pp. 352-53.

telegraphers of the United States and Canada, with the exception of the press and broker operators, for increased wages and improved conditions of work. Two companies, the American Rapid and the Bankers and Merchants, agreed to a 15 per cent advance, the abolition of Sunday work without extra pay, and other conditions, but the Western Union, then controlled by Jay Gould, made a fight. On July 28, the general executive board issued an appeal to the Order for the Telegraphers, but only $1,640.65 came in and the board, on its own responsibility, advanced a further $2,000 from the funds of the General Assembly. This, too, was inadequate, and on August 17 the strike was called off and the men ordered back to work by the district assembly. They went back completely disorganized and were forced to sign the iron-clad promising to abandon "any and all membership, connection or affiliation with any organization or society whether secret or open which in any wise attempts to regulate the conditions of my service or the payment thereof while in the employment now undertaken." [15]

This was the first strike on a national scale in which the Order was involved and its disastrous ending caused widespread criticism. It was an ambitious undertaking not so much in the number of men concerned as in its nation-wide character and the strength of the corporations, especially the Western Union. The strike was begun without sufficient preparation under the false impression that the Knights of Labor were in a position to support it. Perhaps promises were made, but Powderly denied this and certainly there was nothing in the new strike law nor in the treasury of the Order to warrant any promises of support for a

---

[15] George E. McNeill, *The Labor Movement: The Problem of To-day,* p. 392; *Proceedings,* 1883 General Assembly, p. 456; John Swinton, *John Swinton's Paper,* June 1, 1884.

simple strike for better wages and conditions. It was not a lockout and though a case might be made for nonrecognition and the general executive board might have levied an assessment instead of making an appeal it is very doubtful if more would have been secured in this way than the amount actually paid out.

The Telegraphers were disgusted with the Knights of Labor and swore never to have anything more to do with them. But in 1886, when they began reorganizing secretly there was said to be "every probability" that they would merge with the Order. [16]

One thing is clear, that the Knights of Labor were in no position to carry on a national strike with any prospect of success. Appeals for aid brought in practically nothing and assessments resulted in more requests for exoneration from payment than actual cash. Robert Layton, who succeeded Litchman as secretary, saw this, and proposed that the Order learn from its mistakes as the trade unions were doing. "If a strike is right and inevitable," he said, "support it: if not, ignore it and save trouble to all concerned. But for the sake of truth let us cease to condemn strikes and refuse to assess for them while we just as strongly yet indirectly indorse them by the issuing of those delusions known as appeals." [17] But Powderly was incapable of a realistic approach. All he could do at the 1883 General Assembly was to insist that no promises had been made and therefore none had been broken. [18] He offered a post mortem when what was needed was a policy. He wanted no recriminations but straddled the question of whether the Order was to leave strikes severely alone or support them with all its resources. Either course would have

---

[16] Swinton, *op. cit.*, Mar. 21, 1886.

[17] *Proceedings*, 1883 General Assembly, p. 414.

[18] *Ibid.*, pp. 402-3.

been intelligible but the Order continued to muddle through.

The experience of 1883 with the Telegraphers and others proved conclusively that the lockout law of 1882 was unsatisfactory. The general executive board diagnosed the situation correctly. In 1883 they said:

> It became apparent in the early history of the year just closing that the laws governing strikes and lockouts were totally insufficient as a means of rendering financial support to members out of employment through any cause. The tardy operation of the legal machinery through the aid of which moneys are collected on assessments or appeals; the inability of the L. A.'s to respond to either the one or the other; the meagerness of the ultimate result of this method of furnishing financial aid, the necessity forced upon us to relieve many L. A.'s from the payment of these assessments in order to retain them in the Order, render these provisions useless as a weapon against the present powers of concentrated capital in many industries.[19]

And they proposed the reëstablishment of the Defense Fund.

Even Powderly was forced to make some concession to this sentiment. He in fact was an excellent barometer of the state of opinion in the Order. But his conversion was tempered with an innate distrust. "Even though we do not favor strikes," he said, "we should establish an emergency fund to be used in upholding the rights of oppressed members who may be imposed upon. . . . "[20]

The Defense Fund was reëstablished under the name of Assistance Fund for strike aid. Each local was required to set apart 5 cents per member per month to be forwarded monthly to the district assembly and deposited by the master workman and treasurer subject to withdrawal signed by the chairman and secretary of the general executive

---

[19] *Ibid.*, pp. 457-458.
[20] *Ibid.*, p. 405.

board. Locals attached to the General Assembly were to forward their funds monthly to the general executive board to be deposited and withdrawn on the signatures of three members of the board. No local or district was to be entitled to any benefits from the fund unless it was clear on the books, and the general executive board in conjunction with the grand master workman was allowed to suspend any local failing to collect and forward its quota within a period of three months.

In the establishment of this fund [the law continued] we declare that strikes are deplorable in their effect and contrary to the best interest of the Order and therefore nothing in this article must be construed to give sanction to such efforts for the adjustment of any difficulty, except in strict accordance with the laws laid down in this article. No strike shall be declared or entered into by any L. A. or D. A. without the sanction of the G. E. B. Any L. A. attached to a D. A. having a grievance requiring adjustment shall report the facts of the case in writing to the officers of the district, who shall take the matter into full consideration and use every effort to avoid a conflict. If in their opinion the facts warrant a reference to the Executive Board, the District officers shall submit a full statement to that body who shall upon full consideration determine what further action if any shall be taken in the matter in so far as any disbursements from this fund are concerned.

An amendment was added to this clause covering locals attached to the General Assembly requiring that they secure the sanction of the general executive board before they could receive aid from the fund. In cases of lockouts where twenty-five or more members were involved in any one district or local because of their membership in the Order, the general executive board might after investigation draw upon the Assistance Fund. An amendment stipulated that no aid could be given members who struck without the permission of the general executive board and were then locked out. In every case the general executive board was first to consider "whether practical coöperation" could not be set up as a means of relief and if it should decide that it could, it was to turn over the proper share of the Assistance Fund to the Coöperative Board. An amendment provided that no assistance from the fund would be given until the strike was two weeks old and new locals were relieved for six months from paying their quotas. The law went into effect Jan. 1, 1884. [21]

Thus, in 1883, the Order returned to its original attitude toward strikes, or something like it, and on paper at any rate established anew the strike fund which had been diverted by a secretary with a publicity complex and by enthusiasm for coöperation. The new law gave the general executive board complete control over all strikes and provided for their support when entered upon with due care and consideration. The winter of 1883-84 was one of industrial depression and of unsuccessful strikes against reductions of wages. The Fall River spinners, The Hocking Valley miners, the Troy molders, the Pennsylvania miners, the Philadelphia carpet weavers, the Indiana miners, all lost. Knights of Labor were involved in all these but none except the carpet weavers' was a Knights of Labor strike, while the strikes of the glass workers, the Philadelphia shoemakers and the Union Pacific shopmen, all three Knights of Labor, were completely successful.

In October, 1883, before the new strike law went into effect the general executive board levied an assessment on the Order of 5 cents per member to aid the striking glass workers of Local Assembly No. 300. This was not a success and four canvassers were sent out to solicit further aid. On Jan. 30, 1884, the glass workers concluded a five months' strike, having gained every point and maintained their closed shop over the whole country. This was the

---

[21] *Ibid.*, pp. 509-10 and 517. Substitute for Constitution, Art. XIX.

second national strike of the Order and though it involved no more than 1,500 men it showed that victory was possible. The glass workers gave the Knights the credit for their success and it greatly stimulated the industrial point of view.

In November, 1882, Joseph R. Buchanan joined the Knights of Labor in Denver, and in December issued the first number of the *Labor Enquirer*. The dramatic story of this man's career need not be repeated here. It can be found in his own words in *The Story of a Labor Agitator* somewhat highly colored perhaps, but more interesting than most biographies of labor leaders. On May 4, 1884, the Union Pacific shopmen at Denver went out on strike against a wage reduction without organization, and appealed to Buchanan for aid. Within one day they were organized as the Union Pacific Employees' Protective Association and the entire Union Pacific system was out on strike. Four days later the company capitulated and the wage reduction was withdrawn. Under Buchanan's leadership the shopmen were held together and organized as local assemblies of the Knights of Labor.

This was the beginning of the remarkable success of the Order in the railroad strikes, the first time in the history of the American labor movement that a union was able to deal with a modern corporation on terms of equality. These achievements made the Knights nationally feared and respected. A legend grew, exaggerating their strength, numbers, hidden purposes, and power for good or evil. In three years the Order grew from 50,000 to 700,000 and if it did not reach one million the only reason was that organization was stopped because growth was too rapid. For the first, and probably the last time in labor history, we find the head of an organization minimizing its strength and doing his best to curtail it.

It cannot be said, however, that the successful strike activity of the Knights in 1884-85 and the early part of 1886 was due to the new Assistance Fund or the policy of the Order. The Assistance Fund never amounted to much more than $7,000 and the strikes of 1884-86 were supported chiefly by the old method of assessment and appeal. Strikes were won not by careful planning but by spontaneous revolt which caught the employers unprepared. The first success on the railroads in the case of the Union Pacific was so sudden and complete as to create an illusion that it was easy and could be repeated at will. Others followed but each one found the employers better prepared until finally the Southwestern System turned on the Order and utterly defeated it. None of these strikes was managed by the Order from beginning to end. They began with locals or districts and drew in the general officers only when they showed signs of failure. The general executive board was run ragged in these years settling disputes all over the continent.

Professor Commons has given currency to the impression that the growth of the Knights was due to a stampede of the unskilled into the Order. This question has been dealt with elsewhere but here it is well to note that the great railroad strikes were of shopmen or machinists. The machinists have had an interesting history. Unlike the shoemakers and other skilled crafts, they were a product of the Industrial Revolution. Before machines there were no machinists, only the village blacksmith. But human ingenuity devised machines to make machines and the same substitution of machine for hand work, division of labor, and the development of specialized or semiskilled, are found in the machinist's craft as in those that were carried over from a pre-machine age. The machinist, however, was affected in another way. He had to follow the machines he made and repaired, and as machinery was introduced into every industry the machinist group was broken up, scattered across the continent, so that the old Machinists' and Blacksmiths' Union lost track of its personnel. The railroad shopmen were quite lost to the old union in 1884 when the Knights of Labor offered them a semi-industrial form of organization that was suited to their needs. For a time the trainmen too were in the Order and supported the shopmen's demands. But there was no real community of interest between the two groups and under the leadership of the Locomotive Engineers the alliance with the shopmen was broken. This and the preparedness of the corporations caused the final failure of the railroad strikes. Chief Arthur of the Locomotive Engineers was bitterly attacked by the Knights, especially by Buchanan. But it was a case of *sauve qui peut*. Arthur's first duty was to the Engineers and if the shopmen insisted on running amok, the Engineers could hardly be expected to follow them indefinitely and turn their mistakes into successes.

On Monday, Aug. 11, 1884, a notice of a 10 per cent reduction in wages for fifteen first-class machinists was posted in the Ellis, Kan., shops of the Union Pacific, and twenty men who had been active in the May strike were discharged in Denver. District Assembly No. 82, composed of Union Pacific employees, was not organized until 1885, but it had some sort of existence at that time for on August 13 the executive board called a strike of all the shopmen on the system. On August 18, the company agreed to restore the wages at Ellis, take back the Denver Knights, and discuss and arbitrate other grievances. The second Union Pacific strike was won. [22]

At the 1884 General Assembly, Buchanan was made a

[22] Joseph R. Buchanan, *The Story of a Labor Agitator*, pp. 80-99.

member of the general executive board and returned to
Denver to conduct a partially successful strike of the coal
miners which had broken out in the summer.

Still these successes and others like them were not the
work of the Order, and at the 1884 General Assembly the
rural opposition to an aggressive strike policy even on
paper was clearly seen. As early as 1879 an Iowa representative had tried to do away with the old Resistance
Fund, but his motion was defeated by a vote of 21 to 1.
Again in 1884 the district master workman of District
Assembly No. 28 protested against the assessment for the
window glass workers and the new Assistance Fund. His
letter illustrates the difficulty of discipline and the divergence of opinion in the Order:

To be plain about the matter, D. A. 28 of which I am the
D. M. W. positively refuses to pay either of the above assessments or to comply with the requirements of the law enacted at
the late G. A. at Cincinnati, O. I was a delegate at the late
G. A. and I looked pensively [sic] on and am quite free to say
that there were some good things said and done there, but four-
fifths of the actions of the body was silly twaddle—boy's play.
After January 1, 1884, we being in rebellion so to speak, will not
be entitled to any pass-word emanating from headquarters. We
will then stand suspended. Now, if we can get relieved from
paying these assessments, D. A. 28 will continue to remain a
part and parcel of the Order; otherwise we will reorganize under
the "Improved Order of the Knights." . . . Our people in the
west will not countenance strikes in any shape unless at the
ballot box.

Nothing could more clearly reveal the major conflict of
the Order between West and East, rural and urban, political
and trade purposes. The reply of McClelland, secretary of
the general executive board, is equally informing. He com-
mends the district master workman's candor, deplores
assessments, and suggests that a careful reading of the

Assistance Fund law will show that it will prevent strikes and promote coöperation. "We wish," said McClelland, "to abolish strikes forever and substitute education therefor." It is worth noticing that McClelland does not follow Iowa's suggestion that politics be substituted for strikes. He preferred "education" and this represents the attitude of the Order toward politics.

Another protest was registered, from Cedar Rapids, Ia., against the glass workers' assessment. It shows the underlying source of antagonism between the East and the West. Their interests were different it is true, and their methods. The agricultural or semi-agricultural West could hardly be expected to pay for eastern strikes with enthusiasm, when such strikes could in no way benefit them. But there was more than that. At bottom there was jealousy and envy on the part of the low-paid rural worker of the comparatively well-paid craftsman. It was not often stated so baldly but it was always there: "We don't believe," wrote the Cedar Rapids local, "in paying assessments to help workmen who are receiving on the average twice as much in wages as even the best paid members of our Assembly receive." [23]

The Assistance law was not strictly enforced and large numbers of the locals failed to send in the money.[24] The general executive board was doubtful about the wisdom of continuing it and more than thirty-two documents having to do with its disposition and status were presented to the 1884 General Assembly. By a vote of 48 to 31 it was decided to continue the fund and new laws governing it were passed. The main feature of the new laws was that the moneys received from the locals and de-

[23] *Proceedings,* 1884 General Assembly, pp. 621-22 and 641. McClelland's answer to the local was less conciliatory than his reply to the district.

[24] *Ibid.,* p. 716.

posited by officers of the districts were to be used, not by the general executive board, but by the district assemblies themselves. This was a proper move toward decentralization of the control of strikes and met the complaints of the nonindustrial sections of the Order to some extent. District Assembly No. 28, for instance, was required to establish a district assistance fund, but it was to be used within the district, and presumably, if there were no strikes the law could be ignored. The only control of the fund left to the general executive board was the right to levy an assessment on one district assembly for the relief of another whose funds had been exhausted, but no levy could be made if the fund of the solvent district assembly was less than $100, or that of the local assembly less than $25. Such a levy was to be considered as a loan and to be repaid by the assisted district assembly upon recovery. Executive boards were required to be created by the locals and districts to deal with disputes and call for strike assistance when that was necessary.[25]

The peak of the Knights of Labor success came in 1885 in the Gould strike, where they forced one of the largest railroad systems in the country to accept their demands, and the Wizard of Wall Street to give them his blessing— with his fingers crossed. The Gould system included the Missouri Pacific; Missouri, Kansas and Texas; and the Wabash railroads, about 10,000 miles of line. In October, 1884, a 10 per cent reduction in wages of shopmen and others was ordered on the Missouri, Kansas and Texas, then in the hands of a receiver, and on Feb. 26, 1885, a similar reduction was made on the Wabash. A strike broke out at Moberly, Mo., and spread through the three roads.

---

[25] *Ibid.*, pp. 756-59. In 1885, in the Denver and Rio Grande strike, the general executive board informed the locals concerned that it could not give aid because no district had more than $100 in its fund. (*Ibid.*, 1885 General Assembly, p. 77.)

Joseph Buchanan was sent by the Union Pacific Knights of Labor to Kansas City with the promise of $30,000 to support the strike against these reductions, and he organized local assemblies at Kansas City, Sedalia, Moberly, Hannibal, and St. Louis. The trainmen supported the strikers and the railroads withdrew the reductions in March, 1885, after a conference with the authorities of the three states involved.

This was the beginning of the mushroom growth of the Order. "Every week," wrote Swinton, "trade unions are turned into local assemblies or assemblies are organized out of trade unions and every day new mixed assemblies spring into existence. The numerous strikes East and West during the past twelve months have added greatly to its growth. While the Order is opposed to strikes the first news we are likely to hear after its [the strike's] close is of the union of the men with the K. of L." It made no difference, it seemed, whether the strike was won or lost. The Troy molders formed an assembly after a failure, and after success the Gould shopmen joined the Order "by thousands." [26]

WABASH STRIKE

During April and May, the Wabash railroad laid off members of the Knights and on June 16 their shops were closed down. The executive board of District Assembly No. 93, Moberly, Mo., decided that this was intended to break the union and issued a circular to the effect that the men had been locked out and the second Wabash strike or lockout was on. On June 23, the executive board of District Assembly No. 93 asked the general executive board for help and was told that there was not a district in the

---

[26] Swinton, *op. cit.*, Apr. 12, 1885.

Order with an assistance fund large enough to be assessed
for their benefit; that most of the locals of District Assembly No. 93 were too recently organized to receive help
under the law; that other districts were asking for financial
aid, and that the Wabash affair was not a proper lockout
anyway. The first of these reasons was certainly enough
to warrant the board's refusal of financial aid, but it is not
hard to understand why the others were considered necessary. The general officers were both unable and unwilling
to support a strike of any kind, and their long list of excuses
was more for their own justification than anything else.
On June 29, the executive board of District Assembly No.
93 went to St. Louis to see A. A. Talmadge, general manager
of the Wabash, but he refused to see them as a committee
of the union and insisted on dealing with his employees as
individuals. They again appealed to the general executive
board who "decided adversely." A third appeal brought the
announcement that the Wabash affair could not be considered a lockout solely on account of membership in the
Knights of Labor. "Our great difficulty," the general executive board complained, "is that too many strikes take place
at the same time. It should be regulated so they could be
taken up in detail when support could be rendered sys-
tematically and not as now all strike together!"

Finally Powderly went to Springfield on his way back
from Minneapolis and made a weak attempt to see Talmadge. He failed, and Griffiths was sent from Chicago to
look into the matter. Griffiths couldn't quite make up his
mind what had caused the strike but discovered that three
members of the Order had been jailed for contempt of
court and three more arrested by United States marshals;
that Arthur had ordered the engineers to withdraw from
the Order; that Talmadge had stated positively that he
would treat with no committee and that no union men

would be taken on. About fifty scabs were working in the shops at Moberly, all armed with revolvers and brass knuckles.

Up to this time only the Wabash was involved, but on July 25, the Knights of Labor on the Southwest System, the Missouri Pacific, and the Texas Pacific, met at Parsons, Kansas, and passed resolutions asking the governors of Missouri, Kansas, Illinois, and Indiana to intervene. The Knights on the Southwest System were ready to strike but wanted the support of the Order and District Assembly No. 93 sent an insistent demand to the general executive board to come West. Powderly was too sick to attend, but Hayes, Turner, Bailey, and Buchanan met in St. Louis on August 14. According to Buchanan's report the general executive board was bored with the whole thing and left all the work to him. Buchanan always dramatized matters and never failed to cast himself in the leading rôle, but his description of the St. Louis meeting is worth recording as indicative of the attitude of the board. It is quite in keeping with its previous inaction. " . . . The facts are," wrote Buchanan, "that Turner simply kept the records of the meeting, Hayes looked on and said nothing, Bailey put in most of the time at the window . . . while to the man who had traveled a thousand miles, leaving grave responsibilities behind him, was left the task which was sure temporarily at least to work his own undoing." [27] This man of course was Buchanan.

The "grave responsibilities" to which Buchanan refers was the strike on the Denver & Rio Grande which by that time had been lost, and because of which the stalwart Buchanan was in danger of being lynched by the better element in Denver. And his "task" was the refusal of the general executive board to call out the Southwestern men

---

[27] Buchanan, *op. cit.*, p. 218.

in sympathy with the Wabash strikers. The board tried to see Talmadge but found that he had left St. Louis the morning they arrived and that H. M. Hoxie, general manager of the Missouri Pacific, had also gone East. But they got in touch with Talmadge by wire and were informed that there was no trouble on the Wabash and no need for him to see the board. They then ordered out all members of the Order still working on the Wabash and instructed all Knights on the Union Pacific, the Southwest System, or any other railroad, that they were not to handle any Wabash rolling stock "and if this order is antagonized by the companies through any of its officials, your executive committee is hereby ordered to call out all K. of L. on the above system without any further action."

The general executive board then went to New York to see Jay Gould and on August 26 had a conference with the Wizard and officials of the Wabash and the Missouri Pacific. The board asked that all members of the Order locked out on June 16 should be reinstated and according to their account Gould advised Talmadge to agree. Talmadge asked time for consideration and promised to meet the board in St. Louis on September 3. After the board got home, A. L. Hopkins, vice president of the Wabash and the Missouri Pacific, wrote Powderly asking him, in view of the practical settlement of the strike, to withdraw the order against the handling of Wabash rolling stock by other roads, and Powderly did so. On September 3, Powderly and Turner met Talmadge in St. Louis and agreed to the following: "That no official shall discriminate against the K. of L. or question the right of the employee to belong to the Order. That all employees locked out June 16, 1885, or who came out in their support since that date would be reinstated as fast as possible. That no new person should be put to work by the officials of the company until all the

old employees . . . who desire employment are reinstated."
Powderly agreed that no future strikes would be called until
a conference with the officials of the railroads was held.
The strike was then called off.[28]

This was the most important settlement the Knights of
Labor ever made and was largely responsible for the tremendous growth of the Order in 1886. In the opinion of
the labor public, Jay Gould had been brought to terms and
two important railroad systems had been forced to recognize the Order against their will. "The Wabash victory,"
said the St. Louis *Chronicle*, "is with the K. of L. . . . No
such victory has ever before been secured in this or any
other country." [29]

Jay Gould had said that he believed in labor unions and
wished that all his railroad employees were organized. But
Gould was like that. He had broken the Telegraphers and
was prepared to do the same thing on his railroads. He
forced Talmadge and Hoxie to settle with the Knights because he was not ready to fight them at that time. But
the agreement itself really did not amount to much. It
was an achievement certainly, but it did not involve recognition of the union nor collective bargaining. It said only
that members of the Order would not be discriminated
against nor their right to belong to the union questioned,
and that they would be reinstated as fast as possible. It
is a serious reflection upon the bargaining standards of the
general executive board that they did not even ask for
recognition. They probably would not have got it but no
real labor leader even in 1885 would have been satisfied
with a nondiscrimination clause that company union concerns now have in their regulations. In the eyes of the
public it was a great victory but in actual operation there

---

[28] *Proceedings*, 1885 General Assembly, pp. 84-91.
[29] Quoted in Swinton, *op. cit.*, Sept. 30, 1885.

was no good reason to expect anything from it. "Discrimination" is too vague a word for a contract as the Knights were to discover, and nothing could reveal more clearly Powderly's ineptitude as a bargainer than his failure to demand something more realistic. The fact is that Powderly was essentially a pedagogue and had no interest in, nor equipment for, the major trade union job of negotiation. The general executive board simply wanted to avoid trouble. They were overawed, too, if Buchanan is to be believed, by the importance of the men with whom they were dealing. But even Buchanan, who was aggressive enough, was satisfied with the agreement.

THE SOUTHWESTERN STRIKE

On Mar. 6, 1886, the great Southwestern strike broke out. All through the Wabash strike, the Southwestern men —those on the Missouri Pacific and the Missouri, Kansas and Texas—were restless. They had asked the general executive board to call them out in sympathy with the Wabash men and were refused. They were operating under conditions secured in the short strike on the Gould system in March, 1885. This settlement was applied to shopmen only, but sectionmen, yardmen, bridgemen, etc., were in the assemblies. The real cause of the trouble was overconfidence based on an exaggerated faith in the invulnerability of the Order. Superficially the optimism of the workers was justified. The Order in 1884-85 had engaged in five important railroad strikes and had won four of them. But they were largely flukes. None was properly prepared and in two cases the men were organized after the strike was called. Only on the Wabash was the company in a position to resist and the only aggressive strike—the Denver and Rio Grande—had been lost.

Especially in a public utility, it was one thing to avert a reduction in wages by a poorly organized stoppage of work, but it was quite another thing to get better conditions or resent the attitude of foremen by the same tactics. In the early strikes public opinion supported the strikers and state officials intervened on behalf of the men. But in the Southwestern the public was uninterested at the beginning and then hostile as the strike dragged out to its inconvenience. The men on the Southwest System paid no attention to this. They were blinded by an optimism based on false premises. Their attitude was well illustrated by a letter published on the eve of the strike:

Tell the world that the men of the Gould Southwest system are on strike. We strike for justice to ourselves and our fellow-men everywhere. Fourteen thousand men are out. . . . I would say to all railroad employees everywhere . . . make your demands to the corporation for the eight-hour day and no reduction of pay. Demand $1.50 per day for all laboring men. Demand that yourselves and your families be carried on all railways for one cent a mile. Bring in all your grievances in one bundle at once, and come out to a man and stay out until they are all settled to your entire satisfaction. Let us demand our rights and compel the exploiters to accede to our demands. . . .[30]

When the accounts were finally cast up Martin Irons, district master workman of District Assembly No. 101, was made the "goat," but he was only the spokesman of undue optimism, uncontrolled and perhaps uncontrollable by the general officers of the Order. Early in 1886, five months after the Wabash settlement, Martin Irons issued a circular to the locals in District Assembly No. 101 asking if they would sustain the district executive board in asking for $1.50 a day minimum for unskilled labor and the recognition of the union. Nothing came of this but on February 18, C. A. Hall, a foreman in the Texas Pacific shops at

---

[30] Swinton, *op. cit.*, Mar. 14, 1886.

Marshall, was discharged. Hall was a delegate to the District Assembly and seems to have been given permission to attend its sessions, but the master car builder refused to take him back. The Texas Pacific was in the hands of a receiver and Governor Sheldon was appealed to. He sent Irons to Receiver Brown at Dallas but Irons decided that Marshall was the proper place to hold the conference and wired the Receiver and Col. Noble to that effect. Getting no reply Irons wired again that a strike would be called if no answer were received by 2 P.M. the next day. There was no answer and the strike was called.

In these negotiations Irons was aggressive, and convinced beforehand that the strike was inevitable. The Hall matter gave him his chance but he would have found another. On March 6, the employees of the Missouri Pacific were called out. Hoxie protested to Powderly that this was a breach of the agreement of September, 1885, when the latter promised that no strikes would be called on the Gould system before consultation with the officers of the road. Powderly discovered that the strike had been caused by the discharge of Hall and asked that he be reinstated pending negotiations but Hoxie replied that the Texas Pacific was in the hands of the courts and that he could do nothing about it. He more than hinted that the strike was backed by the short interests on Wall Street.

On March 18, Irons called a conference of District Assemblies Nos. 17, 82, 93, 101, 107, with Powderly in Kansas City, and on the twentieth Powderly and the executive board of District Assembly 101 met the governors of Kansas and Missouri. It was agreed that the governors would use their influence with Hoxie to make some kind of settlement. Hoxie refused to deal with the Order because it had violated its pledge, or because the chance of breaking the Knights seemed good, and Powderly returned to New

York where he had left the general executive board investigating the trouble with the Cigar Makers. On March 27, Jay Gould was asked to submit the Southwest difficulty to arbitration but he refused, insisting that no negotiations could take place until the men were back at work. The next day a conference was held with Gould and the general executive board ordered the men back to work on the understanding that arbitration would follow. But Hoxie still refused to deal with the Order. He would treat only with his own employees actually at work. This the general executive board accepted, having been put in a hole by Gould, and District Assembly No. 101 was ordered to send the men back and select a committee from the Missouri Pacific to meet Hoxie. The board then went to St. Louis and learned that the railroads refused to reinstate members of the Order.

Instructions to return to work were recalled and the strike went on. An appeal was made for funds and Congress appointed the Curtin committee to investigate. A citizens' committee in St. Louis, failing to get Hoxie to agree to arbitration, asked the general executive board to call off the strike in the public interest. This they did on May 4, 1886.[31] It was a complete capitulation and the severest blow the Order had suffered. It came just at the time of the eight-hour strikes and the Haymarket bomb, when the unions were mobilizing out of the Knights. From that date the Knights of Labor lost ground.

After the strike, the railroads, with the help of Pinkerton detectives, brought up 41 members of the Order in St. Louis and East St. Louis on charges of arson and malicious mischief, but all of them were acquitted. Two others were charged with assault with intent to kill and four others with wire tapping. At Pacific, Mo., four men

---

[31] *Proceedings*, 1886 General Assembly, pp. 81-90: Curtin Report.

were charged with train wrecking and at Sedalia 65 indictments were secured, seven of them for train wrecking. On the Texas Pacific, 300 strikers were arrested for contempt of court and charged with killing engines. The Supreme Court decided that letting water out of boilers was not unlawful.[32] At Little Rock there were nine arrests, three indictments and two fines. At Kansas City six men were arrested on the charge of wrecking a freight train and causing the death of two men.

Up to May 1, 1886, the Order was having things pretty much its own way. After May 1, it suffered a long series of reverses. Public sympathy, which had grown steadily in favor of the Knights and the trade unions in 1885 and the early part of 1886, was abruptly alienated by the Haymarket bomb. By August, the Knights of Labor as an organization had practically ceased to exit on the Missouri Pacific system and was dying out rapidly on all the western railroads.

Powderly was bitterly attacked for the failure but it is hard to see what he could have done that would have pleased any one. Martin Irons had put him in a difficult position in view of his promise to Hoxie that no strike would be called without previous consultation with the officers of the Missouri Pacific. But he must have known that he could never have fulfilled that promise. No one had ever consulted him about strikes before they were called, and he could hardly have expected more consideration in the future than he had had in the past. If he had been a capable and vigorous leader he might have gone to St. Louis on the receipt of Hoxie's first wire and called off the sympathetic strike on the Missouri Pacific. The trouble on the Texas could then have been settled and the catastrope averted for the time being. But he was not that, and

[32] *Ibid.*, 1887 General Assembly, p. 1412.

with his inactivity, the aggressiveness of Martin Irons, and the smartness of Gould, the Order suffered.

The Assistance Fund of 1884 failed to provide a surplus for strikes on a national scale controlled by the general executive board. Each district either used up its own fund or failed to collect it, so that the Order was not in a position to assess any one district for the support of another. The constant complaint of the officers was that locals entered strikes without any attempt to have them settled peacefully by the district executive board and then complained when the Assistance Fund was not sufficient for their support. At the same time that one part of the Order was striking, another part was asking to be relieved from collecting the strike fund. At the 1885 General Assembly, the general executive board recommended that the Assistance Fund should be abolished and a sinking fund be established under the control of the general executive board by an assessment of 10 cents per member. But the Order was as yet opposed to the policy of centralization of the control of either strikes or boycotts.[33]

The special session of the General Assembly held at Cleveland, May 25, 1886, was intended to deal with strikes and boycotts, the growth of the Order, and the controversy with the trade unions. Local strikes were endemic and most of them sooner or later involved the districts. The assistance funds of the districts were all exhausted, and when the general executive board was called in, there was nothing to support a strike. Yet the Order was rich. It was about to pay nearly $50,000 for a new headquarters and raise Powderly's salary to $5,000 a year. Again it was not so much a matter of money as of policy. The officers were so emphatically opposed to strikes that any sort of a settlement was preferable, in their view, to their support.

---

[33] *Ibid.*, 1885 General Assembly, pp. 92, 107, 130.

Again in 1886 the control of strikes was placed in the hands of the general executive board and an auxiliary board of six members was added to deal with them. The intention, however, was not to manage strikes but to prevent them altogether if possible; and if not, to settle them on almost any terms. The settlement of the Southwest was an example of how far the general officers would go simply for peace. The settlement of the stockyards strike in the winter was even worse. The policy was a ruinous one for the Order, but the general officers could not see it.

The new strike law passed at Cleveland would practically have made a strike an impossibility had the law been observed. It stipulated that the local or district should take a secret ballot before entering on a strike and required a two-thirds vote to begin it. Any time after that, at the suggestion of the executive board, a ballot might be taken on the advisability of continuing the strike and a majority vote could call it off. No strike was to be started when over twenty-five members were involved, which would require financial or other aid from outside the assembly, until the general executive board had attempted to settle and, failing, had ordered the strike. If the general executive board were not called in no aid was to be given by the Order.[34]

This law left the Assistance Fund in the hands of the districts; and while it gave the general executive board new responsibilities, it left it with no resources and no power to enforce the demands of the members. Powderly asserted that the Cleveland legislation almost put a stop to strikes and boycotts but that employers took advantage of it. "No sooner did our Order place a strong hand on strikes and boycotts than the employers of labor began to

---

[34] *Ibid.*, special session of the 1886 General Assembly, Cleveland, pp. 45, 48, 49.

strike and boycott. Over 200 lockouts have occurred since the employers got the idea that members of our organization could not strike without violating the laws of the Order." [35]

While the Richmond General Assembly was in session, word was received that the Chicago packers had reverted to the ten-hour day and that all the employees were on strike. On May 1, 1886, the packing house employees in Chicago had secured the eight-hour day with no reduction of wages as a result of the eight-hour strike. There were at that time only 3,000 members of the Knights in the packing houses out of a total of 20,000, and the strike was engineered by an eight-hour league composed of Knights of Labor assemblies and trade unions in the stockyards. On March 13, Powderly had issued a circular on behalf of the Order disapproving of the proposed May Day strikes for eight hours, partly because he was temperamentally opposed to aggressive measures, partly because there was no proper preparation, and partly because the Federation of Trades had issued the order. During the summer of 1886, the Chicago packers offered the men nine hours' pay for the eight-hour day and an agreement for one year. This was refused, and the packers on October 11, ordered their men to return to the ten-hour day. The strike followed and Barry was sent from the Richmond General Assembly with instructions to make a settlement without involving the Order financially or otherwise. At that time about 15,000 of the 20,000 employees in the stockyards were members of the Knights of Labor. Barry seems to have made a deal with two of the packing houses that, should the men go back to work at ten hours, these two would break with the Packers' Association later, return to the eight-hour system, and allow a new strike to be called on

---

[35] Swinton, *op. cit.*, Oct. 3, 1886.

Armour, Swift, and the others, with more promise of success. This rather dangerous scheme was carried out and the men ordered back to work on October 18. A committee was appointed "for carrying out the plan agreed upon for the reduction of the hours of labor. . . . " Barry left town but kept in touch with this committee, and on November 1 the strike broke out again. Barry's scheme seems to have been working nicely and there was every chance of a reasonable compromise. Carlton was sent by the general executive board to help Barry—or to watch him—but before the former could get to Chicago, Powderly wired ordering the men back at ten hours "until the Order of the Knights of Labor takes definite action on the eight-hour plan." As usual, Powderly was very energetic at the wrong time. "If the men refuse," he told Barry, "take their charters. We must have obedience and discipline." This dispatch was posted in the Board of Trade at the same time that Barry received it and before Carlton reached Chicago, and of course made further negotiations with the packers impossible.

Powderly was accused of selling out to the packers and of being influenced by the Roman Catholic Church. But both explanations of his perplexing action are unnecessary and possibly false. On October 16, a letter was written him by a Father P. M. Flannigan of St. Ann's Church, Lake, Ill., pleading on behalf of the families of the strikers that he do something to prevent the poverty and misery attendant on such a strike and informing him that the packers would not again consent to an eight-hour day unless it were made universal. Powderly insisted that this letter reached Richmond while he was absent and was not opened for weeks after October 16. If that were so it might have influenced him in November when the strike was actually called off, and it is perfectly possible that it did. But it was probably not a decisive influence because Powderly's own point of view was exactly that of Father Flannigan, and his back was decidedly up over the eight-hour question. He was always for an eight-hour law and against all strikes. The May Day movement had got him into the anarchist trouble and he disliked and distrusted Barry not without reason. Barry seems to have told him nothing of the little scheme to pull the strike under more favorable conditions, and Powderly was probably convinced that the thing was settled in October.[36]

On the eight-hour question Powderly was a ridiculous rationalizer. He called the strike off, he said, because he knew, even if it had succeeded, "it would be but a question of time until the trade would leave Chicago and go to other points where men were working ten hours. The laws of business," declared this astonishing labor leader, "cannot be lightly tampered with. . . . "

In 1887 the Assistance Fund was abolished so far as the Order as a whole was concerned; but local, district, trade, and state assemblies were allowed to create and maintain assistance funds of their own if they so desired.[37]

---

[36] *Proceedings,* 1887 General Assembly, pp. 1477, 1499, and 1419-22. On Nov. 19, 1886, a special assessment of 25 cents was levied due to a "grave emergency." This was about three weeks before the first meeting of the American Federation of Labor. (Swinton, *op. cit.,* Dec. 5, 1886. *Journal,* January, 1887, p. 2252.)

[37] *Ibid.,* p. 1802.

Note: This is not intended as a complete record of the strikes of the Order. Aside from innumerable local strikes, the following were of importance: the Hocking Valley coal strike of 1884-85; the Saginaw Valley strike of 1885; the Augusta, Ga., cotton mill strike of 1886; the coal handlers, New York City, 1886; street railway strikes New York, 1886; the Reading Railroad strike, 1887, and the New York Central, 1890.

CHAPTER VIII

THE ORDER AND THE UNIONS

THE early local assemblies of the Knights of Labor differed little from the trade unions. In the first secret work the charge to new members, drafted by William Fennimore in 1869, read, in part:

We shall use every lawful and honorable means to procure and retain employ for one another coupled with just and fair remuneration, and should accident or misfortune befall one of our number, render such aid as lies within our power to give, without inquiring into his country or his creed; and without approving of general strikes among artisans, yet should it become justly necessary to enjoin an oppressor, we shall protect and aid any of our number who thereby may suffer loss, and as opportunity offers extend a helping hand to all branches of honorable toil.[1]

So far as secrecy and ceremonial were concerned, they were both common in the trade unions of the period though the Knights may have carried them to an extreme.[2] The one distinguishing characteristic of the Order was its principle of solidarity, the belief that all trades should be brought under one banner. As early as 1861 Stephens is reported to have said, "I speak to you of unions as they now exist. . . . They are too narrow in their ideas and

---

[1] *Adelphon Kruptos.*

[2] The Sons of Vulcan (puddlers and boilers); the Brotherhood of the Footboard (later the Locomotive Engineers); the Knights of St. Crispin (shoemakers); the Lasters' Protective Association were all secret societies originally and most of them had ceremonies and high-sounding titles like the Knights of Labor.

too circumscribed in their field of operations. None of them looks beyond a city and few of them look a year ahead." This was before the national unions had developed. "I do not claim," he continued, "any power of prophecy, but I can see ahead of me an organization that will cover the globe. It will include men and women of every craft, creed and color; it will cover every race worth saving. . . . " [3]

"Solidarity" is and has always been a magnificent and powerful ideal. It was and is the rallying cry of the radicals and has a strong popular appeal. Its desirability is obvious and the case for it, both emotional and intellectual, is not hard to make. But "solidarity" means little. It is an ideal, not a program. The real problem is to discover some way in which it may be secured, some form or forms it may properly take. Uriah Stephens probably never faced the question of means. He was a visionary, not a practical man. Any one who insists that he is not a prophet is rightly suspect. Powderly was less a prophet than his predecessor, but by the time he had arrived on the scene the national unions of the sixties had come and gone and the tradition of their ineffectiveness was reënforced by their decline in the depressed seventies. Obviously what was needed was solidarity and the craft unions were incapable of creating it. The Knights took up the task with no very definite idea of how it was to be worked out. They muddled through the major problem of their existence. Craft and labor sentiment divided them. The old national unions revived and drew apart and labor solidarity was destroyed.

The original local of the Knights of Labor was strictly craft and remained so to the end. It could have tried to extend and form a national union of garment cutters, but its leaders had other ideas, to organize all crafts, starting

---

[3] *Proceedings,* 1897 General Assembly, p. 37.

in Philadelphia and ending only on the rim of the world. For this purpose they adopted the practice of initiating members of other crafts in the garment cutters' local, and, when enough of another craft had been admitted, to organize these "sojourners" as a new assembly. In this way craft organization and labor solidarity were both maintained. The sojourner did not participate in the discussion of trade matters nor pay dues. As the name implies, he was taken in partially and temporarily as a nucleus of a new local of his own craft.

From its inception [writes Powderly] Assembly No. 1 was more exclusively a trade organization than any trade union that had existed in the United States. None but garment cutters who could prove that they had served a stated term as apprentices were admitted. The principles of coöperation and assistance were confined to a few who could pass examinations as first-class workmen. The real work of Knighthood had not yet started and the founders of the first assembly, with the exception of Uriah S. Stephens, William Fennimore and Henry L. Sinexon were as much interested in trade matters as any person who belonged to a trade union. Compared with the trade unions of that day the first assembly of the Knights of Labor was far behind them in toleration and fellowship.[4]

The district assembly was originally a mixed body composed of delegates from the different locals in its jurisdiction. It is impossible to discover the date of the first mixed local, though two of them were represented at the first national convention, July 3, 1876. At the end of 1875, Local Assembly No. 88 of Scranton was not only a purely craft local of stationary engineers, but did not even know that sojourners were allowed to be admitted.

The fact seems to be that the idea of the mixed local came from the experiments of the National Labor Union and the Industrial Congresses, the two bodies already

---

[4] T. V. Powderly, *Thirty Years of Labor*, p. 78.

described, which had tried to build an organization from the top downward. The mixed local gained headway only after the formation of the General Assembly in 1878, when Schilling and Powderly, both formerly in the Industrial Congress, imposed upon the Knights many of the ideas of the defunct society. The mixed assemblies grew rapidly, especially in semirural districts where there were often not enough men of one trade to form a craft local. On Jan. 1, 1882, according to a record in the *Journal of United Labor,* there were in the Order 27 working districts and a total of 484 local assemblies. Of the latter, 318 were craft locals and only 116 mixed. The table also gives 13 districts not working, with 140 locals—53 trade and 87 mixed —and 135 locals attached to the General Assembly—67 trade and 68 mixed. Thus, in the working locals, craft organization was markedly predominant. The larger number of mixed locals in the nonworking class shows the impermanence of the mixed as opposed to the trade form. The locals under the General Assembly were found in out-of-the-way places where no districts had been organized.

Another table, with no date but from internal evidence representing the Order near the height of its strength (1886), gives a total of 88 districts and 1,499 locals. Of the latter, 836 were trade and 625 were mixed. This does not include locals attached to the General Assembly, nor 38 locals whose nature is not specified. Including locals attached to the General Assembly the total was 1,088 trade and 1,279 mixed. From this it is evident that the proportion of mixed locals had grown, but a further examination shows that this growth lay outside the older districts of the Order. District Assembly No. 1 of Philadelphia had 20 trade and no mixed locals in 1882, and 54 trade and 6 mixed in 1886 (if that is the proper date). In the latter year it had in addition 2 trade districts, No. 70 shoemakers, and No. 94 leather workers.   District Assembly No. 3, Pittsburgh, had 61 trade and 7 mixed locals in 1882 and 12 trade and 2 mixed in the latter year (the decline of District Assembly No. 3 has already been discussed).   In District Assembly No. 7 the distribution changed somewhat toward mixed locals and in District Assembly No. 13 toward trade locals.   A very decided change is seen toward trade locals in District Assembly No. 16, from 7 trade and 14 mixed in 1882, to 13 trade and 3 mixed in the later year. In District Assembly No. 24, Chicago, there were 2 trade and 16 mixed in 1882 and 16 trade and 4 mixed in 1886. District Assembly No. 57 of Chicago had 12 trade and 4 mixed.   In New York there were four trade districts in the later year (Nos. 64, 75, 85, 91) and District Assembly No. 49 which had 81 trade and 11 mixed locals.   This indicates that the antitrade sentiment of District Assembly No. 49 came from the politicians of the Home Club rather than the make-up of the district itself.   District Assembly No. 30 of Massachusetts had in the later year 93 trade and 77 mixed locals, but, because of its leaders, was known as a center of trade sentiment.[5]

The change in distribution between mixed and trade assemblies is explained, therefore, not by changes in the older sections of the Order, not by the inrush of the unskilled, but by expansion into the agricultural West and South.   Texas had 128 locals in 1886 of which 95 were mixed.   Kansas had 82 locals only 22 of which were trade.   Colorado had only 28 trade locals out of a total of 75.   Virginia had only 14 trade locals out of a total of 66, Tennessee only 9 out of 33.   The total number of locals attached to the

---

[5] The table for 1882 is found in the *Journal*, pp. 189-92.   The later table is in pamphlet form, undated, and was loaned by Mr. Saposs. Locals not described and a few "farmers'" locals have been omitted from both lists.

General Assembly—these were in outlying regions on the whole—was 906 of which 654 were mixed.

Thus, while within the district assemblies the locals were still predominantly trade in 1886 or thereabouts, when the scattered locals attached to the General Assembly are considered the Order was predominantly mixed. The General Assembly was composed of delegates from the district assemblies and from locals attached to the General Assembly, but the real control resided in the district representatives. The district assemblies, being composed in most cases of representatives from both mixed and different trade locals, might be expected to represent the "mixed" point of view, but this was not necessarily the case. There were some definitely national trade districts such as the Telegraphers and Local Assembly No. 300, Glass Workers, and later the Miners, Shoemakers, etc. There were many trade districts not of national spread, and there were districts in regions where one trade so predominated that the few mixed locals did not count. This last was especially true of the mining regions of Maryland, Pennsylvania, Ohio, and Illinois, where many of the so-called mixed districts were composed almost entirely of miners.

The first trade district in the Order was No. 8 of Pittsburgh, founded Sept. 23, 1877, before the General Assembly, and composed of Local Assemblies Nos. 281, 300, 305, 319, 322, 484, all glass workers. It broke up in 1880, but in May of the same year, certain locals, Nos. 300, 308, 322, merged as a trade local and organized the window glass workers all through the country, thus creating a real, national trade union. This action was ratified by the 1880 General Assembly.

District Assemblies Nos. 7 of Ohio, and 9 of Pennsylvania (1877), 25 of Maryland (1879) were miners' districts but not exclusively so. District Assembly No. 45 (1882) with headquarters at Pittsburgh was composed entirely of telegraphers. District Assemblies Nos. 48 (1882) Cincinnati; 63 (1883) Rochester; 70 (1884) Philadelphia; 77 (1885) Lynn; and 91 (1885) New York were all shoemakers' districts long before the formation of a national trade district of shoemakers. Others of the same sort were District Assemblies Nos. 64 (1883) New York, printers; 75 (1884) Brooklyn, street car employees; 82 (1885) Denver, Col., Union Pacific railroad employees; 93 (1885) Moberly, Mo., railroad employees; 101 (1886) Sedalia, Mo., Gould System railroad employees; 85 (1885) New York City, plumbers; 94 (1885) Philadelphia, leather workers; 97 (1885) Washington, D. C., government employees.

Thus there was a large trade element within the Order but it was greater even than this suggests. The General Assembly was controlled to a considerable extent by the largest districts, No. 1 of Philadelphia, No. 24 of Chicago, No. 30 of Massachusetts, and No. 49 of New York; and all of these districts were, in composition, predominantly trade.[6]

There was no reason then, unless the mixed assemblies in these districts were much larger than the trade, why the influence of the large "mixed" districts should have been other than trade. No reason but one—the peculiarities of the district leaders. In Philadelphia, the leaders were representative of the trade composition of the district. In Chicago, the leaders were reformers and politicians. In Massachusetts, the sentiment was balanced but in favor of the trades. And in New York, the Home Club carried all before it in spite of the predominantly trade character of its locals. In the last analysis the scale was turned against the trade unions by a small clique in New York

---

[6] No. 1, 54 trade and 6 mixed; No. 24, 16 trade and 4 mixed; No. 30, 93 trade and 77 mixed; and No. 49, 81 trade and 11 mixed.

City aided by the growing influence of the agricultural West.[7]

In spite of the predominantly craft composition of the Order in its earlier years, and a strong trade union element throughout, the leaders of the Knights after Stephens were not sympathetic toward trade unions either within or without. They believed thoroughly that the Knights of Labor had superseded the open trade unions, and the condition of the latter when the Knights were growing seemed to warrant that belief. They believed further that the exclusiveness and narrowness of the craft unions weakened the labor movement, divided instead of uniting it, and made it unfit to oppose the industrial combinations that were growing up.

It was not impossible, however, for a craft union to establish and maintain itself within the Order, gain by its support, and at the same time lose nothing of craft autonomy. Many trades were formed and nourished behind the veil of the Knights as in a womb. Many others, living precariously outside, entered it. And some of the strongest, the Typographical and the Iron and Steel Workers in particular, seriously considered this step.

The conflict between the Knights and the trade unions which came to a head in 1886 was not an irrepressible one, not due entirely or primarily to structural differences or

---

[7] After 1886, national trade districts were organized in many trades: 1886 National Trade Assembly 135, Miners, with headquarters at New Straitsville, O., and 143 Glass Workers with headquarters at Milwaukee, Wis. In 1887: National Trade Assembly, 151 Filemakers; 189 Lithographers; 190 Textile Workers; 198 Machinery Constructors; 200 Paper Hangers; 210 Shoemakers; 217 Iron and Steel Workers. In 1888: No. 222 Silk Workers; 224 Philadelphia and Reading employees; 225 Cigar Makers; 226 New York City Street Car Employees; 230 Bookbinders; 231 Garment Cutters; 240 Leather Workers; 245 Saw Makers; 247 Carriage Workers; 250 Type Founders; 251 Watch Case Makers; 252 Brass Workers.

points of view. Personal pride and ambition, political intrigue and accident had much to do with it. But the major difficulty was that the Knights, in 1886, became too dangerous by their size and unwieldiness, not for employers and the public alone, but for the trade unions which were growing up beside them.

A part of the misunderstanding of the attitude of the Knights toward the trade unions is due to confusion on the matter of strikes. The early leaders of the Knights were definitely and irrevocably opposed to strikes. They had grown up in the seventies when strikes were consistently lost. But they were not alone in this. All union leaders of the seventies were opposed to strikes and most of them tried to substitute negotiation and arbitration. The Knights had their share of strikes, successful and otherwise, but never with the consent of the older leaders. And though they failed to develop a strong financial reserve and centralized strike policy such as those which were developed by the Cigar Makers, they made attempts to do so.

It is frequently asserted that the Knights were more interested in coöperation and politics than in trade matters, but this is not so. The American labor movement had always been interested in coöperation and politics and the Order, in succeeding the National Labor Union, the Industrial Congresses, eight-hour leagues, and St. Crispins, carried on this tradition with modifications. But they carried on the tradition of the trade unions as well, and in the period of their greatest activity were primarily a bargaining organization and frequently successful against industrial forces of unprecedented strength. They paid much less attention to coöperation than their predecessors. It was a declining practice with a long succession of failures behind it. As for politics, it was avoided by the Order as such with remarkable success until the Knights had ceased to be an industrial organization.

Structurally the Knights contained every form conceivable and in this respect differed not at all from the American Federation of Labor. The mixed local of the Knights is the same thing as the federal union; the mixed district and state assemblies correspond to the trades' assemblies or city centrals and the state federations; the National Trade Assemblies to the national unions, and the General Assembly to the annual convention of the American Federation of Labor. The difference is one of emphasis and center of authority. In the Knights the district assemblies, and in the American Federation of Labor the large national unions, held the balance of power. As for federalism, the autonomy of the district was in fact as great as now is the autonomy of the national union. In theory, the General Assembly was over all. In practice, the districts and even the locals did as they pleased. When a powerful district like District Assembly No. 49 was disciplined, it could always make the General Assembly take it back. If the strength of the American Federation of Labor lies in its weakness, the weakness of the Knights certainly did not lie in the strength of the General Assembly or its officers.

The real difference between the Knights of Labor and the American Federation of Labor is that the former tried to organize all workers in one way or another, while the latter renounced this perhaps overambitious program in order to save the national unions from the wreck. Along with this went a limitation of aims, in theory at least, to purely trade matters and the renunciation of a dream.

In the accepted story of the conflict between the Knights and the trade unions, too much attention proportionately has been given to the place of the Cigar Makers, possibly because Samuel Gompers was of that trade. But it was only by accident that Gompers was a cigar maker, and the "New Unionism" the Cigar Makers were supposed to represent, meant little more than a new and more aggressive leadership. It is worth noting that there was little trouble between the Knights and Cigar Makers in the early stages in or outside New York, and that the trouble in New York originated in a split among the Cigar Makers themselves. The Cigar Makers, under Strasser, with Gompers as his New York lieutenant, were becoming highly centralized in an attempt to control their innumerable sporadic strikes, and in 1882 the radical wing split off under the name of Progressives. The Progressives were politically minded but the Internationals were politicians and held the bag. District Assembly No. 49, under the Home Club, and controlling the Central Labor Union of New York, took the side of the Progressives and finally carried the Order into the fight. As for principle, trade union theory, policy, organization or form, there was little involved on either side. The International was the administration; the Progressives anti-administration. The Home Club was for itself and anything that would tighten its hold on New York. Perhaps in it all, a foreign leadership was disengaging itself from the vaporizings and petty politics of the New York radicals of the eighties, and settling down into a quiet and conservative old age. Strasser was a rigid disciplinarian and when he had won, the Cigar Makers' International Union was a neat little bundle ready to dry up and blow away. But before this happened, it sent Samuel Gompers upon his long and not inglorious career. Gompers was the builder, spokesman, and manipulator of the "New Unionism" which was very old before he was born.

As for ideas, in so far as there were ideas, they came not from the Cigar Makers but from P. J. McGuire of the

Carpenters. McGuire was more intelligent than Gompers but lacked the latter's qualities of leadership. McGuire learned and moved with the times. He passed through all the radicalisms and then turned to an insignificant English benefit union, the Amalgamated Carpenters and Joiners, with a few locals in the United States, and in 1881 built on its lines the Brotherhood of Carpenters and Joiners. Pure and simple trade unionism suited the Carpenters because of the exceptional nature of their craft. Cigars were being made in factories and tenement houses when the Cigar Makers tried to set up craft unionism among the hand workers. But the work of the carpenters was, in the eighties, a craftsman's job and still is to a greater degree than most. A policy suitable to the carpenters was unsuitable to the cigar makers, so that the former have retained their strength and the latter are almost extinct. McGuire went to the English benefit unions for inspiration and to the loose British Trades Congress. But he did so just when the British Trades Congress was leaving its conservatism for a political career.

The Knights of Labor had two origins, as a local society in 1869, and as a national organization in 1878. In 1869 the trade unions were at the height of their power and reaching out into politics. In 1878, they were almost nonexistent after the long depression of the seventies. The explanation of the Knights' success in the seventies is to be found in their secrecy, and the same thing explains their static or declining condition from 1878 to 1881. In other words complete secrecy was an advantage to a group of growing locals and districts, but the threat of a secret society of national proportions drew upon it the unfavorable attention of the Church and press. Once the name of the Order had been made public and changes made in the ritual to mollify the Church, the Knights grew consistently. The trade unions, too, began to recover in 1880, but were again set back by the depression of 1883-85.

The national unions of the fifties and sixties were national only in name. They were loose federations of craft locals having little central authority and less money. The locals made their own agreements with employers with no reference to the national organization and the slightest depression wiped them out. The depression of the seventies left only a handful of national unions, none of which had as many as 5,000 members and few as many as 1,000.

When the national unions began to revive in 1880 they were under a cloud. They had disappeared in the seven lean years and the last remembrance of them was connected with the National Labor Union and the political agitations of the sixties. As late as 1886, the trade unions found it necessary to explain themselves. "It is a mistaken notion," they said, "to imagine that trade unions have failed," [8] and the writer goes on to show that only within the preceding decade had they been given a fair chance. It was admitted that the old organizations of fifteen or twenty years before had failed, but that was because they organized in the flush of good times to get wage increases, or in bad times to resist reductions. The writer, however, does not specify just what times were proper for the organization of unions. "Trade unions are now being organized," he continued, "as they should be—on a permanent basis—as social institutions with high dues, trade benefits and insurance features. . . ." This, of course, was exactly the way in which the English benefit societies had always been organized.

But the New Unionism was not, according to *The Carpenter*—probably McGuire—to be quite pure and simple. " . . . in the future they will become the corner stone of the Co-Operative Commonwealth," and they were to

---

[8] *The Carpenter,* April, 1886, p. 4.

avoid politics only "until such time as the workers through association and acquaintance have acquired that degree of unanimity to act in concert politically." And "being organized on special trade lines they can act on trade matters all the more intelligently and practically as well as speedily than in mixed bodies." In trade disputes or strikes "the entire power and financial reserve of the Brotherhood is concentrated on the support of the union in trouble." [9]

This was the lesson the trade unions learned between the sixties and the middle of the eighties, that a permanent national union should be based on benefits, the high dues which accompany them, a strike fund and the avoidance, for the time being at any rate, of reform and political ambitions. The best example of this sort of unionism in America was the oldest national trade union, the Typographical, which almost alone had survived the Civil War and the depressions. The English influence was of the same sort. The cotton mule spinners of New England were organized and maintained by Lancashire immigrants. English, Welsh, and Scotch miners had organized the American Miners' Association of 1861. In 1864 the Iron Molders had suggested sending a representative to England.[10] The Soft Stone Cutters had borrowed their constitution from the English society and the Granite Cutters in 1877 borrowed theirs from the soft stone organization.[11] The Cigar Makers had corresponded with their fellow craftsmen in England in 1871 and 1876, and when they reorganized in 1878-79, they used as their model the rules of the English union.[12] In the United States, the Amalgamated Society of Engineers (machinists) and the Amalgamated Society of Carpenters

---

[9] *Ibid.*, September, 1886, p. 5.

[10] *Proceedings,* 1864 Iron Molders' Convention.

[11] Granite Cutters' *Journal,* April, 1877.

[12] Cigar Makers' *Journal,* March, April, and December, 1876, and August, 1879.

and Joiners, branches of English unions of the same names, had existed since 1851 and 1860 respectively. Being benefit societies their dues were high, their numbers few, their conservatism beyond belief, and their lives long and uninteresting.

And yet the new American unionism was different from the old English unionism it copied. It was more aggressively a bargaining affair and if it raised its dues for insurance, it raised them too for strikes.

The attitude of the Knights of Labor toward the trade unions, new and old, differed from place to place, from time to time, and from union to union. In a word, it was opportunistic. It began in sympathy and a desire to cooperate, became, with the formation of the Federation of 1881, somewhat superior, and ended, with the growth of Home Club influence, definitely antagonistic. The attitude of the unions toward the Knights was less genial with the rise of Gompers and McGuire, especially the former. Personalities played a part. The new leaders were on the make as new leaders must be. The old ones had either inherited or acquired that respectability which goes with office. Powderly and Gompers could hardly be expected to understand one another. Powderly was Irish, Gompers, Jewish. Powderly was for some years the mayor of an industrial town, accustomed to the seat of authority, strait-laced especially about liquor, middle-class. Gompers was just from the workshop and the political club where things were not quite "genteel." The Knights complained they never saw him sober and, while it was probably equally true that they never saw him drunk, they were not given to making fine distinctions, and their shocked expressions must have offended him. The new leaders had diluted their class consciousness—a characteristic of leaders on the make— into wage consciousness which might or might not rub off in the course of years. At any rate Powderly did not have it. He probably never "sold out," but he undoubtedly was not irrevocably attached to his following as was Gompers throughout his whole career.

In 1893, John Hayes, the business man in the Knights, was going West to solicit advertising for some private money-making venture. He asked Powderly for letters of introduction to Armour, Pullman, and other Chicago business men whom the Order had fought in its heyday. It was a queer business and Powderly was unhappy about it. He warned Hayes not to accept advertisements from unfair firms and those under the boycott of the Order, even though he was

well aware that in too many instances the ban is recklessly placed on an employer and the boycott pushed when prudence would suggest a more conservative and equitable course. Nevertheless the people I serve are deserving of consideration even though in error and I must not sanction anything that would oppose their actions or best interests. . . . This is an arrangement between Mr. Wright, yourself and me. It is in no way related to the Order of the Knights of Labor . . . and whatever we realize on the venture does not go to swell the funds of any organization. . . . I am not receiving sufficient remuneration to enable me to continue the work. . . . I have more friends outside the labor organizations than in them. I would rather it were otherwise but would not smother conviction or a sense of fair play even to gain the good-will of members of a labor organization. It has been my aim to cause workers to look beyond their own surroundings and view those of their employers. Unless they do this they can never realize what the other side is like. I contend that the majority of employers can be approached much easier through a tender of good-will than with a club and having acted on that principle I have made enemies of the advocates of the club. . . . You can easily see that many employers, those who read and think, will recognize in me a friend who can honestly entertain for them a kindly feeling without violating my pledge to the workers who look to me for counsel.

It will be the aim of this work we are now doing to bring the employer and the employee into closer relations.[13]

And he might have added, "and make a little for ourselves on the side." The thing was all wrong and wrapped up in the worst sort of casuistry. Gompers would never have done it.

The early attitude of the Knights toward the trade unions is found in Stephens' address to the second regular General Assembly, January, 1879. After making the rather exaggerated claim that during the year "some trades and callings have so nearly accomplished the complete organization of their entire branch all over the continent within our Fraternity . . . ," he suggested "issuing an address . . . to the trade associations of the continent, calling their attention to the benefits of amalgamation and affiliation with our great brotherhood, and the weakness and evils of isolated effort . . . that the coming year be especially devoted to unifying all labor organizations into one grand consolidated body."[14] Stephens' suggestion was accepted and he was authorized to issue the address and if necessary call conventions of the trade unions "for the purpose of affiliating them with the Order."[15]

That this did not involve the absorption of the trade unions by the Knights is seen from the adoption of a resolution permitting the organization of national trade districts so that "trades organized as trades may select an executive officer of their own who may have charge of their organization and organize local assemblies of the trade in any part of the country and attach them to the District Assembly controlling that trade." Trades so organized might "hold delegate conventions on matters per-

---

[13] Letter from Powderly to Hayes, Apr. 3, 1893.
[14] *Proceedings*, January, 1879 General Assembly, p. 55.
[15] *Ibid.*, pp. 82, 84.

taining to their trade. . . ." [16]   Another resolution, passed
on the motion of Powderly, amended the rules to allow a
trade assembly "to exclude visitors of other trades or callings from the sanctuary" when it wanted to discuss matters
relating solely to its trade.[17]

The beginnings of opposition, though ineffective, were
not wanting. They came from the West. Singer of Missouri asked that "all charters heretofore issued to assemblies of special trades be recalled and that in future charters be granted only to mixed or amalgamated assemblies."
This was rejected on the recommendation of the committee.[18] Singer also asked for a definition of the "sojourner"
which was given as follows: "Sojourners are persons of one
trade initiated into an Assembly of another trade for the
purpose of ultimately forming an assembly of their
own. . . ." [19]

Stephens was not present at the third General Assembly
at Chicago in September, 1879, but his address was read.
"No time should be lost," he wrote, "or money spent in
strikes or the organization of separate trades or callings.
The benefits resulting therefrom are but partial and
evanescent. . . . Our first duty is the consolidation of all
branches of productive labor into a compact whole." [20]

But the antitrade West was in control at Chicago and
the General Assembly completely reversed itself. All laws
permitting the organization of special trades were stricken
out.[21] On a resolution of a Missouri delegate it was agreed
that "locals formed and conducted exclusively in the interest
of any one trade are contrary to the spirit and genius of the

---

[16] *Ibid.*, pp. 69, 72.
[17] *Ibid.*, pp. 70, 72.
[18] *Ibid.*, pp. 50, 69.
[19] *Ibid.*, p. 69.
[20] *Ibid.*, September, 1879 General Assembly, pp. 102-3.
[21] *Ibid.*, p. 140.

Order as founded," and, further, that "locals conducted in the interest of any special trade must in all cases be subordinate to the District Assembly in whose territory they may be located" and must admit workmen of all trades.[22]

This was certainly sweeping enough but rather confused. It repudiated not only trade districts but trade locals. At the same time it tacitly accepted trade locals by ordering them to remain attached to their district assemblies. The Chicago convention marked in theory if not in fact the turning of the Order away from trade unions within and without. It marked too the beginning of the Powderly régime and there may be some connection between the two. In 1880 Powderly declared that the Order "in comparison to isolated trades unions, bears the same relation that the locomotive of to-day does to the stage-coach of half a century ago." [23]

At Pittsburgh, in 1880, the trade union faction recovered sufficiently to ask for a law governing national and international trade unions, "that they may join this Order in a body," [24] and that reciprocity treaties might be made "with the old trade organizations of the country, particularly the Iron Molders." [25] While these proposals were rejected, an opposing resolution "that we disapprove most emphatically of any and all connection . . . with open or public trades unions" received the same treatment on a vote of 20 to 16.[26]

The Federation of Organized Trades and Labor Unions held a preliminary meeting in August, 1881, and organized permanently in November. The first meeting was largely

[22] *Ibid.*, pp. 98, 129, 140.
[23] *Ibid.*, 1880 General Assembly, p. 169.
[24] *Ibid.*, p. 195.
[25] *Ibid.*, pp. 198, 234.
[26] *Ibid.*, 1880 General Assembly, p. 226.

the result of the split in the Knights of Labor and the second had a large delegation of Knights of both trade and antitrade factions. The General Assembly met in September between these two conventions and it appeared that the Order might be absorbed by a larger labor movement. But while the constitution of the new organization, much against Gompers' wishes, allowed representation to the Knights, the latter deserted the Federation after its first meeting. With the return of the trade unionists to the Order in 1882 at the New York General Assembly, one of the first acts was the passing of a resolution in support of the Amalgamated Association of Iron and Steel Workers then on strike. It was more than a coincidence that the Amalgamated withdrew from the Federation that year, and that the Knights' resolution of sympathy repudiated any desire to create division in the ranks of the steel workers "in favor of joining the Knights of Labor." [27]

In 1882, the General Assembly returned to the original attitude toward trade organizations in the Order. It not only permitted but encouraged the formation of trade assemblies. There were a number of reasons for this: the success of the Glass Workers in establishing a strong national trade assembly when even trade locals were prohibited by the law of the General Assembly; antagonism toward the new Federation; the shortcomings of the larger, mixed districts, and the removal of Litchman as secretary of the Order.

The new secretary, Robert Layton, reported that many trade unions had written him that they were "seriously meditating the propriety of coming over to us in a body," [28] suggested reorganizing the shoemakers who had been without a national union since the disappearance of the Crispins,

---

[27] *Ibid.*, 1882 General Assembly, p. 270.
[28] *Ibid.*, pp. 297-98.

and echoed the complaints of locals against the mixed district assemblies.[29] He was supported by the general executive board which recommended giving up the districts and supplanting them by trade and state assemblies. "The growing sentiment of the Order, however," the general executive board reported, "seems to indicate a preference for the formation of Trade Districts."[30]

The New York General Assembly then proceeded to adopt two methods of forming trade districts within the Order. The first provided that when any branch of industry desired to form a trade district the executive board upon request should assemble a delegate convention of the trade "for the purpose of such organization."[31] Once formed, all the locals of the trade were to be attached to the trade district which would then be a national trade union within the Order. The second method provided that locals of one trade might form a trade council composed of three delegates from each, and that all trade matters should be referred to this council "and until acted on by that body shall not be brought before the District Assembly to which said trade locals are attached." Trades organized under the jurisdiction of the Order might form national trade councils by the calling of a convention. "Such convention may enact a code of laws for the government of said Council and if said laws be approved by the G.M.W. and the Executive Board the Grand Secretary shall issue a charter. . . ."[32] Ralph Beaumont in the chair decided that mixed locals could not compel members of trade locals to withdraw from the latter and join the former, and permission was given to form a building trades' district.[33] But

---

[29] *Ibid.*, p. 296.
[30] *Ibid.*, p. 334.
[31] *Ibid.*, p. 364.
[32] *Ibid.*, p. 368.
[33] *Ibid.*, pp. 325, 353-54.

proposals that the executive board call conventions of wood-workers and cigar makers to form trade districts were rejected.[34]

The depression of 1883-85, and the defeat of the Telegraphers' District Trade Assembly No. 45 by the Western Union in 1883 delayed the development of the Order on trade lines made possible by the legislation of 1882. The open unions were defeated all along the line in 1883, the cigar makers, miners, steel workers, printers, Fall River mill workers, New Orleans freight handlers, all lost. Only the New York building trades made gains.[35] At the General Assembly at Cincinnati, in 1883, no serious change was made. The general executive board recommended the formation of national trade councils and a local protest against the formation of trade assemblies was defeated.[36] District Assembly No. 17, St. Louis, the center of anti-trade sentiment up to that time, asked that locals attached to trade districts be compelled to remain under their territorial districts "for unless this is done we see in the near future the abolishment of one of the noblest teachings of the Order, to aid and protect each other." [37] This resolution seems to have been lost in the shuffle but it represented as did others from the same source the opposition of small, mixed districts to the loss of locals because of their withdrawal to enter districts of their trades. Approval was given to all printers and others connected with the printing and publishing industry to join District Assembly No. 64, of New York, the senior printers' district in the Order.[38] The committee reported favorably on trade districts for

---

[34] *Ibid.*, p. 311.
[35] John Swinton, *John Swinton's Paper*, Dec. 16, 1883.
[36] *Proceedings*, 1883 General Assembly, pp. 469, 432, 500.
[37] *Ibid.*, p. 437.
[38] *Ibid.*, pp. 467, 508.

shoemakers [39] and trunk makers [40] and trade influence can also be seen in the change of the prefix of the titles of national officers from "Grand" to "General." [41]

On the other hand, the proposal to put all carpenters in one district was defeated [42] along with the suggestion that trade locals might elect members by a majority vote, and that the building trades should be represented on the executive board.[43] Finally it was decided that no charter should be issued to a national trade district unless "it be demonstrated to the satisfaction of the Executive Board that the members of such trade could not be effectively organized under the system of mixed or territorial districts." [44] The effect of this resolution depended of course on the attitude toward trade assemblies of the executive board which up to that time was strongly trade in its sentiments. Its chairman was Frank K. Foster, at the same time an officer in the Federation of Trades and Labor Unions.[45]

The depression was breaking up many of the weaker trade unions and their members were drifting into the Order. The furniture workers complained in 1884 that the Knights were organizing their membership in new assemblies[46] and while this was true, it was equally inevitable. "Two or three years ago," wrote a correspondent in Swinton's paper, ". . . there were only two or three unions in Troy that amounted to anything. Now nearly every trade is organized. . . . Most of the credit for this improvement

---

[39] *Ibid.*, p. 499.

[40] *Ibid.*, p. 506.

[41] *Ibid.*, pp. 494, 441, 507, 459.

[42] *Ibid.*, pp. 440, 498.

[43] *Ibid.*, pp. 445, 498.

[44] *Ibid.*, pp. 439, 502.

[45] The 1883 General Assembly also appointed a committee to arrange an alliance with other labor and trade unions and asked the general officers to try and bring all trade unions within the Order. (*Ibid.*, pp. 467, 506, 505.)

[46] Swinton, *op. cit.*, July 27, 1884.

should undoubtedly be given to the Knights of Labor. They organized new unions and strengthened old ones till Troy is almost solidly union. . . ." [47]

But if the trade unions suffered from the Knights, the latter had difficulties not unconnected with the trade unions. The miners were about equally divided in their allegiance and when a trade union called a strike, as at Hocking Valley, the Knights had to follow whether there was provision for their support or not. "In a large number of instances," said the executive board in 1884, "the Knights of Labor membership is unwillingly forced to submit to the dictation of the trade unions . . ." and the board wanted to know if "the authorization of a strike by a trades' union with which any number of our members are in affiliation should be deemed as equivalent to the sanction of your Executive Board also?" [48]

But the difficulties with the unions were of less moment than the growth from a new source within the Order of antitrade sentiment. District Assembly No. 49, of New York, was beginning under the Home Club its long and successful attack on the general officers and their friendliness to the trades. In 1883 it presented a list of charges to the general executive board against District Assembly No. 64, New York printers; against a Cigar Makers' local, No. 2458, "Defiance Assembly," of which Gompers was a member; and against District Assembly No. 52 of Brooklyn. It asked that all locals within the territory of District Assembly No. 49 be attached to the district. The general executive board was faced with a nice jurisdictional dispute and decided on the whole against District Assembly No. 49. The printers, it decreed, was a trade assembly and might be allowed to take in lithographers, type founders, pressmen

---

[47] *Ibid.*, Dec. 14, 1884.
[48] *Proceedings*, 1884 General Assembly, pp. 715-16.

and feeders; therefore the protest of District Assembly No. 49 "is not well founded." As to Defiance Assembly "some of the members of the Board think it would be unwise to withdraw the charter from a large body of organized men." [49] But all mixed locals, and trade locals without districts to which they might be attached, were to remain in District Assembly No. 49. This was after the Cuno affair and the suspension and rehabilitation of the New York District. It was at the beginning of the fight with the Cigar Makers.

District Assembly No. 49 also protested the admission of two delegates to the General Assembly from a trade district, No. 75, street railway employees, and of Adolph Strasser, president of the International Cigar Makers' Union, from Local Assemblies Nos. 1629 and 2458. But Strasser was admitted and one delegate from the street railway employees' district.[50]

That was the last of the old general executive board and its trade sympathies. The new general executive board had only three elected members instead of five, and one of them was John W. Hayes nominated by the Home Club. "Boring from within" had begun, and it continued until it finally reached the general master workman.[51]

In spite of District Assembly No. 49, the year 1884

---

[49] *Ibid.*, pp. 617-18.

[50] *Ibid.*, p. 562.

[51] Mr. Hayes says that the Defiance Assembly No. 2458 was framed up by Frank K. Foster and had no "large body of organized men," but was composed of officers of the International Cigar Makers' Union "boring from within" the Knights of Labor and securing the Order's label in large quantities for use on International-made cigars because the employers and the officers of the International all realized that the label of the Knights was infinitely superior to the blue label of the International. This will be dealt with more thoroughly in the chapter on the Cigar Makers.

The new general executive board still had five members—the general master workman and the general secretary were members ex officio.

marks the peak of interest up to that time, in the recognition of the need of national trade districts within the Order. Only the Glass Workers and the Telegraphers had been so organized, the trade element in the Knights being confined largely to locals and trade districts. In 1884 the International Trunk Makers applied to the General Assembly for admission as a body and were taken in.[52] The board, too, levied an assessment of 5 cents per member for Local Assembly No. 300, the national union of Window Glass Workers.[53] Large sums were sent to the Hocking Valley miners and permission was given for the formation of a national union of plumbers.[54] Then, too, District Assembly No. 64 had its say in opposition to District Assembly No. 49 and stated the case for trade assemblies in strict trade union terms, not failing at the same time to mention the inefficiency of the large, mixed districts.[55]

Finally, the new constitution of 1884 provided for the formation of national trade assemblies as follows:

That trades organized under the jurisdiction of the Order may form National Trade Assemblies giving at least three months' notice to each local assembly composed of such trade that a convention would be held for the purpose of forming such national trade assembly. Such convention may enact a code of laws for the government of said assembly and if said laws be approved by the Executive Board, the General Secretary-Treasurer shall issue a charter to such a body on the receipt of the same fee as now charged for a D. A. charter.[56]

This was practically the same as the 1882 procedure, and a second section was added making the joining of the national trade assemblies optional with the locals.

---

[52] *Proceedings,* 1884 General Assembly, p. 619.
[53] *Ibid.,* p. 616.
[54] *Ibid.,* p. 787.
[55] *Ibid.,* p. 702.
[56] *Ibid.,* p. 776.

But while the Knights of Labor were prepared to absorb the trades they did not hesitate to declare their essential divergence from the national unions in spirit and intent. The general executive board that was about to be supplanted by the tools of the Home Club went out with a blast of defiance against "pure and simple" trade unionism. "It is necessary that we recognize," said Foster, McClelland, Campbell, Murray, and Barry, "the essential difference between our Order and Trades' Unions. . . . This essential difference is that our Order contemplates a radical change in the existing industrial system, and labors to bring about that change, while Trades' Unions and other orders accept the industrial system as it is and endeavor to adapt themselves to it. The attitude of our Order to the existing industrial system is necessarily one of war. . . ." [57]

This was not exactly a new note in the Knights of Labor but it had a new tone. The Order had always been "radical" in the sense that it had always opposed the wage system, but it was not until remarkable growth began in 1883-84 that its "radicalism" became aggressive. And here, for the first time, the revolutionary note is struck in revolutionary terms. Shortly after this, men like Martin Irons, Joseph Buchanan, and Albert Parsons were to take the general executive board at its word and act as the officers had spoken. The year 1884 marks the turning point from defense to aggression.

This aggression took two forms, one led by the Home Club against the trade unions, and the other, led by Barry, Bailey, Buchanan, against the railroads, the packers, and combined capital in general. Both had initial success and final failure. The Home Club almost ruined the International Cigar Makers but created the American Federation of Labor. Jay Gould was twice defeated, and the packers

---

[57] *Ibid.*, pp. 716, 717.

forced to grant the eight-hour day. But in 1886 the great Southwest strike was ingloriously lost, the packers, with Powderly's aid, returned to ten hours, and Albert Parsons and four of his companions were being made ready for the gallows as a result of the Haymarket bomb. The year 1886 proved that the wage system was not thus lightly to be overthrown and once this was decided, the trade unions which accepted the *status quo* were able to gather the elect of the labor movement together, retreat to a safe and sane position, and weather the storm.

In 1885 the Knights began their phenomenal growth stimulated by returning prosperity, success in bargaining, strikes, boycotts, and the aggressiveness of the new leaders. Trade sentiment in the Order increased and though Powderly spoke against the national trade districts at the 1885 General Assembly,[58] he wrote in December to the general executive board suggesting that A. G. Denny be sent to the Eastern Glass Bottle Blowers' League to ask them to enter the Order. For a while there was little conflict with the open unions except in New York. A district court in Washington, D. C., decided that a mixed district had no right to initiate members whose crafts were already organized and threatened to revoke the charter of the mixed district for interference with the trade.[59] A printers' local in Philadelphia asked that a granite cutters' local of the same city "square itself with the Granite Cutters' National Union" or have its charter revoked, and the General Assembly ordered the granite cutters' local to return to the national union.[60] So strong was the trade feeling and the entente between the Knights and the open unions that a resolution was introduced, but not passed, refusing admis-

---

[58] *Ibid.*, 1885 General Assembly, p. 25.
[59] *Ibid.*, pp. 102-3, 140.
[60] *Ibid.*, pp. 106, 109, 140.

sion to the Order to "any person who has ever been expelled from any trades' union," [61] and another that no one should be taken into the Knights who was not clear on the books of his trade union.[62] Even the conflict with the Cigar Makers was confined to New York and the 1885 General Assembly was asked to refrain from the use of the Order's general label on cigars. While the committee reported against this, it recommended that the Knights' label should be used on cigars "made by members of the Order only and that the utmost caution be exercised in granting the use of the label." New York protested, but the committee report was adopted with the further stipulation that "no label should be used except upon cigars made at union prices." [63]

The same General Assembly gave the miners permission to form a national trade assembly by means of a convention to be held in St. Louis, Feb. 17, 1886,[64] and the plate glass workers were given permission to form a national district.[65]

Thus, so far as the constitution was concerned, the formation of national trade assemblies was possible from the beginning with the exception of the two years 1880 and 1881. But the actual condition is somewhat confused. The permission of the general executive board was necessary to create a trade district and the decision was often passed on to the General Assembly. The window glass workers formed a national organization when the law prohibited it, because the general executive board thought well of the idea. But after the law was changed in 1882, and again in 1884, to allow the formation of national unions within the Order, there was no great rush to organize in that way.

---

[61] *Ibid.*, pp. 125, 138.

[62] *Ibid.*, pp. 120, 138.

[63] *Ibid.*, pp. 109, 131, 132.

[64] *Ibid.*, 1886 General Assembly, pp. 126-27, 135.

[65] *Ibid.*, pp. 127, 133.

The movement toward the trade district form began to be marked in 1885 for industrial rather than constitutional reasons. Before 1884, the general executive board had been trade unionist in sympathy. After 1884, it was aggressively Knights of Labor, with Barry and Bailey organizing trade districts and Powderly inviting the old trade unions to enter the Order. At the same time the new general executive board under the control of District Assembly No. 49 was fighting the Cigar Makers' International in New York.

The confusion is somewhat relieved when it is understood that the fight against the Cigar Makers' International in New York was not, as Gompers and Strasser asserted, a fight against trade unionism. It began as an internal controversy in Local No. 144, International Cigar Makers' Union, in 1882 over the proper methods to be used to secure the passage of an anti-tenement-house law. The socialists objected to the political methods of Gompers and were able to elect their own man, S. Schimkowitz, president of the local. Strasser refused to recognize the left wing officers, suspended the president, and lectured the socialists upon the methods of the American "school" of "labor reformers." [66] The old officers of No. 144 skipped out with the books and funds of the local when the newly elected officers tried to get them by warrant, and Strasser twice refused funds to the International executive board to go to New York to investigate the difficulty. When money was found the executive board went to New York and decided that Schimkowitz had been duly elected president of No. 144 and that Strasser had suspended him without warrant. It

---

[66] Union dues were also involved. The Progressives wanted lower dues to permit expansion among lower-wage groups, while the International had established relatively high dues and thus tended to limit its membership to the hand cigar makers.

recommended that the left wing should return to No. 144 and a new election be held. Both Strasser and the New York socialists objected to this and the latter seceded and formed Progressive Union No. 1. They appealed to District Assembly No. 49 for support and got it, and from that time on the New York district fought Strasser and Gompers. In doing this, they dragged the Order into a local squabble and drove the trade unions together into the American Federation of Labor.[67]

At the special General Assembly in May-June, 1886, the Cigar Makers presented their complaints to the Knights and P. J. McGuire offered the trade union "treaty" formulated by the officers of the national unions at Philadelphia. Powderly sent an invitation to the Amalgamated Association of Iron and Steel Workers to enter the Order and later attended their convention to support the offer. Complete autonomy was promised the Steel Workers as it was later promised the Glass Blowers and the Typographical. At Richmond in October, the Cigar Makers were expelled from the Order.

The Richmond General Assembly which convened two months before the formation of the American Federation of Labor amplified the constitutional regulations governing national trade assemblies, but made no important change. The new law was promulgated in July, 1887,[68] and revised

---

[67] Cigar Makers' *Journal*, supplement 1883 *Proceedings*, and for executive board's report, June 15, 1882. This is dealt with more fully in the chapter on the Cigar Makers.

[68] *Proceedings*, 1886 General Assembly, pp. 265-66; *Ibid.*, 1887 General Assembly, p. 1800.

Commons and Associates, *History of Labour in the United States*, Vol. II, p. 428 has misinterpreted this new law suggesting that the change in 1887 made it imperative on the part of the general executive board to give a trade charter and that the right of the mixed district to refuse to allow a local to withdraw to enter a trade district was taken away. This is interpreted to mean that the attitude of the

at the 1887 General Assembly. It provided that when a majority of locals of any one trade wanted to form a national trade district, they might apply to the general executive board for a charter, and should the general executive board decide to grant it, the regulations governing the Window Glass Workers should be adopted as far as possible. This new regulation was simply the old law of 1882 and 1884 and it was adopted with some slight changes in 1887.[69]

Nevertheless, after the formation of the American Federation of Labor in December, 1886, there was a rush of the trade element into national trade districts. Nearly every trade in the Order tried to get a trade district charter in 1887, but the general officers were less enthusiastic about this movement than the rank and file. Under the influence of District Assembly No. 49 they expelled the Carpet Workers' Trade District No. 126. When seventeen locals of silk workers in New York and New Jersey asked

Knights toward trade districts changed markedly after the formation of the American Federation of Labor.

The facts are that no such change was made. The general executive board continued to exercise the right to reject an application for a trade charter and the mixed districts never had had the right to refuse permission of a trade local to join a trade district. Mr. Perlman was confused by a change from "may" to "shall" in the new law which referred, not to the general executive board's power to grant trade charters, but to the duty of the trade assemblies to ask for them after they had decided they were wanted. (*Proceedings*, 1886 General Assembly, p. 265; *Ibid.*, 1887 General Assembly, pp. 1736, 1800.) The misinterpretation is understandable as the matter was confused. Local Assembly No. 300 brought in amendments to a document that had been published the previous year and was not reproduced in the *Proceedings* in which it was amended. It is important to get it straight, because it involves the question as to what extent the Order was driven toward trade districts by the American Federation of Labor. Under the general executive board interpretation of the new law, the mixed districts did not lose, but actually gained, the right to refuse trade locals permission to withdraw to enter trade districts. (Swinton, *op. cit.*, June 12, 1887.)

[69] *Proceedings*, 1887 General Assembly, p. 1800.

for a trade charter the general executive board held the
matter up, because the New York district assembly had
not given its permission to the locals to withdraw from
its jurisdiction, though there was no indication that any
New Jersey district had been consulted in the matter.[70]   A
national trade charter was asked for by the bricklayers of
Philadelphia, but District Assembly No. 1 protested and
the charter was refused.[71]   The National Trade District of
Machinists, No. 198, included machine helpers, blacksmiths,
etc., but when District Assembly No. 49 refused to allow
a blacksmiths' local to enter the trade district, the board,
while admitting that blacksmiths were covered by the Machinists' charter, upheld District Assembly No. 49.   The
board's interpretation of the new law in this case read that
the trade locals could join a trade district only after receiving permission from the mixed district to which they had
formerly belonged, but that if any subdivision of the trade
later wanted to form a separate trade district no such permission was required.[72]   The same thing happened with
the machinery constructors.   They were given a trade district charter but the board decreed that "no local assembly
can withdraw from a district assembly without first having
received its *approval* and *clearance*." [73]   The rubber workers wanted to form a trade district in 1887 and applied to
the general executive board.   Not receiving a prompt answer they wrote again and threatened to withdraw.   The
general executive board expelled them because of their impatience and the fact that "their application did not bear
the seal of the District Assemblies to which these locals
were attached, nor the permission for withdrawal."   "Ac-

---

[70] *Proceedings,* 1887 General Assembly, p. 1418.
[71] *Ibid.,* p. 1291.
[72] *Ibid.,* p. 1372.
[73] *Ibid.,* p. 1357. The new law mentioned only "clearance"; "approval"
seems to have been the board's own idea.

cording to the law," the general executive board continued, "this permission was necessary before a charter could be granted. . . ." [74] Even when there was no technical difficulty in the way, the board showed no enthusiasm about granting trade charters. Resolutions from the machinery constructors were presented, threatening to withdraw from the Order by Jan. 1, 1887, if they were not given a trade charter, but the general executive board ignored them and reported "no action necessary." [75]

On the other hand, trade district charters were granted to firemen and engineers,[76] horse car drivers,[77] lithographers,[78] painters, paper hangers and decorators,[79] machinists and machinery constructors,[80] etc., and in St. Louis a German district was formed covering the territory of District Assembly No. 17.[81]

The fact seems to be that the general officers remained unenthusiastic about trade units in the Order and paid little attention to the possibility of inroads by the American Federation of Labor. It was rather the members themselves who pressed toward trade organization. Powderly, who had been influenced by the Window Glass Workers to invite the Eastern Bottle Workers' League into the Order, and who went to Pittsburgh in the summer of 1886 to wean away the Iron and Steel Workers from the trade unions, had always at heart opposed the trade sentiment. After the split with the unions was sealed by the formation of the American Federation of Labor, he made a weak attempt

---

[74] *Ibid.*, pp. 1299-1300.
[75] *Ibid.*, p. 1298.
[76] *Ibid.*, p. 1428.
[77] *Ibid.*, p. 1381.
[78] *Ibid.*, p. 1387.
[79] *Ibid.*, p. 1410.
[80] *Ibid.*, pp. 1418-19.
[81] *Ibid.*, p. 1388.

to reconcile his personal feelings with the trade tendency of the Order,[82] but it did not last long.   In 1889 he wrote Hayes, "I will tell you frankly I don't care how quick the National Trade Assemblies go out.   They hinder others from coming to us and I am strongly tempted to advise them all to go it alone on the outside and see how it will go to turn back the wheels of the organization for the benefit of a few men who want to be at the head of something." [83]

But the national trade districts formed after 1886 were seldom successful.   They sooner or later withdrew from the Order and, as open trade unions, affiliated with the American Federation of Labor or disappeared altogether.

The early trade sentiment in the Knights declined for a time after the first General Assembly, revived in 1882, and reached its peak in the expansion years of 1885-86. Immediately after the formation of the American Federation of Labor there was a rush to form trade districts but the General Assembly was unsympathetic.

The attitude of the general officers is less readily summarized.   On the whole, they were opposed to trade formations within the Order.   Powderly, Litchman, and the older officers were opposed on principle, but the general executive board which was ousted in 1884 was sympathetic.   The new men, Hayes, Barry, Bailey, under the control of District Assembly No. 49, opposed the open unions, but, with the exception of Hayes, they were anxious to create trade units within the Order with which to fight them.   Powderly went with the general executive board for a while in his attempts to get some of the national unions into the Order.   But when the split was made irrevocable by the creation of the American Federation of Labor, they all

---

[82] *Ibid.*, p. 1535.
[83] Letter from Powderly to Hayes, Feb. 9, 1889.

seem to have become skeptical of trade districts and re-verted to the mixed district point of view.

The Order itself was much more trade in its sympathies and connections, especially in the East, than the general officers or the General Assembly.

CHAPTER IX

THE UNIONS AND THE KNIGHTS [1]

THE GLASS WORKERS

THE best example of trade unionism within the Knights of Labor was that of the Window Glass Workers.[2] For nearly twenty years this strict trade society lived comfortably and successfully within the Order, helped by its general strength and helping it financially and in other ways. The Window Glass Workers' Union was a small one and probably never had more than 1,700 members, but it controlled every factory in the United States and a number in England, Belgium, France, and Italy. The glass workers were able to maintain a standard of production of forty-eight boxes a week, their idea of the needs of the market, on the condition of which they were well informed. They worked nine hours a day and five days a week and had two months' vacation in the summer when the fires were drawn. Their wages were $30 to $40 a week for single-strength, and $50 to $70 for double-strength blowers. They were at that time unaffected by machinery, though specialization had crept in and under intelligent leadership they maintained standards that were impossible in other trades. Their work was highly skilled, requiring some knowledge of the chemistry of glass, the lung capacity of a prima donna, and the heat-resisting qualities of a stoker. They

---

[1] The Cigar Makers will be taken up in the discussion of the origin of the American Federation of Labor.

[2] Included flatteners, cutters, blowers, and gatherers. (*National Labor Digest*, November, 1922, p. 21.)

had the most complete labor monopoly of any union in the country and when this was threatened by the importation of English, French, and Belgian glass workers, President Cline went to Europe and organized assemblies there. They were the most aggressive union in pushing the anti-contract-labor law through Congress.

On Sept. 23, 1877, District Assembly No. 8 [3] of the Knights of Labor was organized in Pittsburgh of Local Assemblies Nos. 281, 300, 305, 319, 322, and 484. This was the first trade district in the Order and existed before the General Assembly was created. It lapsed early in 1880, but in May of the same year certain locals, Nos. 300, 305, and 322, were merged as Window Glass Workers' Local Assembly No. 300. They immediately organized their craft throughout the United States directly under the Pittsburgh local and applied to Powderly to regularize the practice. The general executive board took the matter before the 1880 General Assembly, stating explicitly that the Glass Workers "are held together by trade interests mainly and are simply a centralized trade union . . . of an exclusive nature inside the Order"; that they had their own traveling organizers unauthorized by the grand master workman; formed branches in cities where the Order had assemblies; and that their members would not join these assemblies nor take out charters as trade locals under the districts. "Those branches declare," said the general executive board, "that they belong to Local Assembly No. 300 of Pittsburgh," and initiate only glass workers.

They say that their members speak so many languages that only trade interests can hold them together now, but that in due time when they learn more of our principles of Universal Brotherhood they will adopt our liberal methods. Their organization is so powerful that it rules in every window glass

[3] Glass workers.

factory and dictates its own rate of wages. If that trade centralization should be destroyed by us . . . the window glass workers will be at the mercy of the employers. Pittsburgh is the center of the glass trade and Pittsburgh price rules the market throughout the land, therefore the Pittsburgh brothers must have control of all the glass workers in America.[4]

This was said to the General Assembly which revoked all the earlier legislation in favor of trade assemblies, and though the general executive board pretended that it was a special case, it was special only in the way it was handled.

But even the general executive board had not been quite ready to accept the arrangements the glass workers had made for themselves. It had suggested that in cities where there were more than forty glass workers they should open their assemblies to other trades, initiate members of all trades as sojourners, and comply with all the rules of the Order. This last did not mean much because the Order had so many rules and these were so conflicting from year to year and even at the same time, that only Powderly, who was a lawyer at heart, knew what they were. A further conference with the glass workers removed the last doubt of the executive board and it reported that trade centralization was absolutely necessary, but that the union must conform to the rules of the Order "wherever possible." Rules for the trade were drawn up by Litchman, approved by Powderly, and promulgated May 15, 1880.

Under these rules Local Assembly No. 300 was required to make the usual quarterly reports to the grand secretary on membership and the Resistance Fund, and pay the arrears of the per capita tax and the special assessment of 1879. Members were to be elected and initiated in the usual way but a candidate living too far away from Pittsburgh to be initiated in No. 300 was to be initiated in the nearest

---

[4] *Proceedings,* 1880 General Assembly, p. 184.

local assembly on the presentation of a certificate of fitness from the Pittsburgh local. After initiation, this member was attached to Local Assembly No. 300. The latter was required to take in sojourners and was attached to the General Assembly. It was also allowed to elect its own officers and nominate organizers to the general master workman.[5]

Other glass workers were not so fortunate. Local Assembly No. 1496 composed of window glass layers-out and layers-in applied to the 1880 General Assembly for permission to withdraw from District Assembly No. 3, follow the example of Local Assembly No. 300 and organize as a national union with Local Assembly No. 1496 "the head of the window-glass layers-out of the United States." They also wanted permission to strike for a 15-cent increase, asserting that they had been discriminated against in wage adjustments in comparison with the teasers. They complained, too, of the exclusiveness of Local Assembly No. 300.[6]

Their requests were flatly rejected [7] on highly constitutional grounds, but the ordinary mortal is left somewhat confused before what, on the surface, seems to be quite opposite treatment of two craft groups seeking the same thing. This suggests the weakness of a legalistic interpretation of a labor society and perhaps of any other. Laws, in the Knights of Labor at least, were made to be useful and not necessarily to be used. When the officers wanted to do a thing a way could always be found to do it. The general executive board gave Local Assembly No. 300 a new constitution without "by your leave" from the General Assembly and then cajoled that august body into a semblance of acceptance. But when the layers-out came in

---

[5] *Journal*, p. 14.
[6] *Proceedings*, 1880 General Assembly, pp. 233-34.
[7] *Ibid.*, pp. 250-51.

a constitutional manner before the General Assembly and asked for the same thing they were, with great parading of the constitution, given the air.

Many explanations suggest themselves: the opposition of District Assembly No. 3 which affected the layers-out but not Local Assembly No. 300 because the latter had previously been organized in a trade assembly; the criticism of Local Assembly No. 300, and the request for strike aid when strike aid, if not strikes, was frowned upon. But the most satisfactory explanation is probably to be found in the way in which the two groups acted. Local Assembly No. 300, ignoring the law and the constitution, presented the general executive board with a *fait accompli*, while Local Assembly No. 1496 asked permission first. In the Knights of Labor it was always well to take action and then ask for authority. There, as elsewhere, nothing succeeded like success. The unfortunate layers-out suffered for their regularity.

The entente between Local Assembly No. 300 and the Order shows conclusively that there was no inherent, irrepressible conflict between labor and trade organization or point of view. But it shows, too, that accidental circumstances peculiar to this situation were of importance. And there was opposition. District Assembly No. 2 of Camden, N. J., complained bitterly of the new arrangement [8] and the rules were amended to require window glass workers outside of Pittsburgh to remain full members of the local assemblies in their neighborhoods, while only half, instead of the whole, initiation fee was to go to the trade local.[9] This was repealed at the 1881 General Assembly and the window glass workers were permitted to organize "preceptories" outside Pittsburgh having no connection with

[8] *Ibid.*, pp. 189, 244.
[9] *Ibid.*, pp. 244-46.

other locals or districts.[10] This probably did not satisfy the Camden district, but it was said in 1882 that the Window Glass Workers of New Jersey was the only large body of workers in the state "who have steadily maintained a trade organization during the whole past 15 years." [11]

Wages for window glass workers were 20 per cent higher in the Pittsburgh region than in the East and in July, 1882, the union decided to raise eastern rates 10 per cent. A strike was called. The Window Glass Manufacturers' Association had twenty-one men arrested under the Pennsylvania conspiracy laws, and began to import Belgian glass blowers at $30 a head.[12] The Belgians were organized by Local Assembly No. 300 as fast as they arrived. Then the Belgians were arrested by the Manufacturers' Association and upon appeal to their consul at Washington got legal advice. The glass manufacturers were asking Congress for higher protection against imported glass, and Local Assembly No. 300 decided that it needed protection against imported glass workers. In August, 1883, it prepared an anti-contract-labor law and presented it to the Cincinnati General Assembly in September.[13] Here appears the value of a combined trade and labor society like the Knights and the significance of the initiative of a trade within it. Immigration, voluntary and subsidized, was affecting many industries besides the glass workers, but only they and the iron and steel workers, because they had the organization, the intelligence, and the funds, took measures to control it. The great mass of the Knights of Labor could not lead, but they could follow and, when the glass workers appealed to them, the whole force of the Order was thrown behind their demands. Between 50,000 and 100,000 signa-

---

10 *Ibid.,* 1881 General Assembly, pp. 294, 303.

11 New York *Herald,* Apr. 23, 1882.

12 John Swinton, *John Swinton's Paper,* December, 1883.

13 *Proceedings,* 1883 General Assembly, pp. 432, 500.

tures were placed on a petition to Congress [14] and on Feb. 1, 1884, Powderly, Turner, Barry, eight glass workers and representatives of the Amalgamated Association of Iron and Steel Workers, appeared before the Committee on Education and Labor in support of the Foran bill which attached a penalty of $1,000 to the importation of labor under contract. The bill passed the House but was not reached in the Senate.

In 1884 the General Assembly added to its platform the following: "that the importation of foreign labor under contract shall be prohibited," and in January, 1885, Powderly wrote Congress asking in the name of the Order that the bill be dealt with. It was passed Feb. 2, 1885, but had been denatured in the process. It was amended in 1887 and again in 1888.[15]

In the summer of 1883 the Glass Workers struck and were locked out. Their first strike had cost them $75,000 and they asked the Order for assistance. The general executive board levied an assessment of 5 cents per member in October, 1883, but it was not a success and four canvassers were sent out to solicit further aid.[16] A conference with the manufacturers in November failed to reach a settlement, but on January 30, 1884, after five months, the strike was won and 1,500 [17] men returned to work under a satisfactory agreement. Two months later Local Assembly No. 300 advanced $2,000 to the Order to take over the Cannelburg Coal Company.

The Glass Workers had gained every point: "last year's wages, limit of production under our control, the apprentice system intact, no extra work and our lines unbroken";

---

[14] *Ibid.*, 1884 General Assembly, p. 623.
[15] Senate committee on education and labor, 48: 1: No. 820. House committee, 48: 1: No. 444.
[16] *Proceedings*, 1884 General Assembly, pp. 615-16, 620.
[17] The number is variously given as 1,200, 1,500, 1,700, and 3,000.

and they attributed their gains entirely to the Order. "Had it not been for the Knights of Labor," they wrote to the *Journal,* "Local Assembly No. 300 would not have been successful," and the letter grew lyrical in praise of the Knights.[18] In May, the Glass Workers were able to boast that "We absolutely control the production of window glass in this country," and proceeded to elaborate the philosophy of restrictive trade unionism: " . . . Recognizing the fact that time has changed the weapons of warfare from the rude club and clenched fist to reason and argument based on the state of the trade, production, stocks, cost and the state of the world's market, we have . . . succeeded in getting a nearly perfect system of gathering and compiling statistics relative to production and consumption, stocks, number of factories and pots operating, factories building or to be built, numbers of men in the trade and apprentices, probable consumption and possible output, we regulate production." They were paid $120 for twenty days' work.[19]

The success of the Window Glass Workers so impressed others that the Plate Glass Workers were allowed, in 1885, to follow their example [20] and form a national trade union under Local Assembly No. 3616.

In 1884, President Cline went to Europe and established an International Window Glass Workers' Association. At Pittsburgh, in July, 1885, the first convention was held with delegates from England, Belgium, France, Italy, and Portugal.[21] This was perhaps the nearest thing to an international union the United States had had. In 1886 the Alpha Assembly of Glass Workers, Sunderland, England, had 1,000 members and there were other locals at St. Helens, Liverpool, London, Birmingham, and Glasgow.

---

[18] *Journal,* p. 644.
[19] Swinton, *op. cit.,* May 4, 1884.
[20] *Proceedings,* 1885 General Assembly, pp. 127, 133.
[21] Swinton, *op. cit.,* July 19, 1885.

There was a glovers' local in Brussels and a glass workers' local at Charleroi.[22]

The success of the Window Glass Workers was not lost on other glass workers, nor on the Order. In 1885 it was said that the Flint Glass Workers, Bottle Glass and Druggist Glass Blowers' League was ready to enter the Knights. In 1886, Powderly recommended that A. G. Denny of Local Assembly No. 300 be sent as special organizer to bring all glass workers into the Order. He went himself to the convention of the Eastern Glass Bottle Blowers' Association in July and invited them to join. "We do not beg you to come in . . ." he said, "but I ask you for your own sake. In doing this you are not asked to surrender the right to regulate your trade in your own way . . . we should not interfere with your right to strike. That is your own affair, but if you are doubtful of the result, call on the General Executive Board and let them have a chance to settle the matter. . . . Beyond that manage your own affairs." The convention voted forty-two to twenty-six to join the Order.[23] This attitude was a little strange for Powderly, but it is explained by the success of the Window Glass Workers and the conflict with the trade unions which had become acute by the summer of 1886. The Glass Blowers' League, eastern division, received a trade district charter and became District Assembly No. 149. In 1887 a split occurred in the new district and the district master workman resurrected the League in New Jersey. Denny reported that two-thirds of the members had gone back to the open organization.[24]

Factional difficulties within Local Assembly No. 300 and financial troubles with the general officers of the Order

---

[22] *Journal*, September, 1885, p. 1087.
[23] Swinton, *op. cit.*, July 25, 1886.
[24] *Proceedings*, 1887 General Assembly, pp. 1334-36.

cropped up at the New Orleans General Assembly in 1894, and in 1896 the Window Glass Workers settled their accounts and withdrew from the Order. They returned again in 1897, according to Hayes, but this probably meant little. The story of their difficulties with the Knights in decline is not worth recording.[25]

THE SHOEMAKERS

The importance of the shoemakers in the Knights of Labor can hardly be overestimated. They were the largest single craft group in the Order, from them came at least four of the most prominent leaders of the Knights, Ralph Beaumont, Charles Litchman, Richard Griffiths, and James P. Wright, and they carried over into the new organization certain very definite ideas out of their experience with the Knights of St. Crispin.

The Knights of St. Crispin, from 1868 to 1870, was the largest and strongest trade union in the United States. Catching the manufacturers unawares it had a remarkable but temporary success with strikes. The employers organized, and from 1870 strikes were consistently lost. Cooperation was attempted all through this period but its success was short lived. In 1875 an attempt was made to revive the Crispins with a policy of "arbitration" in place of strikes. The revival was a failure and by 1878 the shoemakers were without a union.

Four of the thirty-three delegates at the first General Assembly of the Knights of Labor in 1878 were shoemakers and they brought their experience, and what they believed to be the lessons from that experience, with them. They had seen an aggressive strike policy fail before organized capital in an industry that was being rapidly mechanized,

---

[25] *Ibid.*, 1896 General Assembly, pp. 27-30, 43-4; 1897 General Assembly, pp. 28-30.

and this had converted them to "arbitration." They had tried coöperation and had had a flurry in politics but were not completely disillusioned about either. And they had failed as an isolated trade union.

The ideas of the Knights of Labor so dovetail into this experience that it is not an unwarranted supposition that the new Order built upon the ruins of the old. The new Order was opposed to strikes and in favor of arbitration. It was interested in coöperation and in politics. And above all it stood for the solidarity of labor against isolated trade unions.

In 1873 shoemaker sojourners left Local Assembly No. 1 and organized a shoemakers' local, No. 64, in Philadelphia, with Harry Skeffington as master workman. A second shoemakers' local, No. 280, was formed in Cincinnati in 1877, and the first woman's local in the Order was Garfield Assembly No. 1684, organized at Philadelphia in September, 1881. In 1882 Secretary Layton saw the opportunity of organizing a strong group of shoemakers' locals in Massachusetts and the next year District Assembly No. 63 was formed in Rochester, N. Y., of shoemakers' locals. A movement toward a national trade district began in July, 1883, when Local Assembly No. 64 of Philadelphia asked permission to withdraw from District Assembly No. 1 and attach itself to District Assembly No. 63. To this, District Assembly No. 1 objected and Local Assembly No. 64 was persuaded to ask for a shoemakers' district in Philadelphia.[26] At the same time three requests to form shoemakers' districts were granted.[27]

The cause of this movement toward a national trade

[26] *Ibid.*, 1883 General Assembly, p. 455.
[27] *Ibid.*, pp. 438, 443, 499, 502.
From District Assembly No. 24, Chicago; District Assembly No. 63, Rochester—already in effect a trade district—and from Local Assembly No. 1715.

district of shoemakers is to be found in part in the failure
of District Assembly No. 1 and the general officers to protect the shoemakers at Allentown, Pa. On Jan. 16,
1883, a wage scale was presented to the five shoe shops in
Allentown and rejected by three of them. One shop refused to reëmploy the men unless they agreed to leave
the Order. The general executive board was asked by
Secretary Turner of District Assembly No. 1 to assess the
Knights to protect these men, but refused, because of
the uselessness of such an assessment on the one hand and
of the stringent laws of the Order on the other. The laws
were always stringent when it was considered useless to
do anything. District Assembly No. 1 did what it could to
support the locked-out shoemakers and the general executive board imported good Knights from Cincinnati to place
in the shops to convert the scabs or get them to quit. In
this way "a large number of scabs were transported"—
it is to be hoped to a better place—and the firm was "pre-
vailed upon to withdraw its objection provided the men
would return quietly as individuals." These are the words
of the board which seemed to regard this as a reasonable
compromise. But it is hard to discover what objections
the firm had withdrawn when it took the men back "as
individuals." This is as good an illustration as any of
the weakness of the general officers in trade disputes. They
regarded themselves as arbitrators and were so impartial
that they settled any way just to maintain peace. The
shoemakers of Allentown however refused to return on
those terms, District Assembly No. 1 withdrew its support,
"and the men have since been left almost to their own
resources." [28]

No stronger argument for trade districts in the Order
could have been made than the experience of the Allen-

---

[28] *Ibid.*, p. 456.

town shoemakers. The mixed district was unable to support its local on the basic demand for recognition and the general executive board did not seem even to realize that an agreement that the men should go back "as individuals" was far worse for the Order than no agreement at all. For a union to be beaten and the men forced to return as individuals is one thing, but when it agrees to be beaten on the question of recognition it should cease pretending that it is a union. It is a tribute to the shoemakers' patience that they remained in the Order and a tribute to their intelligence that they established trade districts as fast as possible.

In June, 1884, thirteen shoemakers' locals in Philadelphia withdrew from District Assembly No. 1 and organized trade district No. 70 [29] and in January, 1885, a trade agreement was drawn up between the Philadelphia manufacturers and the Knights providing for a joint board of arbitration to deal with disputes. Pending negotiation and arbitration, strikes and lockouts were prohibited.[30] This machinery broke down in 1886 because of "illegal" strikes called "vacations," and in 1887 the Philadelphia employers combined to lock out the vacationists and broke the union.[31]

By September, 1884, there were five district assemblies of shoemakers in the Knights, and District Assembly No. 70 decided to call a convention to form a national trade district. This convention was postponed, perhaps because of unfavorable replies, and a second call was sent out March 16, 1885, citing the Window Glass Workers as an example of what could and should be done by the shoemakers under the constitutional provisions made in 1882 and 1884 for national trade districts. This convention

---

[29] Swinton, *op. cit.*, June 15, 1884.
[30] A. E. Galster, *The Labor Movement in the Shoe Industry*, pp. 55-6.
[31] *Ibid.*, pp. 65, 73.

was held in Philadelphia, June, 1885, and the Executive Council of Shoe and Leather Workers, Knights of Labor, was organized. It decided to hold a meeting in Detroit in 1886.[32]

At Haverhill, Mass., July 20, 1885, District Assembly No. 30 ordered a strike in the leather factory of Clerk and Lennox against a foreman, a suspended member of the Knights, "obnoxious" to the men. The factory started a branch in Wilmington, Del., to escape the Order but Local Assembly No. 3947 of Wilmington succeeded in organizing the branch. The strike was won, wages advanced, and the foreman and twenty-five nonunion workers were discharged.[33] Even if this is an exaggerated account, it shows the value of the widespread organization of the Order to a trade within it. A national union under the same circumstances would have had to organize the Wilmington branch after it was established on nonunion lines, for the firm would certainly not establish a branch where the union already existed. With the Knights it was almost impossible to find a place where there were no locals at all.

The only important trade union in the industry outside the Knights of Labor was the Lasters' Protective Union organized in 1869 and confined to New England. With this organization the Knights worked in unusual harmony for some years. On Nov. 12, 1885, forty-two shoe manufacturers of Brockton issued a statement expressing their belief "in the individual right of all, to hire or discharge whomsoever he may choose, as well as the workman's right to work whenever and wherever it is for his interest so to do." [34] The sentiment like the language may have been somewhat archaic but the intention was clear

---

[32] Swinton, *op. cit.*, June 21, 1885.

[33] *Journal*, July, 1885.

[34] George E. McNeill, *The Labor Movement: The Problem of To-day*, p. 209.

enough. The Lasters struck and with the aid of the Knights of Labor forced the forty-two combined individualists to change their philosophy. The "Philadelphia Rules" were adopted: the right of the employer to hire and fire provided that no employee was fired for membership in a labor society; the ten-hour day; the joint committee of arbitration; the outlawry of strikes and lockouts; [35] the standard scale for piece workers; and the settlement of day and week work wages by individual agreement. This agreement was signed by the Knights of Labor, the Lasters' Union, and the Trimmers and Setters. In 1886 the Lasters' Union of Lynn asked the general executive board "how they might be identified with the Knights of Labor and still keep their organization entire." They were told they might organize assemblies of their trade and form a trade district.[36]

But this harmony between the Lasters and the Knights was too good to last. In Worcester, Mass., in January, 1887, nineteen manufacturers combined to establish "individual" bargaining because they were tired of being pestered by union committees. They gave each employee a list of twenty questions which may or may not have been the origin of the "Ask Me Another" craze. Among them was the rather ambiguous, "Are you a member of any labor organization and what?" The Lasters struck, perhaps as the only answer they could find to this question. The Knights followed suit [37] but not completely. District Assembly No. 30 seems to have supported the strike, but the general executive board did not. It was lost, and the Lasters, according to a prejudiced source, predicted that

---

[35] This outlawry of strikes and lockouts is by no means the fifty-fifty proposition it may appear on the surface. The employer can always discharge men individually without resort to a lockout to achieve his end. It is not so easy for the union to camouflage a strike by withdrawal of its members as individuals.

[36] *Proceedings,* 1886 General Assembly, p. 106.

[37] *Journal,* March, 1887, pp. 2337-38.

"at the conclusion of this struggle many branches of the shoe trade will withdraw from the Knights of Labor and become trades unions like ourselves." [38] McNeill, who was a member of the Order and usually very fair to both sides, blamed this defeat on Powderly, who, he said, had declared that if he had only 5,000 men left "they will go where I say or they will not go anywhere." [39]

It must be noted, however, that both McNeill and Powderly were budding authors at this time and had quarreled as authors will about precedence. The labor movement had become a subject of sufficient interest to impress publishers. Books on it were in demand and there was a rush to get into print. McNeill got there first and published his book in 1887, a compilation of accounts by trade union leaders, edited and partly written by himself. He put Powderly's name at the head of the associate editors though the articles on the Knights of Labor were written or compiled by himself. Powderly's contribution was a short thing on unemployment, probably a reprint of some newspaper or magazine article. Powderly protested vigorously that he had no connection with any man's book and McNeill evidently felt that this had hurt his sales. It is just possible that author's pique may have had something to do with the breach between the two men though Powderly was quite capable of saying but not doing the thing McNeill reported.

Whatever the source there is no doubt about the fact that dual unionism in 1887 was causing trouble. The American Federation of Labor and the Knights were fighting it out all along the line and the Knights were getting the worst of it. The impression left by this struggle has been that dual unionism is unworkable. It is certainly difficult,

---

[38] Cigar Makers' *Journal,* May, 1887.
[39] Swinton, *op. cit.,* July 3, 1887.

but before 1887 the Knights were able to get along in many places with all sorts of unions and with some unions everywhere. The destruction of the Knights did not end jurisdictional disputes, and the troubles between the Knights and the unions after 1887 were more frequent and severe than before, largely because war had been declared between the two national organizations. Before 1886 the conflicts between the Knights and the unions, aside from the Cigar Makers, were less violent than many recent jurisdictional disputes in the building trades.

The difficulty was real enough if not inherent in dual organization. At Alton, N. H., the Lasters called a strike in which they seem to have been joined by one Knights of Labor assembly.[40] A representative of District Assembly No. 30 and a representative of the Lasters made a settlement with the firm and the former recommended that in future no assembly should strike to sustain the Lasters' Union before a conference was had between representatives of the two organizations, "and all other means of adjustment had failed and upon the Lasters' Union pledging itself to support the Knights of Labor under similar circumstances." He also recommended that no member of the Lasters' Union should be allowed to vote in an assembly on a request to strike coming from the Lasters.[41]

But at Brockton the Lasters and the Knights continued to work together. On Aug. 6, 1887, forty-three lasters struck in the William L. Douglas factory. Douglas had been a member of the Knights and asked them to take the places of the lasters. Their reply was in the very best manner of the time. "We consider," they said, "his invitation to members of the Knights of Labor to take the place of the union lasters on strike an insult to the organiza-

---

[40] No. 4801.
[41] *Proceedings,* 1887 General Assembly, pp. 1329-30.

tion." [42]   That this item was published in Gompers' paper proves conclusively that chivalry, though sore beset in many quarters, still lived.

The executive council of the Shoe and Leather Workers drifted away from the Knights, and the shoemakers themselves began to split along the lines created by machine specialization. On Nov. 10, 1886, the "Boot and Shoe Cutters International Assembly of the U. S. and Canada," all Knights of Labor, was organized at Philadelphia,[43] evidently an attempt on the part of a skilled group in the industry to disengage itself from the mass but remain in the Order, and a last attempt to create a national district of shoemakers within the Order was made at Brockton in June, 1887, when District Assembly No. 70 again called a convention to meet in conjunction with the executive council of the Shoe and Leather Workers. The result was the formation of National Trade Assembly No. 216 of the Knights of Labor [44] with H. J. Skeffington at its head. But it was too late. In trying to get the shoe assemblies together Skeffington had trouble with District Assembly No. 30, Massachusetts, and District Assembly No. 48, Cincinnati. He was cited for suspension by the 1888 General Assembly, but received instead a reprimand by the grand master workman to which he submitted under protest.[45] Probably Skeffington had been less than diplomatic in Cincinnati but Powderly's reprimand which ended "go and sin no more" [46] was an absurd and insulting statement to make to any man before the General Assembly.

Previous to this, at the convention of the National Trade Assembly 216 at Rochester, it had been decided to "adhere

---

[42] *Union Advocate,* September, 1887.
[43] Swinton, *op. cit.,* Nov. 14, 1886.
[44] Shoemakers.
[45] *Proceedings,* 1888 General Assembly, pp. 61, 64, 66 and 79-82.
[46] *Ibid.,* p. 97.

to the Knights of Labor if harmony is maintained and difficulties cleared up," but at the same time authority was given to the officers to form a national trade union under the name "United Boot and Shoe Workers National Trade Assembly" after taking a vote of the locals.[47]

Powderly's ridiculous or perhaps vindictive reprimand of Skeffington was not likely to maintain harmony nor to clear up difficulties and one month after the 1888 General Assembly, a convention of National Trade Assembly 216 was held at Indianapolis to which Powderly was invited but did not go. On Feb. 19, 1889, Skeffington issued a circular asking all assemblies in the shoemakers' district to surrender their charters as Knights of Labor and organize as locals of the Boot and Shoe Workers International Union, affiliated with the American Federation of Labor.[48] The cutters remained Knights of Labor some time longer.

There seems to be no moral here, but it is true, for whatever reason, that the shoemakers have never since been so thoroughly organized as they were under the Knights of Labor. Specialization has driven them apart and destroyed the solidarity for which the Knights stood.

THE MINERS

The Knights of Labor organized early among the miners and the latter remained in the Order longer than any other large trade group. The two industrial unions of the American Federation of Labor, the Miners and the Brewers, grew up in the Knights, severed their connections late and the explanation of their industrial character is to be found in this relationship.

The reason for the success of the Knights among the miners was that the former grew strong when the open

---

[47] Galster, *op. cit.*, pp. 62-3.
[48] *Ibid.*, p. 63.

unions in the mining regions were destroyed. The open unions revived, however, and they and the Knights coöperated, fought, and finally united to form the United Mine Workers of America, until very recently one of the two largest unions in the United States.

The miners' unions have had the most varied experience both as to numbers and extent of organization of any large industrial group. The soft coal area of the United States is so widespread that national organization has never been completely attained except in name. Organizations have grown in one state or district and another, and have come together as "national" unions but even this modified national spread has never been of long duration as compared with other industries. The soft coal industry will be one of the last to reach the stage of large-scale production and the control of output. As Hamilton and Wright have shown, it is the best existing example of how the competitive system, so lauded by the older economists, does not work.[49]

The American Miners' Association was organized in 1861 in Illinois and Missouri with Daniel Weaver as president. In 1863, the Massillon Miners' Association was formed in the Tuscarawas Valley of Ohio. The latter was broken up in 1867-68 by unsuccessful strikes, and an attempt to revive it in 1869-70 failed. In 1871, the Illinois Miners' Benevolent and Protective Association was founded but did not survive.

In the Pennsylvania anthracite region the Miners' and Mine Laborers' Benevolent Association was organized in Schuylkill County in 1868. It spread into Ohio in 1869, and under the leadership of John Siney, through Pennsylvania, Ohio, Maryland, and Indiana. In October, 1873, Siney organized the National Association of Miners at Youngstown, Ohio, and absorbed the Miners and Mine

---

[49] W. H. Hamilton and H. R. Wright, *The Case of Bituminous Coal.*

Laborers. This first "national" union among the miners was said to have a membership of 21,200 in 1874. It was modeled after the British union and its leaders were opposed to strikes and interested in arbitration and coöperation. A wage increase was arbitrated in Ohio but the union failed to live up to the decision. This, and repeated strikes, and the arrest of Siney and Parks in Clearfield County, Pa., broke up the organization. Siney retired discouraged and John James closed the affairs of the National Association of Miners in 1876, after an attempt at coöperative mining in Tennessee. Meantime the Molly Maguires had run their course. The "long strike" in 1874-75 among the anthracite miners had destroyed their organization. There was nothing but the Knights of Labor, and in 1875-76 the miners began to flock into the Order.

In Maryland, District Assembly No. 25 was practically a trade district of miners and throughout the mining regions the secret assemblies of the Knights replaced the open locals which had lost their national and district organization. Christopher Evans went into Hocking Valley in 1875 to collect funds for the Pennsylvania miners in the "long strike." He went as a member of the open union but he held at the same time a commission as organizer for the Knights of Labor, issued by John Davis of the Pittsburgh District Assembly No. 3. He organized Local Assembly No. 120, at New Straitsville, Ohio, in October, 1875. This was later attached to District Assembly No. 7 which, with District Assembly No. 9 became almost exclusively miners' districts.[50] In 1877, H. W. Smith organized thirty assemblies in Illinois.[51]

The revival of mining and the miners' organization began

---

[50] Christopher Evans, *History of the United Mine Workers of America*, p. 78.

[51] Andrew Roy, *A History of the Coal Miners of the United States*, p. 135.

in 1879 along the Monongahela and Youghiogheny rivers in District Assembly No. 9. A strike was called to recover some part of the reductions made during the depression, and was about to be lost when David R. Jones learned that coal reserves were low. He held the men out until they gained their increase and became the absolute head of the miners in the district. In 1880, under John McBride, the miners of the Tuscarawas Valley got an increase and in April formed the Ohio Amalgamated Association. In March, 1882, District Assembly No. 45 went on strike for nearly eight months against a reduction and the iron-clad. They sent Myles McPadden to Clearfield, Pa., and in July the Clearfield miners strucⁱ for the Maryland scale. McPadden and thirteen Knights were arrested. The Order retained counsel for their defense but the strike in Maryland was lost.[52] In November, 1882, the Colorado and New Mexico miners were organized by the Knights [53] and in 1883 "a practical coal miner" was appointed by the grand master workman "for the purpose of organizing the coal miners of the United States into the Knights of Labor." [54] At Pittsburgh, the same year, a national organization was formed on paper but the Hocking Valley strike, June, 1884, to March, 1885, destroyed the open union in Ohio and the Knights' locals with it.[55]

The National Federation of Miners and Mine Laborers,

---

[52] *Proceedings,* 1882 General Assembly, pp. 323-24.

[53] *Journal,* p. 863.

[54] *Proceedings,* 1883 General Assembly, p. 438.

[55] There was a suggestion here of possible trouble growing out of dual unionism, but it amounted to little at this time. McClelland, reporting to the 1884 General Assembly for the executive board, "called attention to the controlling power of the Miners' Association [Ohio] who for better or for worse draw our members into difficulty. . . ." But he asked that the regular order of business be suspended to take up the question of helping the Hocking Valley miners and on a motion of Horan of New York a call was made on the Assistance Fund for District Assemblies Nos. 7 and 9. (*Proceedings,* 1884 General Assembly,

the second so-called national open union in the period, was organized at Indianapolis, Sept. 9, 1885, by John McBride, Daniel McLaughlin of Illinois, John H. Davis, and Chris Evans, all Knights of Labor. With the coöperation of one of the operators, W. P. Rend, a joint conference with the operators was held at Pittsburgh in December, 1885. At Columbus, Feb. 23, 1886, the Pittsburgh scale—establishing differentials for all fields covered by the agreement—was adopted, and a national board of conciliation and arbitration was set up.

After this the conflict between the Knights of Labor and the miners' open national union became acute. Chris Evans, who was active in the formation of the open union, makes much in his history of the precedence of the National Federation in point of time over the Knights of Labor National Trade District 135. He insists that this district was formed after the Federation and in order to fight it. It is possible that the organization of the Federation speeded up the Knights, but they had moved toward a national trade district of miners a year before the Federation was organized. At the General Assembly, September, 1884, representatives of the miners' assemblies had resolutions asking for the calling of a convention of the miners for this purpose but the resolutions were mislaid. On Oct. 25, 1884, a notice was inserted in the *Journal* asking all miners' assemblies to vote on the proposal for a national convention and send the returns to Bailey who was to call such a convention not later than February, 1885.[56] Although the National Trade District 135 was not completed until 1886 and may have

p. 567.) Meanwhile $2,000 was sent to these districts. (*Ibid.*, p. 655.) Another complaint of the same sort came from Du Bois, Pa. (*Ibid.*, p. 641) and District Assembly No. 11 said that because of the importation of Hungarians, the use of detectives, and religious controversies the miners' assemblies were breaking up. (*Ibid.*, p. 624.)

[56] *Journal*, p. 823.

been brought to a head by the organization of the Federation, it was tardiness more than anything else that prevented its formation in February, 1885, at least six months before the formation of the Federation. Evans later went into the American Federation of Labor and his history is somewhat influenced by the ancient controversy.

When the National Federation was formed in 1885 there were hundreds of miners' assemblies all through the mining states which had, for some time, regarded the Order as the national representative of the miners, and at the Hamilton General Assembly of 1885, held in the same month as the miners' federation was formed, the Knights of Labor miners received permission to organize a National Trade Assembly like that of the Glass Workers.[57] This was carried out at St. Louis, May 20, 1886, and William H. Bailey, a member of the general executive board, and one of the new men among the general officers was made master workman. The first convention of this National Trade Assembly 135, Miners and Mine Laborers, was held at Indianapolis, September, 1886. Bailey expressed the point of view of the Knights in a communication to the *Journal*.

Heretofore we have been content to remain Knights of Labor in the primitive meaning of the name, mingling with other crafts, learning their grievances and sources of oppression, exchanging sympathy, ideas and aid, and imbibing that true spirit of social equality and fraternal feeling that must characterize every trade and calling if we would rise to the true dignity of labor. But along with the above our Order demands and our own interest compels us to have an intelligent and thorough knowledge of matters pertaining to the mining interest. The rapid increase of miners and mine laborers in the Order indicated that the time had arrived to unite all of our calling into a distinct body based upon the substantial principles of the world's educator—the Knights of Labor.[58]

---

[57] *Proceedings*, 1885 General Assembly, pp. 126-27.
[58] *Journal*, July, 1886, p. 2113.

It is not necessary to take this at its face value. Bailey was no more disinterested than any other labor leader seeing his organization being taken away from him. But his is a good statement of the trade point of view within the Knights, even if it came late enough to suggest that the activity of the open unions forced it upon the Order.

The center of the new movement was New Straitsville and Shawnee, Ohio, Local Assemblies Nos. 120 and 169 under District Assembly No. 7, but a similar demand came from Sedalia, Mo. It seems, however, to have been more successful in the Pittsburgh district where the Amalgamated Association was weak. Costello, president of the Amalgamated Association, was made organizer for the Knights, and at Banksville, Dec. 3, 1886, the Amalgamated disbanded and went over to the Order.[59]

Thus, while the miners had been without a national organization from 1876 to 1885, they found themselves with two in 1886—the National Federation and National Trade District 135. It is impossible to say which was the stronger numerically, but the open union by its joint conference with the operators was in a better position. The early attitude of the Federation toward District 135 was one of pained surprise which developed quickly into open antagonism. At the second convention at Indianapolis in 1886, the Federation declared, "We will not tolerate any organization that seeks to destroy trade unions," and refused to take District 135 representatives into the joint conference. But Bailey was a fighter and loyalty to the Order was strong among the miners. Organizers were sent out and a disastrous internecine war began. The Federation became alarmed and invited the district into the joint conference but this was refused, and in January, 1887, the Ohio Miners' state convention ordered its members to withdraw from the

<hr>

[59] Swinton, *op. cit.*, Dec. 12, 1886.

Knights if the war were not stopped.[60] In April, however, the Federation again approached District 135 and a joint meeting of the two unions was arranged for June 3. But the joint conference between the Federation and the operators was held in May, so that District 135 could not participate in the agreement for the following year.[61]

At the Cincinnati convention of National Trade District 135 in June, 1887, Bailey resigned and was succeeded by William T. Lewis. Bailey had trouble within the Order as well as outside. Mixed districts in mining regions were protesting that the withdrawal of the miners' locals to enter 135 meant their destruction and some miners' locals were reluctant to enter the miners' district.[62] Powderly was antagonistic. He refused to allow miners' locals in his own district, No. 16, to be transferred to 135.[63] The two "B's"— Bailey and Barry—were the pet abominations of the general master workman and he was able to get rid of them in time.

Lewis seems to have tried to turn his organization over to the Federation. A conference was held Dec. 5, 1888, to discuss amalgamation, but the Knights would agree only to coöperate with the open union, while the latter would agree only to a change of name. Negotiation was proceeding when the Federation seems to have demanded that

---

[60] *Ibid.*, Jan. 30, 1887.

[61] The above account is taken largely from Roy and differs considerably from Evans who is less reliable. Evans has it that McBride wrote Bailey in April suggesting a meeting of the two organizations before the joint conference in May, but in the same letter McBride said he had no confidence in Bailey. The latter replied that he would meet the Federation in June at the regular convention of National Trade District 135 at Cincinnati. The officers of the Federation refused to go but suggested that No. 135 pass resolutions showing their readiness to amalgamate with the Federation. (Evans, *op. cit.*, Vol. I, p. 236.)

[62] *Proceedings*, 1887 General Assembly, pp. 1700-1.

[63] *Ibid.*, 1888, General Assembly, p. 10.

the Knights should give up their identity altogether. Lewis and his following went into the Federation which was reorganized with John McBride, president, as the National Progressive Union. Lewis was made secretary and the new organization joined the American Federation of Labor.

But National Trade District 135 remained with John W. Rae, master workman, and Robert Watchorn, secretary-treasurer. Roy says that the miners' Federation made a mistake in "peremptorily" ordering the Knights to disband "their splendid national district," and that no compromise could have been satisfactory that did not admit 135 on an equality with the open Federation. "When the Progressive Union was ready to do this the way was clear." Evans' story of the same period is so involved and incomplete as to be unintelligible. He first gives the impression that the defection of Lewis was a bona fide amalgamation and later gives the story of the real amalgamation of 1890 without explaining why the first did not work out.

Because of the continued split between the miners' unions, the joint conference with the operators in February, 1889, broke up without accepting a scale. In September, at Wilkes-Barre, 135 proceeded to call a meeting of all organized and unorganized miners in the United States to take action on various matters of which the consolidation of the miners' unions was one. The Progressive Union joined with the Knights and asked their members to send delegates to Columbus, Jan. 22-24, 1890, to vote on the following:[64]

1. Unification under one head without the sacrifice of the essential features of either union.

2. The maintenance of national, district, and local unions, either secret or open as the members desired.

---

[64] Evans says that the Progressive Union issued the call for this convention and the Knights approved it but it matters little one way or the other. The above is Roy's account.

3. Equal taxation.
4. One staff of officers.

The conference met at Columbus on Jan. 23, 1890, and with the blessing of both Gompers and Powderly all four propositions were accepted. The new organization took the name, United Mine Workers of America, and elected John Rae (Knights) president, William Turner (Progressives) vice president, and Robert Watchorn (Knights), secretary-treasurer. The United Mine Workers remained affiliated with both the American Federation of Labor and the Knights of Labor.

Thus dual unionism of five years' standing was finally settled, largely because the split had almost destroyed both organizations. At the time of the amalgamation there were not quite 17,000 members in the two unions, 60 per cent of whom seem to have belonged to District Assembly No. 135 and 40 per cent to the Progressive Union. By the end of 1890 the membership was said to have doubled and the increase was about equal in each branch.[65]

At the first convention of the United Mine Workers, Feb. 16, 1891, their own success at amalgamation led to an attempt to take the rival parent organizations by the hand. They proposed a treaty between the Knights of Labor and the American Federation of Labor on the basis of the mutual recognition of working cards and labels, and coöperation in dealing with expelled members. But it is significant that the name of the miners' new organization was changed back to the "United Mine Workers of National

---

[65] These figures are not necessarily reliable. The official reports give the membership as follows:

1890	23,573
1891	26,665 (May)
1892	14,595 (Jan.)
1893	24,023 (Mar.)

(Evans, *op. cit.*, Vol. II, p. 257.)

District Assembly 135, Knights of Labor, and the National Progressive Union." That surely covered everything.

In June, 1892, Rae resigned as president and was succeeded by John McBride. According to Evans there had been a great falling off in membership under Rae which was quickly recovered under McBride. At any rate, under the latter the miners were becoming more an open and less a Knights of Labor organization, and at the 1892 General Assembly, Powderly complained and asked that District 135 withdraw from the Order. This recommendation with Hayes' amendment as to how National Trade Assembly 135 should be reorganized was passed; but a more drastic amendment of Hicks, District Assembly No. 253, that all members of the Order holding cards in unions affiliated with the American Federation of Labor, withdraw from one or the other, was defeated after Powderly had spoken against it.[66] Rae and Watchorn had promised Powderly when the amalgamation was agreed to in 1890, that the United Mine Workers in two years would become completely a Knights of Labor organization. They probably intended that it should, but it did not, and Powderly felt cheated.

The villain in the play seems to have been John Hayes, general secretary-treasurer of the Order. He not only misled Powderly in 1892, but in 1890 he seems to have conspired with Watchorn to bolster up the strength of 135 so as to secure a larger representation than it was entitled to when the amalgamation with the Progressives was consummated. On Oct. 29, 1889, Hayes wrote Watchorn that District 135 was entitled to only three delegates to the General Assembly as its numbers were about 10,000. But the District actually sent seven delegates which would indicate a strength of double what it actually had. Watchorn seems to have been responsible for this, but Hayes must

---

[66] *Proceedings*, 1892 General Assembly, pp. 7, 8, 53-56.

have agreed to it because he was afraid that the district would be "scooped up" by the Progressives in the amalgamation. Later Hayes wrote Watchorn "your seven delegates racket has skinned us out of $88—on mileage. Can't you get up some sort of scheme to make 135 pay it back to us?" [67]

In 1893 Powderly confessed to the General Assembly that he had been misled and withdrew his recommendation made at the previous General Assembly that 135 leave the United Mine Workers.[68] McBride accepted the apology but under him the Knights of Labor element in the United Mine Workers was disappearing. The arrangements made in 1890 were only technically carried out and 135 was being absorbed by the open union. Powderly was defeated in 1893 and under Sovereign the General Assembly of 1894 went back to the Powderly recommendation of 1892 which he had withdrawn. The committee to which the matter was referred stated positively that there was no such organization as District 135, that the so-called National Trade Assembly was "dominated and controlled" by officials of the United Mine Workers, and that the 1890 General Assembly had not ratified the amalgamation. On its recommendation, after a long fight, most of the delegates from National Trade District 135 were refused admission to the assembly, the resolutions of 1892 to reorganize a pure and simple Knights' district were readopted, and the Progressives were invited to join the Knights "with a view to reorganizing the now disorganized miners of the country." [69]

The United Mine Workers had practically disappeared in the strike of April, 1894, which lasted eight weeks and was lost. At the beginning of the strike, which was intended to

---

[67] Evans, *op. cit.*, Vol. II, p. 322-24.
The letters are reproduced.
[68] *Proceedings*, 1894 General Assembly, pp. 125-26, 131.
[69] *Ibid.*

reduce the coal reserves and maintain the wages of 1893, a hopeless prospect in view of the panic, the union had only 13,000 paid-up members and 24,000 in good standing. Nevertheless, 124,000 struck and later additions brought the number up to 180,000, or practically the entire mining community of the country. At the end of the strike there was a return to district agreements and the national union disappeared.[70]

District 135 having been thrown out of the Knights seems to have led or joined an Independent Order in 1895. What was left of it and the old Progressives remained together as best they could through the depression, and in 1898 the United Miners of America revived under the name it had taken in 1890 unhyphenated by reference to its constituent parts. The Order attempted to reorganize the miners but with little success.

THE BREWERS

The Brewers' was the second industrial union within the American Federation of Labor to emerge in that form from the Knights of Labor and to retain it because of their long connection with the Order. They had been organized in local benefit societies in the fifties, but had no bargaining union until 1879 when a Cincinnati local asked the employers for a ten-and-one-half-hour day in place of the thirteen hours they had been working, a minimum wage of $60 a month, and the reduction of hours on Sunday from eight to four. The brewers were mostly Germans and worked under conditions brought over from Europe in a semidomestic type of industrial organization. The Cincinnati movement failed and the union disappeared. In 1881, a similar attempt failed in St. Louis, and in New

---

[70] Evans, *op. cit.*, Vol. II, p. 372.

York, the same year, the Brewery Workers' Union of New York and vicinity was organized. It struck in June for a ten-hour day, two hours on Sundays, and a wage of 50 cents an hour, and was helped by a boycott by the Central Labor Union and the central committee of the Socialist Party. But the strike was lost after five weeks and the members of the union were blacklisted. Many of the leaders had to leave New York.[71]

The statistician of the insurgent Brooklyn local of the Knights of Labor, No. 1562, reported that the New York brewers had come "to the conclusion that their open organization had been a sad failure. Their strike has scattered the men in all directions and their best men cannot find employment because they are placed on the blacklist. They have resolved to join us in a body. Over 800 men are ready to form a trades' assembly. They see the necessity of organizing secretly. Capital in the large cities is too powerful; we cannot fight it openly. . . ."[72] The men in the Kuntz brewery decided "after the defeat and destruction of the Brewery Workers' Union to form a secret organization" and established a local assembly of the Knights. But "several years elapsed before the brewery workers of New York recovered from the defeat of 1881 and even then an open organization was not to be thought of."[73]

In 1884 the New York brewers appealed to the Central Labor Union to help organize them, and the *Volks-Zeitung* published a notice asking brewers to send their names and addresses to the organizing committee. But the fear of discharge was so great that it took weeks to get a meeting together in secret, and then it disbanded to meet again

---

[71] Where not otherwise specified this record is taken from Herman Schlüter, *The Brewing Industry and the Brewery Workers' Movement in America*.

[72] *Journal*, p. 141.

[73] Schlüter, *op. cit.*, p. 108.

down town "where no one need be afraid of meeting acquaintances." This meeting was held Aug. 10, 1884, and created the Brewers' Union No. 1 of New York, out of which later grew the United Brewery Workmen of America. No. 1 was a secret trade union and at the same time Local Assembly No. 1672, of the Knights of Labor.

In November the secretary of the new union was discharged by his employer and, in 1885, other members were let out by Peter Doelger. The Central Labor Union, under the control of the Home Club, boycotted Doelger's beer and he was finally compelled to recognize the union and pay $1,000 for the cost of the boycott.[74]

The New York Brewers were socialists, and while the secrecy of the Knights was helpful to them in the early years, there was no other bond of union between the two groups. As the Brewers gained strength they left the Order, especially in New York. They complained against the intrigues of District Assembly No. 49 and especially against its insistence that they strike in sympathy with the coal handlers in 1887. They felt strong enough to have an open union and had little use for the secret work. But another reason was Powderly's temperance policy which, if not enthusiastically agreed to by the Order, was long tolerated. In 1889 the General Assembly was asked to boycott the "pool beer" of St. Louis, but the committee reported against it as being "inconsistent and unwise to place the General Assembly on record as legislating on the subject of beer." [75] Personally and professionally the Brewers were offended by

---

[74] Schlüter, op. cit., pp. 115-16. This practice of making the employer pay the cost of a boycott later got the Knights into trouble in the Theiss beer garden boycott and in the Rochester clothing market. In 1886, and later, the courts construed it as blackmail and James Hughes of the Knights' cutters and others were sent to jail. The Knights regarded it as a legitimate practice so long as the money went to the organization.

[75] Proceedings, 1889 General Assembly, p. 53.

these utterances, and this alone no doubt would have led them sooner or later to withdraw from the Knights. In New York, the Ale and Porter Brewers remained as Local Assembly No. 8390 long after the others had left.

In 1886 the brewers were organized in Newark, Baltimore, Philadelphia, St. Louis, Cincinnati, and Chicago. The first society in Newark was Enterprise Assembly Knights of Labor which later became Local Assembly No. 2 of the open union. In St. Louis the Gambrinus Assembly, No. 7503, was started by the Central Labor Union. In Philadelphia the United German Trades organized the brewers into the Knights of Labor and in Cincinnati the Brewers' Union joined the Order. But difficulties soon arose. The Knights were too busy in 1886 to pay much attention to the brewers or any one else. The New York local protested to the general executive board against the action of District Assembly No. 17 of St. Louis in refusing to support a boycott and was curtly informed that District Assembly No. 17 was right "as the fight was with a trade union and not with the Knights of Labor.[76] In 1887, Local Assembly No. 7503 asked permission to leave District Assembly No. 17 and join the German district, No. 191. Bailey was sent to settle the matter and reported that all the complaints of the local were groundless and uncalled for and that he had ordered them to remain in 17.[77] This was the same Bailey who organized the national trade district of miners, No. 135.

The Brewers' National Union was organized in Baltimore, Aug. 29, 1886, and at its convention, Sept. 11, 1887, it adopted resolutions against the Knights because of their stand on temperance. "The Order," it said, "did not support us in any way . . . and we cannot show a single victory which was due to the Knights of Labor." But, in spite of

---

[76] *Proceedings*, 1886 General Assembly, p. 131.

[77] *Ibid.*, 1887 General Assembly, p. 1379.

this, several locals "declared that they were not yet in a position to turn their backs on the Knights of Labor." [78]

In Philadelphia, Local Assembly No. 7086 and the Brewers' Union No. 5 carried on a six months' strike which the Knights boasted ended in an agreement with the employers' association to recognize the Order "to the exclusion of all other labor organizations." [79] The Brewers insisted that the Knights of Labor and the boss brewers had combined to betray the men.[80] The New York *Sun,* then vigorously opposed to the Order, declared that

this action has its counterpart in other matters. . . . Strikes have been declared off and if the local assembly . . . does not obey the order immediately, the assembly is suspended. This was the case with the slaughter-house men in Chicago, the railroad strike in East St. Louis, the tailors' unions in this city. . . . At the present time the Knights oppose granting a charter to a trade district. They oppose open trade unions. They oppose the Central Labor Unions. . . . It is nothing more nor less than the Home Club which is a secret, iron-clad, oath-bound body within the Order of the Knights of Labor controlling and ruling it with a rod of iron.[81]

Louis Herbrand, secretary of the Brewers' National Union, said that Local No. 5 had received $18,000 from the national organization while the assembly, No. 7086, had got no help "moral or financial" from District Assembly No. 1, but was pressed for back dues while supported by the open union.[82]

In Milwaukee, in 1887, the Gambrinus Assembly withdrew from the Order because of the temperance policy.[83]

---

[78] H. Schlüter, *op. cit.,* p. 136.
[79] E. A. Cook, *Knights of Labor,* illustrated, p. 19, not a very reliable source.
[80] *Brewers' Journal,* Jan. 1, 1887.
[81] New York *Sun,* Jan. 1, 1887.
[82] *Union Advocate,* July, 1887.
[83] Swinton, *op. cit.,* July 17, 1887.

In New York all the assemblies withdrew after District Assembly No. 49 had ordered them to support the coal handlers. "But they will resume their connection," said Swinton, "with the Knights of Labor if a charter for a trade district can be obtained. . . ." [84] The Ale and Porter Brewers remained in the Order and in 1888 a strike, boycott, and lockout in one, was decided by arbitration in favor of the men in the employ of Leavy & Britton Brewing Co.[85]

But the matter was still far from settled. In 1889, the general executive board of the Knights of Labor endorsed a boycott on the Anheuser-Busch Company of St. Louis and forced it to capitulate because of their boycott strength, especially in the South. The Knights claimed that this was the first success the Brewers had had after their break with the Order, and the St. Louis assemblies asked the Milwaukee unions in 1892 to return to the Knights.[86] In the same year the Brewers' national convention passed a resolution that, "our organization at the same time form a national trade district within the Knights of Labor so that each local union in case of a struggle may enjoy the support of the American Federation of Labor and the Knights of Labor." This was put to a vote of the members and a great majority were for it. But the American Federation of Labor rejected the proposal and threatened the Brewers with expulsion, and the Knights, while at first insisting that the American Federation of Labor charters be given up, later agreed to the dual affiliation. A brewers' trade district, No. 35, was organized in the Order in 1893, and a considerable number of the locals of the United Brewery Workmen went into it, including those of New York City, which maintained a dual affiliation from 1894 to 1896.

---

[84] *Ibid.*, Feb. 20, 1887.
[85] *Proceedings*, 1888 General Assembly, p. 82.
[86] Schlüter, *op. cit.*, p. 178.

The usual conflict developed within the Order between trade and mixed districts, and in 1894, the trade district asked for complete control of all brewers in the Order. The American Federation of Labor took advantage of this controversy and refused to support the Brewers' label and a boycott in Pittsburgh, until the national union gave up its connection with the Knights. In 1896 the American Federation of Labor ordered the Brewers to dissolve National Trade District 35 or leave the Federation. They dissolved the district "with regret" and the national union, while forced to demand the return of the district charter, advised the locals to join the mixed assemblies of the Order. In retaliation a proposal was made in the 1896 General Assembly to withdraw all Knights from organizations in the American Federation of Labor, but was defeated.[87] Some local brewers' assemblies withdrew from the national union and remained in the Order. In Rochester, N. Y., Local Assembly No. 1796, which was said to have had a contract with the employers' association for fifteen years, refused to leave the Knights and was supported by the city trades' and labor assembly. But "The National Union, assisted by that so-called nothing the American Federation of Labor decided to place a boycott on the beer manufactured in the city of Rochester. . . ."[88] Later some of the employers, probably hurt by the American Federation of Labor boycott, deserted the Knights, and in 1898, Hayes advised what was left of the Order, themselves to boycott Rochester beer. With both organizations refusing to drink the same amber "intoxicant" for different reasons, the Rochester brewers were put in a difficult position, but the cause of temperance was no doubt advanced.

---

[87] *Proceedings,* 1896 General Assembly, p. 97.
[88] *Ibid.,* 1897 General Assembly, p. 46.

Organization among the iron and steel workers began in 1858, when a few puddlers and boilers came together in Pittsburgh and formed a society called the Sons of Vulcan. This expired at once, but was again revived in 1861 and expanded into the National Forge of the Sons of Vulcan, Sept. 8, 1862. In 1867 the union had 1,514 members in 36 forges (locals), but it declined the next year. It established centralized control over strikes in 1870 and built up a strike fund. The membership was 2,000 in 1871 and 3,500 in 1873.

The Associated Brotherhood of Iron and Steel Heaters was formed in August, 1872, and later took in rollers and roughers. It was never large and practically disappeared in 1874-76. At the last convention of 1876 it had only 412 members.

The Iron and Steel Roll Hands Union, including rollers, roughers, catchers, and hookers, was organized June 2, 1873, with 473 members. The industry was shot through with craft exclusiveness and one of the first acts of the Roll Hands was to decide to have nothing to do with the puddlers' and heaters' organizations. It was formed on the eve of the depression and in 1875 had so declined that it sought amalgamation with the other unions in the industry.

The United Nailers never formed a national organization.

At the Columbus convention of the Iron and Steel Roll Hands Union in 1874, the first step toward amalgamation was taken, and in July, 1875, delegates from the Roll Hands attended the Heaters' convention at Covington, Ky. A committee was appointed by the Heaters to confer with both the Roll Hands and the Boilers, and as all of them were in bad shape, the prospect of amalgamation was good. The Boilers seem to have favored amalgamation but took no action. In August, 1875, a joint convention of the Heaters and the Roll Hands was held in Philadelphia while the Boilers' convention was there in session. On Dec. 7, 1875, a joint committee representing the three unions met in Pittsburgh and on Aug. 3, 1876, a joint convention was held with 68 delegates in attendance, 46 from the Sons of Vulcan, 15 from the Heaters' union, 6 from the Roll Hands and one from the Nailers. Here the Amalgamated Association of Iron and Steel Workers was organized.

The Amalgamated had a bad time in 1878-79 with a series of strikes against wage reductions, but in 1879 the industry came out of the long depression of the seventies and the union picked up. Again in 1881 strikes and internal dissension left it weak and it entered the first convention of the Federation of Organized Trades and Labor Unions for support. John Jarret, president of the Amalgamated, was made chairman and secured the adoption of a protection plank. The Federation dropped the protection plank the next year and the Amalgamated withdrew, not to return.

In 1884-85 under President Weihe the Amalgamated declined. The Nailers withdrew in February, 1885, but returned in 1886. Weihe was chairman of the committee of trade union leaders which struggled with the Knights in 1886 and finally formed the American Federation of Labor, but the Amalgamated voted in June of the same year to have nothing to do with the Federation of Trades. Jarrett could give no explanation of this "unless it be that the Amalgamated Association expect the Knights of Labor will eventually represent or what is more proper, actually be the Confederation of Trades." [89]

It was probably this action of the Amalgamated convention which caused Powderly to invite the steel workers

---

[89] McNeill, *op. cit.*, pp. 268-311.

to form a national trade district within the Knights. Immediately after the special session at Cleveland he followed up this invitation by a visit to the Amalgamated convention at Pittsburgh. If the Amalgamated would enter the Order, he promised, "it will retain its separate identity, maintain its system of government, control its own officers and in no wise lose any of its privileges." [90] The convention decided to put the question to a vote of the lodges and the proposal was defeated. It is surprising that it was considered at all in view of the exclusiveness of the steel workers' organization.

Barry had patched up a difficulty between the Amalgamated and a Knights' assembly at Scottsdale, Pa., in 1886, but a further conflict developed at Braddock and Mingo Junction, which, along with the activity of Bailey in organizing assemblies in the steel mills, was instrumental in deciding the Amalgamated to keep out of the Order. In June, 1887, the Amalgamated ordered its members not to join the Knights after April 1, 1888, and decided to go into the new American Federation of Labor.[91] As early as May, 1887, it was reported that the Knights of Labor was trying to organize a national district of iron and steel workers,[92] and the activity of Bailey could always be regarded with suspicion in a case of this sort. This would explain the rapid change of the Amalgamated from a receptive to an antagonistic attitude and the nullifying of Powderly's conciliatory work. It would help too to explain the latter's intense dislike of Bailey.

There was some difficulty in getting a national trade

---

[90] New York *Tribune,* June 5, 1886.

[91] *Proceedings,* 1886 General Assembly, pp. 92-93; J. S. Robinson, *The Amalgamated Association of Iron, Steel and Tin Workers,* Johns Hopkins University Studies, 1920, p. 50; the *Union Advocate,* July, 1887; Swinton, *op. cit.,* June 26, 1887.

[92] Cigar Makers' *Journal,* May, 1887; *Union Advocate,* July, 1887.

district charter for the steel workers, but on June 4, 1888, the first convention of the National Trade District 217, Iron, Steel and Blast Furnacemen, was held. It admitted all workers around the mills and might have forced the Amalgamated to modify its attitude toward the "unskilled," if the latter had listened to its own secretary, William Martin. But it did not and not many years later the once most powerful trade union in the United States was defeated and broken by its own exclusiveness, large-scale, mechanized industry, a gentleman named Frick, and the employees of a Pinkerton.

There followed the reign of the sainted Gary, canonized by a lady who had once crowned the Rockefeller with a brick.

THE CARPENTERS

In 1854, and again in 1867, the carpenters had formed national unions which did not last, and in the seventies they were represented only by a small number of locals of the (English) Amalgamated Society of Carpenters and Joiners. In April, 1881, Peter J. McGuire, having tired somewhat of the innumerable socialist cliques and controversies in all of which he had played a part, and fresh from political achievements in Missouri, started a paper, *The Carpenter*, to try again to organize his old trade. Woodworking machinery was taking the place of hand labor; machine-made doors, sashes, moldings, and window frames were being increasingly used. Piecework was supplanting day work and the subdivision of labor was reducing the demand for skilled mechanics. Wages were low and the apprentice system was out of joint. In a word, the carpenters, too, were feeling the effects of the ever encroaching Industrial Revolution.

McGuire worked fast, favored by a short-lived prosperity,

and on Aug. 8, 1881, the first convention of the Brotherhood of Carpenters and Joiners was held with 36 delegates
representing 12 locals and a total of 2,042 members. A
death benefit was adopted in 1882 and sick and accident
benefits were paid by the locals. The union had its ups
and downs, but in 1886 it claimed to have 24,000 members.[93]
McGuire's attitude toward the Knights of Labor was much
more conciliatory than that of the Cigar Makers. He was,
however, quite as active as Gompers or any one else in
the creation of the American Federation of Labor. When
he called the Philadelphia meeting of the trade union leaders in 1886 he may, as he says, have intended no antagonism
toward the Knights of Labor. The Order was stepping
on the toes of the Carpenters along with the rest of the
unions. It could hardly help it and McGuire, who was not
involved in the New York scramble, may have expected
simply to "devise a plan for alliance and submit it to
the Knights of Labor." Certainly the earlier experience
with a Federation in 1881 gave him no encouragement to
lead a second attempt. The treaty that the Philadelphia
meeting produced was far from conciliatory or even reasonable, but McGuire admitted that it was not intended to be
taken seriously. It was a bargaining offer and might have
been whittled down to little more than a pious wish.

At any rate McGuire insisted that the Philadelphia meeting was not called with the intention of fighting the Order.
He pointed out that it would hardly have been held in
Philadelphia, the home of the Knights, had that been the
intention and at the time of the meeting of the general
executive board.[94] The fact seems to be that the fight
between the Cigar Makers and District Assembly No. 49
had reached the stage at which no compromise could have

---

[93] *The Carpenter,* October, 1886, p. 23. McNeill, *op. cit.,* gives the
number as 21,423, pp. 355-60.
[94] *The Carpenter,* May 2, 1886.

been secured from either side, and after June, when the Home Club got control of the Order, the trade unionists could do nothing but set up a dual national organization. But there is a possibility that McGuire did protest too much. There was good reason for the trade unions to break away from the Knights.

If McGuire was not as bitterly opposed to the Knights as was Gompers, he was opposed for the same reason. The national unions were being carried into the Knights. He felt, with some justification, that the Order should restrict its activities to the unorganized field where no trade unions existed. "But where," he said, "there is a national or international union of a trade the men of that trade should organize under it and . . . the Knights of Labor should not interfere." [95] He complained that the Knights "in various localities were urging our local unions to disband and form local assemblies," and that "expelled members of the Brotherhood and men who have been black-balled have been admitted into the Knights of Labor and under the shield of the Order have made every effort to undermine the Brotherhood." He forgot perhaps that he had once been expelled from the Knights but had got back again by the efforts of District Assembly No. 49, which itself was trying to disrupt the Order and destroy the trade unions. And, finally, in a few cases he found that Knights had forced the members of the Brotherhood out of work by refusing to work with them. All unions, he said, were affected in the same way. [96]

The general officers of the Knights promised that these inroads would be stopped, but the trade unionists were skeptical. Powderly they regarded as sincere in his protestations but unable to control the situation, and some

---

[95] *Ibid.*, February, 1886, p. 4.
[96] *Ibid.*, May, 1886, p. 2.

members of the general executive board were known to be ready to absorb or even destroy the unions.

At Troy, N. Y., the Knights of Labor carpenters refused to work with the Brotherhood and McGuire wrote, March 18, 1886, to General Secretary Turner proposing "a mutual interchange of cards between our respective organizations." This was what the Knights later offered the trade union committee, but at this time they made no reply.[97] McGuire claimed the credit for the Philadelphia meeting of the trade unionists called on April 26. "I discovered," he wrote, "a secret and formidable movement of a certain element within the Knights of Labor bent upon hostility to trade unions and aiming to attack them singly and if possible encompass their destruction." [98] It was hardly as bad as that, and if it was a discovery for McGuire it was an old story with Gompers. McGuire saw, however, no cause for alarm. There was to be no bitter war between the trade unions and the Knights of Labor. The sole object of the Philadelphia conference was to draw up a plan of alliance to submit to the Order.[99]

If the plan had been the same as that already offered by McGuire—the mutual exchange of working cards—the trouble might have been settled easily enough. But either McGuire was romancing or he reckoned without the Cigar Makers. The Philadelphia "treaty" was a very different thing and one that the Knights could not accept.

That the inroads of the Knights upon the Carpenters were real and dangerous to the Brotherhood is indicated by McGuire's conciliatory attitude and by other matters. The Brotherhood local, No. 1 of Washington, D. C., was suspended for failure to pay its assessments and went over

---

[97] McNeill, *op. cit.*, p. 359.
[98] *Ibid.*, pp. 355-56.
[99] *The Carpenter*, May, 1886, p. 2.

to the Knights, taking about $2,000 of the Brotherhood's funds. As the 1886 convention of the union was to be held in Washington this was rather embarrassing and another meeting place had to be found.[100]   In October, 1886, there was a movement to merge all carpenters' locals of the Knights into a national trade district to be called the Progressive Carpenters and Joiners.[101]   This followed the decision of the August convention of the Brotherhood to buy only blue label (International) cigars and a resolution to discourage the organization of carpenters in trade locals under the Knights of Labor.[102]

In the May, 1886, strike for the eight-hour day, the carpenters' central council of Chicago, including the Brotherhood locals, nine Knights of Labor carpenters' assemblies, and locals of the Amalgamated Society, had been more successful than any other carpenters' group in the country. They had obtained a signed agreement from the Master Carpenters' Association guaranteeing the eight-hour day. This was renewed in April, 1887, but after a strike of the bricklayers which threw numbers of carpenters out of work, the Master Carpenters went back to the nine-hour day. The Carpenters, including the nine Knights' assemblies, struck, but there were no funds to support the Knights while the Brotherhood came to the aid of its members.[103] This showed, as did other incidents of the same sort, the need of a national trade assembly and the weakness of the Order where one did not exist.   At the same time, a Knights' local in Chicago asked the general executive board if they might accept a joint card in the central council and increase their dues.   Both requests were granted.   A request from New

[100] *Ibid.*
[101] Swinton, *op. cit.*, Oct. 10, 1886.
[102] *The Carpenter,* January, 1887, p. 2.
[103] *Proceedings,* 1887 General Assembly, pp. 1423-24.

York to form a national trade assembly of carpenters and woodworkers "to include framers, stair builders, sash, blind and door makers and wood-working machine work" was also rather ungraciously agreed to.[104]

The entente between the two carpenter groups in Chicago was broken in 1888 and the Knights' Carpenters formed their own general council (Progressives) while the Brotherhood organized under the United Carpenters' Council. These two were reunited, in part at least, in 1890, when the central council, including the Brotherhood, the Amalgamated, and the Knights, supported by the American Federation of Labor, struck for various conditions including the eight-hour day. The Knights' assemblies were not included in the settlement and appealed for assistance to the General Assembly. This was given in 1890 and again in 1894, but by that time it had degenerated into a quarrel between the Order and the American Federation of Labor.[105]

In New York the Progressive Carpenters' Union and the United Order of Carpenters both broke away from the Brotherhood and joined the Knights in 1890.[106]

THE PRINTERS

The International Typographical Union suffered along with other trade unions in the depression of the seventies. The locals lost most of their members and the national organization had never exercised any great measure of control.[107] It was not until 1884 that the Typographical became anything more than a group of locals whose delegates met annually to discuss strike funds and constitutions.

---

[104] *Ibid.*, pp. 1358, 1360.

[105] *Ibid.*, 1890 General Assembly, pp. 5-6; *Ibid.*, 1894 General Assembly, pp. 162-64.

[106] *Journal*, June 4 and July 10, 1890.

[107] George E. Barnett, *The Printers*, p. 38.

In 1881, because of its weakness, the Typographical took the first steps to create a federation of trades, but the national unions did not respond with the exception of the Cigar Makers, who were not immediately enthusiastic, and when the Federation did organize in November it was composed largely of trades' assemblies and the Knights of Labor.

During the early eighties the Knights formed about forty assemblies of printers and in 1883, District Assembly No. 64 of New York, Printers, was organized. The Typographical was still weak, opposed to strikes and a strike fund, and relied largely on the boycott, for the effectiveness of which it depended on the Knights. In 1884 great pressure was brought to bear upon the International to enter the Order, but the long history of the union, its benefit features and craft exclusiveness stood in the way. At the 1884 convention at New Orleans, President Crawford said:

Much has been said and written since our last session with regard to merging our International body into a District Assembly of the Knights of Labor. Being a member and an enthusiastic supporter of the principles and objects of that noble and grand organization I would not say or do anything that would tend to cripple its usefulness or retard its wonderful growth but the careful reasoner cannot but agree with me that to merge an organization that has battled for almost half a century . . . into another organization . . . acknowledging allegiance and bowing obedience to a new grand commander . . . would be suicidal in the extreme. . . . [108]

There were some difficulties between the Knights' assemblies and the printers' locals, the admission of "rats" into the Order being the chief, and the 1884 convention instructed Crawford to see Powderly to iron matters out. In 1885, Big 6 of New York boycotted the *Tribune* for alleged breach of contract in the employment of nonunion men. This boycott was warmly supported by the Knights

---

[108] George A. Tracy, *History of the Typographical Union*, pp. 369-70.

and the General Assembly passed a resolution introduced by District Assembly No. 64, "that this General Assembly call upon the Order everywhere to use every effort to crush out the New York *Tribune* and all unfair or 'rat' newspapers." [109]

But as the International and the Knights both grew stronger, jurisdictional and other difficulties increased, and the 1885 convention of the printers appointed a committee to see Powderly and lay their complaints before him. The General Master Workman received them "courteously and listened attentively," and promised compliance with their wishes. He told them that a law was being prepared that would "in the future cause an avoidance of all complaint." [110]   Powderly's faith in law was as complete as it was unjustified.

In 1886 the Typographical came very close to joining the Order. The majority of delegates at their convention were in favor of it and the election of the president turned on this question alone. William Amison of Nashville who was in favor of amalgamation was elected by a vote of 69 to 45 against Charles Stivers who was against it.[111]   Farquhar counseled the delegates to preserve their individuality and President Wittmer said that "the appearance of the Knights of Labor seemed to present both the method and the occasion" of uniting labor organizations. He continued:

It will not be disputed that it was this motive that led leading members of all the trade unions into the Order. . . . It is therefore clearly not in the interest of any class of labor that the order should be disintegrated or its strength impaired. Its prestige has often been the shield of persecuted unions, and under its protection they have risen when prostrate. [But there was an

109 *Proceedings*, 1885 General Assembly, pp. 126, 163.
110 Tracy, *op. cit.*, pp. 385-87.
111 Swinton, *op. cit.*, June 13, 20, 1886.

element in the Order opposed to the trade unions.] Ignoring the variety of interests and the difference in skill and intelligence existing in all ranks, and the sub-division of society to conform to all conditions, they would make labor organizations the only exception to the rule established by experience! [112]

Isaac Cline and A. M. Dewey were sent by Powderly to this convention to invite the Typographical to enter the Order. After listening to them the convention made its demands of the Knights: that they "will not attempt to dictate the course of action of the distinctive trades," and "that they will not cover with the shield of the order—an order of which all of us are proud and glad to be members of—any man who has been found unworthy to mingle with his fellow craftsmen in good standing." [113] But they refused to surrender "the integrity of this union," and the committee on relations with the Order reported, that in spite of Powderly's promises, conditions were worse instead of better and that he had shown that "he did not keep his promises or that he is unable to control the organization of which he is the head. . . ." [114]

In 1887 the Typographical tried to decide between the Knights and the American Federation of Labor. Gompers and Dewey debated before the Buffalo convention the merits of the rival organizations. The influence of Big 6 was thrown against the Order because of local difficulties with District Assembly No. 49 and the *Sun* boycott. Here again the Home Club was the villain of the piece.

The Typographical had had representatives at the first meeting of the American Federation of Labor in 1886 because they had been in the old Federation and were among the group who brought the new one into existence, but they were not affiliated and their delegates brought in two reports

---

[112] Tracy, *op. cit.*, pp. 382-85.
[113] *Ibid.*, pp. 386-87.
[114] *Ibid.*, pp. 385-87.

to the Printers' convention of 1887. The majority report,
while making no recommendation, was favorable to the
'American Federation of Labor. The minority report was
put in the form of a leading question:

Is representation desirable? The position has ever been held
by the I. T. U. that it derived its powers from its subordinates
and is amenable for its acts to its creators alone and that under
authority thus invested it is the ultimate tribunal of appeal in all
matters typographical. Will it after so many years of usefulness and honest endeavor surrender its prerogatives to the
American Federation of Labor by accepting a charter from
that body? [115]

This was almost exactly the position the Typographical
had taken toward the Knights of Labor in 1884 and 1886.
The committee to which both reports were sent recommended: that the individuality of the International Typographical Union shall be maintained; that the International
Typographical Union shall not take a charter and be
subordinate to any organization; that the International
Typographical Union shall not pay a per capita tax to any
organization to which it may send representatives.[116]
There could be no question of the meaning of these concise
and emphatic recommendations.

But District Assembly No. 49 or the Home Club had
put a boycott on the New York *Sun* for its opposition to
the Order and against the protest of the Printers' district,
No. 64.[117] The *Sun* was a union shop and the Typographical objected on principle to boycotting a paper for its
opinions.[118]

---

[115] It is evident from this that the old federation to which the Typographical belonged, and the American Federation of Labor were very
different types of organization. The old Federation had never attempted to charter its original member organizations.

[116] Tracy, *op. cit.*, pp. 397-404.

[117] *Proceedings*, 1887 General Assembly, p. 1764.

[118] George A. Stevens, *New York Typographical Union No. 6*, p. 399.

The American Federation of Labor convention at Baltimore, in 1887, made changes in its constitution to placate the "individuality" of the Typographical. Instead of chartering the older unions they were given "a certificate of affiliation," as evidence of the fact that they had "allied, affiliated or federated themselves together for certain purposes in which all are supposed to have an equal interest," and it was "specifically set forth in the constitution that each is to remain supreme in the control of its own trade affairs." [119]

The Typographical continued to send delegates to the American Federation of Labor conventions but paid no per capita tax. They were still worried about their "individuality," but in 1889 they decided to pay their share of expenses in the past and the per capita tax from June on.[120]   At the Boston convention of the American Federation of Labor, the International Typographical Union advocated a reduction of the per capita tax and reiterated its "determination to preserve its autonomy and jealously guard and control matters pertaining to our craft as illustrated by its refusal to lose its identity in the Knights of Labor or take a charter from any other organization." The American Federation of Labor in 1889 proposed an assessment to aid the eight-hour movement, of 2 cents per member per week for five weeks. The International Typographical Union delegates took no action on the short-hour program or on the assessment, and "there being no authority for the payment of this money it remains unpaid." A further assessment of 8 cents also remained unpaid. Gompers wrote May 16, 1890, and was told that the Typographical officers were not authorized to pay the assessment and the matter would be brought before the next convention. The

[119] Tracy, *op. cit.*, pp. 420-21.
[120] *Ibid.*, pp. 428-29.

next convention of the Typographical Union ordered the assessment paid.[121]

The Carpenters had been helped by the American Federation of Labor in their eight-hour movement in 1890, and the Typographical asked that they be selected for 1891. The Miners, however, had a prior claim and the Printers were put off. The officers of the Typographical asked the convention of 1891 to amend the constitution to allow them to pay the Federation assessments and this was done.[122] The International Typographical Union was thus finally in the Federation but by no means completely satisfied with it. Its delegates to the American Federation of Labor in 1891 suggested reorganization on a wider basis in the near future "and it was contended that its then narrow lines of action would never be successful in emancipating labor." [123]

---

[121] *Ibid.*, pp. 436-39.
[122] *Ibid.*, pp. 446-47.
[123] *Ibid.*, pp. 462-63.

CHAPTER X

THE FEDERATION OF ORGANIZED TRADES AND
LABOR UNIONS, 1881-1886

WHILE the Knights of Labor was slowly building up a single national union capable of including men of all crafts and of none, there remained outside the Order a small group of national trade unions so-called, each covering single crafts and reaching out toward some sort of union. Only a few of these nationals had survived the depression of the seventies and those few were in a sorry condition. But with the return of prosperity in 1879 they began to improve. The oldest was the International Typographical Union. The newest and largest was the Amalgamated Association of Iron and Steel Workers. And the most energetic was the Cigar Makers' International Union.

Previous attempts at federation of national unions had invariably run into politics, sometimes under the leadership of national officers, sometimes led astray by "reformers," and sometimes both, when the national officer and the reformer happened to be the same person or when they joined forces for one reason or another.

In 1878 a secret society sprang up in Indiana calling itself the Knights of Industry. It combined with another secret organization, the Amalgamated Labor Union, to call a convention at Terre Haute on Aug. 2, 1881.

In 1879, at its Washington convention, the International Typographical Union, looking for help in its weakened condition, instructed its secretary to communicate with the national unions for the purpose of federation.[1] The idea of the Printers was to educate other workers to support union printing offices and to force union papers to employ union men. A committee was appointed which, in 1880, drew up a platform for a proposed "Continental Federation of Trades." As indicative of the temper of the trade unionism of the period, two of the planks in its platform are worth noting: one, to encourage productive and distributive coöperation, and another, to "propagate strictly trade union doctrines wherever possible." [2]

At the Toronto convention of the Typographical in June, 1881, the secretary reported "the almost utter failure" of his efforts toward federation. He had written to the other unions asking them to appoint delegates to a convention, the time and place of meeting to be arranged later. The other unions were: the Amalgamated Association of Iron and Steel Workers; Carpenters; Locomotive Engineers and Firemen; Cigar Makers; Coopers; Granite Cutters; Iron Molders; Miners, and the International Labor Union. He had received encouraging replies from Strasser (Cigar Makers), Arthur (Locomotive Engineers) and Fitzpatrick (Molders). But the Cigar Makers were the only ones to commit themselves by a resolution and even they, "in the hurry attending the closing hours of their session, neglected to elect delegates." [3]

The Printers, still undiscouraged, arranged to have representatives attend the annual conventions of the national unions further to stimulate their interest in federation and the city trades' assemblies were included in a renewed invitation. But on the fourth day of their convention an announcement was made of the calling of the Terre Haute

---

[1] George A. Tracy, *History of the Typographical Union*, p. 315.
[2] *Ibid.*, pp. 323-24.
[3] *Ibid.*, pp. 328-30.

meeting for August 2 by the Amalgamated Labor Union. The purpose of this meeting was "to effect a preliminary organization of an international Amalgamated Union." The Printers then appointed L. A. Brant of Detroit, the retiring corresponding secretary, to go to Terre Haute.[4]

Again, as in 1864, the initiative toward federation had been taken by the trades' assemblies rather than the national unions. The vain attempts of the Printers showed that the national unions were as yet impotent or uninterested. Along with the trades' assemblies was the Amalgamated Labor Union, composed of disaffected members of the Knights of Labor.

The Terre Haute convention met as scheduled on Aug. 2, 1881. The delegates were: P. J. McGuire from the St. Louis Trades' Assembly; Richard Powers, Lake Seamen's Union, Chicago; Mark L. Crawford, Chicago Typographical Union No. 16; Thomas Thompson, Dayton, Ohio, Iron Molders' Union No. 181; James Pierce, Simon Neale, F. M. Light, Terre Haute Coopers' Union No. 16; George W. Osborne, Springfield, Ohio, Iron Molders; Mark W. Moore, Terre Haute Typographical Union No. 76; John E. Coughlin, Chicago, President of the National Tanners' and Curriers' Union, but representing a trades' assembly; Samuel Leffingwell, Indianapolis Trades' Assembly; W. C. Pollner, Cleveland Trades' Assembly; Lyman A. Brant, International Typographical Union; five representatives of the Amalgamated Labor Union and three more from the Terre Haute Iron Molders' local.

This representation shows clearly that the national trade unions had little to do with the Terre Haute convention.

---

[4] *Ibid.*, p. 332. Strasser reported to the Cigar Makers in 1881 that the efforts of the Printers to call a trades convention were not a success, the Cigar Makers' International Union being the only organization that responded. (Cigar Makers' *Journal*, Oct. 10, 1881.)

It was a repetition of the movement of 1864 of the trades' assemblies, because of the weakness or nonexistence of the national unions after the depression. The only bona fide representative of the national unions was Brant of the Printers, and of the twenty-one delegates, twelve were from Terre Haute. What Brant called a "crude plan" of organization was submitted to the convention. It was evidently the work of the Amalgamated Labor Union for Brant complained that it would have compelled the trade unionists to withdraw. Its preamble contained a declaration against trade union organization and the expressed intention of the new movement to force trade unions out of existence. It was intended to establish another secret society of workingmen. The majority of the convention was in favor of this plan but adjournment was achieved and a committee of five appointed to call a second meeting at Pittsburgh for November 15. The committee was composed of Brant, chairman; Moore, Terre Haute Typographical; Crawford, Chicago Typographical; Pollner, Cleveland Trades' Assembly, and McGuire, St. Louis Trades' Assembly.[5]

Brant's story is a little confused. If the convention was, as he says, in favor of the Amalgamated Labor Union program, it is rather strange that the committee had no representatives of that organization. Possibly the convention split and the Printers with some of the assemblies called the November convention on their own. The call was issued, citing the British Trades' Union Congress as a proper example for an American federation, and signed by Brant, Coughlin, Powers, McGuire, Thompson, Osborne, Pollner,

    [5] *Ibid.,* p. 339. McGuire was at this time a member of the Knights of Labor and an active socialist politician. The Brotherhood of Carpenters and Joiners was not organized at the time of the Terre Haute convention. It was organized August 8 and held its first convention in 1882.

Leffingwell, and Backus, the last the only representative of the Amalgamated Labor Union.

The first convention of the Federation of Organized Trades and Labor Unions met at Pittsburgh, Nov. 15, 1881. One hundred and seven delegates attended. The largest national trade union representation was from the Printers with 14 delegates. The Amalgamated Association of Iron and Steel Workers had 10; the Molders, 8; the Glass Workers, 6; the Cigar Makers, 5; and the Carpenters, 5. The rest came from the trades' assemblies and the Knights of Labor. John Jarrett, president of the Amalgamated Association of Iron and Steel Workers, was made chairman, and Samuel Gompers was made chairman of the committee on plan of organization. This committee reported in favor of a purely trade federation under the name "Federation of Organized Trades' Unions of the U. S. and Canada," to be composed of "trades' unions" only. This of course started a row. The American labor movement was not then ready for "pure and simple" trade unionism, the national unions had been too weak to lead, the trades' assemblies were mixed bodies, while the Knights of Labor had probably the largest representation in the convention, perhaps 50.

A colored delegate pointed out what later became very clear, "that it might be dangerous to skilled mechanics to exclude from this organization the common laborers, who might in an emergency be employed in positions they could readily qualify themselves to fill." Another delegate asserted in Knights of Labor terms: "We recognize neither creed, color nor nationality but want to take into the field of this organization the whole labor element of the country." Robert Layton, who became secretary of the Knights, said: "There seems to be something singular about the manner in which we are changing base. This Congress was widely advertised as a labor congress and now we are talking about trades. Why not make the Knights of Labor the basis for the federation?" And he threatened that the Knights would withdraw.[6]

After much debate the trade federation idea was defeated and the name changed to "Federation of Organized Trades' and Labor Unions, etc." The usual platform was adopted covering incorporation of unions, compulsory education, child labor, apprenticeship, eight-hour day, convict labor, the store order, mechanic's lien, repeal of conspiracy laws, national bureau of labor statistics, immigration. The only unusual measure was a protection plank inserted on the insistence of the steel workers. A legislative committee was elected which included Gompers.

At the second convention of the Federation at Cleveland, November, 1882, there were only 19 delegates in place of the 107 of the previous year. The Knights of Labor had withdrawn though individual members of the Order remained. Samuel Leffingwell was made president and the article on protection was dropped for protection from cheap foreign labor. This offended the steel workers and the Amalgamated withdrew. It voted at its next convention against entering the Knights of Labor. The basis of representation to the Federation was changed so as practically to leave out the Knights of Labor assemblies and a letter was presented from P. J. McGuire, which is one of the early adumbrations of the later "pure and simple" idea. He advised the delegates "to work for issues we comprehend" and to seek not political but industrial unity, "not by prescribing a stereotyped, uniform plan of organization for all, regardless of their experience or necessities, nor by antagonizing nor aiming to destroy existing organizations, but by

---

[6] A. P. James, *The First Convention of the American Federation of Labor*, quoting the *Evening Chronicle*, November 17.

preserving what is integral in them and by widening their scope so that each without submerging its individuality, may act with the others." This was evidently intended for the Knights of Labor but it was a good summary of the later Federation point of view.

A per capita tax was supposed to be paid to the Federation but the Typographical never paid it and the presumption is that others did not. They paid simply a pro rata share of the expenses of the convention the total of which never amounted to more than $700 and was usually much less. The Federation issued no charters to its constituent members and its only job was political.

The third convention met in New York with Gompers as president. There were twenty-six delegates. The legislative committee reported a bill for the incorporation of national unions, a Seaman's bill in Congress and the passage by the New York legislature of an anti-tenement-house cigar making law. It also noted that the activity of the organizers of the Knights of Labor in "proselytizing" among the trade unions had somewhat abated. Having failed as a federation of trade unions, a proposal was made to widen out into a united federation of labor, to include "the laboring elements of the whole population" for political purposes, "to provide and put in operation the requisite political machinery to secure by legal enactments through state and national legislatures full protection of labor against the encroachments of organized capital." And it was suggested that a committee be appointed to confer with the Knights of Labor and "kindred organizations."

But Gompers would have nothing to do with the Knights of Labor and he introduced a substitute motion, "that the legislative committee is hereby instructed to enter into immediate correspondence with the proper officials of national and international labor organizations of all descriptions for the purpose of obtaining their views. . . ." [7] This might have included the Knights but it was evidently intended to keep them out. The convention thought Gompers' plan too vague and likely to cause delay, which was perhaps the intention, and Frank K. Foster, at that time chairman of the general executive board of the Knights of Labor, offered an amendment to appoint committees to confer with labor organizations. This was not much better but it passed, and nothing came of it,[8] though in the same year the Knights of Labor had approved the appointment of a committee to draw up a plan for alliance with other labor organizations and to confer with their representatives,[9] and another to have the general officers try to bring all trade unions into the Order.[10]

The Cigar Makers' conflict showed up in a resolution of the Federation that workmen should ask for none but union-label cigars, "and see that the little blue label is pasted on every box." [11] As the Knights' label was white this amounted to a delicate suggestion that the Knights cigar makers were not union.

Finally, the 1883 convention added some trade planks to its platform: for a record of strikes; the eight-hour day by union action; to increase union dues and accumulate a fund; insurance; and the consideration of a system "by which one trade can assist another in time of trouble financially as well as morally." [12]

There were only twenty-five delegates at the 1884 convention at Chicago. Gompers was absent and was succeeded as president by W. J. Hammond. The Cigar Makers

---

[7] *Proceedings*, Federation, 1883, pp. 10-11.
[8] *Ibid.*, p. 13.
[9] *Proceedings*, 1883 General Assembly, pp. 467, 506.
[10] *Ibid.*, p. 505.
[11] *Proceedings*, Federation, 1883, p. 16.
[12] *Ibid.*

wanted to establish a central strike fund and the Carpenters to fix May 1, 1886, for a general "movement" of all trades for the eight-hour day. Delegates from the Progressive Cigar Makers were refused admission and the Federation was on its last legs. In the three years of its existence it had done nothing, had added no important unions to its roll, had even lost some. It had tried to expand and had failed. "I am conscious," said the secretary of the legislative committee, "that the chief interest will consist of the future possibilities it [the report] suggests rather than in its record of objects attained." The Federation of Trades he thought was the key to the solution of the labor problem and he believed that "this present Congress can initiate such a movement.[13]

The depression of 1883-84, the loss of three great strikes—the Telegraphers, the Hocking Valley Miners and the Fall River Spinners—were reflected in the dejection of the 1884 convention. Strikes were to be avoided if possible, but "we do not hold with those theorists who would ignore present social conditions and who strive to direct the labor movement in pursuit of some will-o'-the-wisp millennium grounded neither upon the capabilities of human nature nor the dictates of common sense. We must walk before we can fly and we believe the gaining of higher wages and shorter hours to be the preliminary steps toward great and accompanying improvements in the condition of the working classes." [14] And in this they were undoubtedly right.

No replies had been received from the Federation's advances toward unification of the labor movement except from their own members, and the conclusion was drawn from this that "the radical differences in the views of the

---

[13] *Ibid.*, 1884, pp. 15-17.
[14] *Ibid.*, p. 18.

different societies preclude the idea of unification excepting among the genuine unions." [15] This was a rather broad statement in view of the fact that there were only seven "genuine" (national) unions in the Federation, only three of which—Printers, Cigar Makers and Carpenters— amounted to anything, while the Miners, Iron and Steel Workers, Shoemakers, and dozens of others were outside. The fact is that the trade unions of the country hardly knew the Federation existed and even those who sent delegates to its conventions realized its impotence. In July, 1886, the Iron Molders' convention took steps toward the formation of a federation of trades and Swinton had to explain to them that such a Federation was already in the field. [16] Either the Molders did not know about the Federation, or they did know it was on its last legs. When the American Federation of Labor came to be formed, the committee ignored the old Federation altogether and the latter was so unrepresentative a body that Gompers simply changed the date and place of its meeting so that he could transfer it body and soul to the new organization.

The 1884 convention put a new article into the constitution, but not into practice, providing for a centralized strike fund under the control of the legislative committee, if and when approved by a two-thirds vote of the members of the constituent unions. [17] It was not approved and was never put in operation. [18]

Finally, a motion was passed that was to have far-reaching effects, not because of the Federation's act, but because of the labor upheaval in 1886. In its expiring hours, the 1884 convention decided "that eight hours shall constitute a legal

---

[15] *Ibid.*, p. 21.
[16] John Swinton, *John Swinton's Paper*, Aug. 1, 1886.
[17] *Proceedings*, Federation, 1884, pp. 7-8.
[18] *Ibid.*, 1885, p. 16.

day's work from and after May 1, 1886." [19]   This innocent-appearing decision, with no slightest provision to put it into effect, was the one act of the old Federation that had results. A similar resolution had been passed by the Industrial Congress on its deathbed, but nothing had come of it. It was a shot in the dark. May, 1886, was nearly two years off and under ordinary circumstances the whole thing would have been forgotten by then. But ordinary circumstances did not prevail in 1886. The labor movement under the Knights took a tremendous bound forward. The railroad strikes were won and lost. A state of mob-mindedness was created into which the idea of a May Day strike fitted perfectly. As May Day approached, socialists, - anarchists, Knights, trade unionists, saw the chance of a great demonstration of labor's new power. The Federation had said nothing about a strike and made no effort to have one. But strike mania swept the country and out of the agitations connected with it came the Haymarket bomb and the judicial murder of four men. The chief sufferers from this incident were the anarchists and the Knights of Labor. With its innocent resolution the responsibility of the Federation ended. The Knights bore the brunt of public disapproval because their members were involved, and of trade union disapproval because Powderly refused to be drawn into it. The unions came off with banners flying though their gains were slight and the Federation was so insignificant that nobody bothered either to praise or blame it.

The Knights of Labor were invited to coöperate in the "movement" for the eight-hour day [20] and the 1885 General Assembly at Hamilton referred the matter to the general executive board to do all "they lawfully could" in this direction.[21]

---

[19] *Ibid.*, 1884, pp. 24-25.
[20] *Ibid.*, p. 31.
[21] *Proceedings*, 1885 General Assembly, pp. 128, 135.

There was little real conflict between the Knights and the Federation, largely because the latter was ignored by the Order. Many of the delegates to the Federation were also in the Knights and some of the officers, including McGuire, Gompers, and Foster. In 1885, District Assembly No. 41 of Baltimore ordered all its locals to withdraw from the Federation, but on an appeal from Local Assembly, No. 1649, the general executive board decided that the district had no right to do this and the locals continued to send delegates to the other body.[22]

Meanwhile the Federation continued to slip downhill. There were only eighteen delegates to the 1885 convention and McClelland of the Amalgamated Engineers (English) resigned the chairmanship of the legislative committee, possibly in protest against the proposed assessment for a strike fund. No reply had been received from the Knights of Labor about the eight-hour movement and the strike fund proposal was defeated by a vote of 28 to 14. Because of the small vote it was decided to postpone the period for receiving returns to March 1, 1886. The vote of the membership on the eight-hour proposal was 2,197 to 510, and of the local unions 69 to 9 in the affirmative. Many locals were said to be in favor of the eight-hour day but doubted the success of the May Day movement. California already had the nine-hour day and preferred to let well enough alone. The response was certainly not encouraging, considering that every one would want the eight-hour day if they could get it without a reduction of wages. No organized effort was put behind the "movement" by the Federation. It simply invited some sort of action by somebody, but it did specify a date. That was the one definite thing about the whole matter and the thing that caused all the trouble. For the first time in American history, May

---

[22] *Ibid.*, p. 73.

Day became what it is in Europe, a moment of revolutionary demonstration when the pent-up antagonism of the year might be let loose. But America did not like it and it has not happened again.

Up to 1885, the Federation had been a quiet little family showing unusual unanimity under Gompers' somewhat desultory management. But the conflicts of the outside world could not forever be excluded from even so quiet a spot. When the Cigar Makers asked the 1885 convention to endorse the label of the International Cigar Makers only, Emrich, representing the German Furniture Workers, protested. His union was in sympathy with the Progressive Cigar Makers and he asserted that the latter had been unfairly treated by the International. On the understanding that the difficulties between the International and the Progressives would be patched up he agreed to the proposal. [23]

The Typographical, too, was dissatisfied. Although it had been the real creator of the Federation it felt "that the Federation of Trades as constituted at that time was little more than an informal conference of labor representatives." And it did not like the company. "Attention was called to the character of some of the delegates admitted to the deliberations of the Federation." President Wittmer said "it is all important that . . . working men should not be compromised by affiliation in any degree with that class of irreconcilable agitators, who failing to appreciate the opportunities of free institutions, advocate principles and methods foreign to trade unionism." And it was "earnestly recommended that representatives of the International at the next convention of the Federation of Trades be instructed to oppose the admission of representatives from any but recognized bodies of organized labor." [24]   In 1885,

---

[23] *Proceedings*, Federation, 1885, pp. 27-28.
[24] Tracy, *op. cit.*, p. 388.

Gompers was made president and the next convention was set for October, 1886, in St. Louis.

No such convention was ever held. The struggle between the Knights and the unions came to a head in 1886 and in that struggle the expiring Federation had no place. The American Federation of Labor was organized in December, 1886, at Columbus, Ohio, upon a call from the trade union committee which had carried on the negotiations with the Knights during the year. A week after this call was sent out, Gompers announced that the old Federation would meet at Columbus, December 7, instead of St. Louis in October. "The change," he said, "is brought about by the fact that the trades' union conference committee have called a convention of all national and international unions to meet at Columbus, December 8, which promises to be largely attended." [25]

The last session of the old Federation met as Gompers decided. Only twelve organizations were represented. The Knights were blamed for the failure of the eight-hour movement in May, and on December 9, the second day of the convention, the old Federation dissolved and, headed by Samuel Gompers, marched in a body to "the trade union conference." They were accepted as delegates by the new organization under the following agreement:

1. The Trade Union conference has founded an organization to be known as the American Federation of Labor with a constitution better protecting the interests of trade unions.

2. We have agreed that all moneys, papers, and effects of the old Federation be turned over to the officers of the new organization and that all per capita tax due the old be collected by the new.

3. That the new organization agrees to publish the proceedings and reports of this federation in the official *Proceedings*. The recommendation, "that the Federation do now merge into

[25] Swinton, *op. cit.*, Nov. 28, 1886.

the American Federation of Labor and affiliated bodies likewise," was adopted.[26]

For three years the American Federation of Labor dated its organization from 1886, but in 1889 it became genealogically inclined and changed its dating so as to make 1881 its year of origin. There was no harm in this very human act, but it has had the unfortunate effect of giving a totally incorrect impression of the nature of the old Federation. Unquestionably Gompers and McGuire were trying to build up a federation of skilled trades as their own ideas were clarified during the early eighties. But the old Federation never was that, it never was much of anything. The American Federation of Labor had a separate origin, a much wider base, a stricter craft content, and, in a word, became a federal organization, not simply an annual meeting. Aside from the legislative committee, the old Federation had no real organization at all.

---

[26] *Proceedings,* Federation, 1886, p. 10.

CHAPTER XI

THE CIGAR MAKERS

THE so-called "new unionism" of the Cigar Makers was new only in the sense that it was temporarily successful. The object of every national union of the middle of the last century was to break down the independence of the locals and establish centralized control, especially over strikes. The national unions of the early sixties were without authority or funds and had no administrative functions other than those connected with the annual conventions. As the sixties advanced they all, with the exception of the Typographical, tried to establish national strike funds and some of them national insurance features. The panic of 1873 and the depression which followed wiped these out, but with the revival of 1880, the tendency toward centralization by control of finances revived too. The Carpenters and the Cigar Makers were more successful than any other trade union. The Knights tried but failed. So did the Federation of Trades. But there was nothing new about it. Local autonomy had to go sooner or later if national unions were to be had at all, and the "money power" was the obvious and only centralizing control that had any chance of success. The Cigar Makers' benefits, strike fund, equalization of funds were just this. It was only by chance that a strong, military-minded German, Adolph Strasser, came to be head of the Cigar Makers and was able to do, in a perhaps necessarily high-handed way, what every one else was doing with less success.

It was personality, too, that made the connection of the Cigar Makers with the origin of the American Federation of Labor more intimate than that of other unions with the possible exception of the Carpenters. Practically every trade union in the country had complaints to make against the Knights of Labor in 1886, but it was the Cigar Makers' conflict which created an open break and made an amicable arrangement impossible. This was not because the Cigar Makers were more wage conscious than the other trades or more independent. The Typographical was far more touchy about its independence, and craft consciousness, a more rigid and restricted sentiment than wage consciousness, had always been the outstanding characteristic of the trade unions. The importance of the Cigar Makers in relation to the origin of the American Federation of Labor was due primarily to the fact that Samuel Gompers was a cigar maker. Had Gompers been a carpenter or almost anything else, that trade would have been foremost in the movement toward federation for the simple reason that Gompers was the kind of person who is determined to lead. Yet circumstances had to prepare for him. His first venture in 1881 failed miserably, but when, in 1886, a critical situation developed, when the trade unions had their backs to the wall, and the Knights were encompassing and swallowing them up, he got his chance as a man of destiny, not because he was a cigar maker but because he was an aggressive and able trade union leader.

But when all this is said, it remains true that Strasser and Gompers were cigar makers and that the conflict among the Cigar Makers themselves and between them and the Knights brought the American Federation of Labor into being.

The National Cigar Makers' Union was organized June 21, 1864, and in 1867 changed its name to the Cigar

Makers' International Union. The cigar-making industry in the sixties and seventies went through the same changes experienced by the shoemaking industry in the fifties and sixties. The troubles of the shoemakers in the fifties were due to the development of the factory system without machinery, whereby the independent shoemaker, working in his "ten-footer"—a shed behind his house—was displaced by the wage-earner who went to work in a factory owned and operated by the new merchant manufacturer. In the seventies the shoemaker became a shoe operative because of the introduction of machinery and the consequent further division of labor. The same thing happened to the cigar maker a decade later. In the sixties the cigar maker was drawn from the small shop and his direct connection with the consumer, into the factory. And in the seventies he suffered from the introduction of the mold and the division of labor. The tenement-house system arose later to take advantage of cheap labor, low costs, and nonunion conditions. The mold was a tool and not a machine in the proper sense of the word, that is, it was operated by hand and not by "power." But it had much the same effect on the cigar maker's operation. It did not speed him up as much as the power machine had a tendency to do, but it did subdivide his work and break down his special skill. The old cigar maker made the bunch, molded it by hand, and rolled it. The introduction of the mold after 1867 split up the operations into bunch making and rolling, and made it possible partially to replace the cigar maker by unskilled and female "filler" or "bunch" breakers. In 1870, the union, by constitutional amendment, ordered its locals to refuse to allow union members to work with "filler breakers."[1] This meant not only that the International

---

[1] Commons and Associates, *History of Labour in the United States*, Vol. II, p. 72.

was opposed to the mold, but that it was to exclude all but the hand cigar makers.

The International had grown from 984 members in 1864, to 5,800 in 1869, its high point for many years. The exclusion of the filler breaker in 1870 was not completely carried out and it turned many of the locals against the International. The membership declined to 3,771 in 1873 before the panic, to 2,167 in 1874, and to 1,016 in 1877. From 1875 to 1877 the national organization practically ceased to exist. [2]

In 1872 the restriction policy was carried a step further and members of the union were prohibited from working not only with filler breakers but with nonunion men. The strike fund was increased as the numbers declined. In 1873 the constitution was again amended to allow union members to work in shops where filler breakers were employed but not "in conjunction with filler breakers." [3] This meant the breakdown of opposition to the mold, but left the union restricted to the declining number of hand cigar makers.

In New York City, rollers and bunchers were taken into the local in spite of the prohibition in the constitution of the International, but the strike of 1873 drove cigar making into the tenements and destroyed the union. It reorganized in 1874 and called a strike against the tenement-house system in 1877. This was lost and the local again disappeared. [4]

The International was unable to control the striking proclivities of the locals, or to support strikes when called. In

[2] George E. McNeill, *The Labor Movement: The Problem of To-day,* appendix.

[3] Commons *et al., op. cit.,* Vol. II, p. 73.

[4] *Ibid.,* p. 178. In 1883 New York state passed a law against the tenement-house manufacture of cigars, but it was declared unconstitutional in 1885 as having no relation to health. (Commons *et al., op. cit.,* Vol. II, p. 178, footnote 36.)

1873 it was decided to substitute arbitration for strikes, but it was of no avail. In 1875 the few remaining unions "were only awaiting their death blow in the form of a reduction or a special assessment of a few cents weekly," [5] the International was forced to take in bunch breakers and rollers and a number of locals seceded or broke up in protest.

With only 1,016 members the organization reached its lowest point at the 1877 convention. Adolph Strasser was made president by a vote of 3 to 2. Two years later, with only 1,250 members, a reorganization was achieved that put the International on its feet. This reorganization is what has been called the "new unionism." [6] It involved a loaning system for traveling members, equal dues and initiation fees, the equalization of funds, which allowed the International officers to order a prosperous local to transfer a part of its funds to a local in distress, and the centralized control over strikes by means of a strike fund of $2 per member.

Improved industrial conditions and the administration of Strasser were responsible for the growth of the Cigar Makers from 1880 on. The membership was 4,409 (or 3,870) in 1880, the year in which the blue label was adopted and sick and death benefits were revived. In 1881 the membership was 12,709 [7] and because of the large number of strikes during the year (69) and the consequent depletion of the treasury, strikes were prohibited from November, 1881, to April, 1882, and the strike assessment raised from $2 to $2.50.

After the 1881 convention, the Progressive Cigar Makers' Union seceded from the International and almost destroyed

---

[5] McNeill, *op. cit.*, appendix.

[6] Commons *et al.*, *op. cit.*, Vol. II, pp. 306-7.

[7] These figures are computed from the Cigar Makers' own record in McNeill, *op cit.*, appendix.

the latter organization in New York. [8] This was the blow
that drove Gompers, president of Local Assembly No. 144,
into the Federation of Trades and Labor Unions, and it
marks the beginning of his antagonism to the Knights. The
difference between the Progressives and the International
was simply one of how the political campaign against the
tenement-house cigars should be carried on. The Progressives were socialists and the Internationals were
politicians. A committee of Local Assembly No. 144 was
elected in September, 1881, to "agitate" for the abolition
of tenement-house cigars. The Progressives felt that the
proper way to "agitate" was to agitate, *i.e.*, hold mass meetings, parades, and so on. But the committee, representing
the International point of view, supported a "shyster"
lawyer, [9]

a man who has been and belonged to parties of all shades and
colors,[10] communist, Socialist, Greenbacker, Democrat and
finally he has been nominated by the independent republicans.
To such a man and such tactics a big majority of the members
objected, they said if the organization wishes to go into Politics
it shall be pure Labor-Politics and no bargains to be made with
politicians. For that opinion those members were most shame-
fully treated through the columns of the Official Journal of the
Ci'g Int. Union and circulars issued by Adolph Strasser. Since
that time there was always trouble within the ranks of the
Union.

In April, 1881, the regular election of the officers of the Union
took place, in which the men who were opposed to the schemes
of A. Strasser & Co. to dicker in politics were elected by majorities ranging from 2 to 700.

Whether these were the majorities or not, it is a fact that
Gompers and his officers in Local Assembly No. 144 were

---

[8] *Ibid.*, pp. 585-95.

[9] This is the way the Progressives put it. (MSS. presented to District
Assembly No. 49 undated, from Local Assembly No. 2814.)

[10] Some punctuation has been put in this document to make it intelligible, but otherwise it is reproduced as written.

defeated, and a Progressive elected as president. Gompers and his crowd refused to hand over the offices and were sustained by Strasser. The Progressives appealed against Strasser to the International executive board, asking that the latter be sent to New York to investigate. The board asked Strasser for mileage and were refused on the ground that there was no trouble. But money was found and the board went to New York. It recommended that a new election be held and the Progressives claimed that, had this recommendation been followed, peace would have returned.

The other side of the story is given by Strasser. [11] He said that the new president elected by the Progressives was a manufacturer and therefore ineligible, but he did not explain how so strict a craft union as the International purported to be, should have had a manufacturer in one of its locals. He said, too, that the Progressives refused to accept the suspension of the new president, or the order of the executive board to turn over the funds and await a new election.

The probability is that Strasser and Gompers were influenced less by law and justice than by personalities. It would seem that their procedure was unconstitutional, unfair, and high-handed. They were that kind of people. Unquestionably the local was anti-administration in sentiment. But there were other factors involved, the chief of which was the character of the left wing forces. They were certainly radical, probably incompetent to manage the affairs of a conservative business institution like the International and needing to be put down. They had a good case, but "democracy" can be carried too far. Strasser called them "anarchists" and "tenement house scum" but this was after they had ceased to be members of the Inter-

---

[11] Cigar Makers' *Journal*, supplement, 1883 *Proceedings*. For executive board report, see *Journal*, June 5, 1882.

national. And anyway Strasser was no democrat, nor Gompers either. The former was a militarist and the latter a realist. Democrats are made of different clay. The Progressives got a bad deal, but the organization came through. It might have come through anyway, but as this was not attempted, there can be no certainty about it.

The Progressives left the International and spread rapidly among the rollers, bunchers, packers, and even tenement-house workers. For a while they greatly outnumbered the Internationals in New York and established a real national union.

The first cigar makers' local in the Knights of Labor, Local Assembly No. 53, Philadelphia, was organized some time in 1873 and by January, 1882, there were 4 such assemblies, 1 each in Philadelphia, Pittsburgh, Wheeling, W. Va., Baltimore, and St. Louis. By 1886, there were 21 cigar makers' locals, 1 of cigarette makers, 1 of cigar packers, and 2 of tobacco workers. When the Progressives broke away from the International in 1881-82 in New York, they appealed to District Assembly No. 49 for support. This was readily granted by the district which, under the Home Club influence, was anxious to gain complete control of the labor movement in the city. The district was at that time anti-administration and unrepresentative of the Order.

In Cincinnati the International had the same trouble as in New York. In 1883, and again in 1885, the Cincinnati locals went on strike and refused to recognize the authority of Strasser or accept his advice. In the latter year two of these locals issued circulars attacking Strasser, and he ordered that any local making charges against an officer between conventions and failing to substantiate them would lose its charter. In Chicago a like situation arose, but District Assembly No. 24 refused to be drawn into the internal troubles of the Cigar Makers.

The conflict between the International and the Knights originated in no question of principle and in one place only. The Knights were not opposed to trade unions in general, nor to the International in particular. There was opposition in the Order to the trade form of organization within itself and this was strongest in the West and in New York. But even in New York, it was more personal than anything else. There were three trade districts in the city and the mixed district, No. 49, was composed largely of trade locals. The whole thing was, in the beginning, a personal quarrel between the inner ring of District Assembly No. 49, and Gompers, with Strasser behind him, over the ousted Cigar Makers. This ring had fought Powderly as fiercely as it fought the International.

On Dec. 4, 1883, District Assembly No. 49 appealed to the Order for some expression against the treatment given the Progressives by the International, but with no result. The district declared with unnecessary boasting that the matter could be settled only by the Knights of Labor, because of the intensity of feeling between the "paid officers" of the rival Cigar Makers' unions. The appeal was signed by John Caville, the man who had led the first anti-administration fight in support of Theodore Cuno. [12]

On Jan. 21, 1883, Local Assembly No. 2458, Defiance Assembly, Cigar Makers, New York, had been organized. John Hayes asserted that it was chartered by Frank K. Foster, then chairman of the general executive board, for the express purpose of aiding the International. According to Hayes, it was composed of three officers, including Gompers, from each of the five locals of the International in New York, for the purpose of getting the Knights of Labor white label to be used on International-made cigars. It is true that Strasser and Gompers were both members of this

---

[12] *Journal*, p. 609.

local, and that the general executive board gave the charter in opposition to District Assembly No. 49. Strasser
was admitted to the 1884 General Assembly as delegate
from Local Assembly No. 2458 over the protest of District
Assembly No. 49, but the board, when upholding the valid-
ity of the 2458 charter, spoke of a large body of working
men, which suggests that there was more to it than the
International officers. The general executive board refused
the request of District Assembly No. 49 that the charter of
the new Cigar Makers' local should be revoked. [13]

But a change was taking place. Frank Foster refused
renomination to the general executive board in 1884,
perhaps because the "conspiracy" between him and Gompers was a fact, and perhaps because the Home Club was
sure to beat him, and the old board was thrown out. John
Hayes, Joseph Buchanan, and William H. Bailey were
elected as the new general executive board. [14] Hayes was
nominated by Lloyd of New York, one of the old anti-
administration crowd, and has himself stated with no apolo-
gies that he was put in by District Assembly No. 49.
Buchanan was nobody's tool, but Bailey's later activities
suggest that if he was not a Home Club man, he came
under its influence. Barry replaced Buchanan in 1885 and
acted like Bailey. Turner, then general secretary-treasurer,
was a Home Club man. Thus, after the 1884 General
Assembly, the general officers, except Powderly, were
largely under the influence of District Assembly No. 49.

In 1880 the International had adopted the blue label for
cigars. The Knights had a white label for general use but
they also had a blue label for cigars as early as 1880 in use
chiefly, if not solely, in the Pittsburgh region. At the 1883
General Assembly, a cigar makers' local of Allegheny

[13] *Proceedings,* 1884 General Assembly, pp. 562, 653-54, 727.
[14] *Ibid.,* p. 747.

County, No. 1374, asked "that the system of boycotting so successfully carried on for the past three years by using the 'Union Blue Seal'" be approved "as heretofore"[15] and on November 4, the *Journal* stated:

We have already in our Order many local assemblies of cigar makers. For the proper protection of their trade against nonunion and cheap Chinese labor they are using a union label or seal. The Cigar Makers' International Union also have a union label. Both organizations have a common purpose. . . . We trust that the members of the Knights who use the weed will see to it that the box from which they purchase cigars has a union label upon it. If our members cannot get Knights of Labor cigars take those made by the C. M. I. U. just as freely and assist that organization in its gallant fight against cheap labor.[16]

At the 1884 General Assembly more than five resolutions were introduced protesting against the issue of labels by the Order for use on cigars. Two of these came from District Assembly No. 24 of Chicago, which more than hints that there was no irrepressible conflict between the mixed districts and the trade unions. One resolution came from District Assembly No. 65, Albany, N. Y., protesting against any other than "the label now so widely used all over the country issued under the authority of the Cigar Makers' International Union. . . . "[17] At the same time the general executive board reported that the Knights of Labor label on cigars did not compete with that of the International and recommended the continued use of the former. "We believe, however, that no discrimination should be made in purchasing goods contained in packages bearing the label or seal of any recognized trade organization," and while a white label was adopted for general use, a resolution to adopt a special Knights of Labor seal for cigars was

[15] *Ibid.*, 1883 General Assembly, p. 435.
[16] *Journal*, p. 355.
[17] *Proceedings*, 1884 General Assembly, pp. 684-690, 691.

defeated.[18]   Even the Knights' old blue seal which was
allowed in 1883 to live, was in 1884 discouraged.   When
Local Assembly No. 53, Philadelphia, the oldest cigar
makers' assembly in the Order, asked support for the
"blue seal label" there was so much opposition to it that a
meaningless resolution had to be accepted "confirming the
action of the 1883 General Assembly."[19]   Certainly there
was nothing in all this to indicate any ill feeling on the part
of the Order against the International.

In February, 1884, eight months before the friendly
actions recorded above, the firm of Straiton and Storms,
New York, reduced wages on certain brands of cigars and
the Progressive Union called a strike.   This the International refused to support, and three hundred hand cigar
makers remained at work, while 1,500 Progressives went
out.   "It was hoped," said Swinton, "by the friends of both
unions that the International would have joined with the
Progressives to sustain prices."   And again: "There is a
decidedly strong feeling against the action of the International Union among the various trade unions in the city."[20]

A boycott was placed on Straiton and Storms by the
Central Labor Union and District Assembly No. 49.   The
general executive board consented to the boycott only on
the representation from District Assembly No. 49, that
members of the Order were being discharged and scabs put
in their places.   When the general executive board discovered that the "scabs" were members of the International
it repented its action but the harm was done.   "The Board,"
it admitted, "labored under a misapprehension with reference to the employment of scabs and were not aware that
the men designated as such or any number of them were

---

[18] *Ibid.,* pp. 439, 493, 624-25, 716.
[19] *Ibid.,* pp. 682, 763, 765.
[20] John Swinton, *John Swinton's Paper,* Feb. 24 and Mar. 9, 1884.

members of the Cigar Makers' International Union." [21]
The strike was lost and so impartial an onlooker as Swinton
felt that the International was to blame. [22]   But the boycott remained.   The Central Labor Union refused to withdraw it, District Assembly No. 49 pushed it through the
summer [23] and the Order failed to lift it until 1886. [24]   That
was one of the troubles with boycotts—putting them on was
more important and easier than taking them off.

In Albany, N. Y., the Knights and the International were
on the best of terms.   The Albany assembly was one of the
many to protest to the 1884 General Assembly against the
use of the Knights of Labor white label on cigars, and in
July, 1885, the International local, No. 68, appealed to all
trade unions and the Knights to support a boycott. [25]

---

[21] *Proceedings,* 1884, General Assembly, p. 642.

[22] Swinton, *op. cit.,* Mar. 2, and May 25, 1884.

[23] *Journal,* pp. 701, 765.

[24] *Proceedings,* 1886 General Assembly, p. 75.

[25] Swinton, *op. cit.,* July 5, 1885.   The opposite of this occurred in
Syracuse, N. Y., in the winter of 1886.   An International local laid a
boycott in December, 1885, and was supported by the trades' assembly
and a mixed local of the Knights.   A Knight named Daley and a
member of one of the boycotted firms named Barton went to the
general executive board and received permission to organize a cigar
makers' local in the Barton shop, though the general master workman
had prohibited further organization for forty days.   Daley was expelled
from the trades' assembly, two-thirds of whom were members of the
Order, and a committee went to the general executive board to protest.
But this was the new general executive board and after the struggle
with the Cigar Makers in New York had broken out into open war.
Hayes and Bailey gave the committee no satisfaction and Barry was
sent with instructions to undo nothing the general executive board had
done.   Powderly was then approached and expressed astonishment at
the "high-handed action of the Executive Board in overriding the
will of the G. M. W."   Finally, after the special session at
Cleveland where the Home Club got complete control, the general
executive board ordered recognition of the "employers'" assembly, the
rescinding by the protesting local of the resolution boycotting Barton,
and other disciplinary measures.   The local refused to comply and
Turner and Barry revoked its charter (pamphlet).   All this, however,
was after the International in February, 1886, had issued a boycott on
all cigars which did not bear the International label.

A partial reconciliation between the Progressives and the International was achieved in New York in January, 1886. The Progressives voted 1,100 to 700 in favor of reëntry into the parent organization, but the Progressive officers were opposed and insisted that a four-fifths vote was needed. Some members went back but the formal split continued. [26] In February, during a lockout involving both unions, the International laid a boycott on all cigars which did not bear its label. This of course meant the boycotting of Knights of Labor cigars, and in March the manufacturers settled with the Progressives and District Assembly No. 49, getting the white label and the privilege of using the "bunching machine" in exchange for a promise to do away with tenement-house manufacturing. On March 14 the Progressive Union entered District Assembly No. 49 as Local Assembly No. 2814. [27]

It is necessary to remember that this New York quarrel was being carried on when the Knights of Labor were involved in the Southwest strike, which they regarded as a life-and-death struggle with labor's strongest enemy, Jay Gould, and one of the largest combinations of capital in the United States. Powderly and the general executive board were overwhelmed with work and Strasser showed little patience. There was some reason in the Order's complaint that the International officers "violated every principle of unionism by charging in our rear, while the militia of Illinois, in obedience to the order from corporate wealth, were drowning the cry of the oppressed in the roar of musketry and of the hungry with cold lead and steel." [28] And if the metaphors were slightly mixed it is not too much

---

[26] Swinton, *op. cit.*, Jan. 3, 1886.

[27] *Journal*, February, 1886; *The Order and the Cigar Makers*, a pamphlet containing the Knights' side of the controversy; Cigar Makers' *Journal*, March, 1886, with the International's side.

[28] Pamphlet.

to attribute the incoherence in some degree to justifiable indignation.

The Order as a whole was drawn into the New York cigar makers' troubles for the first time in January, 1886, in the strike and lockout already referred to. It is difficult to get at the true facts of this situation in view of the conflicting testimony, but because of its later importance, as clear a story of the matter as is possible must be gleaned from the records. On Jan. 2, 1886, the United Cigar Manufacturers of New York with 16 shops employing 6,000 men reduced wages to compete with tenement-house-made cigars. There were at that time in New York two cigar makers' local assemblies of the Knights of Labor, the Progressive Union, and five locals of the International. District Assembly No. 49 and the Central Labor Union, which was then under the former's control, contended with the International for jurisdiction over the cigar makers. When the wage reduction was made, all these groups were ready to strike, but it is difficult to discover where the strike started. According to the Knights of Labor story, the Progressive Union wrote the International locals on January 4, asking for a conference for united action but received only one reply and that was unsatisfactory. On January 13, a joint committee of the Central Labor Union and the Progressives held a conference with a committee from the International, but they could not agree upon united action. On January 15, Levy Bros., one of the sixteen factories involved, was struck by the International, which at the same time asked the Progressives to call out Love's shop. The Progressives failed to call out Love's, where they had 500 men, but called out Brown and Earle's instead, and on January 18 the United Cigar Manufacturers locked out the workers of all shops. The Knights asserted that just before the lockout, the International made an agreement with Kirbs & Spiess to make that factory an International closed shop, and that, as a result, eighty Progressives and 300 nonunion workers were discharged.

The lockout was about two weeks old when a committee of the Central Labor Union and Progressives met the manufacturers at the Grand Hotel. The International was not represented and said it had received no notice of this conference. An agreement was made which seems to have reduced wages in Levy's, McCoy's, and Brown and Earle's factories and maintained or even increased them in some others, and on February 12 the lockout was declared off. The members of the International did not return to work and those who returned, including the Progressive Union members, were organized into the Knights of Labor. The firms were given the white label which the International was boycotting.

Both Progressives and the International seem to have carried on a cutthroat competition for shops. Local Assembly No. 2458 which the Order said had been organized by officers of the International to get the Knights' label, was suspended by the general executive board on March 15, and on July 4 its charter was revoked. [29] The strike committee of the International was composed of Gompers, Herman, and Strasser, all members of this assembly, and Haller, who seems to have been a suspended member of Local Assembly No. 2814. This committee issued a number of circulars attacking the Order and its officers.

On March 3 Strasser and Kirchner visited Philadelphia and held a conference with the general executive board and Powderly. The board agreed to visit New York and investigate the charges made by the International against District Assembly No. 49 and Powderly asserted that Strasser offered to bring the International into the Order as

[29] *Proceedings,* 1886 General Assembly, p. 97.

a local assembly. Strasser returned to Buffalo and three days after the conference, March 6, he wrote Powderly protesting against the Knights' interference in New York, insisting that the strike was still on, and that "scabs" in the shops of Levy Bros., McCoy, and Brown and Earle "have been organized as members of the Knights of Labor." This was more than two weeks after District Assembly No. 49 had settled with these firms and the lockout ended so far as the Progressives were concerned. "Should you fail," wrote Strasser to Powderly, "to denounce the action of your organizers in New York City you will merit the condemnation of the C. M. I. U. and of every national trades union in the country. . . . Should you fail to listen to the warning contained in my letter the C. M. I. U. will be compelled to protect itself against unscrupulous employers and so-called labor reformers." [30] Powderly said that this letter did not reach him until May 26.

On March 14, Hayes, Barry, and Bailey, to all intents and purposes a Home Club general executive board, went to New York to investigate the cigar makers' troubles. They took some evidence and then had to rush to Troy on another matter. On their return to New York, they were joined by Powderly who had to go to Kansas by March 18, because of the threat of the extension of the Southwest strike. The board remained in New York ten days and had then to go to St. Louis to deal with the dangerous situation the Southwest strike had created.

During the general executive board investigation in New York, J. D. Kirchner, fourth vice president of the International, presented the demands of the Union: "In all matters affecting the cigar makers its jurisdiction is second to no other organization," he said, and "if it is not supreme

---

[30] *Ibid.*, special session of the 1886 General Assembly, Cleveland, pp. 28-32.

it is at least co-equal and will not permit the settlement of a strike inaugurated by its members unless such settlement has been concurred in by the International Union." This would seem reasonable enough. It was admitted that the International had called the strike in Levy's shop and that the Knights had settled with that firm without the International's consent or coöperation. In all the complications this stands out clearly and whatever criticism may be made of Strasser's impatience and high-handedness, the International was entitled to complain of this act. Kirchner asked the general executive board to "denounce" District Assembly No. 49, to issue no more labels, and to get rid of members taken into the Order after the settlement. And he proposed a joint conference of the International and the Knights of Labor to arrange to admit the International into the Knights on the following terms:

1. That the proposed national trade local should be governed by the existing constitution of the International.
2. That the International blue label should replace all others.
3. That all cigar makers shall enter the new local.
4. That the new local should observe the laws of the General Assembly.
5. That the officers of the new locals should be the officers of the International.

The assertion that such a proposal was made comes from the Knights of Labor general executive board, and it is hard to believe in the light of Strasser's belligerent letter of March 6 and of Gompers' attitude from the beginning. The particulars increase its credibility, however, as does the statement of Powderly that Strasser made the same offer.[31] If it were actually made and had been accepted the whole

---

[31] A similar proposal was made by Cigar Makers' locals of Chicago to the Cleveland special session. (*Proceedings*, special session of the 1886 General Assembly, pp. 67-68.)

course of the labor movement in America might have been changed, but assuming that it was offered, Hayes, Barry, and Bailey were not the men to accept it. They were Home Club men, riding the wave of the Knights' success that for the moment made them of more importance than their merits deserved. Power had gone to their heads and there is their own admission that they rejected a proposal that was reasonable and from which the Order had everything to gain and nothing to lose. In their refusal they signed the death warrant of the Knights of Labor as an industrial body.

"We hardly think," said the board with sanctimonious self-assurance, "that the millions of the Knights of Labor whose Order was founded by the sainted Stephens for the very purpose of counteracting the selfish sectarianism of the trade unions are yet prepared to step down and out in favor of a few organized cigar makers who do not even constitute a majority of the trade." [32]

And so the "sainted Stephens" was dragged in to cover a multitude of meannesses and petty jealousies, to support the intrigues of the Home Club and its tools, and to promote the egoism of three men who by a toss of fortune held in their hands for the moment the destiny of the labor movement in America.

And yet one cannot be too sure that a different attitude would have changed matters. Other unions were being endangered by the Order's advance, and growing restless under the increasing shadow of the one big union. It cannot be questioned but that an integration of the labor movement in 1886 was desirable. It is true too that there were no insurmountable difficulties of structure, function, or ideas. But there were willful and ambitious men in the Order and outside, and they were as much a part of the situation which

---

[32] Circular, July 2, 1886, *The Order and the Cigar Makers.*

created a split where an integration was desirable as any other thing.

The breach with the Cigar Makers was partly responsible for the coming together of the trade unions out of which the American Federation of Labor grew, as recorded in another chapter.

On Sunday, Aug. 1, 1886,[33] when most of the delegates from District Assembly No. 49 were absent at a meeting of their own, the Central Labor Union of New York agreed to the amalgamation of the Progressive Cigar Makers and the International Union.[34] On the following Sunday with District Assembly No. 49 delegates back in the Central Labor Union, an attempt was made to rescind this action which resulted in a free-for-all fight of the two hundred "wriggling, screaming and fighting delegates" as described by the disgusted Swinton.[35] And he drew the logical moral—"better a thousand times would be the formation of a Federation of trade unions apart from the great Order as proposed by the recent national convention of Iron Molders." On Tuesday, August 10, the Progressive Cigar Makers in national convention dissolved and went back into the International. Articles of amalgamation were drawn up on Wednesday and both unions agreed to put the matter to a vote of their members. The amalgamation was completed September 10 [36] and Strasser and Gompers led a rejuvenated International into the American Federation of Labor in December.

---

[33] In April the general executive board adopted a "blue seal label" for cigars made by Knights of Labor (*Journal*, April, 1886, p. 2054) and after the special session at Cleveland in May, the Order decided to "support and protect all labels and trade marks of the Knights of Labor in preference to any other trade mark or label." (*Proceedings*, special session of the 1886 General Assembly, p. 73.)

[34] Swinton, *op. cit.*, Aug. 8, 1886.

[35] *Ibid.*, Aug. 13, 1886.

[36] *Ibid.*, Sept. 19, 1886.

On August 15 the Central Labor Union broke up over the leadership of a parade. Typographical Union No. 6 objected to J. P. Archibold at the head, "as an active member of an organization which has shown itself antagonistic to the principles of trade unionism." [37] The Central Labor Union was reorganized in 1887, freed from the control of District Assembly No. 49.

Meanwhile Strasser and Gompers carried their complaints to the special General Assembly at Cleveland in May. The committee on the state of the Order listened to them courteously, but dealt with the larger problem of the relation of the Knights to the trade unions. At the regular session in Richmond, however, the General Assembly endorsed the action previously taken by District Assembly No. 49 ordering "all cigar makers, packers or whoever may be employed in the cigar trade who are members of the Knights of Labor and also members of the International Union, to withdraw from said Union or leave the Order." [38] This action was promulgated over Powderly's signature as coming from the general executive board in February, 1887.[39] It pleased no one but the "rule or ruin" element in District Assembly No. 49 and the irreconcilables in the International. "The mask of friendship," said the latter, "toward the trade unions has at last been thrown off. The unions . . . now know whom they are dealing with . . . one good thing has been accomplished. The Knights of Labor have exposed themselves in their true colors—as enemies of the trade unions." [40]

The protests from within and without the Order at the expulsion of the Cigar Makers were so loud and so general

---

[37] *Ibid.*, Aug. 22, 1886.
[38] *Proceedings,* 1886 General Assembly, pp. 200, 282.
[39] Swinton, *op. cit.*, Feb. 27, 1887.
[40] Cigar Makers' *Journal,* November, 1886, p. 6.

that Powderly reneged as early as February, 1887,[41] and the general executive board by May of the same year. "The G. E. B. of the Knights of Labor," said the Boston *Labor Leader*, organ of McNeill and Frank K. Foster, "have finally decided that the order against the International Cigar Makers shall be interpreted as applying only to those who are hostile to the Knights of Labor or the general officers." [42] Outside New York the order was never carried out. Buchanan issued a public blast against it, and at the 1887 General Assembly, where Powderly declared the expulsion of the Cigar Makers was unconstitutional, the work of the Richmond assembly was undone too late.

---

[41] *Proceedings*, 1887 General Assembly, pp. 1528-31.
[42] Quoted in Swinton, *op. cit.*, May 8, 1887.

CHAPTER XII

In 1885-86, when the Knights of Labor were making their phenomenal gains, the national trade unions were adding to their numbers more slowly but more surely. At the same time all the national unions felt the effect of the expansion of the Order, and in the early part of 1886 there was much talk of a united labor movement to be achieved by their entry into the Knights.

The old Federation was on its last legs. It had never been representative of the national unions and was quite ignored in the new plans and proposals. It is doubtful if, under any circumstances, the national unions, when it came to the point, would have joined the Knights, but when the New York Cigar Makers' difficulties reached Powderly and the general executive board, the matter was settled and the trade union leaders were ready to follow Strasser, Gompers, and McGuire in an attempt to bring the Knights of Labor to time.

On April 26, 1886, a circular was issued by McGuire (Carpenters), Strasser (Cigar Makers), Dyer (Granite Cutters), Fitzpatrick (Iron Molders), and W. H. Foster, secretary of the old Federation, calling a trade union conference at Philadelphia for May 18, "to protect our respective organizations from the malicious work of an element who openly boast that 'trades unions must be destroyed.' " This element of course was in the Knights of Labor, but "as far as we can learn, without authority from that body." Its "malicious work" was that " 'rats' [a newspaper term for 'scabs' and intended to interest the Typographical] scabs and unfair employers are backed up by this element—suspended and expelled members of trades unions are welcomed into their ranks and these elements use the Knights of Labor as an instrument through which to vent their spite against trade unions. . . ." The Cigar Makers and the Typographical were cited. Specifically the purpose for which the May meeting was called was to draw up a plan "to submit to the General Officers of the Knights of Labor" to cause them "to cease this hostility and antagonism toward trades unions." [1]

On the same day that the five trade unionists sent out their call for the Philadelphia meeting, Powderly called a special session of the General Assembly of the Knights of Labor for Cleveland, May 25, to deal with three matters all growing out of the "unhealthy" growth of the Order: the control of the boycott; the further centralization of control over strikes; and the trouble with the unions.

The Philadelphia meeting of the trade unionists was held May 18, while the general executive board of the Knights was in session. It was attended by 22 representatives, and William Wiehe (Amalgamated Association of Iron and Steel Workers) was made chairman, possibly because of the estrangement of the Amalgamated from the old Federation. Each representative went to the conference with his list of grievances against the Knights, and all of them were in the same vein: that the Order was organizing trade union members and capturing whole locals; that it was indiscriminate in its expansion, taking in "rats," and "black-legs"; that the general officers were opposed to trade unions and kept up the refrain, "the trade unions must go," "the day of the trade unions is over"; and, finally, that

---

[1] *Proceedings*, 17th session International Cigar Makers' Union, p. 6.

trade union officers were being snubbed by the general executive board.

All of these accusations were true if not as important as they seemed at the time. The Order had gained about 500,-000 members in one year in spite of the fact that, officially at least, it had stopped organizing for 40 days. In its triumphant march it stepped on every one's toes, inadvertently in most cases, but in one important case, the Cigar Makers, so far as the general executive board was concerned, with obvious intent. The labor movement was being monopolized by one inflated union, which after some remarkable successes was beginning to run into danger and defeat.

The Philadelphia conference [2] decreed that

inasmuch as the National and· International trades unions have a historical basis, and in view of the success which has attended their efforts in the past, we hold that they should strictly preserve their distinct and individual autonomy and that we do not deem it advisable for any trade union to be controlled by or to join the Knights of Labor in a body, believing that trade unions are the best qualified to regulate their own internal affairs. Nevertheless we recognize the solidarity of all labor interests;

Whereas it has become the avowed purpose of a certain element in the Knights of Labor to destroy trade unions;

Whereas some plan is necessary to stop this and establish harmonious relations;

Resolved: that we draw up a treaty to present to the Special General Assembly at Cleveland May 25.

A committee of five—William Wiehe, Christopher Evans, Adolph Strasser, P. J. McGuire, P. F. Fitzpatrick, with David P. Boyer as alternate—was appointed to draw up the

---

[2] The following unions were represented: Typographical, Bakers, Cigar Makers, Furniture Workers, Bricklayers, Iron Molders, Granite Cutters, Iron and Steel Workers, Carpenters, Typographia (German), Tailors, Boiler Makers, Miners and Mine Laborers, Miners' National Federation, Lasters, Metal Workers, Nailers, Shoe Stitchers, and New York Stereotypers.

"treaty," and it was further decided that an annual conference of the chief officers of the trade unions would be held to promote trade union interests.

The committee drew up the following "treaty" which was presented to the general executive board at the special session at Cleveland, May 25, 1886:[3]

In our capacity as a committee of six selected by the conference of the chief officers of the National and International trade unions held in Philadelphia, Pa., May 18, 1886, beg leave to submit for your consideration and with hope of approval the following terms with a view to secure complete harmony of action and fraternity of purpose among all the various branches of organized labor:

TREATY

1st. That in any branch of labor having a National or International Trade Union, the Knights of Labor shall not initiate any person or form any assembly of persons following a trade or calling organized under such National or International Union without the consent of the nearest Local Union of the National or International Union affected.

2d. No person shall be admitted to membership in the Knights of Labor who works for less than the regular scale of wages fixed by the trade union of his craft or calling, and none shall be admitted into the Knights of Labor who have ever been convicted of "scabbing," "ratting," embezzlement or any other offense against the union of his trade or calling until exonerated by said union.

3d. The charter of any Knights of Labor Assembly of any trade having a National or International Union shall be revoked, and the members of the same be requested to join a mixed Assembly or form a local union under the jurisdiction of their National or International Trade Union.

4th. That any organizer of the Knights of Labor who endeavors to induce trade unions to disband or tampers with their growth or privileges, shall have his commission forthwith revoked.

5th. That wherever a strike of any trade union is in progress, no Assembly or District Assembly of the Knights of Labor shall

---

[3] It was addressed to the General Assembly.

interfere until settled to the satisfaction of the trade union affected.

6th. That the Knights of Labor shall not establish nor issue any trade mark or label in competition with any trade mark or label now issued, or that may be hereafter issued by any National or International Trade Union.[4]

The extreme severity of these demands is a little difficult to understand in view of the relative strength of the trade union group and the Knights of Labor. The total strength of the trade unions represented in the Philadelphia conference could not have been more than 140,000 against about 700,000 in the Order. Yet these national unions, which were so concerned about their autonomy, did not hesitate to lay down with great particularity the exact conditions upon which the Knights of Labor might go out of business. They told the Order what it might and might not organize, in what form and with whose consent. They told it what forms of organization it must break up and what to do with the personnel of the defunct bodies. They made rules as to how and why to remove organizers, and to cap it all, they decreed that the Knights might not issue a label, not only in competition with labels already in the field, but with any that might "hereafter be issued by any national or international union." This last was a *reductio ad absurdum* and throws suspicion upon the whole document. The "treaty" was in no sense what it purported to be, a basis for coöperation with the Knights. It was either a bargaining offer, which the unions were prepared to whittle down, or a declaration of war. The probability is that for most of the trade unionists, including McGuire, it was a bargaining offer, and for Strasser and especially Gompers it was a declaration of war.

The date of the Philadelphia meeting, May 18, is of im-

---

[4] *Proceedings*, 1886 General Assembly of the Knights of Labor, Cleveland, p. 12, and original MS.

portance. While it is true that the Knights of Labor reached their peak strength so far as outward appearances were concerned, in October, 1886, at the Richmond convention, it is also true that their real decline began about May 1 with the loss of the Southwest strike, the May Day fiasco, and the Haymarket riots. Gompers and some others found no difficulty in reading the handwriting on the wall. The Order was already in retreat.

Then, too, so far as the Cigar Makers were concerned there could be no compromise with the Knights of Labor. They had almost wrecked the International and were prepared to complete the job. But before that conflict had become acute, Samuel Gompers had made up his mind to create a pure and simple trade union federation. He had tried it in 1881 and had failed. He was not the kind of man to be stopped by one failure or a dozen. In 1886 conditions were more favorable and though few of the trade union leaders would at that time have undertaken to supplant the Knights of Labor, they were all dissatisfied enough to support a gesture to that effect.

The attitude of P. J. McGuire was probably more nearly that of the active trade union leaders at Philadelphia than was the purpose of Gompers. For McGuire the treaty was a bargaining proposal. He had already suggested an exchange of working cards between the Knights and the Carpenters and this was probably as much as he expected to get. The general executive board had refused this or ignored it, and was later to repent. "In the presentation of our demands," said McGuire, "we have used diplomacy. Of course we do not expect to get all we ask, but by asking boldly for all we want, we will be able to make concessions when the Knights have submitted a counter proposal. . . ." [5]

---

[5] New York *Tribune*, May 30, 1886. The same interview appeared in the *Herald*.

How far the trade unionists would have gone in the modification of the impossible terms of the treaty it is of course
impossible to say. The rigidity of the general officers of
the Knights of Labor under the control of the Home Club
made even negotiation impossible, and Gompers was always
in the background, strong willed and determined to destroy
the Order.

The special General Assembly met at Cleveland on May
25, 1886, to deal with the general trouble in which the
Order found itself because of its growth, and the broad and
reckless strike and boycott practices into which it had been
drawn. The trade union difficulty was only one of its
major problems, but the presentation of the treaty made it
the most important. Immediately the trade and antitrade
forces in the Knights lined up. McNeill of Massachusetts,
though far from being a strict trade unionist, was one of
the most influential men in the Order on the trade union
side. The anti-unionists were led by T. B. McGuire and
other representatives of District Assembly No. 49. McNeill
at once moved that the treaty be referred to a special
committee to confer with the trade union committee which
had brought the document to Cleveland. This, however,
was laid on the table on McGuire's motion until the general
executive board should report its negotiations with the trade
unions. Knowing the attitude of the general executive board
and its connection with the Home Club, the intent of this
move to prejudice the General Assembly is sufficiently revealed.

The General Assembly then went on with its business, a
part of which was to receive the report of the general
executive board on its activities during the year. The
general executive board detailed its dealings with the Cigar
Makers and presented the treaty without recommendation
to the General Assembly. It explained that it could make

no recommendation on the treaty as it had received it "just previous to the opening of the session" and had not known its contents until it was read at the session by Powderly. Robert Schilling moved that the report of the general executive board be referred to the committee on the state of the Order, and Powderly made a long speech quoting Strasser's letter of March 6 and the Cigar Makers' circular of March 16 and complaining that he had been given no time to deal with the Cigar Makers' complaints. A long and excited debate followed, taking up most of Friday afternoon and Saturday, when temporary relief was secured by a recess to listen to a talk on woman's suffrage. On resumption of the controversy, Schilling read a telegram from his Milwaukee district demanding that "rather than assent to the proposed treaty" or any part of it, he vote to disband and return home. The debate was closed by the adoption of a resolution inviting all labor organizations to enter the Order.[6] This was referred, along with the general executive board report including the treaty, to the committee on the state of the Order.

The chairman of the committee on the state of the Order was Frank K. Foster, formerly chairman of the general executive board, a member of the old Federation, and a trade union man. Schilling was a member, and McNeill. The trade union committee with Gompers in attendance, though he was not a member, was cordially received by the Knights' committee and negotiations began which promised to develop into something like an entente.

Back in the General Assembly, Powderly was reading a long message to be sent to the Amalgamated Association of Iron and Steel Workers in convention at Pittsburgh, extending to them the olive branch and inviting them to enter the Order. "No surrender of principle nor of identity need

[6] *Proceedings,* special session of the 1886 General Assembly, p. 34.

attend such a step," he declared. " . . . No interference
in the management of your crafts or their affairs will result.
With the aid of Knights of Labor wherever found in the
vicinity of mill, shop or factory, your numbers will be increased, and your power to regulate the iron and steel business of the United States will be increased in a corresponding
degree." [7] Denny of the Glass Workers was dispatched
with this message which was answered politely, inviting
Powderly to visit the Pittsburgh convention and "give us a
few words." [8]

This Napoleonic move revealed the policy the Knights
were to pursue. It was a policy of "divide and conquer"
and was not the kind of thing Powderly would do on his
own account. There can be little doubt but that the general
executive board was behind it and the Home Club behind
the general executive board. The Amalgamated was the
strongest organization in the country. It had broken away
from the old Federation in 1882 and, although its president,
William Wiehe, was chairman of the Philadelphia meeting
of trade unionists and on the committee which drew up the
treaty, he had been put there because his organization was
in the doubtful column. The Amalgamated, however, was
one of the most rigid of craft organizations and was constantly being warned by William Martin, its secretary,
of the danger of this in view of the rapid mechanization of
the industry. Powderly or his advisers offered the Knights
as an organization of the unskilled in the steel industry and
outside, in support of the boilers, puddlers, rollers, and
heaters in the Amalgamated. It was a clever appeal and
represented the real value of integration. "Do not be
prejudiced," he said, "against our organization because our
Constitution says the 'Knights of Labor is not a mere trade

---

[7] *Ibid.*, p. 38.
[8] *Ibid.*, pp. 65-66.

union.' The Knights of Labor is not a trade union—it is a union of all trades and callings; it furnishes the great heart through which the life-giving current may flow strong and healthy to every part of labor's mighty frame. ...." [9]

Powderly had been converted to this policy by advisers and the experience of the year.[10] An attempt was made to carry it further and send similar communications to all trade union conventions, but McNeill objected because the committee on the state of the order was ready with a report "embodying the spirit of the General Master Workman's letter." [11] The committee on the state of the Order then reported that they had interviewed Strasser, Gompers, and McGuire, had received their complaints and suggestions, and it recommended the exchange of working cards between the Knights and the unions, and the appointment of a special committee of five to confer further with the trade union committee. These recommendations were adopted and a circular prepared to be sent to the unions. It was the failure of the general officers to act as the General Assembly decided that caused the breakdown of negotiations and the formation of the American Federation of Labor. The important clause of the circular required that a commmittee of five "be appointed" to confer with the trade unions.[12]

Before the adoption of this circular, the General Assembly went into the election of an auxiliary general executive board. The business of the Order had grown so great that the old general executive board of three elected members,

---

[9] *Ibid.*, pp. 38-39.

[10] Dec. 28, 1885, Powderly had recommended that A. S. Denny be sent to the Flint Glass Workers, the Bottle Glass Blowers, and the Druggist Glass Blowers' League to invite them into the Order. (*Proceedings,* 1886 General Assembly, Richmond, p. 76.)

[11] *Proceedings,* special session of the 1886 General Assembly, pp. 39, 67.

[12] See Appendix III.

the general master workman, and secretary was incapable of handling it, and it was decided to add six auxiliary members to lighten the burden. This election was the crux of the special session. In it the trade union faction in the Order was defeated by the Home Club, and out of this defeat and the later action of the general officers, which nullified the action of the General Assembly on the trade union question, came the open rupture in the labor movement and the downfall of the Order. The Home Club was able to elect four out of the six auxiliary members of the general executive board: James E. Quinn, District Master Workman of District Assembly No. 49, New York; Hugh Cavanaugh, District Master Workman, District Assembly No. 48, Cincinnati; W. H. Mullen, Richmond, Va.; and D. R. Gibson, Hamilton, Ont. The Home Club already controlled the regular general executive board, Hayes, Bailey, and Barry and the general secretary, Turner, and seems for the time being to have influenced Powderly. The two remaining positions on the auxiliary general executive board were filled by Joseph Buchanan and Ira B. Aylsworth.[13]

"The trade unionists feel," said Swinton, "that the result of the election is a knock-down blow for them and they are predicting war between the Knights of Labor and the unions." [14] And before the convention closed their prediction began to be fulfilled. On a motion of T. B. McGuire the general executive board was instructed to "issue a command to the Order, instructing our members to support and protect all labels or trade marks issued by the Knights of Labor in preference to any other trade mark or label." [15] That the Cigar Makers had done the same thing to the Knights was no justification for so sweeping a decla-

---

[13] *Proceedings,* special session of the 1886 General Assembly, pp. 57-65; John Swinton, *John Swinton's Paper,* June 6, 1886.

[14] Swinton, *op. cit.,* June 6, 1886.

[15] *Proceedings,* special session of the 1886 General Assembly, p. 73.

ration of war on all unions using labels, and was completely
out of harmony with the previous action of the General
Assembly toward the unions. But the Home Club was
riding high and wide, prepared to rule or ruin, not only in
New York but over the whole country.

When the Cleveland special session broke up, June 3,
1886, it was the duty of the general officers to appoint the
committee of five to meet the trade union committee and
try to reach some agreement on the basis of the circular
addressed to the national unions. On June 12, P. J. Mc-
Guire, who seems to have handled the treaty while Gompers
and Strasser confined themselves to the Cigar Makers' demands, wrote Powderly to ask if and when the committee
would be appointed. Powderly answered that it would be
difficult to get five men together for the purpose, but that
the general executive board would act as the committee.
"I feel confident," he wrote, "that much better results will
follow the action at the hands of the Board than at the
hands of a new and inexperienced committee." [16]

Powderly had no business to be confident about any such
thing. When he found it to his interest he was the most
rigid constitutionalist. Time and again he refused to exceed his powers or to let any one else exceed theirs. The
law was sacred to him and his most imposing statements
had to do with the proper exercise of authority. Often his
legal-mindedness was annoying when common sense would
have been a better guide, and often it was useful to him
when there was something he did not want to do. But he
had always preached that the General Assembly was the
supreme authority in the Order—when it spoke all had to
obey. It had spoken on this subject with complete clarity
saying that "a committee of five be *appointed*." The general executive board was elected by the General Assembly,

---

[16] *The Carpenter*, Nov. 28, 1886, p. 3.

and Powderly's hedging could mean nothing else than that he had agreed to disobey the General Assembly, perhaps against his will, at the behest of the inner ring that gained control of the Order at the Cleveland session and before. He must have known, too, that reference of this matter to the general executive board as then constituted, meant not agreement but war with the trade unions. Powderly's act was a breach of trust with the General Assembly and made an entente with the unions impossible. His excuse that five men could not be got together was as weak as his position.[17]

On Sept. 28, 1886, the trade union committee met a part of the general executive board, Hayes, Turner, and Barry, in Philadelphia. The trade unions asked that the treaty be "given due consideration," that in case of future difficulties the facts should be made known to the head of the union concerned, and by him sent to Powderly or the general executive board, and that a special committee of five be appointed to investigate past grievances and secure evidence for suitable legislation. Powderly is said to have agreed to present these demands to the General Assembly at Richmond the following month,[18] but late in October no special committee had been appointed.[19]

Meanwhile, in July, at its annual session in London, Ont., the Molders' Union declared: "We are of the opinion that the time has arrived for the great national and international unions of North America to come together and by a solemn compact engage to sustain each other in efforts for the material advancement of the least of its members . . ." but leaving "to each, the internal management of its own af-

---

[17] It was said that the general executive board had appointed a committee at its first session after Cleveland, but if so the unions were not informed of it. (*The Carpenter*, November, 1886.)

[18] *The Carpenter*, November, 1886, p. 3.

[19] *Ibid.*, October, 1886.

fairs." This was one of the first overt suggestions looking toward the formation of the American Federation of Labor and a committee was proposed "to call a convention of delegates from all the national and international unions in North America not later than January 1, 1887." The rules of the Molders were amended to allow their funds to be used to help other unions on strike,[20] and this was the situation in which the Richmond General Assembly of the Knights of Labor was held.

The greatest assembly of the Order of the Knights of Labor met at Richmond, Va., Oct. 4, 1886, with more than 800 delegates representing more than 700,000 members. No such delegate body of labor had met before on American soil. Its numbers, influence, reputation (good, bad, and indifferent) were unsurpassed. Outwardly the Order was just coming into its own. In two years it was expected with good reason to have two million men. The General Assembly was greeted by the Governor of Virginia, Fitzhugh Lee, to whose oration Powderly replied after he himself was introduced by Frank J. Ferrell, a negro delegate from District Assembly No. 49, a compromise arrangement made by the grand master workman with Quinn of District Assembly No. 49 who wanted Ferrell to reply to Fitzhugh Lee.

But the peak of the real strength of the Knights had been reached five months before, and after May, when the eight-hour movement ended in disaster, the Haymarket bomb was thrown, the Southwest strike was lost, and the unions began gathering their skirts about them to withdraw from the mass, the Order had in reality been going to pieces. The Richmond General Assembly lasted sixteen days, a week of which was taken up with speech making and organization. The general executive board reported its hundreds of activities during the year which had kept it

---

[20] Swinton, *op. cit.*, Aug. 1, 1886.

running from one part of the country to another. A new law was drawn for national trade districts, the Cigar Makers were thrown out of the Order, and the gathering trade unions were ignored. Powderly's salary was increased from $2,000 to $5,000 and the term of the general officers extended from one to two years, possibly in return for their support of the Home Club and its aggressive policy against the national unions.

Powderly was said to have promised to bring the revised demands of the trade unions before the Richmond assembly but he did not, and three weeks later, Nov. 10, 1886, the trade union committee issued a call for a convention at Columbus, Ohio, Dec. 8, 1886, to organize a new Federation of the trades. The call read:

On May 18, 1886, a conference of the chief officers of the various national and international trade unions was held in Philadelphia, Pa., at which twenty national and international unions were represented and twelve more sent letters of sympathy tendering their support to the conference. This made at that time thirty-two national and international trades unions with 367,736 members in good standing.[21]

Since then quite a number of trades union conventions have been held, at all of which the action of the trades union conference has been emphatically and fully endorsed and a desire for a closer federation or alliance of all trades unions has been generally expressed. Not only that but a great impetus has been given to the formation of national trades unions and several new national unions have recently been formed, while all the trades societies with national or international heads have increased in membership and grown stronger in every respect.

The time has now arrived to draw the bonds of unity much closer together between all the trades unions of America. We need an annual Trades Congress that shall have for its object:

1. The formation of trades unions and the encouragement of the trades union movement in America.

---

[21] This is a mistake or a gross exaggeration, for there were probably not more than 138,000 members at this time.

2. The organization of trades assemblies, trades councils or central labor unions in every city in America and the further encouragement of such bodies.

3. The founding of state trade assemblies or state labor congresses to influence state legislation in the interest of the working masses.

4. The establishment of national and international trades unions based upon the strict recognition of the autonomy of each trade, and the promotion and advancement of such bodies.

5. An American Federation or Alliance of all national and international trades unions to aid and assist each other and iurthermore to secure national legislation in the interest of the working people and influence public opinion by peaceful and legal methods in favor of organized labor.

6. To aid and encourage the labor press of America and to disseminate tracts and literature on the labor movement.

There were two differences between this proposed Federation and the Knights of Labor, and two only. The new Federation was called and was evidently to be controlled by the national unions instead of the district assemblies, and it was to be less highly centralized, in theory at any rate, than the Order. There was no new idea in the "call." It was a repetition of the attempts of the national unions from the beginning, to establish a federation in which they would dominate. The difference between this and previous attempts at the same thing came out later when the American Federation of Labor succeeded in doing what the others had failed to do. The time was ripe. The man of destiny was there. The same man, Samuel Gompers, had been there five years before when the same thing had been tried. Five years before he had failed. The time was not then ripe. In 1886 he succeeded, which suggests perhaps that both the situation and the individual are important in the making of history.

The basis of representation to the Columbus convention was as follows: National and international unions with less than 4,000 members, 1 delegate; 4,000 or more, 2 delegates; 8,000 or more, 3 delegates; 16,000 or more, 4 delegates, and so on. Each local trade union not having a national union, one delegate.[22]

This move of the unions seems to have forced the Knights to act, and a committee was finally appointed which met the trade unionists at Columbus, December 8-10, during the first convention of what became the American Federation of Labor. The two committees met. The treaty was again presented. The Order offered an exchange of working cards. Fitzpatrick asked if the "substitute" offered at Cleveland would be considered. No, that had been disposed of. Howes (Knights of Labor) was asked what were his powers and instructions. He had no instructions and little authority. He was asked if he would make some arrangements for the future. His answer was that he had no proposition to make but would consider one made by the unions. The unions had many grievances and could have brought thirty pounds of documents, but they did not know the Knights of Labor committee was to be there. Howes would do his best to prevent trouble, but could not allow another organization to tell the Order "who should constitute their membership," and much more besides.[23]

It was too late. Both sides were obdurate, the Knights more than the unions, perhaps because of their position and the influence of New York. The first convention of the American Federation of Labor declared the blue label of the International Cigar Makers to be "the only union label in that trade," and, further,

Whereas the Knights of Labor have persistently attempted to undermine and disrupt the well-established trades unions [have]

---

[22] Swinton, *op. cit.*, Nov. 21, 1886.

[23] Report of the committee of conference of the Knights of Labor and the trade unions, Dec. 8, 1886; *Proceedings*, 1886, American Federation of Labor, pp. 17-18.

organized and encouraged men who have proven untrue to their trade, false to the obligation of their union, embezzlers of moneys and expelled by many of the unions and conspiring to pull down the trades unions . . .

Resolved: That we condemn the acts above recited and call upon all workingmen to join the unions of their respective trades and urge the formation of national and international unions and the centralization of all under one head, the American Federation of Labor.[24]

The new organization also refused to seat Denny of Local Assembly No. 300, Window Glass Workers, because his organization was "affiliated" with the Knights of Labor, "and is not a trade union within the meaning of the call for the convention." [25]

In 1889 the Knights and the American Federation of Labor tried again to get together. The American Federation of Labor wanted assistance in the eight-hour movement and the Knights' numbers had declined from 700,000 in 1886 to 220,000, making the numerical strength of the two organizations about the same. Powderly, Hayes, and A. W. Wright offered, on the part of the Order, mutual recognition of working cards, mutual recognition of labels, mutual exclusion of suspended or expelled members or those in arrears for dues and assessments,[26] and a circular was sent out by the Locomotive Engineers and other non-American Federation of Labor unions, the American Federation of Labor, and the Knights of Labor, telling the world how far they had gone toward peace. The American Federation of Labor proposed that the Knights "discountenance and revoke the charters of all trades assemblies or districts within the Order," and, in return, the Federation would "urge its members and all working people to become members of the

[24] *Proceedings*, 1886, American Federation of Labor, p. 19.
[25] *Ibid.*, pp. 14-15.
[26] *Proceedings*, 1889 General Assembly, p. 36.

Knights of Labor." [27]   This was the old deadlock, but new times. The Order still could not accept euthanasia, which this would have meant. It preferred the same thing in its own way. And in 1894 the American Federation of Labor decided that "no meeting or conference with the Knights of Labor officials should be held until they declare against dual organization in any one trade." [28]

From 1887 to 1894 the American Federation of Labor and the Knights of Labor spent most of their energies in fighting one another. Slowly the new organization consolidated its forces and the old declined. By 1890 their numbers, according to official records, were about equal, and while the decline of the old organization after 1890 was rapid, the growth of the new was slow. The official figures for the American Federation of Labor in this period are not very dependable but even these show an increase of only 40,000 members from 1890 to 1896.

The Federation, too, had a serious internal fight with the socialists which culminated in the defeat of Gompers in 1894, the one year in which he was not president from 1886 until his death.

---

[27] In 1892 the same proposal was made again. Gompers said the American Federation of Labor could not act for the national unions on the Knights' offer, but he found no difficuly in making a counter proposal. (*Journal,* June 16, 1892.)

[28] William Kirk, "The Knights of Labor and the American Federation of Labor" in Hollander and Barnett, *Studies in American Trade Unionism,* p. 36. But in 1891-92 the United Garment Workers, supported by Gompers, had organized in Rochester, N. Y., while the Knights of Labor were boycotting the products of the members of the Clothing Exchange.

CHAPTER XIII

THE EIGHT-HOUR MOVEMENT AND THE ANARCHISTS

FROM the beginning of the American labor movement, the problem of the number of hours in the working day has run second only to the question of wages. Wage control, however, until recent years, remained in the industrial field, while hour control early carried the labor movement into politics. There was perhaps no good reason for this, unless it was the greater susceptibility of hours to standardization. Up to 1860, ten hours a day was the standard set to be established as a maximum for all workers, while special crafts were able to improve on that. After 1860 eight hours became the standard, and in recent years it has been further lowered to the forty-four- and the forty-hour week.

In 1840, President Van Buren signed the ten-hour law for government employees, and in the forties and fifties the state legislatures were besieged to regulate the hours of labor for all employees, but especially for women and children in the New England mills. Numerous state laws were passed, but none of them was enforceable nor intended to be. In 1868, Congress passed an eight-hour law for federal employees, and the labor reformers of the time were kept busy for some years, seeing that the heads of government departments employing labor obeyed the letter and spirit of the law. State eight-hour laws were also passed, but like the ten-hour laws of the fifties were unenforced or unenforceable.

Along with this political movement there went a more or

less continuous attempt by individual unions to shorten the hours of labor by industrial action, but with little success, and the Industrial Congress, at its last convention in 1875, set aside July 4, 1876, as the date for the eight-hour system to go into effect by a "united movement on the part of the working masses of the United States."

This was probably the first suggestion of a mass movement to establish the eight-hour day and the nucleus of the idea of a general strike. Political action had failed and industrial action by individual unions had not succeeded. There remained only "united movement." The Industrial Congress did not attempt to define the nature of this movement. It meant by implication a general strike, but it might have involved nothing more than a general request for the eight-hour day, which might or might not result in success, compromise, or strikes. But the congress disappeared in 1875 and the idea was left for others to take up.

In 1871, Stephens recommended the reduction of the hours of labor by "a universal movement to cease work at 5 o'clock on Saturday,"[1] but the original platform of the Order said nothing about the method by which the eight-hour day was to be secured. It simply advocated[2] "the reduction of the hours of labor to eight per day so that the laborers may have more time for social enjoyment and intellectual improvement and be enabled to reap the advantages conferred by the labor-saving machinery which their brains have created." In 1879 Stephens reverted to the legislative point of view and Powderly held to that throughout. But the Knights of Labor were not committed to any single method or approach.

A resolution was offered in the General Assembly of 1881 to set aside the first Monday in September, 1882, "for the

---

[1] Powderly, *Thirty Years of Labor,* pp. 85-86.
[2] Article XIV.

workingmen of this country to make a general demand for eight hours to constitute a legal day's work," [3] but it was rejected as inexpedient because of the weakness of the Order—this was its worst year—and the danger of making its weakness public. A similar proposal was made in 1882 to set the first Monday in May, 1883, as the time when "all branches of labor throughout the country shall make a demand upon employers that thereafter eight hours shall constitute a legal day's work . . . and that upon the success of this movement immediate steps shall be taken to demand and enforce legislation recognizing such to be justice, and secure the permanency of the same by legal enactments." [4] Again in 1883 the same resolution was introduced, though no action was taken. [5] But in 1884, the preamble of the constitution was changed and Article XXI was substituted for Article XIV. The new article read: "To shorten the hours of labor by a general refusal to work for more than eight hours." [6] No date was set for action so that the new article was quite innocuous.

In October, 1884, the Federation of Organized Trades and Labor Unions took up and passed a resolution that "eight hours shall constitute a legal day's work from and after May 1, 1886." [7]

There was then little difference between the attitude of the Knights of Labor and the Federation on the eight-hour question. They both wanted the eight-hour day, and by 1884 they both proposed to get it by a stoppage of work. The Order, however, was the outstanding labor society in the country and had it passed the resolution that had been offered three years in succession, it would have meant a

---

[3] *Proceedings*, 1881 General Assembly, p. 309.
[4] *Ibid.*, 1882 General Assembly, p. 312.
[5] *Ibid.*, 1883 General Assembly, p. 509.
[6] *Ibid.*, 1884 General Assembly, p. 769.
[7] *Ibid.*, Federation, 1884, pp. 24-25.

general strike, for which it was not prepared. The Federation could afford to be reckless. It was on its last legs anyway and any general movement for the eight-hour day would have had to rely upon other organizations for its effectiveness. [The Federation was incapable of organizing an eight-hour movement and, in fact, made no effort to do so. It cast its resolution upon the waters and after many days the responsibility for it returned upon the head of the Knights of Labor.] By a stroke of fortune, a resolution passed in the dull times of 1884 reached fruition in the revolutionary year of 1886 and became a rallying point and a battle cry for the aggressive forces of that year.

The Federation did not contemplate a general strike for 1886 when it passed the resolution of 1884. It had no clear ideas on the subject at all. It was little more than a gesture, which, because of the changed conditions in 1886, became a revolutionary threat. It invited the Knights of Labor to coöperate, but received no response. It took a vote of its members which was so small—about 2,500—that a second vote was decided upon. The Carpenters' attitude was typical. They were in favor of the resolution but felt they were not strong enough to put it over, and decided to assist those who were. [8] But at the same time that Edmonston was telling the Federation that the Carpenters could not order a general enforcement of the resolution, he was asking the Knights to attempt it. [9]

Powderly would have nothing to do with any proposal that might involve strikes. He was not in sympathy with the new eight-hour plank in the constitution of the Order "to shorten the hours of labor by a general refusal to work more than eight hours," and on Dec. 15, 1884, he issued one

---

[8] *The Carpenter*, January, 1886; Edmonston's report to the Federation, 1885.

[9] *Proceedings*, 1885 General Assembly, p. 135.

of his troublesome secret circulars protesting against the eight-hour agitation and the waving of red and black flags. He quoted the new eight-hour clause and then proceeded to dilute it to suit his taste. "The general refusal," he said, "must be preceded by a general agitation and that agitation must be begun by this Order. I ask that every assembly take up this question at once. Let each one have its members write short essays on the eight-hour question."[10] And the essays were to be published on Washington's birthday! At the 1885 General Assembly, Powderly insisted that the eight-hour question was a political one and advised the Order to discontinue the May Day scheme.[11]

The explanation of Powderly's attitude is to be found in his allegiance to the older American point of view—that hour reduction should be secured by legislation—accentuated by the fact that a new and alien element had, by 1885, attached itself to the American labor movement. This new element was small but exceedingly articulate and up to that time had exercised its talents chiefly in argument and internal bickerings.

The United States has always seemed to European radicals a promising field for their experiments and ideas. They have thought of it as a new page in the story of the human race, clear of the outgrown traditions of the old past, without fixed institutions, monarchy, feudalism, the Church, and capable of being molded near to the heart's desire.

When their ideas failed of a sympathetic welcome in the old land they turned readily to America with renewed hope. But there was a basic weakness in their logic and in that of their followers. Their ideas all involved in one form or another a high degree of social organization, and while America was to some extent free from entangling alliances

---

[10] Powderly, *op. cit.*, p. 246.

[11] *Proceedings*, p. 15.

with the past, she was very much involved in individual activities in the present. There was no established church in the way, no monarchy, no feudality, but there was something just as strong if not stronger—the individual, human desire to better one's self in a country offering exceptional opportunity. Thus European socialism, in spite of a superficially favorable condition, has always been dud in the United States in comparison with its position at home. And there was no such thing as American socialism. The only bona fide American radical tradition was anarchy, and that, in spite of Thoreau, has been much less a doctrine than a fact. The American pioneer was temperamentally an anarchist and when he disappeared the tradition was carried on by the American business men—old style—the men who would have said "the public be damned," if they had thought of it.

While it is true that socialism and anarchism are philosophical opposites it is also true that socialists and anarchists were frequently the same people. As neither of their ideals was likely to reach fruition in the immediate future, their common opposition to the *status quo* was often of more importance than the divergence of their philosophies. When a socialist turned anarchist or vice versa, it meant simply that his antagonism to the actual was stronger than his allegiance to the ideal. And this is as it should be. Radicalism is much more effective as a protest than as a program and the more lightly the radical holds his ideal, the more successfully will he promote his fundamental purpose to make the world a better place to live in.

To some extent the above is an apology for refusing to enter into the tangled skein of socialist politics and philosophies. The squabbles of the Lassalleans and Marxians had little to do with the American labor movement. The fact that the Marxians thought of trade union organization as a means of setting up the socialist state, while the Lassalleans wanted a socialist state in order to set up trade unions, or something to that effect, means nothing. The important thing is that they, and the anarchists with them, possessed a class philosophy and propagated it vigorously among workingmen with some success. Their actual achievements were of little consequence, could be of little consequence unless they gave up their philosophies. Their strong point was agitation by word and deed, and the proposed May Day strike for eight hours gave them their chance. The eight-hour day was to them anathema, or should have been, but the chance for a demonstration against the established order was a godsend.

Socialism in America began with Robert Owen and his paternalistic community at New Harmony, Ind. This was preceded by the communism of the Shakers and Rappites but they were religious bodies whose economic practices were subordinate. Owen was followed by his son Robert Dale Owen, by the agrarianism of George Henry Evans, a follower of Spence, by Albert Brisbane's Fourierism and the Marxianism of Joseph Weydemeyer. The Civil War wiped out all these movements and even the ideas had difficulty in bridging the gap of 1860 to 1865. In 1870, three sections (German, French, and Bohemian) of the International Workingmen's Association (socialist) organized a central committee in New York, and by 1871 there were eight sections and 293 members of the International in the United States. Two American sections were added in 1871 under the leadership of William West, Victoria Woodhull, and Tennessee Claflin, but they were thrown out of the International the same year, and, in 1872, organized the American Confederation of the International at Philadelphia. At the Hague congress of the International in 1872, West's credentials were rejected and the followers of Bakunin thrown out. The general council of the International was moved from London to New York to keep it out of Bakunin's reach, and while the International declined, its New York headquarters made a nice toy for American socialists to play with. The last congress of the International was held in Geneva in 1873, but the general council (New York) was not represented. The unemployment parades in Chicago and New York in the winter of 1873-74, the latter ending in the Tompkins Square riot, were organized by socialists, but on July 15, 1876, at Philadelphia, the International Workingmen's Association was officially dissolved.

The Social Democratic Party of North America (Lassallean) was formed in May, 1874, with Adolph Strasser secretary, and P. J. McGuire a member of the executive board. It was represented by McGuire at the convention called by the Junior Sons of '76 (Greenbackers) at Tyrone, Pa., Dec. 28, 1875, and again at Pittsburgh, April 17, 1876. On July 19, 1876, at a congress at Philadelphia, the old International, the Social Democrats, the Labor Party of Illinois, and the Social Political Workingmen's Society of Cincinnati, fused to create the Workingmen's Party of the United States. The dead hand of the International was thus removed and the first united American socialist party was formed with an American, Phillip Van Patten, as secretary. In 1877, the socialists entered the local elections in New Haven, Cincinnati, Milwaukee, and Chicago. In Chicago, Albert R. Parsons, one of the few American socialists and a member of the Knights of Labor, ran for alderman in the fifteenth ward. Among his supporters were Karl Kling, Kraus, and Winnen. At a convention at Newark, Dec. 26, 1877, the name of the organization was changed to the Socialist Labor Party and officially it supported the candidacy of Weaver for President in 1880.

In 1875, the Chicago German socialists had organized a

Lehr and Wehr Verein, a workingmen's military society, which was copied in other places. This action was repudiated by the national executive committee in June, 1878, and after the election of 1880 the German, Bohemian, and Scandinavian subsections and the radical members of the English-speaking subsection in Chicago, decided that a new national executive was needed. The central committee of the Chicago section along with the agitation committee of the Grand Council of Armed Organizations, issued a call to all "revolutionists and armed workingmen's organizations in the country" to get ready to "offer an armed resistance to the invasions by the capitalistic class and capitalist legislatures." This was the beginning of the revolutionary movement in America. It grew out of and in opposition to the Socialist Labor Party and was composed of recently arrived immigrants, mostly German, many of them refugees from the German antisocialist laws. In New York a social revolutionary club was organized and affiliated with the International Working People's Association, the Black International, organized in 1881 by European anarchists. On Oct. 21, 1881, these revolutionary groups formed a national organization at Chicago. Among the delegates were Justus Schwab of New York, and Winnen, Parsons, August Spies, and Petersen of Chicago. The new International, in spite of the Chicago influence, rejected a political program and declared for direct revolutionary action. It called itself the Revolutionary Socialist Party. At the second convention at Pittsburgh, Oct. 19, 1883, the New York group was represented by Johann Most and Chicago by Parsons, Spies, Meng, and Rau.

Most was born in Augsburg in 1846. In 1864 he left Germany, and in 1870 was arrested in Vienna for revolutionary propaganda and sentenced to five years' imprisonment. He was released in 1871 after a political amnesty, but was expelled from Austria. He returned to Germany, was sent to jail for eight months in 1873, and ended up the year in the Reichstag. He was again arrested in 1877 and 1878, and on his release was forced to leave Germany. He went to London in December, 1878, and began publishing *Die Freiheit*, but his views were so extreme that Liebknecht repudiated his organ on behalf of the Social Democratic Party and Most turned anarchist. He wrote in praise of the assassination of Alexander II and London put him in jail. On his release in December, 1882, he reached New York and proceeded at once to advocate his "propaganda by deed." This was too much like murder and destruction to suit the Chicago anarchists, but New York, with its notorious gullibility, swallowed the Mostian nonsense whole.

The Pittsburgh convention issued a manifesto proposing to establish a free society by force. It advocated the destruction of the existing class rule by

energetic, relentless, revolutionary and international action, the establishment of a free society based on coöperative organization of production; free exchange of equivalent products by and between the productive organizations without commerce and profit-mongery; the organization of education on a secular, scientific and equal basis for both sexes; equal rights for all without distinction of sex or race, and the regulation of public affairs by free contracts between the autonomous communes and associations resting on a federalistic basis.[12]

The name of the organization was changed to the International Working People's Association and it achieved a momentary fame in the hysteria which followed the Haymarket bomb.

This sudden emergence of a revolutionary philosophy in the America of 1883-86 requires some explanation, but not nearly as much as appears on the surface. Aside from the

---

[12] This record is taken from Perlman, in Commons and Associates, *History of Labour in the United States*, Vol. II.

belligerent tone in which it was uttered, and this was unquestionably the tone of Johann Most who had been in
America less than a year, the philosophy was in keeping
with that of the older American tradition. Robert Owen,
Brisbane, Evans, even Horace Greeley, would have felt
themselves at home in this talk of a free society based on
coöperative production, non-profit-making exchange of
commodities, secular, scientific, and equal education, equal
rights, and federalism. Anarchism was in fact a reactionary
philosophy. It aimed to retrace the steps taken by modern
industrialism back into a simpler and perhaps a happier
past. It came chiefly out of Russia where medievalism
longest retained its hold in sharp contrast with an alien industrialism. Modern socialism on the other hand grew out
of the established industrialism of England where Karl
Marx learned that the Industrial Revolution could not be
stemmed and turned back, but might be forced on to an
impasse.

The new and alarming feature of the Black International
had to do, not with its purposes, but with its methods. It
had become evident by 1883 that political action in America
on the part of the "proletariat" was a dismal failure. The
campaigns of the seventies were flashes in the pan. When
the farmers were miserable they would rush into politics,
and when the workers were depressed they, or their leaders,
would do the same. But their respective miseries seldom
synchronized, were in fact of such a nature that synchro-
nization was almost impossible. The wage-earners were hurt
and the farmers benefited by high prices, while high wages
put the shoe on the other foot. Only in long periods of depression was their misery common, as in the seventies, and
then they seldom wanted the same thing. But America was
predominantly agricultural and a pure and simple labor
party had no chance at all. Politics then was a washout,

and disappointment with politics turned the American wage-earner and his foreign adviser in other directions. Trade unionism was a possibility, but the trade unions were unsympathetic toward the alien and seemed to have achieved nothing. The Germans organized some unions of their own, but many of the immigrants were intellectuals and knew no trade but that of propaganda. The Knights of Labor was open to them and they went into it freely, but were unable to capture it from the Irish-English clique in control.

From impotent politics to arid trade unionism the foreign intellectuals were driven, until in desperation they listened to the voice of anarchy out of the oppressed past, and America was suddenly confronted with the black flag of assassination and terror.

American anarchism was represented by the International Workingmen's Association, the Red International, so-called because of the color of its membership card. It was organized in San Francisco by Burnette G. Haskell in 1881 and gained a following because of the anti-Chinese agitation. It spread east as far as Denver where the Rocky Mountain division was formed by Joseph R. Buchanan in 1883. The Red International was quite innocuous, but Haskell and Buchanan managed by their aggressiveness to make Powderly uncomfortable and that, in the opinion of some, was sufficient justification for the existence of the society.

It was this situation which confronted Powderly in 1884-85, when the Federation of Trades and Labor Unions threw out its suggestion for an eight-hour strike on May 1, 1886. Powderly, in addition to being a careful if not timorous man in action, was the head of a large organization which would have to bear the burden of an eight-hour strike almost alone. He was not the kind of man to take the thing in hand and put it over, and unless he did, it was certain to degenerate into mass demonstrations under the leadership of radicals for whom an occasion of that sort was exactly made, not for eight-hour but for propaganda purposes.

It is true that Powderly with his essays on the eight-hour question was about as ridiculous as a man could be. He was afraid, and as it turned out, his fear was well founded. He was non-class conscious and greatly influenced by the press, and the press was talking about five men, the general executive board, being able to stop the industry of the country, and computing the membership of the Order in millions. Powderly was perhaps the only labor leader who ever underestimated the strength of his organization, and because justice has a streak of poetry in it, the more millions he denied the more he was credited with.

But the fat was in the fire and nothing Powderly might do could prevent some sort of demonstration on May Day, 1886. His opposition, however, helped to prevent effective and concerted action. The situation was greatly confused. The International Bricklayers' Union, for example, decided to ask for a nine-hour day, but the United Order of Bricklayers and Stonemasons of Chicago, an assembly of the Knights of Labor, decided on eight hours,[13] and many local assemblies passed resolutions in favor of "the action of the General Assembly" in fixing May 1, 1886, for the eight-hour strike. Others, understanding that the General Assembly had taken no such action, endorsed the plan of the Federation.

The trade unions were quite as confused as the Knights of Labor on the matter. Swinton said:

It is questionable whether the eight-hour movement will be a success in this city [New York]. . . . The building trades of New York and Brooklyn have adopted the nine-hour rule . . .

---

[13] John Swinton, *John Swinton's Paper*, Feb. 14, 1884.

and the sash and blind makers have fallen into line. The clothing cutters declared last Sunday they were not prepared to put
the eight-hour day in force. The cabinet makers and cigar
makers appear to be the only trades that will make an effort
to adopt the eight-hour day on May 1 and already many unions
in the latter organization have presented amendments to the
constitution some providing for a nine-hour day and others leaving it optional with the local unions. The former trade is
closely affiliated with the carpenters and many cabinet makers
say that the carpenters by adopting the nine-hour day have
spoiled the movement.[14]

The only thing done by the Federation to organize the
May Day movement was to send out printed agreements
to the unions requiring an eight-hour day, with instructions
to present them to employers on May 1.[15]

Early in 1886, the organization of new Knights of Labor
assemblies was stopped for forty days and on March 13
Powderly issued a secret circular warning the Order against
too rapid growth, strikes, and the May Day demonstration.
"No assembly," he declared, "must strike for the eight-hour
system on May 1st under the impression they are obeying
orders from headquarters, for such an order was not and
will not be given. . . ."

It is evident from this circular that Powderly was fright-
ened. The Southwestern strike had just begun. The Order
was growing too rapidly for its health or the health of the
trade unions, which were knocking on Powderly's door and
asking him to call off his organizers. The anarchists within
the Order and without were making themselves heard. And
the Church, ever a danger to the Knights, was again looking
askance at its power and possibilities. "I am neither physically nor mentally capable of performing the work required
of me," Powderly complained, and he proposed to resign,

---

[14] *Ibid.*, March 21, 1886.
[15] *The Carpenter*, February, 1886.

because the members of the Order were putting him in a false position before the public.

The eight-hour movement of May 1, 1886, was a flop, but it had some success in Chicago, especially among the packing-house workers, and gave occasion to the Haymarket bomb and its reverberations throughout the world.

THE HAYMARKET BOMB

The conflict between the Cigar Makers and the Knights of Labor in New York had its counterpart in Chicago, and in each case it was primarily an internal rupture within the Cigar Makers' organization itself. The difference between the two cities was that in New York, District Assembly No. 49 took the part of the Progressive Cigar Makers against the International, while in Chicago both the International and District Assembly No. 24 kept out of the controversy. The Chicago anarchists who entered the Black International in 1883 were socialists driven to advocate direct action by their failure at the polls and the brutality of the Chicago police. Unlike the New York anarchists, they were in close touch with the trade unions especially those composed chiefly of German, Scandinavian, and Bohemian workers. In February, 1884, the Progressive Cigar Makers of Chicago held a mass meeting, and under the influence of Spies and Grottkau passed a resolution for "open rebellion of the robbed class." In June they seceded from the Amalgamated Trades and Labor Assembly of Chicago and organized, with the German metal workers, the carpenters and joiners,[16] the cabinet workers, and the butchers, the Progressive Central Labor Union. By the end of 1885 the Central Labor Union was nearly as large and strong as the old Amalgamated and on friendly terms with the Black International.

---

[16] An anarchist secession from the Brotherhood of Carpenters and Joiners.

The Central Labor Union began to agitate for the eight-hour day in November, 1885, and united the labor movement of the city in an eight-hour league composed of the Amalgamated Assembly, the Socialist Party, the Knights of Labor, and the Central Labor Union. On the Sunday before May 1, 1886, an eight-hour demonstration was held of about 25,000 people addressed by Parsons, Spies, Fielden, and Schwab. Chicago was in a state of terror, but May Day passed without serious trouble. The only marked success of the eight-hour movement was among the packing-house workers.

In February the workers in the McCormick Harvester Company had been locked out, and on May 3 occurred one of a series of encounters between the police and the locked-out workers. The men were holding a meeting near the McCormick plant with Spies as their speaker. They attacked the strike breakers as they were leaving the works and the police rode into them, killing four and wounding many others. Spies rushed to the office of the *Alarm* and issued a call to all workmen to "arm yourselves and appear in full force," at a demonstration the next night at Haymarket Square on the West Side, to "denounce the latest atrocious act of the police."

A crowd of perhaps 3,000 gathered near Haymarket Square at 7:30 P.M., May 4. They were addressed by Spies, Parsons, and Fielden. The Desplaines Street police station was just half a block away, and there Captain John Bonfield and a body of reserves waited for trouble. Mayor Carter Harrison attended the meeting and between ten and eleven o'clock, after Spies and Parsons had spoken, rain set in and the crowd began to break up. Mayor Harrison left and stopped at the Desplaines Street station to tell Bonfield that the meeting had been peaceful and there was no further danger. The Mayor out of the way, Bonfield marched 280 police out of the station and into the crowd of perhaps 200 people who remained listening to Fielden. Fielden protested and as Bonfield ordered the crowd to disperse a bomb was thrown among the police, throwing sixty to the ground and wounding seven of them fatally. The police reorganized and fired into the crowd. ⌈The Haymarket bomb, coming as it did at the end of a long series of strikes, agitations, and threats threw the nation, and Chicago especially, into a panic of fear and hatred and the city was combed for victims of the general lust for revenge.⌋ The police, notoriously brutal in the past, with the added provocation of their comrades' deaths and the encouraging hysteria of the community filled the jails, and out of the haul, eight men—August Spies, Michael Schwab, Samuel Fielden, Adolph Fischer, George Engel, Oscar Neebe, Louis Lingg, and Albert R. Parsons—were finally sent up for trial. There was not a shred of evidence to connect these men with the Haymarket bomb throwing. They were anarchists, and had talked wildly of violence and revolution at one time or another, and on these grounds they were found guilty of "murder in the manner and form charged in the indictment." It was a case of Society against Anarchy with revenge as the motive.

Neebe was sentenced to imprisonment for fifteen years and the other seven to death. A motion for a new trial was denied by the trial judge, Joseph E. Gary, and the date of the execution set for Dec. 3, 1886. Under a stay of execution the case was carried to the Illinois Supreme Court which, after six months' consideration, unanimously denied a writ of error. The United States Supreme Court was appealed to and affirmed the legality of the forms under which the Chicago court had proceeded. Governor Oglesby was appealed to and he intimated that clemency would be extended at least to Parsons if he would petition for it, but Parsons refused because it would injure the chances of his comrades. Lingg, Engel, and Fischer also refused to petition for clemency. On Thursday, Nov. 10, 1887, the Governor commuted the sentences of Fielden and Schwab to life imprisonment and Lingg committed suicide in his cell. And on Friday—the real Black Friday in American history—Parsons, Spies, Fischer, and Engel were hanged until they were dead. On June 26, 1893, Fielden, Schwab, and Neebe were pardoned and set free by Governor John Peter Altgeld.

The only direct connection between the Chicago anarchists and the Knights of Labor lay in the fact that Parsons was a member of the Order. He had joined Local Assembly No. 400, the first local in Chicago in 1877, and was transferred when it dissolved in 1885 to Local Assembly No. 1307 of which he was a member until his execution. But this connection was enough, under the circumstances, to blacken the name of the Order and drive thousands of members out of its fold. Coming on top of the Southwest strike, the attack of the trade unions, and the revival of the opposition of the Catholic Church, it left the Knights dazed and defenseless. Powderly, and the Order as a whole, were caught up in the general panic, and not only failed to go to Parsons' aid, but by their loud repudiation of his opinions did him some harm and themselves no good. No more hysterical outburst could be found in the most capitalistic of the "capitalist" press than the following from the Chicago *Knights of Labor*:

Let it be understood by all the world that the Knights of Labor have no affiliation, association, sympathy or respect for the band of cowardly murderers, cutthroats and robbers, known as anarchists, who sneak through the country like midnight assassins, stirring up the passions of ignorant foreigners, unfurling the red flag of anarchy and causing riot and bloodshed.

Parsons, Spies, Fielden, Most and all their followers, sympathizers, aiders and abettors, should be summarily dealt with. They are entitled to no more consideration than wild beasts. The leaders are cowards and their followers are fools.

Knights of Labor, boycott them. If one of the gang of scoundrels should by any mistake get access to our organization expel them at once. Brand them as outlawed monsters . . . as human monstrosities not entitled to the sympathy or consideration of any person in the world.

We are sure we voice the sentiments of the whole organization when we say that we hope Parsons, Spies, Most, Fielden and the whole gang of outlaws will be blotted from the surface of the earth.[17]

On July 2, 1886, District Assembly No. 24 of Chicago voted to expel all anarchists including Parsons from the Order, but Local Assembly No. 1307 refused to expel Parsons and theirs was the final word.[18] In November, District Assembly No. 24 reversed itself and sent representatives to the Governor to prevent the execution.[19] At Richmond, in October, the General Assembly received a resolution from Quinn of New York expressing sorrow at the "intended execution of seven workingmen in Chicago," and appealing for mercy on their behalf. This was a very mild request five months after the Haymarket incident, but Powderly spoke against it. "Under no circumstances," he said, "should we do anything that can even by implication be interpreted as identification with the anarchist element."[20] A substitute for Quinn's motion was passed that was more in the nature of an apology for the Order than a plea for the anarchists: "While asking mercy for the condemned men," it read, "we are not in sympathy with the

---

[17] Chicago *Knights of Labor*, May 8, 1886, quoted by E. A. Cook *Knights of Labor*, illustrated, p. 16. The paper later changed its tone, spoke of the "so-called anarchists," called them "martyrs," and their execution "judicial murder."

[18] Swinton, *op. cit.*, July 11 and 25, 1886.

[19] *Ibid.*, Nov. 28, 1886.

[20] Powderly, *op. cit.*, p. 280.

acts of the anarchists nor with any attempts of individuals or associated bodies that teach or practice violent infractions of the law, believing that peaceful methods are the surest and best means to secure necessary reforms." [21]   In November, Mrs. George Rodgers told Powderly that District Assembly No. 24 had passed resolutions of sympathy with the anarchists and proposed to call a joint meeting of District Assemblies Nos. 24 and 57 to appropriate money for their defense. Powderly replied that no anarchist resolutions were to be passed and no money raised. The resolution of District Assembly No. 24 denounced the verdict of the Chicago court "as the result of capitalistic and judicial conspiracy," which Powderly decided was not called for by the circumstances.[22]

At the Minneapolis convention in 1887, James Quinn offered another resolution in support of the anarchists, protesting against capital punishment in general and proposing that the Order use its influence to secure a commutation of sentence. Powderly ruled the resolution out of order, but was forced to give his reasons on an appeal against his ruling. Extreme caution marked his statement, and extreme fear of public opinion. This was a year and a half after the bomb throwing and a month before the execution. The panic had passed. Thousands had changed their views and there was a considerable agitation for clemency. Yet Powderly could think of nothing but the danger of associating the Order with anarchy. "Better," he said, "that seven times seven men hang than to hang the millstone of odium around the standard of this Order in affiliating in any way with this element of destruction." He talked of "sniveling" anarchists when the men who were about to die were refusing to petition the Governor for mercy. "For Parsons,"

---

[21] *Proceedings,* 1886 General Assembly, p. 287.
[22] *Ibid.,* 1887 General Assembly, pp. 1499-1513.

he said, "and the other condemned men let there be mercy. I have no grudge against them. In fact I would never trouble my head about them were it not for the welfare of this Order." [23] After the speech, Powderly's ruling was sustained and the Order made no effort to aid Parsons and his associates.

This, however, was the official Powderly, in what he considered the defense of the Order of which he was head. As a private individual he was a more kindly and sympathetic person, which goes to show what officialdom will do to humanity. "Four of the poor fellows walked the plank to-day," he wrote to Hayes on November 12. "I have never felt so stirred before. I have more respect for Parsons, Fischer, Engel, and Spies than ever. They were sincere, and say what you will of Lingg by Heaven he died true to his teachings even though they were damn bad teachings." It is well to know that they had his respect at last, but unfortunate that he could never have had theirs.

[The Haymarket bomb put an end to the eight-hour movement for the time being and what gains were made were lost before the end of the year.] In 1889, Gompers wrote the International Typographical Union that "in the present condition of organized labor" no movement looking to a general strike upon so early a date would receive his countenance or support, and decided that one union should be selected to attempt to establish the eight-hour day. The Knights of Labor were asked to support the Federation program and replied by asking the Federation "to indicate the trade or trades . . . which are prepared to successfully inaugurate the eight-hour movement on May 1, 1890, confident that the Knights of Labor will lend their moral support. . . ." [24] That was all the support it had left to offer.

---

[23] Powderly, *op. cit.*, p. 283-86.
[24] *Proceedings*, 1889 General Assembly, pp. 51-52.

CHAPTER XIV

COÖPERATION

Four main strands are discoverable in the American labor movement: fraternalism, collective bargaining, coöperation, and politics. While it is assumed to-day that collective bargaining is the major function of a labor union, it took nearly half a century of agitation and experiment to reach this assumption, and even now it is accepted in some quarters with reservations and in a few, not at all.

The reluctance of the labor movement to accept collective bargaining as its major function was due largely to the fact that this involved an acceptance of the wage system. Before the Civil War the wage system was a fact, but not necessarily an irrevocable one, and attempts to escape from it or replace it by something else were not so obviously hopeless as they later became. Thus the communities of Owen and the Associationists were less fantastic in their time than they may seem to-day, and the coöperative tradition which derived from them, seemed to make sense in an industrial community of small shops and stores. With the growth of large-scale production, producers' coöperation became increasingly anachronistic, but the tradition persisted because of an obstinate idealism that would not admit the reality and stability of the wage system.

Coöperation was an adaptation of the communities of Owen and the Associationists to meet the needs of wage-earners who were not free to pick up and move into a new, specially created environment. In the communities both production and consumption or exchange were on a coöperative basis and complementary, but coöperative production was the more vital and revolutionary because it struck at the wage system, which consumers' coöperation did not. When, instead of setting up a coöperative community, the workers began to coöperate at home they had to choose between producers' and consumers' coöperation, between the shop and the store. They tried both, but while the store was easier and more successful, the older coöperators looked upon it as a poor thing. It provided cheap groceries and may have operated to keep down the level of wages. Some of the Associationists tried to use the stores to promote producers' coöperation by charging market prices for goods and saving up a reserve to use in coöperative shops. But, as the store coöperators who paid market prices for their goods were seldom the same people who were set up with the surplus in coöperative shops, the plan failed.

The coöperative philosophy rested upon a fallacy common to the early economics, namely, that the production of tangible goods is a superior function to the rendering of less tangible services. This was due to the fact that in a simple economic society the producer, capitalist, and distributor were one and the same person and when they became separated it seemed to the producer at least that his was the most, if not the only important function involved. Coöperation tended then not to eliminate the capitalist and the middleman but to revert to the simpler nonspecialized situation in which all three functions were lodged in one group of persons. For productive purposes this has never worked. No shop or factory has been able to maintain efficiency where the workers themselves own and operate the plant. If the business succeeds the original workers become managers and stockholders, employing new men in a purely wage capacity, or some sort of paternalism is set up such as profit sharing and copartnership. But usually the business fails.

The coöperative store is another matter. Based on Rochdale principles it is capable of a conservative success at least with a wage-earning class that is not dominated by its women and the desire to keep up with the Joneses. The outstanding success in consumers' coöperation, the English and Scotch coöperatives, are sound and unprogressive. Their premises and stocks are unattractive but they have met the requirements of the English and Scotch working people in the past and will in the future, at least until the Englishman's castle becomes his wife's boudoir. In the United States, where style and smartness take precedence over quality, and where women dominate the market, the coöperative store of the conventional sort can hardly hope to succeed.

The Knights of Labor was not a coöperative society, as has been sometimes asserted, nor did it emphasize coöperation in any special way. It had a coöperative plank in its platform, but, as has been pointed out, this platform was borrowed *in toto* from the Industrial Congress, and any general trade or labor society of that period would have had a similar provision. Coöperation was in the air and could not be avoided. Local and district assemblies ventured upon coöperative enterprises, stores, mines, mills, and factories, but without much theoretical background and usually as a result of unsuccessful strikes. The most common coöperative practice of the assemblies was the building of their own quarters with a coöperative store underneath, in part because they had nothing much else to do, and in part to get away from the traditional workingman's club, the saloon. The Order engaged in one rather large coöperative experiment but this was forced upon it. It established a coöperative board but it established boards for almost everything and the coöperative board was the least effective of them all. Powderly was not a convinced co-operator and though Litchman may have been, he was much more an office-holder and politician. So far as organization went the Order was well adapted to coöperative enterprises and there was some idea that the locals would eventually be productive, and the districts distributive units in a coöperative commonwealth.

Uriah Stephens' thought was that the Knights of Labor had a twofold function: "pure and simple" mitigation of the immediate conditions of the wage system, and the long term job of substituting coöperation for capitalism. The first was to be done by the trade locals and the second by the mixed districts.[1]

This was an interesting proposal and one which differentiates the Knights of Labor from its successor, the American Federation of Labor. The latter definitely repudiated "ultimate" aims. The former, while not ignoring the immediate improvement of the condition of the wage-earner, retained not only a general purpose but a specific organization for achieving that purpose. The mixed district assembly was, in Stephens' view, the organ through which labor's idealism would take form and create the nucleus of the new coöperative society that was to be born.

Stephens' position, then, was a compromise between the early idealism of the labor movement which tended to ignore the wage system and work only for the coöperative commonwealth that was to displace it, and the later acquiescence of the American Federation of Labor which repudiated idealism for immediate and practical achievements within the wage system itself. And if the Knights

---

[1] *Proceedings*, 1879 General Assembly of the Knights of Labor, St. Louis, p. 56.

of Labor failed to hold even the balance between practicality and idealism it is no less than most human institutions have done.

But Stephens' idea was never seriously considered by the Order. The districts did not take up coöperation and when the founder dropped out, his plan was forgotten.

Powderly was not at heart a coöperator, though he paid lip service to his predecessor's ideal. Powderly inherited from the agrarian individualism of George Henry Evans, and what he really believed in was not coöperation but independence. In 1880, under the head of "colonization," he spoke of men banding together "for the purpose of securing the greatest good for the greatest number and place the man who is willing to toil on his own homestead." [2] At the same time he spoke of coöperation "which will make every man his own master—every man his own employer. . . ." The first was agrarianism; the second producers' coöperation. The first had Powderly's profound allegiance; the second only his official ukase.

As has been pointed out in another chapter, one of the first steps taken by the Order was the arrangement for a resistance or strike fund at the first General Assembly. This fund was to be collected and held intact until 1880. In the meantime Powderly became grand master, the anti-strike sentiment increased and Litchman predicated most of the fund for publicity. In 1880, the name was changed to Defense Fund and the general executive board recommended its theoretical sum to be distributed as follows: 10 per cent for organization; not more than 30 per cent for strikes, with the recommendation that on approved strikes "brothers be assisted into self-help by coöperative enterprises if possible"; 30 per cent for coöperation; and 10 per cent for education. But the coöperative counsels were

---

[2] *Ibid.*, 1880 General Assembly, p. 171.

confused and the general executive board suggested holding up the imaginary 30 per cent for coöperation, because, while it "is the order of human progress . . . imperfect ideas prevail in reference to its vital principle."

But the 1880 General Assembly was more strongly coöperative than the general executive board and decided that 30 per cent of the Defense Fund should be used for strikes, 10 per cent for education, and the remaining 60 per cent held for productive and distributive coöperation after 1881. Between 1880 and 1881, however, Secretary Litchman spent most of the Defense Fund for a printing press. What remained was credited to the assemblies on their per capita tax, and the Defense Fund disappeared.

Litchman was deposed in 1881 and his recommendation to create a compulsory coöperative fund was not sent to the committee on laws nor reported to the General Assembly. The Order seemed to be on its last legs anyway and was especially tired of funds which somehow never reached their destinations. A committee, however, was appointed to revise the constitution and deal with any question brought forward by the general officers or committees which might have been neglected by the General Assembly. Under this authority the constitution was revised to include Litchman's compulsory Coöperative Fund.[3] This fund was to be under the control of a coöperative board to be invested in worthy coöperative projects on instructions from the General Assembly.

There was a great deal of criticism of the compulsory feature of the Coöperative Fund, and of the way in which it had been put in the constitution, and the 1882 General Assembly, while appointing a coöperative board, made contribution to the fund voluntary. The board reported in 1883 that it had not held a meeting during the year and

---

[3] *Journal,* p. 282.

that only $400 had been paid in. Its secretary found his services "comparatively honorary." The board had no power to start or assist coöperation, and no money if it had had the power. All it could do was write letters, advising local coöperators how to proceed.

While coöperation by the Order was in name only, coöperation by the locals was very low. In 1883, only nineteen locals reported anything in answer to the grand statistician's question on coöperation and "none of them reported as being in a very flourishing condition." [4]   The trouble in Texas was an interesting one. Coöperative stores could not get going because so many Knights had stores of their own.

The simple fact was that, while the older generation was more or less interested in coöperation, the membership of the Order was not, and the matter resolved itself into a conflict between immediate, pure and simple needs of the rank and file and the philosophical purposes of the labor reformers, with the general officers inclined toward coöperation but forced into collective bargaining and strike aid.

In 1883, contribution to the Coöperative Fund was left voluntary, a Board of Trustees was created to take charge of it, and Henry E. Sharpe was made president of the coöperative board. It was beginning to be evident, however, that people would not voluntarily contribute to a general fund from which they would get no direct benefit and over which they would have no control, and Sharpe proposed a grandiose scheme of a guild for integral coöperation, productive and distributive, "of the Order, for the Order and by the Order." [5]   On Jan. 1, 1884, Sharpe called in the coöperative funds of the locals, but the response was not enthusiastic and the board of trustees had to write to the

---

[4] *Proceedings*, 1883 General Assembly, pp. 429-30.
[5] *Ibid.*, 1884 General Assembly, p. 608.

assemblies, pointing out that the coöperative funds did not belong to the locals but to the Order as a whole. The result was that by Sept. 1, 1884, the Coöperative Fund in the hands of the trustees amounted to $969.55.[6]

The Knights' passion for lawmaking had got them into the peculiar fix that their coöperative law was standing in the way of coöperation. A local was unable to collect money to coöperate on its own account and unwilling to raise it for coöperation by the Order. And if it asked for aid from the Order for the purpose of coöperation, it was told that "the Coöperative Board could take no action in the matter."[7] But with less than $1,000 the coöperative board could not launch any large scheme for integral coöperation, and the net result of the whole arrangement was just correspondence. With Powderly furiously writing letters at Scranton throughout his whole career, with Litchman keeping his presses hot at Marblehead, and the coöperative board writing and printing of coöperation in England, France, Germany, and Timbuctoo, the Knights of Labor was probably the greatest propaganda agency of its time.

Henry Sharpe's integral coöperation closely resembled the ideas of the Associationists of the forties and in the early part of 1884 led him to establish a coöperative colony at Eglinton, Taney County, Mo. Here the usual quarrels arose and Sharpe was suspended by the general executive board and later reinstated with the agreement of the local court. But the colony broke up as colonies of that sort have a habit of doing.

The committee on coöperation of the 1884 General As-

---

[6] *Proceedings*, 1884 General Assembly, pp. 679-80. This later increased probably with interest to $1,033.97 and was never used. It was returned to the subscribers in 1888. (*Proceedings*, 1888 General Assembly, pp. 23-24.)

[7] *Proceedings*, 1884 General Assembly, p. 616.

sembly reported against compulsory contribution to the Co-operative Fund but recommended the formation of the voluntary guild, and the General Assembly voted against compulsory coöperation and refused the guild a charter. Sharpe resigned in disgust and was succeeded by John J. McCartney with John Samuel as secretary.[8]

The new committee turned from coöperation by the Order to the encouragement of local coöperative enterprises. It had no money to help these, but made some attempt to find out what was being done. Turner found coöperative hat companies at Haverhill, Mass., and at South Norwalk, Conn., a Co-operative Knitting Company at St. Louis, and the National Coöperative Tobacco Company at Raleigh, N. C., all needing funds.[9] In 1886, the coöperative board had fallen so low that the expenses of its members had to be paid out of the general fund. There was not even enough in the Coöperative Fund to pay postage. Another attempt was made to force compulsory coöperation on the Order, but was forestalled by a provision that $10,000 per quarter for the following year would be set aside for the co-operative board from the general receipts of the Order.[10] But on December 9 the general executive board decided to keep the money for itself and notified the coöperative board that it had no power to loan money.[11] Coöperation, how-ever, was active in 1887 and a great deal of information was collected and published regarding it.

In 1890, the majority of the coöperative board suggested that coöperation be given up and that the Order join with the Farmers' Alliance and "kindred industrial organizations in independent political action." Over the protest of the

[8] *Ibid.*, p. 788; *Journal*, p. 790.

[9] *Proceedings*, 1885 General Assembly, pp. 36, 93.

[10] *Ibid*, 1886 General Assembly, p. 292.

[11] *Ibid.*, 1887 General Assembly, p. 1590.

last of the Knights' coöperators, Henry A. Beckmeyer, this self-denying ordinance was adopted.[12] A committee of three was appointed on coöperation in 1892, politics having promised more than it performed, and in 1893 the coöperative board was reëstablished.

THE CANNELBURG COAL MINE

While the Knights of Labor talked and legislated about coöperation by the Order as a whole, there was only one specific instance of their doing anything about it. The Cannelburg Coal Company came into the hands of the general executive board in what amounted to liquidation. It was no part of the policy of the Order. It was not managed by the coöperative board. And its failure and cost were responsible for the reluctance of the Order to take on any other such ventures in spite of the theoretical belief in coöperation as a solution of the problems of the wage-earners.

In the winter of 1883, eight miners were locked out by the Buckeye Cannel Coal Company of Cannelburg, Ind., for membership in the Knights of Labor. They leased land adjoining the Buckeye mine and entered the same vein. Back forfeits were due on the leases amounting to $1,200 and the men assigned their property to a lawyer of Washington, Ind., to meet them. They appealed to the general executive board to help them carry this obligation, carefully explaining that the forfeits were returnable out of royalties when the property was worked. The mine head was only one-half mile from the railroad and during the winter they hauled their coal by wagon. But in the spring, when they asked for help, the wagon road was impassable, their notes were due, and a promising venture in coöperation was coming to an end. The general executive board

---

[12] *Ibid.*, 1890 General Assembly, pp. 52-54.

appealed to the Glass Workers, always financially sound and just out of a long victorious strike for which they gave the Order the credit, and $2,000 was forthcoming. The miners' notes were taken up and the Knights of Labor found itself with a fine coal property on its hands. The general executive board incorporated itself as the Union Mining Company of Cannelburg, Ind., in trust for the Order, and the experiment was launched.

The experiment was launched with a great flourish in April, 1884, and explains the wave of enthusiasm for coöperation that swept the Order in that year. It was discovered that the founders had intended in the beginning that the Order was to be the means of transition from the wage system to the coöperative system, and that some day the Knights of Labor "shall be a great industrial union, possessing sufficient natural resources and so industrially organized that its members shall through their own labors supply themselves with all those things necessary to the comfort of their lives. . . ." But while this ideal was to be kept firmly in mind, it would not do to rush indiscriminately into coöperation—the general executive board was thinking of its treasury. They must begin in a small way and the Cannelburg mine was evidently it. The capital for the new company was to be $10,000, and as no compulsory assessment could be made for it, an appeal was sent out for a loan from the assemblies.

Debentures were issued in $5.00 denominations and the following rules were laid down:

1. The workers shall receive current wages.
2. All necessary incidental expenses and repairs will be paid.
3. Debenture holders will receive 5 per cent interest per annum and "what remains after paying the foregoing shall be styled profit and shall be divided as follows": 10 per cent to be set aside for the furtherance of coöperation; 10 per cent as a sinking fund to retire the bonds; 3 per cent as a local education

fund, and the balance "to be divided equally between capital
and labor—that is to say, between the workers of the mine and
the debenture holders, in the ratio of the amount represented by
wages paid to the amount paid in for debentures."

The Knights of Labor fell for the fifty-fifty fake by
dividing the surplus between wages and capital which are
not comparable, instead of between wages and interest
which are. But no tears need be shed over that. There
was no surplus to divide.

The bonds of the Union Mining Company did not sell
and a 20-cent assessment was levied to put the mine
in shape. A year after the general executive board had
taken over the property, the half-mile switch to the Ohio
and Mississippi Railroad had not been built. The Buckeye
company was making no attempt to fight. It was hemmed
in by the leases originally acquired by the eight coöperators
and offered to sell out. The general executive board refused and finally acquired a right of way and had the
switch built. The railroad graded for a sidetrack but
failed to lay the rails, and work had to be stopped at the
mine until the coal on the surface was disposed of. The
ordinary bituminous was sold locally, but the cannel coal
had to be shipped. The return from the assessment was
slow and the board had to advance money from the general
fund. They had sunk a new shaft, built the switch, put in
machinery and pumps, and were ready to buy a switch
engine as soon as the railroad connected them with its
sidetrack.[13]

There is no certainty here that either the Buckeye company or the railroad wanted to ruin the coöperative experiment of the Order. The Buckeye company, though it was
referred to as a flourishing capitalist concern, was evidently neither very prosperous nor very alert. It was an

[13] *Ibid.*, 1885 General Assembly, pp. 55-57, 67-68.

old mine and the company had never taken the trouble to secure the leases to the south. When the original coöperators picked these up for a song they had the Buckeye people in a pocket. The latter seem never to have offered to buy, but they were quite willing to sell or amalgamate the two properties and sell to a third interest. The railroad was doubtful about the ability of the Union Mining Company to make a success of their project and delayed the laying of a sidetrack to connect the mine switch to the main line. It refused to supply a switch engine on the grounds that it would not pay the road. But until the Knights had failed there was no suggestion that the railroad deliberately killed their scheme. It was killed by lack of funds and uncertainty of management.

The original coöperators had sunk a shaft into an ordinary soft coal vein. When the general executive board took over the property they sent in a manager who was not a practical miner and started a new shaft. Later they sent William T. Lewis to take charge and he finished the new shaft on Nov. 17, 1884, striking a vein of cannel coal which could not be marketed locally or used for domestic purposes unless broken up by machinery. The market for cannel coal was limited and Lewis admitted that there was not room for both companies. The board had spent $20,000 and would need $4,000 more for an engine. "When that is accomplished," they complained, "we will have to enter the market in competition with a bitter opponent who has been fighting us since the opening of the mine, and, considering the opposition from a great number of the Assemblies to the payment of the assessment . . . " they recommended that the mine be sold or leased.[14] Of course the Buckeye mine and the railroad company were blamed for the delay, but Lewis found the management inefficient;

---

[14] *Ibid.*, p. 92.

and the difficulty in securing a right of way for the switch was probably due simply to the normal reluctance of the farmers to cutting up their lands and their exaggerated ideas of the value of something wanted badly by some one else. No capitalist conspiracy was needed to make the farmers hard-boiled.

The Buckeye company insisted throughout that there was not room for both mines and offered to amalgamate, giving the Knights control and management of the mining and keeping the merchandising and finance for themselves. This would have made an interesting experiment, but the General Assembly rejected it because one of the original co-operators was opposed. He later changed his mind but the General Assembly had spoken and the general officers could not reverse its decision.

The mine could not be sold, and in 1886 it was leased to the Mutual Mining Company, composed of members of the Order. It seems to have brought in some return for a few years, but played out and in 1897 was sold for $4,000 cash.

CHAPTER XV

THE BOYCOTT

THE boycott was the most successful form of union activity found in the Knights, and the Order was the most successful boycotting organization in the history of American labor. Hundreds of boycotts were managed by locals and districts and a few by the general executive board, while numbers of others were laid by open trade unions and their effectiveness secured by the coöperation of the Order.

Yet the boycott was not mentioned in the preamble nor thought of by the early leaders. The boycott, like the strike, was forced upon the general officers but, unlike the strike, they pushed it in one case at least with vigor and determination. They had a strong prejudice against strikes growing out of the experience of the seventies while the boycott was of comparatively recent origin. It is true that in the beginning of the American labor movement there had been boycotts against nonunion workers but it was not until the influence of the Irish was felt that the boycott began to be used generally against employers.

In the eighties the boycott had the obvious advantage over the strike in that it was cheap and easy, and any suffering it might cause to other workers was indirect and concealed. Then, too, it took some time for the courts to get around to it. Its disadvantages appeared later. A boycott was more easily imposed than lifted; it threw men out of work; and it involved in most cases action by a group that was not directly involved, against individuals and concerns which had committed no direct offense.

The unusual success of the Knights of Labor with the boycott can be attributed in part to the fact that they were as much a consumer as a producer body. The trade unions, too, used the boycott effectively in the eighties, but often because of the assistance of the Knights, and fundamentally the success of the boycott in the eighties was due, aside from the slowness of the courts and the consumer character of the Order, to a social condition that has largely passed away—a condition of labor solidarity and class consciousness.

It is commonly supposed that class consciousness is increasing rather than diminishing in this and other countries. This is in fact the basic assumption of socialist, communist, and anarchist thought. But so far as the United States is concerned this supposition is open to serious criticism. It would be out of place and unwarranted here to suggest that class consciousness will not increase in the future. It is ordinarily assumed that with the disappearance of free land and the growth of large-scale production, the wage-earner is or will be more and more relegated to a fixed status from which there can be no escape, and that such a condition is bound to create class consciousness and labor solidarity. This study is, however, not concerned with what may happen in the future but with what has happened in the past.

Before the Industrial Revolution had well developed, class consciousness was found only among the well-to-do and the "well-born." Cheap land was plentiful and business was small. The Industrial Revolution opened up avenues, through which a new class might break into the sacred preserves earlier established by family and land or commercial wealth. From the Civil War to 1890 the United States got along without an "upper class" but developed a labor class out of the old artisans and mechanics, demoted to wage-earners, and Irish, German, and other immigrants. By 1896 class consciousness among wage-earners had reached a relatively high point and found expression in the labor solidarity of the Knights of Labor and in the trade unions. It is true that the older leaders found the imported doctrines of class warfare hard to swallow, but the facts of the situation were equally hard to contradict. The laborer, if not being forced down in the social scale, was at least not moving up at the same rate at which the new plutocracy was rising. By the nineties a sort of upper class had become established in this country, and a sort of lower class. There were distinct and separate standards of living, habits of thought, ways of life, and expectations or the lack of them. The Industrial Revolution had created what seemed to be, on the surface, a social situation out of which "class" had emerged, and it was this that made the boycott successful. There were workingmen's commodities and there were middle- and upper-class commodities. Beer, cheap cigars, rough, ready-made clothing, cheap grades of house furnishings, were made for workingmen and sold in workingmen's districts. A boycott of beer, cheap cigars, or other workingmen's commodities meant something. It was capable of ruining the manufacturer or the recalcitrant retailer.

Now there is no beer, nearly every one smokes cheap cigarettes, and while there is cheap clothing and expensive clothing, house furnishings, etc., there is no workingmen's clothing or furnishings. America has gone through a social revolution in which a large, consumer middle class has been created in place of the large workingmen's class that existed in the eighties. A dress is bought in Paris for $300, copied to sell at $65, copied again to sell at $30, and still again at $15. Superficially it is the same dress worn on Park Avenue one day and Grand Street the next. The communists may rave as they please, but it is quite impossible to be as class conscious in silk stockings as in cotton, and the use of women's garments as illustration suggests one reason for the revolution that has taken place in America in the last thirty years.

Before 1890, the workingman's woman either stayed at home or went into a factory. She, too, wore working-class clothes and held more or less her husband's and father's opinions, or at least suppressed her own. She went shopping with her husband on Saturday night, if he brought anything home to shop with, and she was not permitted to buy boycotted goods. It is common knowledge that since then women have advanced themselves greatly in the world, especially in the neighborhood markets. It is now the woman who buys, whoever may pay, and women are not as notoriously class as they are clothes conscious. From women it has spread to men, so that workingmen's commodities, in response in part to consumers' demand, no longer exist.

At the same time large-scale production and distribution have destroyed the local identity of commodities. When the Knights boycotted Browning's clothes in New York, they knew what they were doing and all that was needed was a local labor solidarity to make the boycott effective. To-day the same clothes may be sold not at all in New York but in large quantities in San Francisco. Present-day distribution of commodities requires a wider and deeper labor solidarity to boycott successfully.

This, it must be repeated, does not mean that labor solidarity or class consciousness may not recover, but only that it was of slow growth, reached its highest point in the eighties, and has declined at least since the War. But when and if labor solidarity recovers, it will not find the boycott its chief weapon as it did in the eighties. The wage-earner as a consumer has merged into a larger non-class, consumer group which buys on the basis chiefly of style and price. We are not likely to return to class commodities and it is well that we should not. If a new class consciousness appears it will be of producers and not of consumers.

The general officers of the Knights of Labor were not opposed to the boycott on general principles as was the case with strikes. They had, in fact, no boycott policy whatsoever. Boycotts began to be practiced by locals and districts, and in 1880 the General Assembly laid a boycott on a Pittsburgh newspaper because it published an account of the secret proceedings of the assembly. But no protest seems to have been made when Litchman took it upon himself to ignore the instructions of the General Assembly, because of the danger of prosecution under the stringent conspiracy laws of Pennsylvania.[1]

Local boycotts became popular in 1880, and in 1882 Layton, who succeeded Litchman as grand secretary, took the first official step, so far as the general office went, by promulgating a boycott on the Duryea Starch Company of Long Island at the instigation of Theodore Cuno. This gave rise to the Cuno affair which has been discussed in another chapter and served to make the general officers more cautious about the boycott by the Order as a whole. Powderly repudiated the Cuno boycott and after investigation it was withdrawn.

In 1883, two locals asked permission of the general executive board to boycott two Pittsburgh newspapers, but were told that it was a local matter and needed only the district's consent,[2] and in the same year the general executive board, after considering the boycotting of the East Liverpool pot-

[1] *Proceedings,* 1880 General Assembly of the Knights of Labor, p. 236.
[2] *Ibid.,* 1883 General Assembly, p. 454.

teries, decided against it on the ground that it would throw other pottery workers out of employment.[3]

But strikes and lockouts were increasing, the iron-clad was being applied. The Telegraphers' strike had been a ghastly failure and the boycott was the only instrument left to the general executive board when their good offices as conciliators were rejected. Thus, in 1884, though the General Assembly refused to "adopt a general system of boycotting instead of strikes," the general executive board took its first step in the direction of a general boycott policy.

In the winter of 1883, the John S. Perry Co. of Albany, N. Y., laid down certain conditions for the stove mounters which the latter regarded as too severe or as discrimination against the Order. After a long controversy between the firm and District Assembly No. 64, the general executive board was called in, and according to its own statement was "treated with contempt." There was no law about boycotting by the Order, but there was no law against it; so the general executive board, forgetting the Cuno affair and Litchman's caution at Pittsburgh, decided to issue a boycott circular against Perry stoves. Perry protested in May and the boycott was raised on Oct. 15, 1885. But the *Journal of United Labor* found a great many labor papers still carrying the boycott notice and many members obeying it as late as Feb. 25, 1886.

The boycott was getting out of hand. Swinton declared:

This new business of boycotting will have to be organized somehow. . . . The other day we received a circular boycotting five of the dry goods firms of this city. It did not appear by whose direction or by what organization the circular was issued. . . . Again, a few days ago handbills boycotting Frank Tousey's publications were put in circulation

[3] *Ibid.*, p. 453.

though the boycott was raised two months ago after his failure, by Typographical Union Number 6. . . . In the Knights of Labor a boycott can originate only with the proper committee and this is the only fit way. . . .[4]

Swinton was somewhat charitable to the Knights. Their control of the boycott was no better and no worse than that of other unions. "There has been," complained Local Assembly No. 3185, "an awful lot of boycotting done of late and it is really impossible to keep the names of all boycotted firms in memory, for which reason Local Assembly No. 3185 has ornamented the hall with a large blackboard on which in plain letters are written the names of the boycotted firms. . . ."[5] Complaints were made that the Knights of Labor was being deluged with requests from the open unions to support boycotts.[6]

There was no question of the success of these operations. Their success was, in fact, too great. The Tousey company referred to by Swinton had been forced into bankruptcy by the Printers and the Knights combined. The firm was reorganized some time in March and the boycott raised, but Swinton reported circulars being issued in May, and the *Journal* of the Order did not officially call off the Tousey boycott until July.[7]

On April 29, 1884, Fuller and Warren Co., stove manufacturers, Troy, N. Y., proposed a reduction of 20 per cent to its stove mounters, and according to the men, refused to recognize any union committee. A strike followed and members of the Knights were blacklisted by the Stove Manufacturers' Association. A committee of District Assembly No. 68 got the men back, but after the season it was said that their places were filled by scabs from other

[4] John Swinton, *John Swinton's Paper*, May 17, 1885.
[5] *Journal*, p. 1040.
[6] Swinton, *op. cit.*, June, 1885.
[7] *Journal*, p. 1032.

cities. This time the committee was given no consideration and District Assembly No. 68 instituted a boycott on Fuller and Warren stoves in April, 1885.[8] The boycott was effective, the firm sent a representative to the general executive board and on March 9, 1886, an agreement was signed, providing that there should be no discrimination against members of the Order, that members of the district expelled for returning to work should be suspended by the firm until disciplined by the district assembly, and that no new men should be employed until all former employees belonging to the Knights had been reëmployed. On these conditions the boycott was to be removed.[9] But there was a hitch in the proceedings and in August, the *Journal* notified the Order that the boycott was reëstablished. The Order insisted that the firm had not carried out its agreement and the boycott remained on its products as late as 1888, when the Iron Molders' Union, which had made peace with the firm, characterized the company as a friend of organized labor.[10]

The Dueber Watch Case Company of Newport, Ky., was another victim of the Order's boycott. About June 30, 1885, William Bailey was sent to Newport, Ky., to look into a complaint of Local Assembly No. 3487 and was told by Dueber that the men had been locked out because of membership in the Order. Bailey's report was followed by a special meeting of the general executive board in Cincinnati on July 13, when a visit was made to the Dueber works across the river. But Dueber was even less amenable at the second visit and "peremptorily ordered" the board out of his office. This was too much for the dignity of the general

---

[8] *Ibid.*, pp. 962-63.
[9] *Ibid.*, March, 1886, p. 2018.
[10] *Proceedings*, 1886 General Assembly, pp. 83, 98-101; *Journal*, August, 1886, p. 2138; *Ibid.*, February, 1887, p. 2300; Leo Wolman, *The Boycott in American Trade Unions*, p. 30.

executive board, an assessment of 5 cents per member was levied on the Assistance Fund and the first strictly general executive board boycott was ordered on Aug. 1, 1885. The board declared its intention to boycott the company out of existence and proceeded to do the same with unusual vigor and heat. They published a statement that Dueber had imported Swiss watchcase-making machinery on the persons of contract laborers declared at customs as their individual tools, thus robbing the United States government of its well-earned rake-off; that the aforesaid Dueber was arrested by keen-eyed customs officials and had paid $7,000 to keep out of the courts. They published, too, the Dueber trade marks, the fact that Dueber was arrested in Philadelphia for conspiring to obtain trade secrets of another firm, and that he assisted in a boycott by Knights and trade unionists upon a competitor in Brooklyn. The general executive board was in fact very hot, and one is left with the suspicion that it was due less to the lockout of the Dueber employees than to the ignominy with which they had been ejected from the Dueber offices. It was, as they said, "the first instance of a boycott emanating directly from the General Executive Board" and they intended to make it stick.[11]

On March 4, 1886, Dueber capitulated and signed an agreement with the Knights, reinstating all the employees who had been locked out because of their membership in the Order. He promised that in future no discrimination would be made against Knights of Labor and no children employed under the age of fifteen years.[12]

A further aid to the boycott policy was the adoption of the Knights of Labor white label in February, 1884. Labels for specific products such as cigars, gloves, cans, etc., were

---

[11] *Proceedings,* 1885 General Assembly, pp. 78-90.
[12] *Journal,* March, 1886, p. 2018.

also adopted by locals and accepted by the General Assembly at various times. The can makers asserted that machine-made goods and child labor were combining to destroy them and poison the consumer.[13]

In 1885, Powderly pointed out that no legislation existed in the Order covering the boycott and advised some uniform plan for its control. "Too much indiscriminate boycotting," he said, "has been indulged in. . . . To declare a boycott for every trifling thing is not only foolish but dangerous. The boycott is a two-edged sword and should receive as careful consideration as the strike before being resorted to. The power to decide upon embarking on a boycott crusade should be placed in the hands of the Executive Board. . . ."[14]

A boycott committee was appointed and recommended that local, district, and state assemblies be left with the power to boycott within their own localities, but when other localities were likely to be affected the matter must be referred to the general executive board with the right to institute a general boycott after negotiation. The general executive board was given the right to compel all subordinate assemblies and individuals to carry out a boycott properly instituted under penalty of loss of charter or expulsion from the Order.[15] After the new rules went into effect, up to February, 1886, the general executive board had 700 requests for permission to lay boycotts and Powderly had to repeat his warning against overdoing it. At the same time the unfair list of the *Journal* rarely contained more than six names.[16]

The special session of the General Assembly at Cleveland in May 1886, tried to curb the use of the boycott. It put

---

[13] *Proceedings,* 1885 General Assembly, pp. 156-57.

[14] *Ibid.,* p. 19.

[15] *Ibid.,* pp. 162-63.

[16] *Journal,* February, 1886, p. 2006.

all boycotting powers in the hands of the general executive
board and ordered that the boycott be issued and withdrawn secretly.[17] It is difficult to discover what was
intended by this, unless it was to avoid the prosecutions
that were beginning to be directed against the Order. In
July, Swinton noted that the New York courts "are disposed
to draw the lines around the boycott tighter and tighter as
if the intention were to strangle it.[18] The courts were in
fact dealing with the boycott as they had dealt with the
strike at an earlier period. It was being brought under the
category of conspiracy which, if it did not apply to the
thing itself, might be made to apply to the methods by
which it was carried out. Some of these methods were
questionable, one especially, the collection of a fine for the
cost of the boycott from the defeated employer, was simply
blackmail, but it seems to have been allowed to flourish by
the general officers in good faith. In March, 1886, a local
assembly of the Knights of Labor, the Carl Salm club, boycotted the Theiss beer garden after an unsuccessful strike.
They were joined by the waiters and bartenders and supported by the Central Labor Union and District Assembly
No. 49. The place was picketed and George Ehret, the
brewer, Theiss, and an interested baker settled the matter
for $1,000 to pay the cost of the boycott. Theiss later
brought action for extortion and intimidation, and Judge
Barrett ruled that the distribution of boycott literature and
speaking to passers-by constituted intimidation and that the
"fine" under the circumstances was extortion. The jury
found all five men guilty and they were sentenced to prison
for from one and a half to nearly four years. Their sentences were commuted and they were released [19] on Oct. 11,

---

[17] *Proceedings,* special session of the 1886 General Assembly, pp. 44-45.
[18] Swinton, *op. cit.,* July 18, 1886.
[19] *Ibid.,* July 11, 1886; Commons and Associates, *History of Labour in the United States,* Vol. II, pp. 444-45.

1886. A similar case was the Rochester clothing boycott which sent James Hughes to jail.

The Cleveland rules against the boycott had little effect. Districts and locals continued to use it with or without the permission of the general executive board. But after the formation of the American Federation of Labor the boycott degenerated into an instrument of jurisdictional warfare and internecine strife.

Newspapers had always been peculiarly defenseless against the boycott and when the Knights and the Printers joined forces against the New York *Tribune* under Whitelaw Reid, they were able, so they said, to defeat Blaine and elect Cleveland in 1884. But the Printers' interest in newspapers was solely a producers' one, while the Knights boycotted as readers as well. Thus the Knights were likely to boycott a paper because of its editorial policy, especially its attitude toward the Order, while the Printers had always avoided action on those grounds. This led to a split, especially after the International Typographical Union had thrown in its lot with the American Federation of Labor.

The Knights and the Brewers worked together with great success as late as 1890, the Knights and the Clothing Workers (cutters) as late as 1891. In 1893, Liggett and Meyers succumbed to a six-year boycott and in 1894 the Knights of Labor supported the American Railway Union's boycott on Pullman cars. As late as 1896 the Knights placed a boycott on machine-made shoes. But in 1896 members of the United Garment Workers' Union replaced Knights of Labor cutters, and in 1897 the Brewery Workmen's Union boycotted a Rochester brewery because it employed Knights of Labor. The Knights retaliated by boycotting the Brewery Union.[20]

---

[20] Wolman, *op. cit.*, pp. 28, 31, 32, 34, 78.

CHAPTER XVI

WOMEN AND THE ORDER

THE Knights of Labor was the first general labor body to encourage the organization of women. The original constitution however made no provision for their admission. It demanded in the interest of male wage-earners that they should be given equal pay for equal work.

Trade and labor unions have objected to the admission of women on two grounds, one economic and the other social, and it is not easy to say which has been the more important. On economic grounds women represented an attack upon the men's standard of wages accompanying the introduction of machinery and, even without machinery, as competition of a lower wage class. In the early stages of the Industrial Revolution women's work had no market price. Men's wages were customary and based crudely upon the assumption that they had families to support. Even when women took over exactly the same work as men had performed, it was assumed that they could work for less because they had no comparable family responsibilities. Most women, however, were introduced into industry along with machinery and the antagonism of men to women was a part of their antagonism to the machines. By the eighties with few exceptions women and machinery were both recognized as inevitable in industry, but there remained a strong social prejudice against women in unions and the prejudice was not confined to the men. Men in that period at least did not want women around when they were engaged in "serious" matters. And women did not want to be around.

They knew their place and kept it. If they were exploited—
and they were—it was but part of the general scheme of
things. They had been exploited by their fathers and
expected to be exploited by their husbands. Feminism was
nothing to them.

But if women could not enter men's unions they could
have unions of their own, provided some one could be found
to take the initiative. This some one was Phillip Van Patten,
the outstanding socialist in the Order who, in September,
1879, asked that working women should be admitted to the
Knights and allowed to form assemblies under the same
conditions as the men.[1] The committee reported in favor
of the resolution, but before the vote was taken Powderly,
acting general master workman in the absence of Stephens,
decided that it involved an amendment to the constitution
and therefore could not pass without a two-thirds majority.
The first vote was 12 to 7, just short of two-thirds, but a
second vote was taken which resulted in a two-thirds
majority, 14 to 6. This should have settled the matter, but
instead it was laid on the table until the next General
Assembly.[2]

Evidently the Knights in 1879 were not quite as enthusiastic about women as they later became. In 1880 an interesting suggestion came from Oceola, Pa., that "for the
protection of labor in manufacturing districts . . . women
should be admitted into this Noble and Holy Order . . .
under a provision that they shall have Local Assemblies of
their own *governed by male officers* and that they shall *not*
be entitled to full privileges of this Noble and Holy
Order. . . ."[3]

No attention was paid to this brilliant suggestion and the

---

[1] *Proceedings,* 1879 General Assembly of the Knights of Labor, Chicago, p. 125.

[2] *Ibid.,* p. 131.

[3] *Ibid.,* 1880 General Assembly, p. 194. Italics are the author's.

committee reported in favor of the admission of women.
But again there was a hitch. An amendment was adopted
to create a committee to prepare ritual and regulations
"with full powers to put the same into immediate operation." [4] This looks like an attempt to delay matters and
either no committee was called or Powderly decided that no
special ritual and regulations were necessary for women,
for no report was made to the following General Assembly.

In the meantime, Harry Skeffington took the bull by the
horns and organized the first women's local, the Garfield
Assembly No. 1684 (shoe operatives) at Philadelphia, in
September, 1881. From this local Mary Sterling was elected
to District Assembly No. 70 and to the 1881 General
Assembly. Powderly was confronted by a *fait accompli*
and ruled that no special ritual and regulations for women's
assemblies were needed. In 1882 the General Assembly
regularized the affair by permitting the initiation of females
not under sixteen years of age.[5]

The Knights from then on were very polite to the ladies.
They appointed a women's committee in 1885 to gather
statistics about women's work. At the special session in
1886, Mary Hanafin replied to the address from the
W.C.T.U. And at Richmond a permanent committee on
women's work was organized and Leonora Barry was made
general investigator with pay. Mrs. Barry's job was to
investigate the conditions of working women, instruct the
members in the mysteries of the Order and "organize female
locals when it will not conflict with more important work."
It was agreed that "any abuse which a female local would
be delicate [sic] in mentioning to the general executive
board may be communicated to the President of the Committee on Women's Work." [6]

---

[4] *Ibid.*, p. 226.
[5] *Ibid.*, 1882 General Assembly, pp. 309, 347.
[6] *Journal*, January, 1887, p. 2247.

There were 16 women delegates at the Richmond convention, among them Mrs. Master Workman Rodgers of Chicago with her "new-born babe." [7] There were 192 women's locals at that time of which 19 were among shoe operatives.[8]

Mrs. Barry was an energetic woman but her lengthy reports about the conditions of women in industry were almost as kaleidoscopic as those of Cuno as general statistician. She had no right to enter factories and when she did visit them she got her friends employed there into trouble. Investigation was being done in a somewhat more systematic way by the Bureaus of Labor Statistics and she rightly turned to propaganda and organization. In 1887 she was made a general officer of the Order. She did some lobbying for a factory inspection law in Pennsylvania and helped found coöperative shirt factories in New York and Baltimore. She tried unsuccessfully to set up a benefit system for women in Rhode Island and other places. And she made speeches everywhere. The Colorado Knights gave her a purse of gold, a painting, and a poem of thirty-two lines. If all the lines were as bad as the first four she was underpaid however much there may have been in the purse.[9]

In 1889 Mrs. Barry refused longer to head the women's department, which, "owing to the failure of the women to organize more thoroughly, does not exist except in name." [10] And in 1890 she sent a brief letter to the General Assembly asking that the department be continued, but not under her, and signing "L. M. Barry Lake."

Marriage, a depleted treasury, and the failure to arouse women to the need of organization explain the defection of a good Knight when good Knights were getting scarce.

---

[7] *Ibid.*, December, 1886, p. 2229.
[8] A. E. Galster, *The Labor Movement in the Shoe Industry*, pp. 51-52.
[9] Details from MSS. loaned by David Saposs.
[10] *Proceedings*, 1889, General Assembly, p. 6.

CHAPTER XVII

POLITICS AND FARMERS

AMERICAN labor has been a spectacular failure in the field of politics. While the French labor movement has been more successful politically than industrially; while in England a strong political party has grown out of an alliance between the trade unions and the socialists; while in Germany the two forms of behavior have gone hand in hand, in the United States innumerable excursions into politics by trade unions and labor groups have been ineffective and destructive of the organizations themselves. It is true that many laws originally proposed by labor are now on the statute books, but it is equally true that some of the most important of them have been used chiefly against labor.

The attitude of the American Federation of Labor and especially of the late Samuel Gompers has left the impression that the American labor movement has been nonpolitical. This is a mistake. The American labor movement like others has swung between industrial and political action, but on the whole its political and reformist behavior has outweighed its activities in the economic field. In the early years, whenever the movement spread out, it became political. Pure and simple trade unionism was always a minor note. Coming down the century the political attitude has declined and the economic has gained. The National Labor Union was quite as political as the land-reform congresses of the fifties. The Industrial Congresses were slightly less so. The Knights of Labor was more "industrial" than its predecessors and the American Federation of Labor has been the least political of all.

The reason for this trend is obvious. Politics in the United States has been bad medicine for labor organizations, not because there is any fundamental or necessary antipathy between labor and politics, but because America and American labor are what they are.

The three main reasons for the ineptitude of American labor in politics are: the early date at which the American worker secured the vote, the political importance of the American farmer, and the immigrant.

On its face it would seem that the American worker's long experience with the vote would have made for political effectiveness, but this is a superficial view. The vote was secured by the worker in this country before he became a wage-earner and without effort as such. He voted first as a citizen in a comparatively non-class community on general political issues and developed a party allegiance in advance of a wage status. When his wage status was fixed he was already strongly attached to one or the other major political party.

The immigrant has been of two sorts, the peasant without political background and unable to think in political terms, herded into one party or another by ward heelers and *padrones;* and the intellectual, with a decided political background but little knowledge of that of the United States. The peasant has been useless to the American labor movement for political purposes, and the foreign intellectual has on the whole been doctrinaire and disruptive. But the immigrant intellectual, unlike the peasant, was able to learn. Robert Owen did not stay in America long enough and would probably not have learned much anyway. Brisbane, though born in the United States, came back from France with a complete system and needed to know no more. G.

H. Evans, though born in England, was the originator in America of the "nonpartisan" political practice much later made famous by the American Federation of Labor. P. J. McGuire, Adolph Strasser, and Gompers learned less from the American labor movement than from the English benefit societies, but they learned from the foreign intellectuals in New York the undesirability of their sort of politics. By tying up the ideas of the English fraternal societies with those of similar organizations in the United States, of which the Typographical was the chief, they arrived at pure and simple trade unionism with nonpartisan political action, derived through the Knights of Labor from the pre-Civil War land reformers. Thus both groups of immigrants have had a negative political influence upon the American labor movement in spite of, or partly because of, the fact that socialists like Sorge, anarchists like Most, and industrial unionists like De Leon, not to mention McGuire, Strasser, and Gompers in their early stage, were predominantly political.

The American farmer like the wage-earner had early party attachments that made it difficult for him to act politically on economic lines. In addition, he was essentially an individualist unlike the peasant of continental Europe. And in the United States, if only because of his numbers, he could not be ignored. In American political history, labor and the farmers have come together as a result of a long depression, a short deflation, or on some single issue like cheap money or antimonopoly. But labor's interest in cheap money grew out of the belief that the proper business of the wage-earner was to become a capitalist, and it therefore declined as this point of view was outmoded, while the negative policy against monopoly was not an especially strong bond of union, because the farmers were opposed to those corporations only which either transported or purchased their products—the railroads, mills, and packing houses.

Thus there was no real community of interest between farmer and wage-earner, and they could get together only as the result of some accidental condition which burdened them both. But such a condition is not found in the ordinary business cycle. The business cycle begins with rising prices and industrial activity, which tend to drive the wage-earners together into collective bargaining and the farmers apart into competitive selling. In the second stage of the business cycle, when business falls off and prices drop, the farmers are driven together for protection, while the wage-earners rest on their laurels and let the lag between wages and prices advance their real standards of living.

Labor enters politics after industrial reverses, but these have no necessary connection with the business cycle. Farmers enter politics as the result of depression which may or may not affect manufacturing industries. But there is this further connection. An industrial depression will bring wage cuts and strikes which are likely to be ineffective. These may drive the wage-earner into politics, and in that case, he will find the farmer with him. This is what happened in the seventies. The farmers were in politics quite independent of the wage-earners in 1877. In 1877 occurred the Great Upheaval among the railroad workers and miners because of a series of wage reductions during the depression. Strikes and riots gained nothing, and in 1878 the wage-earners went political. But in 1886 the labor movement went political again, though there was no depression, because of its successes in 1885-86 and the reverses and disasters to labor of May of the latter year. The farmers went political two years later when the wage-earners were out of politics.

Thus the alliance is ephemeral in the nature of things. The causes of difference are more persistent than the conditions making for common action. Fundamentally the farmer needs high-priced agricultural commodities and cheap manufactures, while the wage-earner needs the opposite, high wages, which usually mean higher-priced manufactures, and low living costs, which require cheap farm products. Only three conditions, all of them exceptional, are likely to bring the farmer and wage-earner together in the political field: a very long depression like that of the seventies, an issue like that of cheap money, and a sudden deflation like that of 1921.

The Knights of Labor, though it grew up in the depressed seventies and achieved national organization just before business recovery, was not a political organization, but more nearly a pure and simple labor society than any of its predecessors. Its platform contained demands which could be gained by political action, but this was borrowed from the Industrial Congress; it is in the nature of platforms to make such demands, and the platform is perhaps the least important part of any society. It is seldom that a new organization knows what it is going to want or to do, and its platform is likely to be traditional.

The early leaders of the Knights were politically minded. Stephens, Powderly, Litchman, Wright, Blair, Schilling had all run for political office. But that was true of nearly all the early labor leaders, especially in the seventies, and it never dragged the Order into politics. The reason for this is not far to seek. Politics had failed to do anything for these men or their constituents. Litchman was defeated after one year in the Massachusetts legislature. Stephens failed of election to Congress. Wright was defeated in Pennsylvania and Powderly was elected to a minor office. Their political ambitions had to be postponed, and they determined to build up a strong labor movement and prepare it for political action some time in the future—a future more and more remote as they became involved in industrial activity. The wage-earner, in their opinion, was too strongly attached to his party idols to act effectively in politics. He needed a long education in labor ideas and policies, and when that was completed, the political problem would solve itself.

During the seventies the Knights of Labor was non-political in spite or because of the fact that its most prominent leaders were absorbed in politics. The first General Assembly in 1878 found Stephens, Wright, Powderly, Litchman, and Blair all in the Greenback-Labor campaign. But the first General Assembly left politics severely alone. At the second General Assembly in St. Louis, January, 1879, Stephens said simply that the campaign of 1878 had settled nothing, perhaps because he had failed of election to Congress, but it was decided that local assemblies might take political action in elections "as may be deemed by them best calculated to advance the interest of the Order,"[1] and a proposal that the general officers keep out of politics was defeated.[2] The strongest indication of political interest is seen in the change of the date of the General Assembly from January to September with the evident intention of influencing legislation. But a decision of the general master workman was approved declaring that the Order "is not a political party. It is more and higher and must be kept so. It is the parent of principles. In it are born and crystallized sentiments and measures for the benefit of the whole people. . . . Political action cannot be taken in the L.A.; that must be done outside in club or party organization

---

[1] *Proceedings*, January, 1879 General Assembly of the Knights of Labor, p. 57.
[2] *Ibid.*, p. 71.

through which political sentiment may be crystallized into statute law." [3]

At the third General Assembly, 1879, at Chicago, the political element in the Order was in the ascendency. The growth of trade assemblies was checked and, at the instigation of Phillip Van Patten, secretary of the Socialist-Labor Party, after a heated debate, political action was recommended to the local assemblies on a "nonpartisan" basis. The locals were permitted to act "with that party in their vicinity through which they can gain the most," but in no case were they allowed to enter a political campaign unless three-fourths of the members supported political action. No member was compelled to vote with the majority.[4]

Powderly carried on the nonpolitical tradition of Stephens and one of his first decisions after election was: "Our Order is above politics and electioneering for any candidate in the sanctuary must not be practiced. . . . Discuss labor in all its aspects but not the merits or demerits of any candidate." [5] At the same time he stated that he always voted for a member of the Order on the general principle that a good Knight would be a good representative of labor, and in explaining his opposition to strikes he asserted his belief that "the evils we now strike against are brought about by bad legislation. . . ." [6]

An attempt was made at the 1880 General Assembly to push the Order into politics by giving its official support in the fall elections to "that political party whose platform most generally embraces the fundamental principles of this Order." The committee to which this was referred was even more explicit and recommended that the General

---

[3] Decisions of grand master workman approved at St. Louis, 1879. (*Proceedings,* 1879 General Assembly, p. 148.)

[4] Article X, constitution.

[5] *Journal,* p. 9.

[6] T. V. Powderly, *Thirty Years of Labor,* p. 66.

Assembly officially notify all local assemblies and district assemblies to support the National Greenback-Labor Party. Both these motions were tabled after long discussion. The failure of the Greenback Party in 1880 discredited politics and the Order remained comparatively free from suggestions of political action until late in its career. In 1881 it was deemed inexpedient to pass a resolution that political action was necessary to accomplish the objects of the Order.

But individual locals and districts, though they were not allowed to discuss politics in the sanctuary, did not hesitate to enter local political campaigns. In Massachusetts, in 1882, a member of the Order was elected to Congress and a number of Knights were at one time or another in the state legislature. Many city officials in Lynn and Lawrence were members of the Order, including at least two mayors in the former and one in the latter city.[7] In 1882, District Assembly No. 41 had a setback in the city elections in Baltimore, and this and other experiences of the same sort discredited political action. Powderly refused nomination on the Greenback ticket for Secretary of Internal Affairs of Pennsylvania in 1882. He was then nominated for lieutenant governor but declined to run. He was afraid that people would say he had used the Order to advance himself politically. "I never belonged to any party," he declared, "and never will." [8] This included the Greenback Party and he always claimed that he was elected mayor of Scranton not as a Greenbacker but as a labor candidate.[9]

Secretary Layton carried on the political tradition of his office and in 1883 protested against the refusal of the locals to discuss politics in the assemblies, though this was in obedience to the rule of the general master workman.

---

[7] *Journal,* pp. 368-69.
[8] *Ibid.,* p. 243.
[9] *Ibid.,* p. 242.

Layton was not so politically minded as Litchman, but the failure of the Telegraphers' strike had influenced him in that direction. Powderly maintained his middle-of-the-road policy. "The moment," he said, "we proclaim to the world that our Order is a political party, that moment the lines are drawn and we receive no more accessions to our ranks from the other existing parties . . .";[10] and he decided again that when a local or district assembly wanted to discuss politics it must first attend to its regular business and then reorganize. After one meeting the political club would be independent of the Knights of Labor assembly.[11] At the same time both Litchman and McNeill were seeking Carroll D. Wright's job as chief of the Massachusetts Bureau of Labor Statistics.[12] But there was nothing unusual in this. These bureaus were regarded by labor leaders as their special hunting grounds. Powderly did his best to be made chief of the Federal Labor Bureau when it was organized June 27, 1884.

The characteristic political behavior of the Knights of Labor as a whole took the form of the lobby, and their first step in this direction was made to support the Window Glass Workers in their demand for an anti-contract-labor law. On Feb. 1, 1884, Powderly, Turner, and eight Glass Workers, supported by representatives of the Amalgamated Association of Iron and Steel Workers, appeared before the committee on education and labor in support of the Foran bill with a petition signed by the Knights. At the 1884 General Assembly an anti-contract-labor clause was added to the constitution and on Feb. 2, 1885, the first anti-contract-labor bill was passed by Congress. At the same time Powderly insisted upon keeping the Order free from

---

[10] *Proceedings,* 1883 General Assembly, p. 409.
[11] *Journal,* p. 407.
[12] *Ibid.,* p. 415.

political entanglements and denied all rumors that the Knights could or would be instructed to vote for either Blaine or Cleveland.[13]

In 1885 Powderly suggested that Knights of Labor lobbies be set up at every state capital and in Washington during sessions of the legislatures, to push labor bills and keep track of the records of the legislators.[14] But Turner warned the General Assembly that "our Order was founded for the purpose primarily of organizing, regulating and consolidating the industrial relations of workingmen. . . ." [15] Turner represented the old Philadelphia tradition and there was no such feeling in the newer, western sections. At Grand Rapids, Mich., the mayor, ten out of sixteen members of the Board of Aldermen, every official of the county, every member of the legislature from the county, and one state senator were Knights of Labor.[16] At Bay City, Mich., the Knights elected the mayor, treasurer and comptroller, three aldermen, three supervisors and three constables, the city surveyor, wood inspector, boiler inspector, and assistant street commissioner.[17] At Cleveland, O., the Knights drew up a platform for a compulsory arbitration law, the exclusion of Pinkerton detectives from labor disputes, the abolition of contract work on state and municipal improvements, and an eight-hour law for municipal employees. These were accepted by the Democratic convention which nominated four men for the state legislature known to be in sympathy with labor.[18] At the 1885 General Assembly a special committee on legislation was appointed.

The labor movement, having gone political in 1878-79,

---

13 *Ibid.*, pp. 763-64.
14 *Proceedings*, 1885 General Assembly, p. 16.
15 *Ibid.*, p. 44.
16 John Swinton, *John Swinton's Paper*, July 26, 1885.
17 *Journal*, p. 982.
18 *Ibid.*, p. 1097.

fell away from Weaver in 1880 leaving him only farmer support. Among the farmers the Greenback sentiment declined to be replaced by an anti-Monopoly or People's Party which nominated Benjamin Butler for President in 1884. Butler was indorsed by what remained of the Greenback Party and secured some labor support, but received little more than one-third the number of votes cast for Weaver in 1880. Politics remained in the background during the depression of 1884-85 and the first part of 1886. The winter of 1885-86 was one of intense industrial agitation led by the Knights of Labor, in which boycotts, strikes, collective bargaining had astonishing success. This activity was typical of a period of economic recovery which lasted until 1891 with a slight recession in 1888. But industrial success came suddenly to an end in the spring of 1886 with the failure of the Southwest strike, the eight-hour movement, and the Haymarket bomb. Public sentiment turned against labor, especially against the Knights.

It looked in mid-summer [wrote Swinton] as though the Money Power had swept all before it and established its supremacy beyond challenge. Jay Gould, the enemy's generalissimo had squelched the railroad strikes of the Southwest and this was followed by the failure of hundreds of other strikes. The eight hour gains of last May in Chicago and elsewhere had been lost. The union men had been blacklisted right and left and a vast conspiracy against the Knights of Labor has shown itself in many localities. The laws had been distorted against boycotting. Pinkerton thugs had been consolidated into petty armies for the hire of capital. Toady judges had served their masters by rancorous pursuit of workingmen. Police outrages on the poor were reported from all sides. The constitutional rights of citizens had been invaded, labor meetings broken up and labor papers threatened or suppressed.[19]

When Ralph Beaumont and John J. McCartney, the Knights of Labor lobby, appeared in Washington in the fall

---

[19] Swinton, *op. cit.*, Nov. 7, 1886.

they found "that the failure of the great Southwest strike coupled with the declaration of Jay Gould that he had broken the back of the Knights of Labor, and further augmented by press reports sent out from Cleveland during the special session of the General Assembly, had the effect of giving the impression that the seeds of disintegration were sown in the Order so strong that it was likely to fall to pieces before the fall elections took place." [20]

The special session of the General Assembly met at Cleveland, May 25-June 3, 1886. The Southwest men had gone back defeated May 4. The Chicago anarchists were awaiting trial and the trade unions were striving to disentangle themselves from the Order under the fire of unjustified public wrath and fear. It afforded the politicians in the Order their opportunity and the Knights took the first step which culminated in the political campaigns of 1886-87.

The special committee on legislation reported to the special session at Cleveland a list of ten political demands, six of them relating to the land, and the remainder for: (1) the abolition of the property qualification for voting; (2) a graduated income tax; (3) a larger appropriation for the labor bureau; (4) the sending of a lobby to Washington. All these recommendations were adopted along with a resolution from Litchman "that we will hold responsible at the ballot box all members of Congress who neglect or refuse to vote in compliance with these demands." Even Powderly was carried away on this political wave. ". . . We should use every means within our power," he said, "to secure for the toiler the right to protect himself upon that day which of all days is important to the American citizen—ELECTION DAY," and he suggested that election day be made

---

[20] *Proceedings*, 1886 General Assembly, p. 139.

a national holiday and that everybody keep sober. At the same time the Order sent an address to the National Grange.[21]

The political campaign of 1886 was the most successful ever conducted by labor in the United States. In New York, Henry George, running on a single-tax platform and supported by Knights of Labor, trade unions, socialists, and what not, received 68,000 votes against 90,000 cast for Abram S. Hewitt (Democrat) and 60,000 for Theodore Roosevelt (Republican). In Chicago, the Union Labor Party received 25,000 votes out of a total of 92,000 and elected a state senator and several assemblymen. In Milwaukee, the People's Party received 13,000 votes and carried the county, electing one state senator, six assemblymen and one congressman. In St. Louis, the workingmen's ticket received 7,000 votes. In Leadville, Colo., the Knights of Labor elected one state senator and three assemblymen. In Newark, N. J., the labor candidate for Congress polled 6,300 votes and one assemblyman was elected. In the sixth congressional district of Kentucky the labor candidate received so many votes that he contested the seat of the Speaker of the House. In the sixth congressional district of Virginia the Knights of Labor candidate was elected. Labor tickets won in Lynn, Mass., Naugatuck and South Norwalk, Conn., Key West, Fla., and Richmond, Va.

Labor candidates running on the tickets of the regular parties had almost equal success. Martin Foran in Cleveland and B. F. Shively, Knights of Labor, in Indiana were elected to Congress as Democrats. Robert Howard of the Spinners was elected state senator in Massachusetts, and other Knights were elected in New York, Connecticut, and New Jersey. Two Knights in St. Louis were elected on the Republican ticket. But John McBride was beaten on the

---

[21] *Ibid.*, special session of the 1886 General Assembly, pp. 41-42, 70.

Democratic ticket in Ohio and Frank Foster in Massachusetts.

The political successes of 1886 pointed unmistakably to a Farmer-Labor Party. As early as September 1, a convention was held at Indianapolis of Knights of Labor, the Farmers' Alliance, the Farmers' and Laborers' Co-operative Union, the Wheel, the Grange, the Greenbackers, the Corn Planters, and anti-Monopolists. A second convention at Cincinnati, Feb. 22, 1887, formed the National Union Labor Party which absorbed the remains of the Greenback-Labor Party. Though the new party indorsed the platform of the Knights of Labor, Powderly recovered from his momentary political enthusiasm and refused to allow the Order as such to become involved in the third-party movement. In answer to a question as to what action the Knights would take concerning the Cincinnati conference he replied, "No action at all as a local assembly. The right of our members to act as they see fit cannot be questioned. But any attempt to make it appear that said conference has the official sanction or patronage of the Order would in our judgment be unwise and suicidal. . . . Let political parties alone as an Order." [22] At the same time he continued to lobby at Harrisburg, Pa., for labor bills. [23]

By the fall of 1887 the political labor movement was distinctly on the wane and Powderly was in a position to exult over his acumen. "I am glad," he wrote, "I didn't talk (for George) this year. I think that now is my time to come out in a ringing article on the folly of 'follying' strange gods and turning the cold shoulder on legitimate labor organizations." [24]

---

[22] *Journal,* February, 1887, p. 2276.
[23] *Ibid.,* March, 1887, p. 2329.
[24] Letter from Powderly to Hayes, Nov. 12, 1887.

A split occurred between the single-tax followers of Henry George, the United Labor Party, and the Union Labor Party, and two national conventions were held in 1888. Neither was a labor party in any real sense. The United convention nominated Robert H. Cowdry for President while the Union Party nominated A. J. Streeter, president of the Northern Farmers' Alliance. Later the United Party withdrew, except in New York, and Streeter's support came almost entirely from the agricultural states.

Through the whole course of the Knights of Labor as an industrial organization, Powderly, with one slight aberration, maintained a nonpolitical stand. He was neither Democrat, Republican, nor Third Party and kept the Order as such out of politics. Individuals, including himself, locals, districts, did much as they pleased. Lobbies were encouraged. Nonpartisan political action was indorsed, but the Order as such remained, until disintegration set in, a labor society. By 1889 the Order had lost its industrial character, and in its decline the western faction and the New York socialists, both politically minded, took charge. Through connections with the Farmers' Alliance it became, in 1889-90, to all intents and purposes a political society and Powderly went along somewhat unwillingly, influenced by his major economic doctrine, the belief in free land.

FARMERS

The American version of English agrarianism advocated in this country by George Henry Evans in the thirties and forties, asserted the right of every individual settler to a quarter section of land, free and inalienable, from the vast resources at the government's disposal. The Homestead Act of 1862 satisfied this demand in part, but the practice of granting lands to railroads, the purchase of lands for speculation, and the settlement of the country after the

Civil War, began to cut off the wage-earner from his traditional avenue of escape. The Knights of Labor took over the land plank of the Industrial Congress, demanding "the reserving of the public lands, the heritage of the people, for the actual settler; not another acre for railroads or speculators." [25]

Powderly was a land crank influenced in part by the American tradition but also by his Irish sympathies and descent. In his view the land question in America was tied up with the problems of the Irish at home. Their one escape was America and with free land gone that avenue was supposed to be shut off. At practically every General Assembly from the time of his election as general master workman, Powderly made long speeches on the land question but little attention was paid to them. He insisted in 1882 that it was "the main all-absorbing question of the hour," and that the eight-hour movement, currency reform, child labor, and even temperance were of little importance as compared with the ownership of land. On this he was radical. He wanted not only to reserve the public domain for settlers, but to expropriate the railroads and speculators, and his reluctance to speak for Henry George in 1886 is explained less by his aversion to politics than by his feeling that the Single Tax was too subtle a solution of the problem.

At the 1884 General Assembly, Powderly asked that the land article be changed by the addition: "that all lands now held for the purpose of speculation by corporation or individual shall be restored to the care of the people," but the General Assembly preferred the Henry George formula and made the article to read: "that all lands now held for speculative purposes be taxed to their full value." [26]

---

[25] Article VI, constitution.
[26] T. V. Powderly, *op. cit.*, p. 176.

At a state convention of the Texas Farmers' Alliance at Decatur in 1885, a committee was appointed to meet the Knights of Labor committee at Dallas, September 1, "to draft resolutions to bring about effective union of the Knights of Labor and the Farmers' Alliance of Texas," [27] and numerous proposals were made at the 1885 General Assembly looking to amalgamation and political action with the Grangers and anti-Monopoly societies. These were lumped with the request of the old Federation to support the eight-hour movement and referred to the general executive board. [28]

The great industrial activity of the Order in 1885-86 was, in the opinion of Powderly, a waste of time. "For three years," he complained, "the attention of the entire Order was diverted in a different direction from that which pointed to the vital question of land reform." [29] But the collapse of the industrial movement gave the politicians and reformers their chance and at the special General Assembly in May-June, 1886, five land planks were adopted along with other political proposals already mentioned. [30]

At the same session an address was drawn up to be sent to the National Grange and Powderly was delegated to deliver it in person. [31] At the Richmond General Assembly a standing committee of three was appointed on fraternal relations with the Patrons of Husbandry, to "report monthly to the General Executive Board of the Knights of Labor such matters as will promote the good of our Order, our country and mankind." In 1887, a committee met a committee of the Farmers' Alliance, agreed with them that both farmer and wage-earner were suffering from "unjust

---

[27] Swinton, *op. cit.*, Aug. 30, 1885.
[28] *Proceedings*, 1885 General Assembly, pp. 100, 106, 125, 128, 135.
[29] Powderly, *op. cit.*, p. 178.
[30] *Proceedings*, special session of the 1886 General Assembly, p. 40.
[31] *Ibid.*, pp. 23, 70.

laws enacted in the interests of chartered corporations,"
and decided that the proper thing to do was to maintain
a dual lobby at Washington, to watch legislation in the
interest of farmers and laborers and to advise their respective organizations of the records of the legislators on
these matters. This was agreed to at the 1887 General
Assembly. [32]

In 1889 the land plank of the Order was again changed
to read: "The land, including all the natural sources of
wealth, is the heritage of all the people and should not be
subject to speculative traffic. Occupancy and use should be
the only title to the possession of the land. The taxes upon
land should be levied upon its full value for use, exclusive of
improvements, and should be sufficient to take for the community all unearned increment." Powderly and A. W.
Wright were appointed a committee to attend the December convention of the National Farmers' Alliance at St.
Louis, where they indorsed the Alliance program and
agreed to the dual lobby and nonpartisan political action.

By 1889 the Knights of Labor had ceased to be an industrial organization and their indorsement of the farmers'
demands could help neither the farmers nor themselves.
But Powderly had at last found his *métier*. On June 10,
1889, he wrote a long agitational letter to the Dakota
Grangers, advising them to get together and throw
"strikes, boycotts, lockouts and such nuisances to the winds
and unite in one strike through the legislative weapon in
such a way as to humble the power of the corporations who
rule the United States to-day." [33]

In 1890 the Knights of Labor went the whole way toward
the formation of a third party. It proposed to call a national reform convention to formulate an independent po-

---

[32] *Ibid.*, 1887 General Assembly, p. 1792.
[33] Letters from Powderly to Hayes, June 10 and June 15, 1889.

litical platform on the principles of the Knights of Labor, [34] and Powderly was instructed to get in touch with the Farmers' Alliance and other organizations and hold a conference on the last Wednesday in July, 1891, in Washington, D. C., to arrange for the national campaign of 1892. Powderly issued the call but little notice was taken of it outside the Order. The Farmers' Alliance meeting at Ocala, Fla., in December, 1890, invited the Knights of Labor to send fraternal delegates and Powderly decided to give up his July meeting in favor of Feb. 22, 1891, at Cincinnati, chosen by the Citizens' Alliance, a political committee appointed at the Ocala convention. The February meeting was postponed to May 19, but by that time Powderly's third-party enthusiasm had disappeared. He wrote to Hayes on May 9, just before the Cincinnati convention, that "the Knights must not be expected to engage in the third party movement except so far as the United States is concerned and then not as an Order but as individuals." He arranged that Wright (Canada) should say this.

On the surface, Powderly's position seems vacillating and uncertain, but fundamentally, his course was entirely consistent. Through his whole career as head of the Knights of Labor he maintained a nonpartisan attitude in politics. He believed in the lobby and in rewarding political friends and punishing political enemies, but at no time did he move to throw the support of the Knights to any political party. He was anxious to tie up with the Farmers' organizations for this nonpartisan program. In 1890 his hand was forced by the politico-agricultural element in the Knights that was growing stronger as the industrial membership fell off. Under the leadership of Beaumont and Sovereign this political faction tried to make him call a third-party convention. He avoided this and allowed Beaumont to join with

---

[34] *Proceedings*, 1890 General Assembly, pp. 70-71.

the third-party faction in the Farmers' Alliance and the Cincinnati convention was called. He attended, but took no part in the proceedings and let it be known that the Knights of Labor would not act as an Order. Perhaps he had no constitutional right to do this because the General Assembly had explicitly and emphatically decided upon independent political action. But that was what he did, and in 1893 the political actionists, led by Sovereign, got rid of him.

Powderly's plan for uniting with the Farmers and other organizations on a nonpartisan program resulted in a meeting in Washington, Jan. 21, 1891, but nothing came of it except the indication that the Knights would not officially support the third-party movement. The Cincinnati convention on May 19 was a farmers' affair, as was the convention at Omaha, July 4, 1892, which nominated General Weaver of Iowa for President, and General Field of Virginia for Vice President of the People's Party. The Omaha convention made an attempt to secure the labor vote by adding labor planks to its platform, and what labor vote it secured was probably from the Knights.

In 1893 Powderly was removed from office on charges made against him by Secretary Hayes, and as the result of an alliance between the Western agrico-political faction and the New York socialist-fundamentalist crowd, the former led by James R. Sovereign of Iowa and the latter by Daniel De Leon and T. B. McGuire. Sovereign was made general master workman and proceeded to elaborate a species of agrarianism that would have sounded well in the forties:

The Order of the Knights of Labor is not so much intended to adjust the relationship between the employer and employe as to adjust natural resources and productive facilities to the common interests of the whole people, that all who wish may work for themselves, independent of large employing corporations and companies It is not founded on the question of adjusting wages, but on the question of abolishing the wage-system and the establishment of a coöperative industrial system. When its real mission is accomplished, poverty will be reduced to a minimum and the land dotted over with peaceful, happy homes. Then, and not till then, will the Order die.[35]

On this assumption, the Order was immortal. But as a matter of fact it was already dead.

---

[35] *Ibid.*, 1894 General Assembly, p. 1.

CHAPTER XVIII

THE DECLINE OF THE ORDER

At the height of its wealth and power the Knights of Labor bought for its headquarters a brownstone "mansion" at 814 North Broad Street, Philadelphia, from Mrs. Mathew Baird. The price was around $50,000. They bought, too, the stables and some of the furnishings. The description of the house, as broadcast to the Order and the world, seems to have left the impression that the general officers had done themselves extremely well and aroused visions among the "horny-handed sons of toil" of Byzantine ease and grandeur, Roman feasts, and houris lounging on piles of satin.

The house was entered by a "broad flight of brownstone steps." The carpeted hall and stairs led up to "a large stained glass window representing the four seasons." The balusters were of carved wood "of unusual thickness" and the newel post was "surmounted by a bronze figure." The south room was forty feet long with three large mirrors framed in "handsomely carved walnut," mantels inlaid with marble, fine lace curtains, walls "frescoed in elaborate designs," and three "immense old gold satin tufted battings" several inches deep and bordered with colored satin hangings. "This room which is to be occupied by G. S. Litchman and his corps of assistants many of whom are ladies . . . is partly separated from a small reception room . . . by huge veneered and highly polished double columns. A magnificent chandelier. . . . The reception room opens through sliding doors . . . upon what was formerly a picture gallery. . . . The floor is inlaid with hard wood, . . . solid marble wainscotting about three feet deep."

The north room, formerly a library, "also handsomely frescoed, . . . two large mirrors, . . . handmade lace curtains, . . . fire-place (gas), red plush hangings, . . . large easy chairs covered with red velvet, . . . massive sofa. . . . " The rear north room, formerly the smoking room, had "a large brown leather sofa, a wine cooler. . . . " Back of this, the dining room, "lighted through an octagon shaped dome . . . " from the center of which was suspended "a double revolving chandelier with twenty-four highly polished and ornamented brass burners. Around the base of the dome carved in wood, a deer with real antlers, a boar, ducks, fish and other specimen of game, . . . eight carved columns, . . . four massive pedestals of marble . . . the meeting place of the General Executive Board. . . . "

On the second floor were "eight large rooms, . . . finely carpeted, . . . lace curtains and satin hangings, . . . large mirrors and stationary washstands . . . ," bathrooms "fitted up in the most complete style." Fourth floor front was a billiard room, with "a billiard table covered with marble"! etc., etc. "The entire building is heated by steam and there are registers in every room. There are also electric call bells, messenger calls and burglar alarms." [1]

It is not suggested that this mid-Victorian grandeur debauched the general officers, that wealth accumulated and men decayed or anything of the sort. But it aroused a storm of criticism not insignificant when joined with other storms from directions already described. Litchman's enthusiastic description was quoted everywhere, but with a sinister twist, and the envy of the mob and their disin-

---

[1] *Journal*, February, 1887, pp. 2289-90.

genuous leaders rose to overwhelm him. "The General Executive Board has squandered the funds of the Order in a reckless purchase of a palace among capitalists and nabobs," was one of the mildest expressions of this hostile feeling.

And there was some truth in it. Power, wealth, prestige, and office had enlarged the breach between the general officers and the rank and file, and Powderly retired to Scranton to write his book and get rid of his enemies. In 1888 the Order lost 300,000 members, and Barry and Carlton were expelled. "I would like to express my regards to Bailey," wrote the general master workman who was "cleansing" the Order of his personal enemies at the Order's expense. ". . . He must go too. Barry is gone. Litchman is shoveling the dirt in on his own corpse and By God every man that stood in the way of the prosperity of the Order must be buried." [2] At the same time, the Order needing money, the general master workman turned to those who had it. "I know there is spirit enough in some of our monied men to assist us now that we have slipped off the snake's skin—its other name is Barry." [3]

In 1889 McGraw and Detwiller were expelled and the financial condition grew worse. Powderly asked James Campbell of Local Assembly No. 300, for a loan of $5,000 to pay off the debts of the general office. [4] The next year: "Something must be done or we must let the sheriff run the concern. . . . The more I think of the past history of the Order the more I am convinced that I was a fool. . . . If I could only resent a thing properly. . . . " [5] In 1892 Powderly lost his own district, No. 16 and wanted to quit. He wrote Hayes: " . . . if there is no money with which to

---

[2] Letter from Powderly to Hayes, Sept. 12, 1888.
[3] *Ibid.*, Dec. 9, 1888.
[4] *Ibid.*, Jan. 1, 1889.
[5] *Ibid.*, March 3, 1890.

meet expenses I must apply for a situation in which I can make a living. . . . I feel that my work don't count any more and desire to end it and take up something new." [6] In his home town, where he had once been mayor and for thirteen years possibly the only figure of national importance, he found that "Sam Gompers is to orate at the trade union picnic here to-morrow. Dan Campbell is to occupy a seat in the carriage with Sam. P. J. McGuire is to be here too and Ben Castles is to ride a horse and wear feathers. I am to occupy a place on the side-walk. . . . I am to have the meeting reported and may find something in it to hang a man on." [7]

Powderly and Wright got out a Labor Day *Annual* as a private money-making venture about this time, and in 1893, Hayes went West to solicit advertising from the monied men. Powderly had written to Armour but was reluctant to give Hayes an introduction to him. "It would not be in good taste and the tone of my letter did not indicate that other solicitations would follow. You have only to call on him taking as little of his time as possible. Feel your way and the rest will be easy. I think the best way to approach Armour would be to drop in and ask for such pamphlets and documents as he can provide concerning his college and art school. Ascertain the name of the institution before entering his presence so that you will commit no error in naming it. . . .

"I enclose a letter to Pillsbury but you must pardon me for not enclosing one to Mr. Allerton. A little matter happened during my career in labor circles which would make it extremely embarrassing for me to introduce any one. . . . You know I have been fifteen years fighting the men we are now asking favors from and it is a trifle against the grain

---

[6] *Ibid.*, July 21, 1892.
[7] *Ibid.*, May 1, 1892.

to write some of them. . . . " [8]   In 1893 Powderly was ousted by a farmer-socialist clique on charges brought against him by Hayes.   He refused to turn the Order's property over to the new officers because they still owed him salary, and for other reasons.   He seems to have tried to start a new movement with Buchanan, his old enemy, and was suspended in 1894.   He sued the Order for past salary and his claims were settled in 1899 for $1,500.

Powderly himself has summed up the weakness of the Knights of Labor under his leadership as well perhaps as it can be done.   Writing to Hayes in 1893 he said:

Your statement confirms the suspicion that has haunted me for some time and which I unwillingly allowed myself to become possessed of more than a year ago, viz.: that the Order was in the throes of dissolution.   Whatever may be or may have been the faults or the virtues of the General Officers it is a conviction with me that no act of theirs could avert the impending fate of the Order.   Teacher of important and much-needed reforms, she has been obliged to practice differently from her teachings.   Advocating arbitration and conciliation as first steps in labor disputes she has been forced to take upon her shoulders the responsibilities of the aggressor first and, when hope of arbitrating and conciliation failed, to beg of the opposing side to do what we should have applied for in the first instance.   Advising against strikes we have been in the midst of them.   Urging important reforms we have been forced to yield our time and attention to petty disputes until we were placed in a position where we have frequently been misunderstood by the employee as well as the employer.   While not a political party we have been forced into the attitude of taking political action.   Our duty in the last campaign was to strike for the success of the People's party and in doing so we naturally offended the successful party.   Now I am besieged with letters every day by our members to sign petitions to be laid before the President whom I opposed on the order of the General Assembly.   All these things have had their effect in reducing our membership but through all the turmoil and mis-

---

[8] *Ibid.*, April 2, 1893.

understanding the Order has stamped deep its impression for good upon the records of the world and should it collapse to-night those who survive it may point to its splendid achievements in forcing to the front the cause of misunderstood and down-trodden humanity. . . . As for a meeting of the Board, I do not know whether that will be necessary for it will but incur additional expense. I shall correspond with them . . . and advise each of them to seek another position where they may earn sufficient to maintain them and their families independent of the Order. . . . It is morning. . . .

Sincerely and fraternally. . . . Yours. . . .[9]

---

[9] *Ibid.*, May 10, 1893.

APPENDIX I

PREAMBLE

"The recent alarming development and aggression of aggregated wealth, which, unless checked, will inevitably lead to the pauperization and hopeless degradation of the toiling masses, render it imperative, if we desire to enjoy the blessings of the government bequeathed to us by the founders of the republic, that a check shall be placed upon its power and unjust accumulation, and a system adopted which will secure to the laborer the fruits of his toil; and as this much desired object can only be accomplished by the thorough unification of labor and the united efforts of those who obey the divine injunction, that 'in the sweat of thy face thou shalt eat bread,' we have formed the Industrial Brotherhood, with a view of securing the organization and direction, by coöperative effort, of the power of the industrial classes, and we submit to the people of the United States the objects sought to be accomplished by our organization, calling upon all who believe in securing 'the greatest good to the greatest number,' to aid and assist us."

When the Knights adopted this preamble they made a few changes. Instead of "the blessings of the government bequeathed to us by the founders of the republic"—a political concept—they said "the blessings of life." Instead of submitting their ideas to the people of the United States they made it "the world" and they of course changed "Industrial Brotherhood" to the five stars.

The changes in the platform were more marked but in the same direction. It is only necessary to summarize the platform of the Industrial Congress and indicate the additions, elisions, and substitutions made by the Knights:

1. To organize "every department of productive industry making knowledge a standpoint for action, and industrial, moral and social worth—not wealth—the true standard of individual and national greatness." The Knights cut out "social" worth.

2. "To secure to the toilers a proper share of the wealth that they create; more of the leisure that rightly belongs to them; more societary advantages; more of the benefits, privileges and emoluments of the world; in a word, all those rights and privileges necessary to make them capable of enjoying, appreciating, defending, and perpetuating the blessings of republican institutions." The Knights changed "societary," an Associationist term, into "society" and "republican institutions" into "good government."

3. A demand from the states and the Federal government for bureaus of labor statistics. Unchanged.

4. "The establishment of coöperative institutions, productive and distributive." Unchanged.

5. "The reserving of the public lands, the heritage of the people, for the actual settler—not another acre for railroads or speculators." Unchanged.

6. "The abrogation of all laws that do not bear equally upon capital and labor, the removal of unjust technicalities, delays and discriminations in the administration of justice, and the adoption of measures providing for the health and safety of those engaged in mining, manufacturing or building pursuits." Unchanged.

7. A law to compel chartered companies to pay their employees at least once a month in full, in the lawful money of the country. The Knights changed this to once a week.

8. A mechanic's first lien law. Unchanged.

9. To abolish contract work by national, state, or municipal bodies. Unchanged.

So far there was little change but Nos. 10, 11, 13, 14 of the Industrial Brotherhood demands were not included in the platform of the Knights of Labor. No. 10 proposed a system of public markets "to facilitate the exchange of the productions of the farmers and mechanics tending to do away with middlemen and speculators," and No. 11 "to inaugurate systems of cheap transportation to facilitate the exchange of commodities." Both of these were farmer planks and had no place in the platform of an industrial organization. No. 13 was against the "importation of servile races," and for the abrogation of the Burlingame Treaty, and No. 14 referred to apprenticeship laws. The Knights were then not interested in Chinese immigration though they later became so. They were evidently not interested in apprentice laws, either because the apprentice system had become obsolete, or because they smacked too much of craft exclusiveness.

In the Knights' platform the remaining planks were retained: the substitution of arbitration for strikes; against contract prison labor; equal pay for equal work for both sexes; the reduction of the hours of labor to eight a day for cultural reasons. The last plank, on money, as adopted by the Knights, asked only for a national fiat currency issued direct to the people without the intervention of banks, to be legal tender for all debts private and public. It dropped the old Greenback idea of interchangeable bonds. And finally, the Knights added one new plank: the prohibition of the labor of children under 14 years in shops, mines, and factories. Changed to 15 years in 1884.

In 1884 both the preamble and the platform were changed. While repudiating politics by the Order, it stated that most of its objects could be obtained through legislation, and "it is the duty of all to assist in nominating and supporting with their votes only such candidates as will pledge their support to those measures regardless of party. But no one shall however be compelled to vote with the majority." New legislative planks were: incorporation of trade unions, etc.; compulsory arbitration set up by law; a graduated income tax; currency inflation in emergencies in place of government bonds; the prohibition of importation of contract labor; postal savings; and government ownership of telegraphs, telephones, and railroads. New or modified non-legislative planks were: coöperative institutions "such as will tend to supercede the wage system"; "to shorten the hours of labor by a general refusal to work for more than eight hours"—presumably per day.

The political strain of 1884 was somewhat toned down by amendments to the effect that the "Knights of Labor deals with the industrial question and not with the political question," and, while a few of its members would try to identify it with a political party, "this Order is in no way bound by the political expression of its individual members," and that "politics must be subordinated to industry." [1] Later additions to the platform up

---

[1] *Proceedings*, 1884 General Assembly of the Knights of Labor, pp. 768-69, 784-85.

to 1893 covered: the referendum in making all laws; land taxes to the full value of the land, exclusive of improvements, and sufficient to take up all the unearned increment; industrial accident compensation; compulsory school attendance between 7 and 15 for 10 months in the year, and free textbooks.[2]

---

[2] Constitution, 1893.

APPENDIX II

THE LOCAL ASSEMBLY

THE first local of the Knights drew up its own constitution eight years before the general constitution was adopted. It named and defined the duties of officers: master workman (presiding officer), worthy foreman (vice president), worthy inspector (doorkeeper), almoner (relief officer), financial secretary, recording secretary, worthy treasurer, statistician (to gather information as to the conditions of the trade), assistant unknown knight (to gather information about proposed members), judge, judge advocate, and clerk of court (a grievance committee for the settlement of disputes among members or to act as a court, if friendly settlement were impossible).

In the original local constitution great emphasis was placed upon ceremonial or secret work, the *Adelphon Kruptos,* which was marked by religious phraseology, and the oath of secrecy. A complicated opening service was laid down which might have been impressive if one were inclined to be impressed. The initiation ceremony was sufficiently alarming and verbose, but it was a solemn affair with no horseplay. In the order of business it was required to ask two principal questions at each meeting: "Are there any vacancies known in the trade to be filled?" and "Are any of our brothers out of employ, seeking engagements or wish to change?" This indicates the craft character of the early local and an important function of employment finding that must have gone on throughout. The only other unusual business was the discussion of labor "in all its interests" and the collection of statistics.

Proposed members were rejected by three or more black balls. When fewer than three were found the matter was postponed to allow the objectors to present their reasons in writing to the master workman without signatures. On the second ballot the objectors were not allowed to vote and one or two black balls would cause rejection. No one under 21 years of age might be initiated and no woman.[1]

When the General Assembly was organized in 1878, constitutions were drawn up for all the units of the Order and the following additions were made to the constitution of the local assemblies: the local assembly could not be formed nor maintained with fewer than ten members, three-fourths of whom must be wage-earners. Persons who had worked for wages might be admitted providing their total did not exceed one-fourth the membership, except lawyers, doctors, bankers, and those who sold liquor or made their living by its sale. In 1882 Powderly rendered a decision that a "capitalist" might be admitted if the assembly so desired.[2] The age limit was lowered to 18 years and initiation fee was to be at least 50 cents.[8] A committee on candidates was established to take the place of the unknown knight. Provision was made for transfer from one local to another and the dues were to be not less than 10 cents a month. The officers remained as they were, and a two-thirds vote was required to expel, suspend, or reinstate a member. By-laws might be enacted if they did not conflict with the constitution of the district assembly or of the General Assembly.

The revised constitution of 1884 dignified the local with a preamble which reflects the political trend of that year, the emphasis upon solidarity and the reformist philosophy of the Order. "The Local Assembly," it declared, "is not a mere trade union or beneficial society; it is more and higher. It gathers into one fold all branches of honorable toil without regard to nationality, sex, creed or color. It is not founded merely to protect one interest or to discharge one duty be it ever so great. While it retains and fosters all the fraternal characteristics and protection of the single trade union, it also, by the multiplied powers of union, protects and assists all. . . . While acknowledging that it is sometimes necessary to enjoin an oppressor, yet strikes should be avoided whenever possible. Strikes at best only afford temporary relief and members should be educated to depend upon thorough organization, coöperation and political action,

---

[1] From a copy of the *Adelphon Kruptos,* undated, but from internal evidence about 1873. Loaned by Davis Saposs, Brookwood College. Women were admitted in 1880.

[2] *Journal,* p. 368.

[8] This was increased to $1.00 in 1880.

and through these the abolishment of the wage system. . . ." [4]

By 1884 the local assemblies, instead of coming together to form districts as was the case previous to 1878, were being set up by organizers recommended by the districts and appointed by the grand master workman. The source of authority had switched from the bottom to the top and the local was required to take the name and number assigned to it by the grand secretary. The age limit for new members was lowered to 16 and doctors were allowed in, but the old rule against liquor dealers, with extensions, and against lawyers and bankers was retained, while professional gamblers and stockbrokers were added to the list of the ostracized. The local was allowed to charge a higher initiation fee for skilled mechanics than for laborers, and for women, a lower. Traveling members were given traveling cards, a password, and a test, a sign of recognition. Besides the original officers there were added a venerable sage (past master workman), inside and outside esquires to guarantee secrecy and decorum, an insurance solicitor, and three trustees to act as custodians of the property of the local.

A large number of locals had been attached to the General Assembly and in 1882 an attempt was made to return all locals to the jurisdiction of the districts. It was stated explicitly that this provision did not apply to trade locals. [5]

In 1886, because of the growing dissatisfaction with the general officers, Powderly issued two orders decreeing that a local or district assembly "which issues a circular or paper in opposition to or contradiction of any command or order from the G. E. B. is guilty of insubordination and may be suspended" and, "circulars, appeals and protests issued from local or district assemblies without the sanction of the G. E. B. must not be read in the assembly to which they are addressed." [6] This was the last word in centralization, but it meant nothing. No one paid it any attention, but it helped to give credence to the charge that the administration of the Order was arbitrary and undemocratic, as it was, in intent and on paper. These two decisions did not appear in the revised and codified decisions of the grand master workman completed up to 1887. They were ignored or rejected by the Richmond assembly.

Powderly himself tells the real story about centralization of

---

[4] *Proceedings*, 1884 General Assembly of the Knights of Labor, p. 780.
[5] *Ibid.*, 1882 General Assembly, pp. 304, 347.
[6] *Journal*, February, 1886, p. 1196.

authority in his circular of March, 1886. There he complains bitterly that no one pays any attention to him, that he says one thing and the members do another, and it all puts him in a very unhappy position before the world. Again the difference must be emphasized between centralization *de jure* and *de facto*. On paper, the Knights moved steadily toward centralization; in fact, they moved unsteadily toward disintegration.

THE DISTRICT ASSEMBLY

As the national unions, especially the larger ones, are the controlling factors in the American Federation of Labor, so the large district assemblies held the balance of power in the Knights of Labor. Here again in theory the powers of the districts were limited by the hegemony of the General Assembly and its officers, while, in the American Federation of Labor, the national unions have almost complete autonomy. Admitting that the powers of the districts were not unlimited, it remains true that the larger and more aggressive of them were able to determine to a considerable extent the policy and behavior of the Order.

Essentially then the difference between the Knights of Labor and the American Federation of Labor is to be found in the character of the district assemblies as opposed to the character of the national trade unions.

It is usually assumed that most of the large districts were "mixed" bodies, composed of delegates from locals of various trades and from "mixed" locals, and that the point of view of the district was therefore necessarily anti-trade union. Superficially there is much to be said for this opinion but upon close examination it is not so sound as would seem. There were five types of district assemblies: the national trade district, the trade district, the mixed district in a locality where one trade so predominated that, to all intents and purposes, the so-called mixed district was trade in fact, the mixed district where the majority of the locals were trade, and the district that was "mixed" in sentiment whether it was so in composition or not.

Of the national trade districts, the Window Glass Workers maintained a national trade organization through nearly the whole life of the Order. There were, too, a large number of trade districts not national in scope like the Printers of New York and the Shoemakers of Philadelphia. Then there were such districts as No. 7 and No. 9 in the coal regions which were so largely composed of miners' locals as to make them in fact trade districts though they had some mixed locals under their jurisdiction. The three largest districts in the Order, No. 30 of Massachusetts, No. 49 of New York, and No. 1 of Philadelphia, all had more trade locals than mixed and this was especially true of Philadelphia and New York. But Philadelphia and Massachusetts were the centers of trade sentiment, while New York was the center of mixed sentiment. Thus the big districts were not necessarily anti-trade union. Their sentiments depended not on their composition but on the cliques, rings, and individuals who controlled the machinery of the districts. The Order as a whole was not anti-trade. Powderly was at heart, but he followed rather than led. The mixed sentiment came from the agricultural West and from two cities, St. Louis and New York, where the district officers were imperialists.

But the district assembly, whatever its character, was primarily a territorial unit and in that respect ill adapted to modern industrial organization. It was of the old American tradition of the trades' assembly, though more homogeneous than its prototype, and its localism stood in the way of labor organization on an industrial and national basis. It was in fact as little adapted to modern industry because of its localism as was the craft union because of its exclusiveness. The technical organization of industry outstripped the social organization of the workers. Both craft and local limitations were anachronisms in the eighties.

The original constitution of the district assembly as laid down by the first General Assembly, provided that it should be composed of representatives from at least five locals, that it was the highest tribunal in the district and should decide all controversies among its constituents, assess taxes for its maintenance, and legislate in the interest of the Order. Locals were represented in the district on the basis of one representative for one hundred members or fewer and one for each additional one hundred members or major fraction thereof. The districts had the same officers as the General Assembly and the district master workman had the power to recommend applications for local charters.[7] At the St. Louis General Assembly in 1879 the basis of representation of the locals to the district was left to the districts themselves, but at Detroit in 1881 it was changed, and the local representation fixed by the constitution. At New York,

---

[7] *Proceedings,* 1878 General Assembly, pp. 35-36.

in 1882, this was abandoned and a compromise adopted giving each local one representative to the district and permitting the latter to fix further representation as it chose.[8]

THE NATIONAL TRADE ASSEMBLY OR DISTRICT

The history of the development of the trade district is given in another place. Here it is only necessary to call attention to the constitutional provision of 1884 permitting the formation of national trade assemblies, to be created by conventions of locals of one trade, and to be given charters on the same terms as other districts. It was not compulsory for any local to join the national trade assembly.[9]

STATE ASSEMBLIES

The conflict within the Order between trade and mixed units was further complicated by a faction that was opposed to both, but particularly to the mixed assemblies because of the greater danger of jurisdictional difficulty. The influence behind the demand for state assemblies was western and political. In the East, with its denser industrial population, the district was confined to a manageable area even when its numbers became too great. But the mixed districts of the West had large territories and comparatively few members, so that the creation of a state assembly was easy and perhaps desirable.

Further, the state was a political unit while the district was not, and the West, especially the small towns in which the locals were found, was more politically minded than the industrial East. Two resolutions from Ohio demanding state assemblies were introduced in the January General Assembly at St. Louis in 1879, and both were rejected. In September, at Chicago, Phillip Van Patten, secretary of the Socialist Labor Party, introduced two resolutions, one to form state assemblies and the other to take political action. The political nature of the proposal for state assemblies is seen in the terms of the resolution: "The District Assemblies cannot conveniently attend to the interests of a territory larger than the usual Congressional district." Van Patten suggested that states having ten or more locals should be governed by one state assembly, leaving the district assemblies

---

[8] *Ibid.*, January, 1879 General Assembly, p. 83; *Journal*, p. 425.
[9] *Proceedings*, 1884 General Assembly, p. 776.

as they were, while states with from five to ten locals should remain with only district assemblies. His political resolution suggested that political action be recommended to all assemblies. The latter was passed but the state assembly proposal was rejected.[10] At the same time a proposal to abolish districts and form state assemblies was also rejected.[11]

Nothing was done toward the formation of state assemblies until 1883, when a committee was appointed to draw up a law governing their formation.[12] But in January, 1884, Michigan took the matter into its own hands, held a state convention at Detroit, and drew up plans for state assemblies to be presented to the next General Assembly. Officers were elected, a charter applied for, and a platform covering the boycott and political action laid down.[13] This is a typical instance of the way in which things happened in this highly centralized Order. The General Assembly would reject or delay until some faction or section would act. Action would then be taken by the General Assembly with as good grace as possible.

The special committee recommended a plan for the formation of state assemblies to the 1884 General Assembly. It was defeated by a vote of 50 to 45, but Powderly ruled that the locals might form state assemblies if they wished! [14]

In June, 1885, a state convention was held at Nashville, Tenn., interested in the boycott, the abolition of the payment of wages in script, and contract prison labor. It asked the trade unions as well as local assemblies of the Knights to send representatives.[15] At the 1885 General Assembly, state assemblies were recognized by a vote of 107 to 28. They were given representation to the General Assembly on the same basis as the districts.[16] In 1897, long after the Order had ceased to be an industrial society, it was decided that state assemblies were not a success, and the charters of all but Arkansas, Colorado, and Michigan were revoked.[17]

---

10 *Ibid.*, September, 1879 General Assembly, pp. 119-20, 130.
11 *Ibid.*, p. 95.
12 *Ibid.*, 1883 General Assembly, p. 500.
13 *Journal*, pp. 723-24.
14 *Proceedings*, 1884 General Assembly, pp. 740-41.
15 *Journal*, July, 1885, p. 1037.
16 *Proceedings*, 1885 General Assembly, pp. 112, 129, 134.
17 *Ibid.*, 1897 General Assembly, pp. 46-47.

The General Assembly of the Knights of Labor had "full and final jurisdiction" and was the highest tribunal of the Order. It alone possessed "the power and authority to make, amend and repeal the fundamental and general laws of the Order; to finally decide all controversies . . . to issue all charters on the recommendation of the district assemblies where such exist, and to issue traveling, transfer and final cards. It can also tax the members of the Order for its maintenance." [18] Originally the General Assembly held its meetings in January of each year, but this was changed to September in 1879, making two regular meetings for that year. It was changed again to October in 1885, and to November in 1888. It held two special sessions, one in 1878 to deal with the objection of the Catholic Church to secrecy and the religious character of the ceremonies, and the other in 1886, required by the problems arising out of the tremendous growth of that year.

The General Assembly had the same offices as the locals and districts with some additions, and used the same titles with the prefix "Grand" later changed to "General." It had a general executive board of five elected officers, which was changed in 1884 to three chosen by election, and the general master workman and the general secretary ex officio. In 1886 six "auxiliary" members were added to the general executive board to help carry the excessive burden that numbers and expansion involved. Uriah Stephens was grand master workman in 1878-79 and was followed by Terence V. Powderly, who was elected at the September assembly of 1879 and remained head of the Order until 1893. He was followed by J. R. Sovereign of Iowa. Various boards and departments were set up to deal with specific activities, coöperation, insurance, women's work. The General Assembly elected the officers and members of important boards. The grand master workman appointed the committees, confirmed the appointment of district organizers, and appointed organizers where no district existed.

The General Assembly was composed of representatives from the national trade assemblies, district assemblies, state assemblies, and locals attached to the General Assembly. Originally each district assembly was allowed one representative for the first 1,000 members or less, and one more for each additional 1,000

---

[18] Article I, constitution.

or major fraction thereof, but no district assembly was allowed more than three representatives. In 1879 this was changed to give one representative for 500 members, and one more for each additional 500. In 1884 the basis of representation went back to the original 1,000 members, and in 1886 the Order had grown so large that 3,000 members was made the basis of representation to apply to all state, national, trade, and district assemblies.

The revenue of the General Assembly came from a per capita tax, district and local charter fees, the sale of the *Adelphon Kruptos,* and transfer, traveling, and final cards. There were also special funds like the Resistance Fund and the Coöperative Fund and returns from assessments and appeals. The original per capita tax was one and one-half cents per quarter, but it was raised January, 1882, to 6 cents per quarter. The Order was usually poor, but with the great membership in 1885-87 it had ample, even excessive funds. Assessments were very hard to collect for any purpose and appeals brought in little. The Resistance and Coöperative Funds were inadequate and badly managed, and the death-benefit plan was never a success.

APPENDIX III

"To the Officers and Members of all National and International Trades' Unions of the United States and Canada, Greeting:

"Brothers in the Cause of Labor:—We, the Knights of Labor, in General Assembly convened, extend our heartiest greeting to all branches of honorable toil, welcoming them to the most friendly union in a common work.

"This organization embraces within its folds all branches of honorable toil and all conditions of men, without respect to trades, occupations, sex, creed, color or nationality. We seek to raise the level of wages and reduce the hours of labor; to protect men and women in their occupations, in their lives and limbs, and in their rights as citizens. We seek also to secure such legislation as shall tend to prevent the unjust accumulation of wealth, to restrict the power of monopolies and corporations, and to enact such wise and beneficent legislation as shall promote equity and justice, looking forward to the day when coöperation shall supersede the wage system, and the castes and classes that now divide men shall be forever abolished.

"We recognize the service rendered to humanity and the cause of labor by trades-union organizations, but believe that the time has come, or is fast approaching, when all who earn their bread *by the sweat of their brow* shall be enrolled under one general head, as we are controlled by one common law—the law of our necessities; and we will gladly welcome to our ranks or to protection under our banner any organization requesting admission. And to such organizations as believe that their craftsmen are better protected under their present form of government, we pledge ourselves, as members of the great army of labor, to coöperate with them in every honorable effort to achieve the success which we are unitedly organized to obtain; and to this end we have appointed a Special Committee to confer with a like committee of any National or International Trades' Union which shall desire to confer with us on the settlement of any difficulties that may occur between the members of the several organizations.

"We have received a communication from a committee of the national officers of some of the National and International Trades' Unions, requesting certain specific legislation at our hands; but as we believe that the object sought and stated in the preamble to the communication above referred to can best be accomplished by a conference between a committee of this Association and a committee of any other organization, and as the propositions contained therein are inconsistent with our duty to our members, we therefore defer action upon said propositions until a conference of committees can be held.

"The basis upon which we believe an agreement can be reached would necessarily include the adoption of some plan by which all labor organizations could be protected from unfair men, men expelled, suspended, under fine, or guilty of taking places of union men or Knights of Labor while on strike or while locked out from work; and that as far as possible a uniform standard of hours of labor and wages should be adopted, so that men of any trade, enrolled in our Order, and members of trades' unions, may not come in conflict because of a difference in wages or hours of labor. We also believe that a system of exchanging working cards should be adopted, so that members of any craft belonging to different organizations could work in harmony together—the card of any member of this Order admitting men to work in any union shop, and the card of any union man admitting him to work in any Knights of Labor shop.

"We further believe that, upon a demand for increase of wages or shorter hours of labor made by either organization, a conference should be held with the organized labor men employed in the establishment where the demand for increase of wages or reduction of hours is contemplated—action upon a proposed reduction of wages or other difficulty to be agreed upon in like manner; and that, in the settlement of any difficulties between employers and employees, the organizations represented in the establishment shall be parties to the terms of settlement.

"Trusting that the method proposed herein will meet with your approval, and that organized labor will move forward and onward in harmony of effort and of interest, we are

"Yours fraternally,

"COMMITTEE."

"We further recommend that a committee of five be appointed to promulgate the above circular, with powers to confer with the trades-union organizations, to report for action to the next General Assembly." [1]

---

[1] *Proceedings,* special session of the 1886 General Assembly, pp. 52-53. There was a newspaper report to the effect that the committee dealing with the treaty was ready to accept sections one and two but rejected number three, which demanded that trade locals and districts be disbanded, and was ready to compromise on the rest. The trade unions were said to be ready to deal with the treaty in the same spirit. (*New York Tribune,* May 30, 1886.)

SELECTED BIBLIOGRAPHY

Adelphon Kruptos (n. d., and 1891).

ALDRICH, M. A., *The American Federation of Labor,* American Economic Association Studies, III, no. 4 (New York, 1898).

American Federationist, Vol. I, pp. 107, 195, 230, 257; Vol. III, p. 217; Vol. IV, p. 96; Vol. V, p. 53; Vol. VII, p. 279; Vol. VIII, pp. 402, 404.

BARNETT, George E., *The Printers,* American Economic Association Publications, 3d series, Vol. X, no. 3 (October, 1909).

BEMIS, E. W., *Coöperation in the Middle States,* Johns Hopkins University Studies, 6th series, III (Baltimore, 1888).

―――― *Coöperation in New England,* American Economic Association Publications, Vol. I, no. 5 (November, 1886).

BROWNE, Waldo R., *Altgeld of Illinois* (New York, 1924).

BUCHANAN, Joseph R., *The Story of a Labor Agitator* (New York, 1903).

Carpenter, The, 1880-97, Indianapolis.

Cigar Makers' Official Journal, 1876-90 New York, Buffalo, Chicago.

COMMONS, John R., and Associates, *History of Labour in the United States,* Vol. II (New York, 1918 ed.).

Constitution of the General Assembly, etc., of the Order of the Knights of Labor, 1887, 1892, 1893, 1895, 1899, 1900, 1901, 1910.

COULTER, J. L., "Organization among the Farmers of the United States," *Yale Review,* Vol. XVIII, pp. 277-98.

Craftsman, The.

Decisions of the General Master Workman, 1887, 1890.

ELY, Richard T., *The Labor Movement in America* (Baltimore, 1886).

EVANS, Christopher, *History of the United Mine Workers of America, 1860-90* (Indianapolis, 1918).

FARNHAM, Henry W., "Die Amerikanischen Gewerksvereine," in Schriften, *des Vereins fur Sozialpolitik* (Leipzig, 1879).

FITCH, J. A., *The Steel Workers* (New York, 1911).

Furniture Workers' Journal, The.

GALSTER, Augusta E., *The Labor Movement in the Shoe Industry* (New York, 1924).

GEORGE, Henry, Jr., *The Life of Henry George by His Son,* 2 vols. (New York, 1904).

GOMPERS, Samuel, *Seventy Years of Life and Labor,* 2 vols. (New York, 1925).

Granite Cutters' Journal, The.

HAMILTON, W. H., and WRIGHT, H. R., *The Case of Bituminous Coal* (New York, 1926).

HINES, Thomas R., *The Anarchists' Conspiracy* (Boston, 1887).

HINTON, R. F., "American Labor Organizations," *North American Review,* 1885, Vol. CXL, p. 48.

HOAGLAND, H. E., "The Rise of the Iron Molders' International Union," *American Economic Review,* June, 1913.

—— "Early Organizations of the Iron Molders," *International Molders' Journal,* Vols. XLVII, XLVIII.

HOLLANDER, J. H., and BARNETT, Geo. E., *Studies in American Trade Unionism* (New York, 1906).

Illinois Bureau of Labor Statistics, 4th biennial *Report,* "Trade and Labor Organizations in Illinois," pp. 145-63; "The Eight-Hour Movement in Chicago, May, 1886," pp. 466-98; "Strikes in Chicago and Vicinity," pp. 261-86.

Iron Molders' Journal, The.

JAMES, A. P., "The First Convention of the American Federation of Labor," reprint from *Western Pennsylvania Historical Magazine,* March 3, 1924. This is a study from the Pittsburgh papers of the convention, November, 1881, of the old Federation of Organized Trades and Labor Unions.

John Swinton's Paper, 1883-87 (New York). The least partisan labor paper of the period, and the best edited.

Journal of United Labor, 1880-1889, Journal of the Knights of Labor, 1880-1917, Marblehead, Mass., Pittsburgh, Philadelphia, and Washington, D. C., the official journal of the Order.

Kansas Bureau of Labor Statistics, 2d annual *Report,* "The Southwestern Strike," pp. 21-72.

KIRK, William, "The Knights of Labor and the American Federation of Labor," in HOLLANDER and BARNETT, *Studies in American Trade Unionism* (New York, 1906).

—— *National Labor Federations in the United States,* Johns Hopkins University Studies, Series XXIV, nos. 9-10 (Baltimore, 1906).

Labor Enquirer, 1883-88 (Denver and Chicago).

Labor Standard, 1876-89 (New York, Boston, Fall River, and Paterson, N. J.).

LESCOHIER, Don D., "The Knights of St. Crispin, 1867-74," *Bulletin* of the University of Wisconsin, no. 355 (Madison, Wis., 1910).

Letters from T. V. Powderly to John W. Hayes, from February, 1887, to 1893. In the possession of Mr. John W. Hayes (Washington, D. C.).

McGUIRE, P. J., "History and Aims of the A. F. of L.," in TRANT, Wm., *Trade Unions* (Washington, 1905).

McNEILL, George E., *The Labor Movement: The Problem of To-day* (Boston, 1887).

Missouri Bureau of Labor Statistics, 8th annual *Report,* 1886. "Official History of the 1886 Strike on the Southwestern Railway System," appendix, pp. 5-117.

National Labor Digest, January, 1921, to March, 1923, containing the beginning of a history of the Knights of Labor by John W. Hayes.

National Labor Tribune, 1874-90 (Pittsburgh).

New York *Herald,* April 23, 1882. The Cuno article.

New York *Sun,* January 1, 1887.

New York *Tribune,* May 30, 1886, and June 5, 1886.

Ohio Bureau of Labor Statistics, 7th annual *Report,* 1883, "Labor Troubles," pp. 213-54.

The Order and the Cigar Makers. Statement of the General Executive Board and evidence taken March 16, 1886, at the Astor House, New York. Pamphlet.

PARSONS, Lucy, *Life of Albert R. Parsons* (Chicago, 1889).

Pennsylvania Bureau of Labor Statistics, 10th annual *Report* 1881-82, "Labor Troubles in Pennsylvania, 1882," pp. 144-92.

PINKERTON, Allan, *Strikers, Communists, Tramps and Detectives* (New York, 1900).

POWDERLY, T. V., *Thirty Years of Labor* (1st ed., Columbus, Ohio, 1889; 2d ed., Philadelphia, Pa., 1890).

Powderly's secret circular, March 13, 1886.

Proceedings, Annual Conference of the Federation of Organized Trades and Labor Unions, 1881-86.

Proceedings, Annual Convention of the American Federation of Labor, 1886-94.

Proceedings, 11th Annual Convention of the Amalgamated Association of Iron and Steel Workers (Pittsburgh, June, 1886).

Proceedings, 34th Annual Session of the International Typographical Union (Pittsburgh, 1886).

Proceedings, 17th Session of the International Cigar Makers' Union.

Proceedings of the General Assembly of the Knights of Labor of America, 1878-95.

Report of the Committee of Conference of the Knights of Labor and the Trade Unions, Columbus, O., Dec. 8, 1886. Author's possession.

"Report of the House Select Committee on Labor Troubles in Missouri, Arkansas, Kansas and Texas," House Doc., 49th Cong., 2d sess., 1886-87. No. 4174.

ROBINSON, J. S., *The Amalgamated Association of Iron, Steel and Tin Workers,* Johns Hopkins University Studies, Series XXXVIII, no. 2 (Baltimore, 1920).

Rochester Democrat and Chronicle, April 18, 1874.

ROY, Andrew, *A History of the Coal Miners of the United States* (3d edition, Columbus, O., 1907).

SCHILLING, George A., "A Short History of the Labor Movement in Chicago," in *Life of Albert R. Parsons* (Chicago, 1903).

SCHLÜTER, Hermann, *The Brewing Industry and the Brewery Workers' Movement in America* (Cincinnati, 1910).

Scrapbook of newspaper clippings, 1887-88, Reading strike, etc. Author's possession.

Secret Circular, undated. Explanation of the signs and symbols of the Knights of Labor. Author's possession.

Senate Committee on Education and Labor, 1883, 4 vols. of testimony, 1885, Vol. 48; 1, no. 820.

Shoe Workers' Journal, "A Review of the Unions in the Shoe Trade of America," p. 8, July, 1910.

SORGE, F. A., "Die Arbeiter Bewegung in den Vereinigten Staaten 1877-1885," *Neue Zeit,* 1891-92, Vols. I, 206, 388; II, 197, 239, 268, 324, 453, 495; 1894-95, Vol. II, 196, 234, 304, 330; 1895-96, Vol. II, 101, 132, 236, 267.

Souvenir Journal of the 1890 General Assembly, Knights of Labor, containing short biographies of the leaders of the Order. Additional notices in 1891 *Souvenir Journal.*

Sozialist, Der, March 3, 1888.

SPEDDEN, E. R., *The Trade Union Label,* Johns Hopkins University Studies, Series XXVIII, no. 2.

Statement of the Progressive Cigar Makers to District Assembly No. 49, MS. loaned by David Saposs.

STEVENS, George A., *New York Typographical Union No. 6, New York State Department of Labor* (Albany, N. Y., 1913).

THORP, Willard L., *Business Annals*, National Bureau of Economic Research Publications (New York, 1926).

TRACY, George A., *History of the Typographical Union* (Indianapolis, 1913).

Union Advocate. The first journal of the American Federation of Labor, ed. Samuel Gompers, June, 1887, to December, 1887.

VILLARD, A., *Les Chevaleurs du Travail*, Académie de Nimes, series 7, Vol. X, pp. 267-87, 1888.

WALTERSHAUSEN, Sartorius von, *Die noramerikanischen Gewerkshaften* (Berlin, 1886).

WOLMAN, Leo, *The Boycott in American Trade Unions*, Johns Hopkins University Studies, Series XXXIV (Baltimore, 1916).

WRIGHT, Carroll D., "An Historical Sketch of the Knights of Labor," *Quarterly Journal of Economics*, January, 1887.

INDEX

INDEX

401